International Regimes

*Published under the auspices of the
Center for International and Strategic Affairs,
University of California, Los Angeles,
and the World Peace Foundation*

Cornell Studies in Political Economy

EDITED BY PETER J. KATZENSTEIN

International Regimes

EDITED BY

STEPHEN D. KRASNER

Cornell University Press

ITHACA AND LONDON

The contents of this book first appeared in volume 36, number 2, and volume 35, number 4, of the journal *International Organization*.

This book first published in 1983 by Cornell University Press.
Second printing, 1984.
Fifth printing, Cornell Paperbacks, 1989.

International Standard Book Number (cloth) 0-8014-1550-0
International Standard Book Number (paper) 0-8014-9250-5
Library of Congress Catalog Card Number 82-19905
Printed in the United States of America

Librarians: Library of Congress cataloging information appears on the last page of this book.

The paper in this book is acid-free and meets the guidelines for permanence and durability of the Committee on Production Guidelines for Book Longevity of the Council on Library Resources.

Contents

Contributors

BENJAMIN J. COHEN is William L. Clayton Professor of International Economic Affairs at the Fletcher School of Law and Diplomacy of Tufts University, Medford, Massachusetts.

JOCK A. FINLAYSON is a Research Associate in the Institute of International Relations at the University of British Columbia.

ERNST B. HAAS is Professor of Political Science at the University of California, Berkeley.

RAYMOND F. HOPKINS is Professor of Political Science at Swarthmore College, Swarthmore, Pennsylvania.

ROBERT JERVIS is Professor of Political Science at Columbia University, New York City.

ROBERT O. KEOHANE is Professor of Politics at Brandeis University, Waltham, Massachusetts.

STEPHEN D. KRASNER is Professor of Political Science at Stanford University, Stanford, California.

CHARLES LIPSON is Assistant Professor of Political Science at the University of Chicago.

DONALD J. PUCHALA is Director of the Institute of International Studies and Professor of Government and International Studies, the University of South Carolina, Columbia.

JOHN GERARD RUGGIE is Associate Professor of Political Science and a member of the Institute of War and Peace Studies at Columbia University, New York City.

ARTHUR A. STEIN is Associate Professor of Political Science at the University of California, Los Angeles.

SUSAN STRANGE is Montague Burton Professor of International Relations at the London School of Economics and Political Science.

ORAN R. YOUNG is Co-Director of the Center for Northern Studies in Wolcott, Vermont.

MARK W. ZACHER is Director of the Institute of International Relations and Professor of Political Science at the University of British Columbia.

Preface

This volume is a synthesis of major arguments that informed the study of international relations during the 1970s. The decade began with a concerted attack on state-centric realist approaches. Studies such as Graham Allison's *Essence of Decision* argued that it was necessary to go inside complex government decision-making networks to secure an adequate understanding of foreign affairs. More germane to the concerns of this present volume were a number of major works from a "liberal" perspective suggesting the importance of transnational and transgovernmental actors in the international system. These actors penetrated national boundaries. They both reflected and contributed to the growing complexity of the international system. The world was understood to be increasingly interdependent. The formal trappings of sovereignty remained, but states could no longer effectively exercise their power because they could not control international economic movements, at least not at acceptable costs. The state-centric realist approach to the study of international relations was rejected as incomplete at best and misleading at worst.

These arguments corresponded with and reflected a major shift in the substantive focus of a significant amount of work in the field. During the 1950s and 1960s students of international affairs were concerned primarily with military and strategic conflict: what has frequently been referred to as high politics. The most important theoretical contributions were associated with systems approaches and nuclear strategy. Questions of national integration attracted less attention, and international law virtually disappeared as a matter of concern. But in the 1970s a number of changes in the focus of public attention altered this situation. Tensions between the Soviet Union and the United States abated. Foreign trade pressures increased. Developing countries made strident demands for a New International Economic Order. A cartel of oil-exporting states quadrupled the price of petroleum. The Vietnam War ended. Global economic performance deteriorated. In short, low politics became more salient for both policy makers and scholars. At first blush the conventional state-centric realist orientation with its emphasis on conflict and the zero-sum nature of international relations seemed inadequate for analyzing this situation.

But the realists quickly counterattacked. They pointed out that the growing disorder in the international system corresponded with a decline in American power. They argued that the stability of the 1950s and 1960s reflected the ability and willingness of the United States to maintain order. The dominant institutions of the postwar period—the United Nations, the World Bank, the International Monetary Fund, the General Agreements on Tariffs and Trade—reflected the values of American central decision makers. The United States had used its material resources and prestige to nurture and sustain these institutions. It was no coincidence from a realist perspective that the world situation deteriorated during the 1970s, for as the costs of providing collective goods for the global system increased, the United States retreated to a more narrowly self-interested policy.

But as the decade progressed, realists also confronted some discomforting empirical developments. While strains increased, the 1930s were not replayed. In 1970, any realist with a modicum of courage who could have foreseen the major events of the coming decade would have predicted a gloomier future than the one that actually unfolded. Tensions with the Soviet Union did not notably increase. The international monetary system performed admirably under enormous pressures. Hostility between industrialized countries and the Third World abated after the initial demands for a New International Economic order in the mid 1970s. In sum, although adherents of various liberal perspectives, which rejected realism, saw their hopes and expectations of an ever more cooperative international system shattered by the difficulties encountered during the 1970s, the realists could hardly gloat about their analytic position. For although difficulties multiplied, international behavior did not deteriorate to the degree that a straightforward realist analysis would have predicted.

This volume confronts these dilemmas. Its authors are scholars associated with both liberal (what I have termed Grotian in my introduction) and realist traditions. The notion of rules of the game or international regimes—of principles, norms, rules, and decision-making procedures—that guide international behavior can be endorsed by both schools of thought. For liberals/Grotians, regimes remain the normal state of affairs in the international system. For realists they are difficult to create, but—at least for the scholars in this volume, with the exception of Susan Strange—once created, they may assume a life of their own. This modified realist argument suggests that the rules of the game established by the United States at the conclusion of the Second World War have persisted despite the changing attitudes and capabilities of American central decision makers. They provide some stability in an international system in which power is becoming more widely dispersed. This mode of analysis, with its emphasis on the need to distinguish periods of regime creation and regime maintenance, does not lead to any Pollyannaish conclusions concerning the future stability of the international order. Most of the non-Grotian authors in this volume are skeptical of the extent to which regimes can persist in the face of alterations in underlying national power capabilities. Nevertheless, a focus on international regimes does open new research agendas, especially those concerning questions regarding the relationship of international institutional structures to underlying power capabilities, and does offer an analytic construct that makes the events of the 1970s more comprehensible for both liberals and realists.

STEPHEN D. KRASNER

Stanford, California
October 1982

Acknowledgments for the special issue of *International Organization*, 1982

Support for this enterprise, both material and intellectual, came from a number of sources. Earlier versions of the papers were presented at meetings held in Los Angeles in October 1980 and Palm Springs in February 1981. These were made possible by grants from the Ford Foundation, the Center for International and Strategic Affairs at the University of California, Los Angeles, and *International Organization*. The Center for International and Strategic Affairs also provided indispensable logistical support for the conferences, with Donna Beltz serving as an extraordinarily capable conference coordinator while at the same time pursuing her graduate studies.

Albert Fishlow, Roger Hansen, Lynn Mytelka, and Peter Katzenstein, acting in his capacity as editor-in-chief of *International Organization*, served as the review committee for this special issue. They read numerous drafts and their suggestions improved all of the essays. Finally, I would like to express my gratitude to the Editorial Board of *International Organization* and especially to Robert Keohane, the journal's editor-in-chief at the time this project was first conceived. Their suggestions and guidance dramatically expanded my vision of this enterprise in ways that I know contributed to my own intellectual growth and, I hope, to the utility of the volume for both its contributors and its readers.

S. D. K.

October 1981

Structural causes and regime consequences: regimes as intervening variables

Stephen D. Krasner

This volume explores the concept of international regimes. International regimes are defined as principles, norms, rules, and decision-making procedures around which actor expectations converge in a given issue-area. As a starting point, regimes have been conceptualized as intervening variables standing between basic causal factors on the one hand and outcomes and behavior on the other. This formulation raises two basic questions: first, what is the relationship between basic causal factors such as power, interest, and values, and regimes? Second, what is the relationship between regimes and related outcomes and behavior? The first question is related to a number of basic paradigmatic debates about the nature of international relations. But for the purposes of this volume the second is equally or more important. It raises the issue of whether regimes make any difference.

The articles in this volume offer three approaches to the issue of regime significance. The essays of Oran Young, and Raymond Hopkins and Donald Puchala see regimes as a pervasive characteristic of the international system. No patterned behavior can sustain itself for any length of time without generating a congruent regime. Regimes and behavior are inextricably linked. In contrast, Susan Strange argues that regime is a misleading concept that obscures basic economic and power relationships. Strange, representing what is probably the modal position for international relations scholars, elaborates a conventional structural critique that rejects any significant role for principles, norms, rules, and decision-making procedures. Most of the authors in this volume adopt a third position, which can be labeled "modified structural." They accept the basic analytic assumptions of

International Organization 36, 2, Spring 1982
0020-8183/82/020185-21 $1.50

structural realist approaches, which posit an international system of functionally symmetrical, power-maximizing states acting in an anarchic environment. But they maintain that under certain restrictive conditions involving the failure of individual action to secure Pareto-optimal outcomes, international regimes may have a significant impact even in an anarchic world. This orientation is most explicitly elaborated in the essays of Arthur Stein, Robert Keohane, and Robert Jervis; it also informs the analyses presented by John Ruggie, Charles Lipson, and Benjamin Cohen.

The first section of this introduction develops definitions of regime and regime change. The following section investigates various approaches to the relationship between regimes, and behavior and outcomes. The third section examines five basic causal factors—egoistic self-interest, political power, diffuse norms and principles, usage and custom, and knowledge—that have been used to explain the development of regimes.

Defining regimes and regime change

Regimes can be defined as sets of implicit or explicit principles, norms, rules, and decision-making procedures around which actors' expectations converge in a given area of international relations. Principles are beliefs of fact, causation, and rectitude. Norms are standards of behavior defined in terms of rights and obligations. Rules are specific prescriptions or proscriptions for action. Decision-making procedures are prevailing practices for making and implementing collective choice.

This usage is consistent with other recent formulations. Keohane and Nye, for instance, define regimes as "sets of governing arrangements" that include "networks of rules, norms, and procedures that regularize behavior and control its effects."[1] Haas argues that a regime encompasses a mutually coherent set of procedures, rules, and norms.[2] Hedley Bull, using a somewhat different terminology, refers to the importance of rules and institutions in international society where rules refer to "general imperative principles which require or authorize prescribed classes of persons or groups to behave in prescribed ways."[3] Institutions for Bull help to secure adherence to rules by formulating, communicating, administering, enforcing, interpreting, legitimating, and adapting them.

Regimes must be understood as something more than temporary arrangements that change with every shift in power or interests. Keohane notes that a basic analytic distinction must be made between regimes and

---

[1] Robert O. Keohane and Joseph S. Nye, *Power and Interdependence* (Boston: Little, Brown, 1977), p. 19.

[2] Ernst Haas, "Technological Self-Reliance for Latin America: the OAS Contribution," *International Organization* 34, 4 (Autumn 1980), p. 553.

[3] Hedley Bull, *The Anarchical Society: A Study of Order in World Politics* (New York: Columbia University Press, 1977), p. 54.

agreements. Agreements are *ad hoc*, often "one-shot," arrangements. The purpose of regimes is to facilitate agreements. Similarly, Jervis argues that the concept of regimes "implies not only norms and expectations that facilitate cooperation, but a form of cooperation that is more than the following of short-run self-interest."[4] For instance, he contends that the restraints that have applied in Korea and other limited wars should not be considered a regime. These rules, such as "do not bomb sanctuaries," were based purely on short-term calculations of interest. As interest and power changed, behavior changed. Waltz's conception of the balance of power, in which states are driven by systemic pressures to repetitive balancing behavior, is not a regime; Kaplan's conception, in which equilibrium requires commitment to rules that constrain immediate, short-term power maximization (especially not destroying an essential actor), is a regime.[5]

Similarly, regime-governed behavior must not be based solely on short-term calculations of interest. Since regimes encompass principles and norms, the utility function that is being maximized must embody some sense of general obligation. One such principle, reciprocity, is emphasized in Jervis's analysis of security regimes. When states accept reciprocity they will sacrifice short-term interests with the expectation that other actors will reciprocate in the future, even if they are not under a specific obligation to do so. This formulation is similar to Fred Hirsch's brilliant discussion of friendship, in which he states: "Friendship contains an element of direct mutual exchange and to this extent is akin to private economic good. But it is often much more than that. Over time, the friendship 'transaction' can be presumed, by its permanence, to be a net benefit on both sides. At any moment of time, though, the exchange is very unlikely to be reciprocally balanced."[6] It is the infusion of behavior with principles and norms that distinguishes regime-governed activity in the international system from more conventional activity, guided exclusively by narrow calculations of interest.

A fundamental distinction must be made between principles and norms on the one hand, and rules and procedures on the other. Principles and norms provide the basic defining characteristics of a regime. There may be many rules and decision-making procedures that are consistent with the same principles and norms. *Changes in rules and decision-making procedures are changes within regimes,* provided that principles and norms are unaltered. For instance, Benjamin Cohen points out that there has been a substantial increase in private bank financing during the 1970s. This has meant a change in the rules governing balance-of-payments adjustment, but

[4] Robert Jervis's contribution to this volume, p. 173.

[5] Kenneth Waltz, *Theory of International Relations* (Reading, Mass.: Addison-Wesley, 1979); Morton Kaplan, *Systems and Process in International Politics* (New York: Wiley, 1957), p. 23; Kaplan, *Towards Professionalism in International Theory* (New York: Free Press, 1979), pp. 66-69, 73.

[6] Fred Hirsch, *The Social Limits to Growth* (Cambridge: Harvard University Press, 1976), p. 78.

it does not mean that there has been a fundamental change in the regime. The basic norm of the regime remains the same: access to balance-of-payments financing should be controlled, and conditioned on the behavior of borrowing countries. John Ruggie argues that in general the changes in international economic regimes that took place in the 1970s were norm-governed changes. They did not alter the basic principles and norms of the embedded liberal regime that has been in place since the 1940s.

Changes in principles and norms are changes of the regime itself. When norms and principles are abandoned, there is either a change to a new regime or a disappearance of regimes from a given issue-area. For instance, Ruggie contends that the distinction between orthodox and embedded liberalism involves differences over norms and principles. Orthodox liberalism endorses increasing the scope of the market. Embedded liberalism prescribes state action to contain domestic social and economic dislocations generated by markets. Orthodox and embedded liberalism define different regimes. The change from orthodox liberal principles and norms before World War II to embedded liberal principles and norms after World War II was, in Ruggie's terms, a "revolutionary" change.

Fundamental political arguments are more concerned with norms and principles than with rules and procedures. Changes in the latter may be interpreted in different ways. For instance, in the area of international trade, recent revisions in the Articles of Agreement of the General Agreement on Tariffs and Trade (GATT) provide for special and differential treatment for less developed countries (LDCs). All industrialized countries have instituted generalized systems of preferences for LDCs. Such rules violate one of the basic norms of the liberal postwar order, the most-favored-nation treatment of all parties. However, the industrialized nations have treated these alterations in the rules as temporary departures necessitated by the peculiar circumstances of poorer areas. At American insistence the concept of graduation was formally introduced into the GATT Articles after the Tokyo Round. Graduation holds that as countries become more developed they will accept rules consistent with liberal principles. Hence, Northern representatives have chosen to interpret special and differential treatment of developing countries as a change within the regime.

Speakers for the Third World, on the other hand, have argued that the basic norms of the international economic order should be redistribution and equity, not nondiscrimination and efficiency. They see the changes in rules as changes of the regime because they identify these changes with basic changes in principle. There is a fundamental difference between viewing changes in rules as indications of change within the regime and viewing these changes as indications of change between regimes. The difference hinges on assessments of whether principles and norms have changed as well. Such assessments are never easy because they cannot be based on objective behavioral observations. "We know deviations from regimes," Ruggie avers, "not simply by acts that are undertaken, but by the intentionality and acceptability attributed to those acts in the context of an intersubjective framework of meaning.''[7]

Finally, it is necessary to distinguish the weakening of a regime from changes within or between regimes. *If the principles, norms, rules, and decision-making procedures of a regime become less coherent, or if actual practice is increasingly inconsistent with principles, norms, rules, and procedures, then a regime has weakened.* Special and differential treatment for developing countries is an indication that the liberal regime has weakened, even if it has not been replaced by something else. The use of diplomatic cover by spies, the bugging of embassies, the assassination of diplomats by terrorists, and the failure to provide adequate local police protection are all indications that the classic regime protecting foreign envoys has weakened. However, the furtive nature of these activities indicates that basic principles and norms are not being directly challenged. In contrast, the seizure of American diplomats by groups sanctioned by the Iranian government is a basic challenge to the regime itself. Iran violated principles and norms, not just rules and procedures.[8]

In sum, change within a regime involves alterations of rules and decision-making procedures, but not of norms or principles; change of a regime involves alteration of norms and principles; and weakening of a regime involves incoherence among the components of the regime or inconsistency between the regime and related behavior.

Do regimes matter?

It would take some courage, perhaps more courage than this editor possesses, to answer this question in the negative. This project began with a simple causal schematic. It assumed that regimes could be conceived of as intervening variables standing between basic causal variables (most prominently, power and interests) and outcomes and behavior. The first attempt to analyze regimes thus assumed the following set of causal relationships (see Figure 1).

BASIC CAUSAL VARIABLES ⟶ REGIMES ⟶ RELATED BEHAVIOR AND OUTCOMES

Figure 1

Regimes do not arise of their own accord. They are not regarded as ends in themselves. Once in place they do affect related behavior and outcomes. They are not merely epiphenomenal.

---

[7] John Ruggie's contribution to this volume, p. 196.

[8] Iran's behavior may be rooted in an Islamic view of international relations that rejects the prevailing, European-derived regime. See Richard Rosecrance, "International Theory Revisited," *International Organization* 35, 4 (Autumn 1981) for a similar point.

The independent impact of regimes is a central analytic issue. The second causal arrow implies that regimes do matter. However, there is no general agreement on this point, and three basic orientations can be distinguished. The conventional structural views the regime concept as useless, if not misleading. Modified structural suggests that regimes may matter, but only under fairly restrictive conditions. And Grotian sees regimes as much more pervasive, as inherent attributes of any complex, persistent pattern of human behavior.

In this volume Susan Strange represents the first orientation. She has grave reservations about the value of the notion of regimes. Strange argues that the concept is pernicious because it obfuscates and obscures the interests and power relationships that are the proximate, not just the ultimate, cause of behavior in the international system. "All those international arrangements dignified by the label regime are only too easily upset when either the balance of bargaining power or the perception of national interest (or both together) change among those states who negotiate them."[9] Regimes, if they can be said to exist at all, have little or no impact. They are merely epiphenomenal. The underlying causal schematic is one that sees a direct connection between changes in basic causal factors (whether economic or political) and changes in behavior and outcomes. Regimes are excluded completely, or their impact on outcomes and related behavior is regarded as trivial.

Strange's position is consistent with prevailing intellectual orientations for analyzing social phenomena. These structural orientations conceptualize a world of rational self-seeking actors. The actors may be individuals, or firms, or groups, or classes, or states. They function in a system or environment that is defined by their own interests, power, and interaction. These orientations are resistant to the contention that principles, norms, rules, and decision-making procedures have a significant impact on outcomes and behavior.

Nowhere is this more evident than in the image of the market, the reigning analytic conceptualization for economics, the most successful of the social sciences. A market is characterized by impersonality between buyers and sellers, specialization in buying and selling, and exchange based upon prices set in terms of a common medium of exchange.[10] Max Weber states that in the market "social actions are not determined by orientation to any sort of norm which is held to be valid, nor do they rest on custom, but entirely on the fact that the corresponding type of social action is in the nature of the case best adapted to the normal interests of the actors as they themselves are aware of them."[11] The market is a world of atomized, self-seeking egoistic individuals.

[9] Susan Strange's contribution to this volume, p. 345.
[10] Cyril Belshaw, *Traditional Exchange and Modern Markets* (Englewood Cliffs, N.J.: Prentice-Hall, 1965), pp. 8-9.
[11] Max Weber, *Economy and Society* (Berkeley: University of California Press, 1977), p. 30.

The market is a powerful metaphor for many arguments in the literature ⟨ A
of political science, not least international relations. The recent work of
Kenneth Waltz exemplifies this orientation. For Waltz, the defining characteristic of the international system is that its component parts (states) are
functionally similar and interact in an anarchic environment. International
systems are distinguished only by differing distributions of relative capabilities among actors. States are assumed to act in their own self-interest. At a
minimum they "seek their own preservation and, at a maximum, drive for
universal domination."[12] They are constrained only by their interaction with
other states in the system. Behavior is, therefore, a function of the distribution of power among states and the position of each particular state. When
power distributions change, behavior will also change. Regimes, for Waltz,
can only be one small step removed from the underlying power capabilities
that sustain them.[13]

The second orientation to regimes, modified structural, is most clearly ⟨ B
reflected in the essays of Keohane and Stein. Both of these authors start
from a conventional structural realist perspective, a world of sovereign
states seeking to maximize their interest and power. Keohane posits that in
the international system regimes derive from voluntary agreements among
juridically equal actors. Stein states that the "conceptualization of regimes developed here is rooted in the classic characterization of international politics as relations between sovereign entities dedicated to their own
self-preservation, ultimately able to depend only on themselves, and prepared to resort to force."[14]

In a world of sovereign states the basic function of regimes is to coordinate state behavior to achieve desired outcomes in particular issue-areas.[15]
Such coordination is attractive under several circumstances. Stein and
Keohane posit that regimes can have an impact when Pareto-optimal outcomes could not be achieved through uncoordinated individual calculations
of self-interest. The prisoners' dilemma is the classic game-theoretic example. Stein also argues that regimes may have an autonomous effect on outcomes when purely autonomous behavior could lead to disastrous results for
both parties. The game of chicken is the game-theoretic analog. Haas and
others in this volume suggest that regimes may have significant impact in a
highly complex world in which *ad hoc,* individualistic calculations of interest
could not possibly provide the necessary level of coordination. If, as many
have argued, there is a general movement toward a world of complex inter-

---

[12] Waltz, *Theory of International Relations,* p. 118.

[13] Ibid., especially chapters 5 and 6. This conventional structuralist view for the realist school
has its analog in Marxist analysis to studies that focus exclusively on technology and economic
structure.

[14] Robert O. Keohane's and Arthur A. Stein's contributions to this volume, pp. 146 and 116.

[15] Vinod K. Aggarwal emphasizes this point. See his "Hanging by a Thread: International
Regime Change in the Textile/Apparel System, 1950–1979," Ph.D. diss., Stanford University,
1981, chap. 1.

dependence, then the number of areas in which regimes can matter is growing.

However, regimes cannot be relevant for zero-sum situations in which states act to maximize the difference between their utilities and those of others. Jervis points to the paucity of regimes in the security area, which more closely approximates zero-sum games than do most economic issue-areas. Pure power motivations preclude regimes. Thus, the second orientation, modified structuralism, sees regimes emerging and having a significant impact, but only under restrictive conditions. It suggests that the first cut should be amended as in Figure 2.

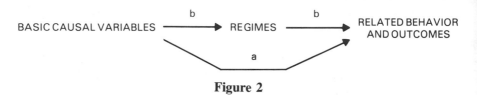

Figure 2

For most situations there is a direct link between basic causal variables and related behavior (path a); but under circumstances that are not purely conflictual, where individual decision making leads to suboptimal outcomes, regimes may be significant (path b).[16]

The third approach to regimes, most clearly elaborated in the essays of Raymond Hopkins and Donald Puchala, and Oran Young, reflects a fundamentally different view of international relations than the two structural arguments just described. These two essays are strongly informed by the Grotian tradition, which sees regimes as a pervasive phenomenon of all political systems. Hopkins and Puchala conclude that "regimes exist in all areas of international relations, even those, such as major power rivalry, that are traditionally looked upon as clear-cut examples of anarchy. Statesmen nearly always perceive themselves as constrained by principles, norms, and rules that prescribe and proscribe varieties of behavior."[17] The concept of regime, they argue, moves beyond a realist perspective, which is "too limited for explaining an increasingly complex, interdependent, and dangerous world."[18] Hopkins and Puchala apply their argument not only to an issue-area where one might expect communalities of interest (food) but also to one generally thought of as being much more unambiguously conflictual (colonialism).

Oran Young argues that patterned behavior inevitably generates con-

---

[16] The modified structural arguments presented in this volume are based upon a realist analysis of international relations. In the Marxist tradition this position has its analog in many structural Marxist writings, which emphasize the importance of the state and ideology as institutions that act to rationalize and legitimate fundamental economic structures.

[17] Raymond Hopkins and Donald Puchala's contribution to this volume, p. 86.

[18] Ibid., p. 61.

vergent expectations. This leads to conventionalized behavior in which there is some expectation of rebuke for deviating from ongoing practices. Conventionalized behavior generates recognized norms. If the observer finds a pattern of interrelated activity, and the connections in the pattern are understood, then there must be some form of norms and procedures.

While the modified structural approach does not view the perfect market as a regime, because action there is based purely upon individual calculation without regard to the behavior of others, the third orientation does regard the market as a regime. Patterns of behavior that persist over extended periods are infused with normative significance. A market cannot be sustained by calculations of self-interest alone. It must be, in Ruggie's terms, *embedded* in a broader social environment that nurtures and sustains the conditions necessary for its functioning. Even the balance of power, regarded by conventional structural realist analysts as a purely conflictual situation, can be treated as a regime.[19] The causal schema suggested by a Grotian orientation either closely parallels the first cut shown in Figure 1, or can be depicted as in Figure 3.

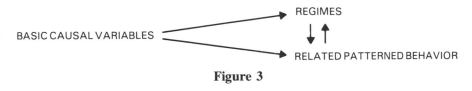

Figure 3

Patterned behavior reflecting calculations of interest tends to lead to the creation of regimes, and regimes reinforce patterned behavior.

The Grotian tradition that Hopkins and Puchala, and Young draw upon, offers a counter to structural realism of either the conventional or the modified form. It rejects the assumption that the international system is composed of sovereign states limited only by the balance of power. Rather, Hopkins and Puchala suggest that elites are the practical actors in international relations. States are rarified abstractions. Elites have transnational as well as national ties. Sovereignty is a behavioral variable, not an analytic assumption. The ability of states to control movements across their borders and to maintain dominance over all aspects of the international system is limited. Security and state survival are not the only objectives. Force does not occupy a singularly important place in international politics. Elites act within a communications net, embodying rules, norms, and principles, which transcends national boundaries.

This minimalist Grotian orientation has informed a number of theoretical postulates developed during the postwar period. Functionalism saw the possibility of eroding sovereignty through the multiplication of particularistic interests across national boundaries. Karl Deutsch's 1957 study of inte-

[19] Bull, *The Anarchical Society,* chap. 5.

gration, with its emphasis on societal communication, made a distinction between security communities and anarchy.[20] Some authors associated with the concept of transnationalism have posited a web of interdependence that makes any emphasis on sovereignty analytically misleading and normatively questionable. Keohane and Nye's discussion of complex interdependence rejects the assumptions of the primacy of force and issue hierarchy assumed by a realist perspective.[21] Ernst Haas points out that what he calls organic theories—eco-environmentalism, eco-reformism, and egalitarianism—deny conventional power-oriented assumptions.

Regimes are much more easily encompassed by a Grotian worldview. But, as the arguments made by Jervis, Keohane, Stein, Lipson, and Cohen indicate, the concept is not precluded by a realist perspective. The issue is not so much whether one accepts the possibility of principles, norms, rules, and decision-making procedures affecting outcomes and behavior, as what one's basic assumption is about the normal state of international affairs. Adherents of a Grotian perspective accept regimes as a pervasive and significant phenomenon in the international system. Adherents of a structural realist orientation see regimes as a phenomenon whose presence cannot be assumed and whose existence requires careful explanation. The two "standard cases" are fundamentally different, and it is the definition of the standard case that identifies the basic theoretical orientation. Stephen Toulmin writes that "any dynamical theory involves some explicit or implicit reference to a standard case or 'paradigm.' This paradigm specifies the manner in which, in the course of events, bodies may be expected to move." It is deviation from that movement which needs to be explained.[22] From a realist perspective, regimes are phenomena that need to be explained; from a Grotian perspective, they are data to be described.

In sum, conventional structural arguments do not take regimes seriously: if basic causal variables change, regimes will also change. Regimes have no independent impact on behavior. Modified structural arguments, represented here by a number of adherents of a realist approach to international relations, see regimes as mattering only when independent decision making leads to undesired outcomes. Finally, Grotian perspectives accept regimes as a fundamental part of all patterned human interaction, including behavior in the international system.

Explanations for regime development

For those authors who see regimes as something more than epiphenomena, the second major issue posed by a schematic that sees re-

[20] See Arend Lijphart, "The Structure of the Theoretical Revolution in International Relations," *International Studies Quarterly* 18, 1 (March 1974), pp. 64-65, for the development of this argument.

[21] Keohane and Nye, *Power and Interdependence,* especially chap. 8.

[22] Stephen Toulmin, *Foresight and Understanding: An Enquiry into the Aims of Science* (New York: Harper Torchbooks, 1961), pp. 56-57. Toulmin's use of the term paradigm is similar to

gimes as intervening variables between basic causal factors and related outcomes and behavior becomes relevant. What is the relationship between
basic causal factors and regimes? What are the conditions that lead to regime
creation, persistence, and dissipation? Here regimes are treated as the dependent variable.

A wide variety of basic causal variables have been offered to explain the
development of regimes. The most prominent in this volume are egoistic
self-interest, political power, norms and principles, habit and custom, and
knowledge. The last two are seen as supplementary, augmenting more basic
forces related to interest, power, and values.

1. Egoistic self-interest

The prevailing explanation for the existence of international regimes is
egoistic self-interest. By egoistic self-interest I refer to the desire to
maximize one's own utility function where that function does not include the
utility of another party. The egoist is concerned with the behavior of others
only insofar as that behavior can affect the egoist's utility. All contractarian
political theories from Hobbes to Rawls are based on egoistic self-interest.
In contrast, pure power seekers are interested in maximizing the difference
between their power capabilities and those of their opponent.

In this volume the essays by Keohane and especially Stein most fully
adopt and elaborate an interest-oriented perspective. Stein avers that "the
same forces of autonomously calculated self-interest that lie at the root of
the anarchic international system also lay the foundation for international
regimes as a form of international order. . . . [T]here are times when rational
self-interested calculation leads actors to abandon independent decision
making in favor of joint decision making."[23]

Stein elaborates two circumstances under which unconstrained individual choice provides incentives for cooperation. The first occurs when
such choice leads to Pareto-suboptimal outcomes: prisoner's dilemma and
the provision of collective goods are well-known examples. Stein refers to
this as the dilemma of common interests. Its resolution requires "collaboration," the active construction of a regime that guides individual decision
making. Unconstrained individual decision making may also be eschewed
when it would lead to mutually undesired outcomes and where the choice of
one actor is contingent on the choice made by the other: the game of chicken
is a prominent example. Stein refers to this as the dilemma of common aversions; it can be resolved through "coordination." Coordination need not be
formalized or institutionalized. So long as everyone agrees to drive on the
right side of the road, little more is needed. (Stein's concept of collaboration

---

Kuhn's notion of an exemplar. See Thomas Kuhn, *The Structure of Specific Revolutions,* 2nd
ed. (Chicago: University of Chicago Press, 1970), p. 187.

[23] Stein's contribution to this volume, p. 132.

conforms with the definition of regimes used here. It is not so clear that coordination involves regimes. Coordination may only require the construction of rules. If these rules are not informed by any proximate principles or norms, they will not conform to the definition of regimes set forth earlier.)

While Stein employs a game-theoretic orientation, Keohane utilizes insights from microeconomic theories of market failure to examine dilemmas of common interests. He is primarily concerned with the demand for regimes, the conditions under which *ad hoc* agreements fail to provide Pareto-optimal outcomes. He maintains that "Regimes can make agreement easier if they provide frameworks for establishing legal liability (even if these are not perfect); improve the quantity and quality of information available to actors; or reduce other transactions costs, such as costs of organization or of making side-payments."[24] These benefits provided by regimes are likely to outweigh the costs of regime formation and maintenance when there is asymmetric information, moral hazard, potential dishonesty, or high issue density. In addition, the costs of forming regimes will be lower when there is a high level of formal and informal communication among states, a condition more likely to be found in open political systems operating under conditions of complex interdependence.

Egoistic self-interest is also regarded as an important determinant of regimes by several other authors. Young argues that there are three paths to regime formation: spontaneous, in which regimes emerge from the converging expectations of many individual actions; negotiated, in which regimes are formed by explicit agreements; and imposed, in which regimes are initially forced upon actors by external imposition. The first two are based on egoistic calculations. Lipson argues that the differential pattern of acceptance of liberal rules in the international trading regime is a function of differential costs of adjustment across industrial sectors; where costs are low, continued adherence to liberal principles, norms, and rules is high. Cohen maintains that the rules of the balance-of-payments financing regime changed in the 1970s because higher oil prices and the petrodollar market altered calculations of interest. Jervis posits that regimes in the security arena will only be formed when states accept the status quo, the cost of war is high, and the spillover into other arenas is substantial. This last point, which echoes Keohane's argument about the importance of issue density, is similar to arguments made by Haas and by Puchala and Hopkins. Haas makes interconnectedness a central element of his analysis: regimes are designed to manage complexity and complexity increases with interconnectedness. Similarly, Puchala and Hopkins maintain that regimes are more likely to arise under conditions of complex interdependence. Hence calculations of egoistic self-interest emerge as central elements in most of the articles in this volume.

---

[24] Keohane's contribution to this volume, p. 154.

2. Political power   *advantage from*
cooperation

The second major basic causal variable used to explain regime development is political power. Two different orientations toward power can
be distinguished. The first is cosmopolitan and instrumental: power is used   *1.*
to secure optimal outcomes for the system as a whole. In game-theoretic
terms power is used to promote joint maximization. It is power in the service
of the common good. The second approach is particularistic and potentially
consummatory. Power is used to enhance the values of specific actors within   *2.*
the system. These values may include increasing power capabilities as well
as promoting economic or other objectives. In game-theoretic terms power
is used to maximize individual payoffs. It is power in the service of particular
interests.

a. Power in the service of the common good

The first position is represented by a long tradition in classical and
neoclassical economics associated with the provision of public goods. The
hidden hand was Adam Smith's most compelling construct: the good of all
from the selfishness of each; there could be no more powerful defense of
egoism. But Smith recognized that it was necessary for the state to provide
certain collective goods. These included defense, the maintenance of order,
minimum levels of welfare, public works, the protection of infant industries,
and standards for commodities.[25] Economists have pointed to the importance of the state for establishing property rights and enforcing contracts;
that is, creating conditions that prevent predatory as opposed to market behavior. The state must create institutions that equate public and private rates
of return.[26] Keynesian analysis gives the state a prominent role in managing
macroeconomic variables. For all of these arguments the purpose of state
action is to further general societal interests.

[25] There is a lively debate over precisely how much of a role Smith accords to the state. Some
(see for instance Albert Hirschman, *The Passions and the Interests* [Princeton: Princeton University Press, 1977], pp. 103–104) maintain that Smith wanted to limit the folly of government
by having it do as little as possible. Others (see for instance Colin Holmes, "Laissez-faire in
Theory and Practice: Britain 1800–1875," *Journal of European Economic History* 5, 3 [1976], p.
673; and Carlos Diaz-Alejandro, "Delinking North and South: Unshackled or Unhinged," in
Albert Fishlow et al., *Rich and Poor Nations in the World Economy* [New York: McGraw-Hill,
1978], pp. 124–25) have taken the intermediate position endorsed here. Others see Smith trying
to establish conditions for a moral society that must be based on individual choice, for which a
materialistically oriented, egoistically maintained economic system is only instrumental. See,
for instance, Leonard Billet, "The Just Economy: The Moral Basis of the Wealth of Nations,"
Review of Social Economy 34 (December 1974).
[26] Jack Hirschleifer, "Economics from a Biological Viewpoint," *Journal of Law and Economics* 20 (April 1977); Weber, *Economy and Society,* pp. 336–37; Douglass C. North and
Robert Paul Thomas, *The Rise of the Western World: A New Economic History* (Cambridge:
Cambridge University Press, 1973), chap. 1.

The contemporary economist who has become most clearly associated with arguments emphasizing the instrumental role of power for cosmopolitan interests in the international system is Charles Kindleberger. In *The World in Depression,* Kindleberger argues that the depression of the 1930s could have been prevented by effective state leadership. An effective leader would have acted as a lender of last resort and provided a market for surplus commodities. In the interwar period the United States was able but unwilling to assume these burdens, and Great Britain was willing but unable. The result was economic chaos. In a more recent statement Kindleberger has listed the following functions that states perform for the international trading system:

1. Protecting economic actors from force.
2. Cushioning the undesirable effects of an open system by, for instance, providing adjustment assistance for import-competing industries.
3. Establishing standards for products. In the absence of such standards inordinate energy may be wasted finding information about products.
4. Providing a national currency that can be used as an international reserve and transactions currency.
5. Constructing public works such as docks and domestic transportation systems.
6. Compensating for market imperfections by, for instance, becoming a lender of last resort when private financial institutions become so cautious that their conservatism could destroy global liquidity.[27]

Despite its emphasis on political action, Kindleberger's perspective is still profoundly liberal. The purpose of state intervention is to facilitate the creation and maintenance of an environment within which a market based on individual calculations of self-interest can flourish. The market, like the human body, is basically healthy, but occasionally the intervention of some external agent (the state, a doctor) may be necessary.[28] A market economy will maximize the utility of society as a whole. Political power is put at the service of the common good.

b. Power in the service of particular interests

The articles in this volume are less oriented toward cosmopolitan ends; rather, they focus on power as an instrument that can be used to enhance the

[27] Charles P. Kindleberger, "Government and International Trade," *Princeton Essays in International Finance* (International Finance Section, Princeton University, July 1978). Adam Smith was less enamoured with leadership. He felt that reasonable intercourse could only take place in the international system if there was a balance of power. Without such a balance the strong would dominate and exploit the weak. See Diaz-Alejandro, "Delinking North and South," p. 92.

[28] Charles P. Kindleberger, *Manias, Panics, and Crashes: A History of Financial Crises* (New York: Basic Books, 1978).

utility of particular actors, usually states. A game-theoretic analogy makes it easier to distinguish between two important variants of the viewpoint of power in the service of particular interests. The first assumes that pay-offs are fixed and that an actor's choice of strategy is autonomously determined solely by these pay-offs. The second assumes that power can be used to alter pay-offs and influence actor strategy.

The first approach closely follows the analysis that applies when purely cosmopolitan objectives are at stake, except that political power is used to maximize individual, not joint, pay-offs. Under certain configurations of interest, there is an incentive to create regimes and the provision of these regimes is a function of the distribution of power. While Keohane focuses on the demand for regimes in his article in this volume, he has elsewhere argued that hegemons play a critical role in supplying the collective goods that are needed for regimes to function effectively.[29] Hegemons provide these goods not because they are interested in the well-being of the system as a whole, but because regimes enhance their own national values.

This emphasis on the need for asymmetric power distributions (supply-side considerations) should be contrasted with Stein's assertions concerning the efficacy of demand. The theory of hegemonic leadership suggests that under conditions of declining hegemony there will be a weakening of regimes. Without leadership, principles, norms, rules, and decision-making procedures cannot easily be upheld. No one actor will be willing to provide the collective goods needed to make the regime work smoothly and effectively. Stein's analysis, on the other hand, suggests that as hegemony declines there will be greater incentives for collaboration because collective goods are no longer being provided by the hegemon. The international system more closely resembles an oligopoly than a perfect market. Actors are aware of how their behavior affects others. When smaller states perceive that a hegemon is no longer willing to offer a free ride, they are likely to become paying customers. For Stein, interests alone can effectively sustain order. Hegemonic decline can lead to stronger regimes.

The second line of argument associated with power in the service of specific interests investigates the possibility that powerful actors may be able to alter the pay-offs that confront other actors or influence the strategies they choose. Here power becomes a much more central concept—the element of compulsion is close at hand. Weaker actors may not be able to make autonomous choices. The values assigned to a particular cell may be changed.

In this volume Oran Young develops the notion of imposed regimes. Dominant actors may explicitly use a combination of sanctions and incentives to compel other actors to act in conformity with a particular set of

[29] Robert O. Keohane, "The Theory of Hegemonic Stability and Changes in International Economic Regimes, 1967–77," in Ole R. Holsti et al., *Changes in the International System* (Boulder, Col.: Westview, 1980).

principles, norms, rules, and decision-making procedures. Alternatively, dominant actors may secure de facto compliance by manipulating opportunity sets so that weaker actors are compelled to behave in a desired way. Keohane posits that in the international system choices will be constrained in ways that give greater weight to the preferences of more powerful actors. Benjamin Cohen notes that the specific rules and institutional arrangements for the Bretton Woods institutions reflected the preferences of the United States much more than those of Great Britain. Jervis points out that weaker states had little option but to follow the balance of power regime of the 19th century with its emphasis on the special role of the great powers. In all of these cases more powerful actors created regimes that served their particular purpose, and other were compelled to accept them because their pay-offs were manipulated or their options were limited.

When a hegemonic state acts to influence the strategy of other actors the regime is held hostage to the persistence of the existing distribution of power in the international system. If the hegemon's relative capabilities decline, the regime will collapse. Young argues that imposed orders are likely to disintegrate when there are major shifts in underlying power capabilities. Hopkins and Puchala suggest that regimes that are highly politicized, diffuse, and biased in their distribution of values are likely to undergo radical transformation when power distributions change. For instance, the norms of the colonial regime collapsed because the power of its supporter, the major European states, eroded. This set of arguments about regime change and hegemonic decline differs from the analysis emerging from a focus on the provision of collective goods for either cosmopolitan or particularistic reasons. Here a decline in power leads to a change in regime because the hegemon is no longer able to control the pay-off matrix or influence the strategies of the weak, not because there is no actor to provide the collective goods needed for efficient regime functioning.

3. Norms and principles

To this point in the discussion, norms and principles have been treated as endogenous: they are the critical defining characteristics of any given regime. However, norms and principles that influence the regime in a particular issue-area but are not directly related to that issue-area can also be regarded as explanations for the creation, persistence, and dissipation of regimes. The most famous example of such a formulation is Max Weber's *Protestant Ethic and the Spirit of Capitalism*. Weber argues that the rise of capitalism is intimately associated with the evolution of a Calvinist religious doctrine that fosters hard work while enjoining profligacy and uses worldly success as an indication of predestined fate.[30] Fred Hirsch has argued that

---

[30] For a recent discussion see David Laitin, "Religion, Political Culture, and the Weberian

without precapitalist values such as hard work, self-sacrifice, loyalty, and honor, capitalist systems would fall apart. Such values are critical constraints on self-interested calculations that would too often lead to untrustworthy and dishonest behavior.[31]

Financing by various pariah groups around the world offers a clear example of the way in which noneconomic norms have facilitated market activity. For instance, bills of exchange were devised by Jewish bankers during the late Middle Ages to avoid violence and extortion from the nobility: safer to carry a piece of paper than to carry specie. However, the piece of paper had to be honored by the recipient. This implied a high level of trust and such trust was enhanced by conventions: established practices were reinforced by the exclusionary nature of the group, which facilitated surveillance and the application of sanctions. The importance of conventions for the use of bills of exchange is reflected in the fact that they were frequently used in the Mediterranean basin in the 16th century but they were not used at the interface with the non-Mediterranean world in Syria where, according to Braudel, "two mutually suspicious worlds met face to face." Here all dealings were in barter, or gold and silver.[32]

In this volume, Hopkins and Puchala make a distinction between the superstructure and the substructure. The superstructure refers to general and diffuse principles and norms that condition the principles and norms operative in a specific issue-area. They note, for example, that balance of power in 19th century Europe was a diffuse norm that influenced the nature of the regime for colonialism. Jervis argues that for regimes to develop in the security area the great powers "must believe that others share the value they place on mutual security and cooperation."[33] John Ruggie's highly original analysis of the postwar economic regime argues that it was founded upon principles of embedded rather than orthodox liberalism. The domestic lesson of the 1930s was that societies could not tolerate the consequences of an untrammeled market. This set of diffuse values, which permeated the capitalist world, was extended from the domestic to the international sphere in the Bretton Woods agreements.

This discussion suggests that there is a hierarchy of regimes. Diffuse principles and norms, such as hard work as a service to God, condition behavior in specific issue-areas. In international relations, the most important diffuse principle is sovereignty. Hedley Bull refers to sovereignty as the con-

---

Tradition," *World Politics* 30, 4 (July 1978), especially pp. 568–69. For another discussion of noneconomic values in the rise of capitalism see Hirschman, *The Passions and the Interests.*

[31] Hirsch, *The Social Limits to Growth,* chap. 11. See also Michael Walzer, "The Future of Intellectuals and the Rise of the New Class," *New York Review of Books* 27 (20 March 1980).

[32] Fernand Braudel, *The Mediterranean and the Mediterranean World in the Age of Philip II* (New York: Harper, 1975), p. 370. For the tie between bills of exchange and Jewish bankers see Hirschman, *The Passions and the Interests,* p. 72, and Immanuel Wallerstein, *The Modern World-System* (New York: Academic Press, 1974), p. 147.

[33] Jervis's contribution to this volume, p. 177.

stitutive principle of the present international system. The concept of exclusive control within a delimited geographic area and the untrammeled right to self-help internationally, which emerged out of late medieval Europe, have come to pervade the modern international system.[34]

In this usage sovereignty is not an analytic assumption, it is a principle that influences the behavior of actors. With a few exceptions, such as Antarctica, Namibia, and the West Bank, sovereignty prevails. Those areas where sovereignty is not applied are governed by vulnerable regimes or lack regimes altogether. Sovereignty designates states as the only actors with unlimited rights to act in the international system. Assertions by other agencies are subject to challenge. If the constitutive principle of sovereignty were altered, it is difficult to imagine that any other international regime would remain unchanged.

4. *Usage and custom*

The last two sets of causal variables affecting regime development are usage and custom, and knowledge. Usage and custom will be discussed in this section, knowledge in the next. Usage and custom, and knowledge, are not treated in this volume as exogenous variables capable of generating a regime on their own. Rather, they supplement and reinforce pressures associated with egoistic self-interest, political power, and diffuse values.

Usage refers to regular patterns of behavior based on actual practice; custom, to long-standing practice.[35] The importance of routinized behavior is particularly significant in the position taken by Hopkins and Puchala and by Young. For these authors, patterned behavior, originally generated purely by considerations of interest or power, has a strong tendency to lead to shared expectations. Patterned behavior accompanied by shared expectations is likely to become infused with normative significance: actions based purely on instrumental calculations can come to be regarded as rule-like or principled behavior. They assume legitimacy. A great deal of western commercial law, in fact, developed out of custom and usage initially generated by self-interest. Practices that began as *ad hoc* private arrangements later became the basis for official commercial law.[36]

In Oran Young's discussion of both spontaneous and imposed regimes, habits and usage play a significant role. Young does not make any strong claims for the specific conditions that lead to spontaneous regimes. However, the literature to which he refers—Schelling, Lewis, and Hayek—

---

[34] Bull, *The Anarchical Society,* pp. 8–9, 70.

[35] Weber, *Economy and Society,* p. 29.

[36] Leon E. Trakman, "The Evolution of the Law Merchant: Our Commercial Heritage," Part I, *Journal of Maritime Law and Commerce* 12, 1 (October 1980) and Part II, ibid., 12, 2 (January 1981); Harold Berman and Colin Kaufman, "The Law of International Commercial Transactions (*Lex Mercatoria*)," *Harvard International Law Journal* 19, 1 (Winter 1978).

is oriented toward a microeconomic perspective focusing on egoistic self-interest. Certain patterns of behavior are first adopted because they promote individual utility. Once established, such practices are reinforced by the growth of regimes. Most American drivers (outside New York City) would feel at least a twinge of discomfort at driving illegally through a red light at an empty intersection. Behavior that was originally only a matter of egoistic self-interest is now buttressed by widely shared norms. Similarly, Young argues that successful imposed orders are bolstered eventually by habits of obedience. (It is not clear that, without these habits, Young's concept of imposed orders conforms with the definition of regime used here.) A pattern of behavior initially established by economic coercion or force may come to be regarded as legitimate by those on whom it has been imposed. Usage leads to shared expectations, which become infused with principles and norms.

5. Knowledge

The final variable used to explain the development of regimes is knowledge. Like usage and custom, knowledge is usually treated as an intervening, not an exogenous, variable. In an earlier study Ernst Haas, in this volume the most prominent exponent of the importance of knowledge, defined knowledge as "the sum of technical information and of theories about that information which commands sufficient consensus at a given time among interested actors to serve as a guide to public policy designed to achieve some social goal."[37] In his essay in this volume Haas points to the potentialities inherent in a stance of "cognitive evolutionism," which emphasizes sensitivity to the consequences of the generation of new knowledge. Knowledge creates a basis for cooperation by illuminating complex interconnections that were not previously understood. Knowledge can not only enhance the prospects for convergent state behavior, it can also transcend "prevailing lines of ideological cleavage."[38] It can provide a common ground for both what Haas calls mechanical approaches (most conventional social science theories) and organic approaches (egalitarianism and various environmentally oriented arguments).

For knowledge to have an independent impact in the international system, it must be widely accepted by policy makers. Stein points out that rules concerning health, such as quarantine regulations, were radically altered by new scientific knowledge such as the discovery of the microbe that causes cholera, the transmission of yellow fever by mosquitoes, and the use of preventive vaccines. Prior to developments such as these, national health regu-

---

[37] Ernst Haas, "Why Collaborate? Issue-Linkage and International Regimes," *World Politics* 32, 3 (April 1980), pp. 367–68.
[38] Ibid., p. 368.

lations were primarily determined by political concerns. After these discoveries, however, national behavior was determined by an international regime, or at least a set of rules, dictated by accepted scientific knowledge. Jervis argues that in the present security arena the possibilities for an arms control regime may depend on whether the Soviet Union and the United States view strategy in the same way. In particular, mutual acceptance of Mutual Assured Destruction (MAD) can provide the basis for a regime. Without consensus, knowledge can have little impact on regime development in a world of sovereign states. If only some parties hold a particular set of beliefs, their significance is completely mediated by the power of their adherents.

New knowledge can provide the basis for what Hopkins and Puchala call evolutionary change, which usually involves altering rules and procedures within the context of a given set of principles and norms. In contrast, revolutionary change, which generates new principles and norms, is associated with shifts in power. As an example of evolutionary change, Benjamin Cohen points out that the fixed exchange rate system agreed to at Bretton Woods was based upon understandings derived from the interwar experience and then-current knowledge about domestic monetary institutions and structures. States were extremely sensitive to competitive devaluation and were not confident that domestic monetary policy could provide insulation from external disturbances. It was much easier to accept a floating exchange rate regime in the 1970s because the knowledge and related institutional capacity for controlling monetary aggregates had substantially increased. In a highly complex world, where goals are often ill-defined and many links are possible, consensual knowledge can greatly facilitate agreement on the development of an international regime. Such knowledge can light a clear path in a landscape that would otherwise be murky and undifferentiated.

In sum, the essays in this volume and the literature in general offer a variety of explanations for the development of regimes. The two most prominent exogenous variables are egoistic self-interest, usually economic, and political power. In addition, diffuse values and norms such as sovereignty and private property may condition behavior within specific issue-areas. Finally, usage and custom and knowledge may contribute to the development of regimes.

Conclusion

In approaching the two basic questions that guided this exercise—the impact of regimes on related behavior and outcomes, and the relationship between basic causal variables and regimes—the essays in this volume reflect two different orientations to international relations. The Grotian perspective, which informs the essays of Hopkins and Puchala and of Young, sees regimes as a pervasive facet of social interaction. It is catholic in its description of the underlying causes of regimes. Interests, power, diffuse norms, customs, and knowledge may all play a role in regime formation. These causal factors may be manifest through the behavior of individuals, particular bureaucracies, and international organizations, as well as states.

The structural realist orientation, which infuses the other essays in this volume, is more circumspect. The exemplar or standard case for the realist perspective does not include international regimes. Regimes arise only under restrictive conditions characterized by the failure of individual decision making to secure desired outcomes. The basic causal variables that lead to the creation of regimes are power and interest. The basic actors are states.

The arguments presented by Stein, Keohane, Jervis, Ruggie, Lipson, and Cohen do press beyond conventional realist orientations. They reject a narrow structural analysis that posits a direct relationship between changes in basic causal variables and related behavior and outcomes, and denies the utility of the regime concept. For this they are taken to task in Susan Strange's critique. However, the basic parametric constraints for these analyses are identical with those applied by more conventional structural arguments. The basic analytic assumptions are the same. Arguments that treat regimes as intervening variables, and regard state interests and state power as basic causal variables, fall unambiguously within the structural realist paradigm. A more serious departure from structural reasoning occurs when regimes are seen as autonomous variables independently affecting not only related behavior and outcomes, but also the basic causal variables that led to their creation in the first place. This line of reasoning is examined in the conclusion to this volume.

Words can hurt you; or, who said what to whom about regimes

Ernst B. Haas

Sticks and stones
Can break my bones,
But words can never hurt me.

I once thought a regime was an arrangement whose members sought to manage and limit conflicts of interests among them because they recognized that complex interdependence makes a game of pure conflict too costly. I also thought that theorists of regimes disagree widely because the words they use to describe conflict and its management come from different normative and philosophical traditions. Some are Marxists, others are radical ecologists. Many are mainstream students of international politics who call themselves realists or structuralists; of these, some profess an attachment to economic liberalism while others prefer to consider themselves neomercantilists. I expected that if these philosophical and normative differences were systematically explored we would understand why we talk past one another when we converse about regimes. I still think so.

I also realized, however, that how one thinks about regimes is a function of how one thinks about learning, about the growth of human consciousness, about social evolution. The ontogeny of theories about regimes recapitulates the history of science. From this adaptation of Haeckel's Law a startling

A version of this paper was read at the 30 August 1980 meeting of the American Political Science Association in Washington, D.C. The paper would not have been written without the very energetic encouragement of Hildegarde Haas, Peter Haas, and John Ruggie. It also owes a large debt to the outstanding comments received from the other contributors to this volume.

International Organization 36, 2, Spring 1982
0020-8183/82/020207-37 $1.50

conclusion follows: the same evolutionary "editing" process that leads to biological adaptation will also bring about a cognitive alignment among theories about international regimes, despite their current disagreements. My purpose is to examine six of these theories in terms of their potential for compatibility or correspondence. Do they have enough in common so that, after a few twists in the evolution of consciousness, we will see them as different approximations to the same purpose? I accept the premise that this will occur.

Since I am not a partisan of any of the familiar philosophical orientations, I must clarify the cognitive stand I take; "evolutionary epistemology" is as good a label as any.[1] This stand suggests that the study of regimes is more than the study of international collaboration as a matter of politics, though it certainly includes the political dimension. The study of regimes is a way of understanding the interactions of *homo politicus* with nature and with culture. It rests on the supposition that our collective understanding of our political choices increasingly depends on how we think about nature and about culture. The study of regimes illustrates the range of past and future choices about international collaboration in a context of changing self-understanding. The politics of collaboration are seen as evolving alongside the evolution of consciousness itself, though not necessarily as an expression of biological evolution. (These evolutions suggest parallels, *not* those isomorphisms between biology, culture, and politics that would enable us to predict a specific evolutionary direction linked to a specific normative order.)

The Law of the Sea (LOS) negotiations illustrate the point. The ocean regime for centuries was based on the norm of maximum open access: outside the territorial sea—whose boundary floated inexorably outward after 1945—any state could do anything. What caused the change toward fisheries conservation zones, pollution-free zones, restrictions on transit, and international controls on the mining of the deep sea? What is responsible for the norm that the oceans are "the heritage of mankind," a public good par excellence? While the evolving regime is far from fashioning rules that recognize this norm in full or institutionalize the public good, it nevertheless represents an evolution in our thinking about fish, chemicals, the price of manganese, and the safety of tankers. These topics, prior to the 1970s, were not thought of as being linked. Unconnected changes in the way we think about resources, development economics, diets, and toxicity have come together in a new syndrome, a new "consciousness" considered "adaptive learning" by those who think these subjects ought to be linked. But the lesson may not

[1] The term and the associated concepts come from Donald T. Campbell, *Descriptive Epistemology: Psychological, Sociological, and Evolutionary* (preliminary draft of the William James Lectures, Harvard University, spring 1977). I have used the 1979 version of the manuscript kindly shown me by Professor Campbell and widely circulated by him. Portions were published as "A Tribal Model of the Social System Vehicle Carrying Scientific Knowledge," *Knowledge* 1, 2 (December 1979).

be final. Some people dispute the legitimacy of the cognitive link. What if science were to suggest that the link is mistaken?

These questions cannot be answered unless somebody's ideas come to be seen as approximating "reality." The study of regimes is a way of mapping the ontogeny and the phylogeny of consensual thought about interactions between man, culture, and nature; it is a way of conceptualizing a shared notion of what really exists—a reality that includes more than the familiar political conflicts among states. My stand, however, implies that we cannot know the reality "out there" because our notion of what it contains changes with every twist of the scientific enterprise. Man-the-knower is the victim of his methods of acquiring knowledge and is therefore condemned to settle for successive approximations to reality. My commitment is nevertheless to an ontogeny postulating that understanding at any given time can be shared and can form the basis for a temporary consensus. My task, the exploration of theories about regimes, is a step in making knowledge capable of being shared. I make no claim that such a sharing of understanding about regimes will preempt evolution of thought or predict the future of actual regimes. On the contrary, my stance implies the permanent evolution of regimes *and* of knowledge about regimes.

For theorist and actor alike everything depends on the concepts learned. I agree with Campbell that "concept learning in all cases is a creative, subjective, presumptive, error-prone process. We cannot convey directly what we mean to others, nor their meanings to ourself, nor learn for ourselves directly of a new real entity existing in nature."[2] Building or changing a regime is a form of human problem-solving that requires actors to learn concepts. The same is true of theorists studying the actors at work, or prescribing for them. Both actors and theorists use many kinds of perceptual short-cuts and screens; both see "the truth as descriptive appropriateness to the world described," synthetic, presumptive, contingent, and conceivably untrue.[3] In short, theorizing about regimes precludes certainty about what we know.

We cannot say with confidence what is "learned" by actors or theorists in building and studying regimes. Learning itself is part of the interplay between studying and doing. It depends on what bits of consensual understanding exist at any one time about the links between politics, culture, and biology; and we know that the bits keep changing. What is learned is the consensus about the linkages, not a final reality—not, to return to the example, a definitive way of managing fish, nodules, chemicals, and tankers under a single norm. The linkage that is accepted in 1981 differs from the knowledge that prevailed in 1960 in including more bits arranged in a nested hierarchy of human concerns, concerns that were not part of our consciousness in 1960. Learning in the perspective of an evolutionary epistemology must be

---

[2] Campbell, *Descriptive Epistemology*, p. 76.
[3] Ibid., p. 13.

open, unspecifiable ahead of events in terms of substance, and as unpredictable as evolutionary adaptation.

My stance, therefore, is not a theory that subsumes various approaches to regimes. It is a point of view chosen to furnish a way of commenting on prevailing views about the dynamics of regimes and to encourage the continued evolution of theories toward an agreed language. My purpose is to foster communication, not to provide true, final theory.

Communication uses words and metaphors, and the language for discussing regimes features many words whose meanings are problematical: among others, order, system, structure, bargaining, equilibrium, cooperation, coordination, costs and benefits, interest, collective goods, organization, equity, efficiency, hegemony, consensus, and interdependence. Each is an aggregation of diverse concepts and semantic associations embedded in some prior view of nature, culture, and man. These views cluster around two long-lived metaphors—the organic and the mechanical. Each word finds its place in a different nested hierarchy of assumptions and beliefs that derives from these metaphors.

The six theories about regimes to be examined here I label eco-environmentalism, eco-reformism, egalitarianism, liberalism, mercantilism, and "mainstream." Each matches a preferred international order to a science-legitimated view of the universe. Each combines acceptance of certain scientific postulates with a set of political values. Each subordinates what it chooses to believe about science to the moral order it prefers. We have no way of telling which one is "right." But since each is used by somebody to define some issue-area to be regulated by collaborative means, we have to dissect each in order to understand how it aggregates issues and variables and arrives at its own nested hierarchy of concerns.

I. The intellectual setting for studying regimes

Order, system, and regime

The Random House English Dictionary defines regime as "a ruling or prevailing system." Others equate the terms order and regime as if they were synonyms. I distinguish between these terms, for if all three words mean the same we are talking not about arrangements that governments make to manage conflict but about all of international politics, all of nature, and all of culture at the same time. The problem is to show how in various approaches nature and culture are thought to relate to politics and eventually to the management of conflict. We need to separate regimes before we can talk about their ties to other things.

Order, system, and regime are not synonyms. Regimes are man-made arrangements (social institutions) for managing conflict in a setting of interdependence because, as Oran Young says, "the growth of interdependence increases the capacity of all relevant actors to injure each other.'' Interdependence implies a network of nonrandom links among actors, links that are organized or structured. Regimes are parts of a system; the system is the "whole," the regimes a few of many parts.

The contributors to this volume have agreed to define regimes as sets of implicit or explicit principles, norms, rules, and decision-making procedures around which actors' expectations converge in a given area of international relations. That differs from what we sometimes call an order in that regimes are artificial creations designed to bring about particular orderings of values among actors; there is no general international "order." The qualities we have in mind when we use the term order in general are those associated with the concept of system. We can only speak of particular orders devoted to equity, efficiency, justice, survival, or whatever we value. Order, then, refers to the benefits a regime is to provide; system refers to the whole in which collaboration toward an order takes place.

This terminological gain is illusory unless we ask a few more questions. Is a competitive or an oligopolistic market a regime? Both could be described to fit our definition, and so could a pattern of strategic interaction among military antagonists in a mixed-motive game—neither instance implies a formal agreement, negotiation, or unilateral imposition. Is the classical balance of power or was pre–1914 imperialism a regime? Was the nineteenth-century Concert of Europe a security regime, is the United Nations one today? Is NATO a regime, are arms control agreements concluded by the superpowers a regime? The burgeoning literature on regimes answers in the affirmative, yet the same arrangements and events are often labeled system and order as well.

Regimes are arrangements peculiar to substantive issue-areas in international relations that are characterized by the condition of complex interdependence: neither hierarchy nor anarchy prevails and states rarely practice self-help. Regimes are all arrangements reflecting "policy contingency," the situation in which actors consider carefully the opportunity costs of disrupting a relationship before practicing self-help. Two kinds of policy contingency exist; Arthur Stein calls them regimes of common interest and regimes of common aversion. In regimes of common interest actors agree that if each followed its own most rational strategy all would eventually be worse off; the second-best strategy—collaboration—then becomes optimal policy. Collaboration calls for agreed rules to abstain from certain behaviors, to behave jointly and positively for certain purposes, and to vest the regime's institutions with powers to monitor and mediate conflicts.

In regimes of common aversion the actors do not agree on a jointly preferred outcome, but they do agree on the outcome all wish to avoid; such regimes merely require policy coordination, not collaboration. Prohibitions on behavior are accepted, central monitoring and conflict resolution are not required, and jointly pursued positive policies are very rare. This accurately describes imperialism, the balance of power, and UN practices for collective security. There is little or no policy contingency between the issues being coordinated and other issues on the international agenda. Hence, situations of common aversion are not, properly speaking, in the realm of regimes.[4]

Why study regimes?

I have argued that we study regimes because they mirror the evolving capacity of man to redefine and perhaps to solve common problems. And I have identified regimes as a dependent variable that concerns all schools of thought. Each prevailing mind-set offers different answers to the same set of questions. What are the questions?

How do regimes originate and change? Since regimes are man-made arrangements we inquire into the objectives of the actors. Self-perceived interests propel them to make agreements on seabed mineral mining or wheat marketing, and these interests change. The analysis of changing interests makes us inquire into the costs and benefits actors associate with a regime. What appeared once to be a benefit may come to be seen as a cost—as happened to the perceived U.S. interest in insisting on a three-mile territorial sea. How do we specify the perception of interests in terms of changing cost and benefit calculations? The theory of public goods is widely used, especially in situations of asymmetrically distributed interests involving goods in joint supply from which no consumer can be excluded. The benefits that the regime is to provide are a good to be managed so as to provide joint gains for all the members. The empirical question about the origin of regimes and their dynamics of change makes use of several key terms: interest, common interest, costs, benefits, and collective goods.

What structural principles explain regimes? This question is analytical: it seeks to pinpoint the nonperceptual features of international relations that constrain actor behavior. Power and hierarchy are core concerns in defining structure. *Structure* is primarily the distribution of capability among states to act autonomously, measured according to the "good exchanged" in a specific regime. The question is embedded in a view that sees states as occupying different positions in a hierarchy of power, balanced differently depending on whether we are discussing wheat, money, armies, or manganese nodules. Regimes arise when the states realize that a desired distribution of "the goods" cannot come about by way of autonomous action. Interdependence, far from being a wholesome mutual need, is thus recognized as a regrettable condition.

Structural analysis seeks to pinpoint the conditions under which states

---

[4] Keohane distinguishes between two other forms of regime: control and insurance. While any specific regime might make use of both forms (and many do) controlling behavior approximates Stein's "collaboration" and insuring against some loss in a setting of varying actor utilities sounds like "coordination." Arrangements that *only* insure against a loss, therefore, do not meet my definitional conditions, though they do meet the lawyer's notion of regime.

calculate interests, costs, and benefits in opting for a regime or abandoning one. The key concepts are *hegemony* and *coalition*. A single state eager to universalize its preferred interest may sponsor and assume the burden of maintaining a regime; if and when its hegemonial position erodes it will wish to alter or abandon the regime that once served its interests. Alternatively, a coalition of weaker states may wish to do the same, sometimes in opposition to a hegemon; their regime will persist as long as the coalition remains intact.

How do regimes work? This question operationalizes concern with interests and structural principles. Goods, collective or private, are delivered by means of agreements that are negotiated (though the negotiation may merely cloak hegemonic imposition); hence bargaining becomes a matter of concern. The negotiators are usually bureaucrats representing organizations and engaged in creating new organizations; as regimes change they may be seen as enacting bureaucratic politics and organizational dynamics. In short, we must focus on notions of *process* in dealing with the question of how regimes actually work, how collaboration is carried out.

What purposes do regimes serve? The teleology of regimes is the core normative question that concerns all schools of thought. Properly phrased, it is the question of order. Marxists, pluralists, ecologists, and liberals may all agree on answers to the three questions discussed above, but they differ sharply on the purpose a given regime is to serve; each prefers a different world order. Marxists and students of dependency are concerned with equity as the norm to be served by a regime. Liberals show more concern with the idea of efficiency or optimality in delivering a good seen as increasing aggregate world welfare. Ecologists are committed to norms of physical and biological survival and with improved global quality of life. Many pluralists, however, also regard the norm of survival as an objective legitimately sought by each state. Survival for them, however, means preserving some degree of national autonomy in the face of complex interdependence, not the survival of the species in the sense of Darwinian evolution.

All approaches to the study of regimes have this much in common. How, then, do they differ?

How to study regimes?

Ontological differences. The theorists I shall examine differ in how they see "reality"; they differ over the kinds of knowledge that exist or can be found to describe reality, and over the concepts that are appropriate for the description of reality. Is reality primarily cultural or biological? If it is both, which dominates? Is politics prior to biology as a body of knowledge, or the reverse? Are there structural principles in nature that also describe culture and human choice? Or are men capable of altering structures through acts of will and wisdom? If so, where do they find that wisdom—in biology, physics, religion, or dialectical materialism?

The answers entangle us in more terminological confusion, because various schools of thought adopt different metaphors. The controversy over regimes is due in part to the fact that some rely on an organic metaphor while others prefer a mechanical one. The choice determines where one places the "system" of which international politics and international regimes are parts. Is the system the political and economic relations among states? Marxists tend to think these relations express prior cultural and economic patterns, but ecologists do not. They prefer an organic perspective to the mechanical metaphor and see politics and economics as expressions of competition or cooperation in the search for ecological niches. It matters, therefore, where one sees one's reality, how abstractly or concretely one describes the system of action at issue. Regimes are supposed to help solve problems, but the problem itself is a function of how one imagines the system in which something problematical is taking place. Key concepts require clarification: system, type of structure, equilibrium, causation, adaptation, and learning.

Not everybody accepts the notion of system as crucial to the discussion of regimes. But among those who use the concept—probably the majority of writers on regimes—some fundamental distinctions must be made. Some analysts, particularly those who borrow their imagery from the natural sciences, think of systems as "real," as factually and conceptually correct ways of describing the reality that shapes regimes; others, primarily from the social sciences, think of systems as heuristic simplifications of a very complex reality. Writers in the heuristic mode must be divided into those who interpret events "downward" from the level of the system and others who describe the system as a result of "upward" pressures exerted by the units that make up the system. Realists work at the level of the system, Marxists and pluralists at the level of the units, and ecologists at both.

Hence, we distinguish between system-dominant and actor-dominant systems, depending on whether the flow of action is seen as upward or downward; the former is "closed," or nearly so, and the latter is "open"— suggesting homeostasis in the first case and what Waddington called homeorhesis in the second.[5] Each view of the system implies a different nested hierarchy of concepts. Closed systems are not subject to manipulation because their underlying structure determines causation and therefore limits the range of adaptive interventions open to man. Open systems, however, can be altered by man—if man is motivated to do so. The consequences produced by regimes derived from these conceptions are clearly going to be different.

The opposing conceptions of structure also contain opposed notions of causation. Do human choices (policies) shape the system or does the system determine the kinds of policies worked out by actors? Does structure

[5] Homeostasis refers to processes that disturb systemic equilibrium temporarily; after the perturbation, the system reverts to its original state. Homeorhesis refers to the continuation of a process that changes a system despite temporary setbacks and interruptions. The term was coined by C. H. Waddington to capture morphogenetic evolution.

precede action or do actions bring about structure? Believers in closed systems hold that the structure of the system sharply constrains human choice: men and states do what they must in order to survive. Causation, then, flows downward from the system to the actors; the whole shapes the parts. The system is animated by its structure and that structure consists of lawlike propositions, derived by the theorist of regimes from physics, genetics, or economics. If the structure is "anarchical," the actors must husband power to assure their ability to practice self-help; if the structure is "oligopolistic," they must mix competition with cooperation to prosper; if the law is natural selection, the actors must compete for limited niches.

But those who see the actions of the parts as shaping the whole—thus reversing the direction of causation—subscribe to a different view of structure. Structure here is just another word for pattern or tendency, not a set of laws describing reality. Structural arguments like the following illustrate this usage: economies (states) enjoying a comparative advantage will seek free trade in the appropriate sectors; foreign investors tend to put their money into activities promising the most rapid return; states with the strongest capabilities in a given issue-area tend to dictate the form of the regime. Weak imputations of causation go along with notions of structure-as-pattern.

Theorists of regimes who identify with closed systems will incline toward a homeostatic view of the interactions between man, politics, and nature. They will opt for a view of the "system in equilibrium" and will tailor their notions of regimes so as to restore equilibrium if it is disturbed. Human adaptation is seen as "learning to live in the system." Those who take the opposing view, however, see in disequilibrium a warning and an opportunity to do better. Adaptation to the system, for them, means learning the kinds of lessons about interdependence among causes that will assure survival to mankind, to specific states, or to a particular form of social organization. Theorists of regimes who reject both views of system also tend to reject notions of structure as predictors of human choices.

Normative and epistemological differences. Different ontological stances lead to different notions of the good and how to realize it. The concept of equilibrium is crucial in separating these competing notions. One can observe and measure—if one agrees on a dependent variable and on appropriate indicators—equilibrium among the parts of the system without passing judgment on the moral implications of the result. To show that nuclear weapons are distributed so as to make a preemptive strike irrational is to make a moral argument only if one also entertains commitments about the desirability of using the weapons and assigns no value preference to any existing social or political order. When these conditions do not apply the observation of nuclear equilibrium contains no moral judgment.

In the discussion of regimes, however, the existence or nonexistence of equilibrium among the parts of the system is often linked to a preference about order. If we argue that the purpose of a given regime is to realize equity—or efficiency, survival, or a certain quality of life—we also tend to argue that disequilibrium means that these purposes are not being realized. The creation or restoration of equilibrium, therefore, becomes a moral statement about a desired state of affairs. This is true of both versions of systems thinking. Believers in open and in closed systems, determinative and nondeterminative structures, tend to associate their notions of equilibrium with moral improvement. Only some mainstream political analysts of regimes who are reluctant to embed their versions of the system in biological, physical, and cultural contexts resist this imputation and confine their view of equilibrium to non-normative observations. The others merge observation, assertion, and moral preference and thereby shape the general discussion of international regimes. Two basic metaphors, the mechanical and the organic, capture these conceptual and semantic associations. The mechanical seeks to minimize disturbance in the system and to return it to equilibrium; it is focused on self-maintenance. The organic seeks to profit from disequilibrium in order to assure continued adaptation to a changing reality; it is focused on evolutionary self-organization.

Before we explore these metaphors further it is (unfortunately) necessary to comment on how theorists use the magic of equilibrium analysis. The attraction of the term equilibrium lies in its presumed generality to all fields of inquiry. But, says Russett, "scientific equilibrium is, whether overtly or only implicitly, a mode of analysis, a research tool, a way of looking at all the complex phenomena of society."[6] It is an epistemological device, not necessarily a substantive doctrine. However, it often *becomes* a doctrine—an ideology—when the theorist transposes the substantive laws of a system, expressed in terms of equilibrating processes in nature, to social processes and then prescribes which kind of regime should set matters right (for which, read "restore equilibrium"). Whether and how this is done are core points on which theorists of regimes disagree. In the meantime, we must take note that the qualifying adjectives—stable and unstable, stationary and moving, static-mechanical and dynamic-organic—have no agreed meanings either in the natural or in the social sciences. These terms refer to different ways of conceptualizing the influence on the system of a myriad of variables that are conceded to be in flux. Stable, static, and stationary do not mean that constant processes of change are absent. They suggest merely that the system remains much the same despite the process. Unstable, moving, and dynamic suggest the opposite.[7]

Each of the two informing metaphors represents a particular view of the

[6] Cynthia Eagle Russett, *The Concept of Equilibrium in American Social Thought* (New Haven: Yale University Press, 1966), p. 10.

[7] My terminology reflects the general confusion documented by Russett, *Concept of Equilibrium*. My juxtaposition seeks to capture how writers on regimes use the concepts; it does not do justice to the variety of meanings and imputations in the natural sciences in which the terms originated and in which they remain controversial now. See Russett, ibid., chap. 10 for instances of this. She also shows, pp. 157ff., that economists continue to disagree as to what they mean by the terms "static" and "dynamic" equilibrium.

overall system in which regimes are embedded and carries with it a particular view of that system in equilibrium. That view implies differences in how change, evolution, and adaptation come about, whether the system is essentially harmonious or conflict-ridden, self-maintaining or self-organizing, as it changes. Moreover, one view is pessimistic while the other sees hope.

The *mechanical* metaphor is pessimistic. It sees the world in steady state, closed, its future determined by its constituent elements and the laws that govern them. Processes of change occur homeostatically; the return to equilibrium after a disturbance means that the system is programmed toward self-maintenance. It is stable, stationary, and static in the short run. Eventually, however, the system must run down; it is doomed to entropy. These assumptions carry with them the image of a zero-sum game over the good things to be had for mankind—conflict is part of the program. But even though conflict is as natural as one school of biological evolutionists paints it to be, it is not necessarily desirable. Short-term disequilibria are often unpleasant and efforts to overcome them should be made. Hence we need regimes. Self-maintenance will be hurt and entropy ushered in sooner than fated if international processes are permitted to follow the positive-feedback pattern. Adaptation, learning, and evolution are helped, therefore, by arrangements that strengthen negative feedback processes. Adaptation means learning to live in a finite system.

The hope held out by adepts of the *organic* metaphor is based on their conviction that the processes embedded in their system are essentially harmonious. The system is open, moving, and dynamic. It incorporates growth and development. The tendency toward entropy can be overcome, and the concept of homeorhesis incorporates this idea. In the short run, to be sure, negative feedback processes foster temporary equilibria. But the fact that the system is programmed for movement implies that in the longer run various states of disequilibrium are to be expected. Because the system is open and dynamic, the exact number and value of the input variables cannot be known and the next equilibrium state of the system remains indeterminate. What should mankind do in such a setting? Disequilibrium, at any given point, means that we have not understood the structure of the system; we permitted the wrong processes to take over. But homeorhetic principles stipulate openness to learn: we are biologically equipped to evolve into better problem-solvers. Adaptation means learning to do better in a dynamic system, which is itself programmed—and we with it—to organize itself toward its own perfection.

One major school of thought, generously represented in this volume, does not completely fit this scheme. Some mainstream political scientists, who are often labeled structuralists, sharply distinguish between the values preferred by the writer and the form of analysis used in the discussion of regimes; hence the preferred order does not necessarily predict the way in which the origins and fortunes of regimes are dealt with. These writers, even though they all accept the mechanical as the applicable metaphor, do not

THEORIST'S PRIMARY VALUE COMMITMENT

		EQUITY	EFFICIENCY	SURVIVAL	QUALITY OF LIFE
	ORGANIC	Egalitarians	?	Eco-Environmentalists	Eco-Reformers
	MECHANICAL	Marxist Egalitarians	Liberals	Mercantilists	Basic human needs
		Mainstreamers: none of the above values			

Theorist's image of system accepts these metaphors

Figure 1. Some theories of regimes

rely on a view of politics derived from natural science. Nor do they consistently adhere to the classical realist view of international politics.

II. Regimes and the organic metaphor

Three approaches exist within the organic metaphor: the eco-environmental, the eco-reformist, and the egalitarian. They share a number of concerns and assumptions. The theory of evolution and the image of turbulent fields underlie the metaphor. The three approaches wish to contribute to the survival of the species. They offer diagnoses of the crisis of mankind and suggestions of the appropriate therapy. Unlike adherents of the mechanical metaphor, eco-environmentalists and eco-reformers think of complexity as both cause and effect. Particular social and political configurations (capitalism, industrialism, democracy) define complexity for egalitarians, liberals, and mercantilists. For ecological thinkers, however, the notion of turbulence suggests multiple feedback processes among the constituents of complexity, thus making that condition much more than an independent variable. The constituents include physical and biological "parts" as well as culture and politics.

Turbulent fields are "environments in which there are dynamic processes arising from the field itself which create significant variances for the component systems. . . . Most significance attaches to the case where the dynamic field processes emerge as an unplanned consequence of the actions of the constituent systems."[8] Whatever their preferred ideology, analysts agree that the actions we prefer to take are constrained by large forces or patterns beyond our will; but analysts also agree that our actions somehow influence those larger forces in ways we neither intend nor wish. This is true whether we want to keep the oceans clean, limit nuclear energy, help the Third World practice self-reliance, preserve or overthrow capitalism, or maintain a military balance of power. The "field" is the sum of international relations in all cross-cutting issue-areas. What makes it "turbulent" is the ill-understood feedback process between systemic constraint and deliberate intervention—the very condition that regimes are intended to manage.

Evolutionary theory relates to this in offering clues to the appropriateness of the interventions we practice. Mankind is part of nature; its consciousness of itself and of nature is seen as part of evolution. As this consciousness expands deliberate intervention can assure survival more (or less) effectively by improving our understanding of the ever-changing feedback processes. The persistence of turbulence is expected to lead either to the entropy of the world system or to its salvation.

These pessimistic and optimistic strands of evolutionary thought entail an important distinction for students of regimes. The pessimists are associated with contemporary sociobiology. Even though they are biologists by profession their assumptions are closer to the mechanical view of the world than to the homeorhetic position. Sociobiologists see evolution as a continuation of struggle between species, and even individuals within species (or ethnic groups, or nations), for food and space. They see the environmental "challenge" as the way in which a breeding population adjusts its size to permanent ecological constraints.[9] The informing metaphor is homeostatic: fluctuations in population size cannot transcend natural limits. Adaptation either can be physical-genetic, as in natural selection, or it can be deliberate and conscious, as when mediated through cultural change. While sociobiologists would see regime construction as an instance of cultural adaptation, they rarely venture into this realm, usually confining their substantive suggestions to population control, agriculture, and the preservation of a diversified gene pool. Sociobiologists are not interested in morally significant regimes. Their homeostatic view of nature merely predicts that the successfully adapting species will find its proper niche. This said, sociobiology is not relevant to our quest; the school rejects the notion of progress.

The theorists who interest us take a different view. The purpose of evolution is to learn to live in harmony with all life forms and all global resources. The world is conceptualized as a huge system of biological and

[8] The term was coined by F. E. Emery and E. L. Trist, *Towards a Social Ecology* (London: Plenum, 1973), from which this quotation comes.

[9] Edward O. Wilson, *On Human Nature* (Cambridge: Harvard University Press, 1978).

physical interdependencies among life forms, about to be destroyed because men have set themselves up as the master form and raped the globe. Instead, they must learn to manage resources wisely, and learning consists of taming politics to make this possible. Regimes are needed to promote cooperation, joint planning, disarmament, human rights, population control, and recognizing the limits of growth. While this sounds like a moral dictum or an ethical insight, ecologists will argue that our positive knowledge supports their view of evolution; moral progress and purpose are considered implicit in science.

A world not subjected to human mismanagement would be in a state of moving and dynamic equilibrium—men's mismanagement is responsible for the current disequilibrium. The world is seen as an organism suffering from pathologies that will end in entropy unless speedily corrected. Eco-evolutionists and eco-reformers are writing the "manual for Spaceship Earth," as Buckminster Fuller put it long ago, and the manual is designed to restore equilibrium in production and consumption, rights and obligations, freedom and authority, participation and hierarchy.[10] No automatic market and no contemporary political system is up to the task of saving the world from men.

The appeal of this way of putting the question, of course, depends on seeing one Crisis of Mankind rather than many crises of different severities and diverse origins. Primarily ecologists identify with this approach because of their penchant for seeing connections among various crises, connections that are less apparent to others. Liberals and mercantilists are uneasy with the approach. Some egalitarians reject it because they think of The Crisis as the contradictions within capitalism, not the arms race, the population explosion, or the exhaustion of natural resources. But other egalitarians accept part of the ecological diagnosis.

Eco-evolutionism

The crisis of mankind, the predicament of man, mankind's survival—these labels sum up the concern of eco-evolutionism. The crisis is seen as an overall disequilibrium of the "world system," which, far from being a synonym for capitalism or imperialism, is the totality of interacting forces. Instead of balancing one another in accordance with the natural evolutionary dynamic, these forces distort each other in the direction of hypertrophic phenomena. A world system in dynamic equilibrium would imply the evolu-

---

[10] Buckminster Fuller, *Operating Manual for Spaceship Earth* (Carbondale: Southern Illinois University Press, 1969). Evolution, following the formulation apparently pioneered by Herbert Spencer, means "an orderly unfolding from simple to complex"; it implies progress and maturation. The organic view of evolution is distinctly morphogenetic; the trajectory is progressive unfolding in the realization of a diverse genetic and an equally diverse cultural-adaptive potential. See Stephen Jay Gould, *Ever Since Darwin* (New York: W. W. Norton, 1977).

tion of mankind toward increasingly complex structures, better adapted to cope with new challenges arising from the ecological environment. But while nature exhibits instances of such equilibria, social evolution is almost always more chaotic: short-run perturbations result in longer-run balances, to be upset later by new short-run perturbations, etc. These perturbations, in the metaphoric language of evolution, can also be seen as challenges posed by subsystems in turmoil. Food and population dynamics fail to match; technology, while creating wealth, also intensifies environmental degradation; wealth-creation results in alienation as well as pollution; peace, harmony, and cooperation are upset by conflict over how wealth ought to be distributed. Imbalance within each of these subsystems disturbs the world system's tendency toward dynamic equilibrium.

The very terms chosen for describing the crisis of mankind give us the principles underlying the diagnosis. The crisis is due to entropic tendencies, which are manifesting themselves in the evolutionary cycle that characterizes all of life; they are the result of man's own mismanaged evolution, his own role in that cycle. It is time to redefine and rechannel that role toward the greater integration of all systems:

> Nature is 'permissive'. . . . It permits the local decrease of entropy if entropy increases proportionately elsewhere. It permits the development of myriad forms and patterns of behavior and organization, it selects from among those which happen to have come about. Evolution could have taken different specific forms—there is nothing necessary about a species called *homo sapiens,* for example. But the many forms it could have (and perhaps has) taken in the vast reaches of cosmos cannot include forms contrary to the general trend of development. *We cannot see how evolution could fail to push toward order and integration, complexity and individuation,* whatever forms it may choose for realization. It sets forth the guidelines and lets chance play the role of selector of alternative pathways for its realization. There is purpose without slavery, and freedom without anarchy.[11]

This formulation explains what is meant by "structure." The term here describes various modes of evolutionary cooperation that result in a new pattern of adaptive complexity. Structures are the patterns or styles of cooperation through which disequilibria in a given system are ended. The word *process* is used rather loosely to say the same thing. One such process is the creation of "organizations"—not the United Nations or the Pugwash Movement but the balance between centralized and decentralized collective problem-solving judged optimal for evolutionary cooperation. The term cooperation is rarely used with any meaning specific to the international activities we normally study. Cooperation means the biological process whereby a species acquires an improved design better adapted for coping

---

[11] Ervin Laszlo, *The Systems View of the World* (New York: Braziller, 1972), p. 52. Emphasis added.

with a particular environmental challenge. It is a judgment on how sym-
bioses between species come about, akin to the Mertonian idea of "latent
functions" associated with social structures.

Eco-evolutionism attaches specific meanings to the words we use in discussing the performance of regimes. The notion of a public good is associated with the survival of the species. However, in determining the costs
and benefits of a given course of action, eco-evolutionists insist that the economic definitions of these terms be scrapped in favor of such criteria as
"social costs," "survival costs," or Boulding's "goodness function."[12]
Neither equity nor efficiency is abandoned here: they are redefined in terms
of a different set of values. The yardstick of a benefit or a cost is not the good
of the firm, the city, or the country, but the capacity of man to survive. The
words management and learning tend to be used synonymously to specify
"good" ways of manipulating processes and structures and designing organizations, not just any way of running activities nonrandomly. "Planning"
and "learning to plan" show up frequently as expressions that denote much
the same thing. All are words to characterize the "right" way of working
toward an "order" that allows for evolutionary survival.

The ultimate inspiration for the eco-environmental approach may be religious. Learning to understand the system so that mankind can resume the
proper evolutionary path combines religion and science in the way Teilhard
de Chardin suggested a generation ago, a combination that is also implicit in
the analogy between Zen and nuclear physics. Evolution is not merely a
scientific theory: it is *the* principle that underlies the cosmos, and it tells us
where everything in the cosmos is going. Religion and science combine to
legitimate the human liberation and emancipation implicit in the unfolding
process.

The bulk of the background knowledge claimed for legitimating the approach, however, comes from the natural sciences. Biological evolutionary
lore, as interpreted by people biased toward nonviolence, cooperation, and
harmony as natural forces, prevails:

> Common characteristics are manifest in different forms on each of the
> many levels, with properties ranged in a continuous but irreducible se-
> quence from level to level. The systems view of nature is one of har-
> mony and dynamic balance. Progress is triggered from below without
> determination from above, and is thus both definite and open-ended. To
> be "with it" one must adapt, and that means moving along. There is
> freedom in choosing one's paths of progress, yet this freedom is
> bounded by the limits of compatibility with the dynamic structure of the
> whole.[13]

Cybernetic principles are used to discover the identity of "the whole." The
organization, storage, and diffusion of information are crucial to this mind-

---

[12] Kenneth E. Boulding, *Ecodynamics* (Beverly Hills, Cal.: Sage, 1978), pp. 269ff.
[13] Laszlo, *Systems View,* p. 75.

set. But since the whole itself is partly a construct of cybernetic operations and only a metaphoric approximation of "the real world," eco-evolutionists agree that the analyst must provide the core value around which "the whole" is to be specified. That core value is ecological balance, in which social harmony, world peace, and the happiness of the individual all find their place.

One might suppose that the realization of ecological balance calls for specific concepts dealing with political behavior, but the eco-evolutionists pay scant attention to interest, hegemony, coalitions, conflict-resolution machinery, and bureaucratic phenomena. Political imperatives are derived from natural systems such as genetics, physics, and cultural anthropology, not from the study of politics and economics. The growing appeal of the mind-set lies in its generality; it claims that international politics is subsumed by a body of knowledge and morality that encompasses all of the cosmos. A regime, as a mere political artifact, is of relatively little interest to eco-evolutionism, though such regime-designers as Julian Huxley, Arvid Pardo, and Michel Batisse are eco-evolutionists.

Eco-reformism

Regimes are a matter of direct interest to eco-reformers because of their reliance on principles of design and social ecology as an important subset of natural principles. While eco-reformers accept the notion of a world system and its constituent subsystems, their analysis is directed to a more concrete level of concern, the mastery of the *problématique*.

> How, then, can we more realistically 'see' reality? If we accept the interlinkage, interaction and dynamics of the problems that are proliferating in our situation it seems that we might approach a clearer view of that situation were we to conceive of these problems as a generalized meta-problem or meta-system of problems—a system which I shall henceforth call the 'problématique.'[14]

The problématique is the problem of all the problems, not merely the sum of the problems of pollution, war, famine, alienation, resource depletion, urban crowding, and the exploitation of the Third World by the First. It is a systemic construct that assumes causal connections among these problems, connections that amplify the disturbance in the metasystem. The empirical or experimental verification of the problématique could constitute the first necessary step in meeting the challenge and fashioning a response. This, of course, requires social science rather than natural science, causal modeling in addition to evolutionary doctrine. Global modeling, made familiar by *Limits to Growth* and its successors, is the knowledge from which the ap-

---

[14] Hasan Ozbekhan, "The Predicament of Mankind," in C. West Churchman and Richard O. Mason, eds., *World Modeling: A Dialogue*, vol. 2 (New York: American Elsevier, 1976), p. 16.

proach derives its recommendations for regimes. Eco-reformers take changes in the material nature of life as basic and given, and draw on the sciences that map them. However, they—unlike most eco-evolutionists—insist on including political and economic lore as additional and autonomous constituents of the knowledge base.

Hence the system of interest to eco-reformers is a much more recognizably human construct than the eco-evolutionists' conception. Their preferred term is "world" or "global" system:

> The world cannot be viewed any more as a collection of some 150-odd nations and an assortment of political and economic blocs. Rather, the world must be viewed as consisting of nations and regions which form a world system through an assortment of interdependencies. . . . Apparently, the emerging world system requires a 'holistic' view to be taken of the future world development: everything seems to depend on everything else.[15]

Physics and biology provide parameters that bound the realm of choice, but they do not define the system itself. Yet the conception remains organic—"living" and "dynamic" are adjectives much used by eco-reformers. The various problems that make up the problématique are problems precisely because they trigger disequilibrium in the world system—when everything depends on everything else the wrong choice can make things much worse. Dynamic equilibrium must be restored; to do this, we must master the problématique first.

Mastering the problématique involves the practitioner in grasping the world system of which everything of interest is a part. But if, by definition, the system is the connection of everything with everything, where do we start? The core value to be maximized—ecological balance—requires us to select variables, or subsystems composed of interacting variables, that speak substantively to this value. One current catch-phrase captures this: economic development that enables us to stay within the earth's "outer" and "inner" limits, or "ecodevelopment."

How do eco-reformers arrive at this principle? They assume an interaction between three different spheres of activity. The material base of life is rapidly changing because of greater resource use, population growth, and physical degradation. Economic activity is characterized by huge increases in production, trade, and investment, which, however, take place by externalizing the social costs of production to poor people in rich countries and, globally, to poor countries. This results in a global division of labor that threatens survival because it goes hand in hand with increasing military confrontations, the diffusion of destabilizing technologies, and the imitation by the Third World of the anti-ecological practices of the First and Second. Global economic inequality is causally associated with the prevailing mode

[15] Mihajlo Mesarovic and Eduard Pestel, *Mankind at the Turning Point* (New York: E. P. Dutton, 1974), pp. 20 and 21.

of production; the vanquishing of inequality, however, implies even more survival-threatening policies of development.

The remedy is the recognition of interconnectedness and the resulting turbulence, which can be controlled if mankind recognizes there are physical ("outer") limits to the amount of malaise, uprooting, alienation, and conflict that we can bear. Ecodevelopment offers a formula for enough industrialization of the right kind to give us a liveable division of labor.

Eco-reformers delight in using the word structure; there are "structural models" of the world system, "structures of production," and "structures of authority." Structures are deep-seated causes of problems, nonrandom behaviors that shape problems and problem sets, as illustrated in the set of interactions summarized above.

> Their commonality of cause has to do with the fact that they are in some considerable measure the products of a relatively small number of deeply rooted social forces; and their commonality of effect has to do with sustainability and limits, and the functional interdependencies and potential for mutual vulnerability that these produce. And they are distinguished as being global in character in the dual sense that they are shaped and conditioned by social forces that themselves constitute a world-system of relations, and their effects increasingly make the productive and regenerative capacities of planetary life-support systems a variable element within this world-system.[16]

This formulation raises the issue of whether we are dealing with structures-as-laws or structures-as-patterns. If it is the former the world system has a life of its own, which limits the choice left to the actor; if it is the latter the system is of the more open variety, in which causation flows from the actors to the constraints. Most eco-reformers prefer to have it both ways. They obviously want the actors to master the problématique, an achievement that depends on choice and will; but they also cherish the legitimacy that comes from being able to argue that "science, our values, and our analysis are all congruent." The imputation given to structures, therefore, partakes of both meanings.

Eco-reformers are not all of one mind on this question. They differ on exactly which variables in which subsystems ought to be selected (as the many global models illustrate). Thus the specification of inner and outer limits remains a matter both of controversy and of the prior definition of key terms. To the Club of Rome this is a big hypothesis to be explored further, but to some students of dependency it is a fact. To the one, a good world order is one able to bring about ecodevelopment, however that may be specified in terms of a particular model. To the other, the good world order overcomes Third World dependency and surmounts the capitalist global division of labor. Order may mean a utopia to be created, to be approximated

---

[16] John Gerard Ruggie, "On the Problem of 'The Global Problématique,' " *Alternatives* 5, 4 (January 1980), p. 526.

and tested by world order models; more modestly, it may mean a new set of rules for international conduct designed to launch mankind toward an unspecified better future.

In either case, eco-reformists agree with eco-evolutionists in their treatment of costs and benefits and in their concern with collective goods that serve the cause of a better quality of life. Theirs is a conception of publicness that seeks to subsume the values of equity as well as the values of efficiency. Eco-reformers are most interested in identifying and managing the commons of this world before they are spoiled by the development drives of separate nations, and hence eco-reformers must take an interest in organizations.

Organizations are efforts at collective adaptation to changed environmental conditions, which try to make the most of what the structure of the system permits. Questions of centralization and decentralization dominate. Collaboration is what actors do within organizations, and both organization and collaboration are ways of specifying processes; management, meanwhile, means the manipulation (through organizational-collaborative processes) of those variables in the system accessible to the actors so as to maximize the value of ecological balance. Management is informed by "learning"; progressively learned lessons improve management. Learning, in turn, implies an unfolding of human consciousness about complexity, about how the system works, and about the way the components interact—it implies a better understanding of cause and effect. The correct identification of causes in a complex system permits the mastery of the problématique, not the mere tinkering with a few visible problems. Hence it promises a more efficient and equitable meshing of ends and means.

This commitment to collaboration and organization, however, implies no well-developed notion of politics or the political process. Process means exercising the right choices within the structural realm left to choice. Eco-reformers pay very little attention to the concrete interests that animate actors, to bureaucratic dynamics, or to coalition behavior. The mind-set is concerned more with consciousness-raising, with demonstrating the need to relaunch mankind on the proper evolutionary course within a reasonably open system. Actors are the objects of sermons, of plans, or of designs, not of behavioral analysis. Though accorded the place of components in the world system, they are not units of analysis. No consensual prescription for a regime to bring about the better order has emerged from this mind-set.

Egalitarianism

To capture the egalitarian viewpoint, one is tempted to quote Kwame Nkrumah's famous advice: "Seek ye first the political kingdom." It is not that ecology and resources and population are forgotten; the problems they pose, however, are to be managed by way of a new morality. Technological solutions are not dismissed; they are subordinated to the values of participation, self-determination, self-reliance, and human dignity, and the admissibility of any specific technical solution is judged by these moral standards. Politics, not biology, genetics or economics, is charged with implanting that morality. The political task is the destruction or supercession of existing forms of domination, of institutionalized inequality, whether willed or "structural."

Evolution implies social reorganization; greater equality among individuals, groups, and nations is an evolutionary-adaptive principle. This is true of Marxist adherents of this mind-set such as the designers of the Bariloche model, of such philosophical-anarchist writers on energy as Amory Lovins, and of the social psychology of peace advocated by Herbert Kelman. It is equally explicit in the non-Marxist egalitarian world scenarios of Reshaping the International Order (RIO) and of the World Order Models Project (WOMP). The value to be maximized is equity, defined as equality in wealth and welfare, power, and access to quality of life. Egalitarians may prescribe socialism, self-reliance, and breaking the bonds of dependency. Or they may be content with reforms that would regulate multinational corporations (MNCs) and subject them to codes of behavior consistent with Third World needs. Egalitarians may embrace full-scale industrialization for poor countries, or preach the virtues of alternative technologies, the primacy of agriculture, and reliance on renewable sources of energy. Like eco-reformers, they identify with aspects of the New International Economic Order (NIEO) as a step toward the preferred regime of global economic reorganization and redistribution. But the NIEO does not take them far, because its program does not constitute a full-fledged attack on all hierarchies in international life.

The system that appears in egalitarian discussions of world order is a looser concept than the one used by eco-evolutionists and eco-reformers. It is not a meta-relationship among all relationships, with its own structural principles; it is a synonym for what we usually call world capitalism, imperialism, or the structure of influence—or some amalgam of all of these, as in the center-periphery formulation. The relationships that interest the analyst result from policies followed by actors: the system is the pattern produced by the interaction of unit-actors. Causation flows "upward," in contrast to the images popular among eco-evolutionists and eco-reformers.

When there are no major contradictions within world capitalism, the system is in equilibrium. Now, when contradictions abound, it is in disequilibrium, which sets the scene for a creative crisis, an opportunity for changing the system. As long as the rich succeed in shifting the contradictions among them to the poor, from the North to the South, the system remains in equilibrium. When the poor are no longer willing to be exploited in this fashion, activities that constituted "good management" from the vantage point of the rich become obsolete. Truly good management—the principles now advocated by the poor—is aimed at equitable international redistribution.

This view of the system has important consequences for the meaning of other standard terms, structure and process. Structures are patterns of dominance associated with particular activities carried on in the system. These can be observed and mapped with the indicators provided by social science and alternatives to the dominant structures can be modeled. Processes are typical behaviors. They have results, or outcomes, which confirm the structures. For instance, egalitarians would say that technology transfer (i.e., the behaviors associated with buying and selling machinery) results in an increasing dependence of "peripheral" buyers on "central" suppliers, thus confirming the structure of dependence. Since the structures of the system result from behavior they are patterns associated with human motivations rather than law-like manifestations of nature. Clearly, the egalitarian mind-set contains assumptions that differ from those of the other devotees of the organic metaphor.

Notions of collaboration and organization follow from these verbal conventions. Behavior for the egalitarian is by no means merely volitional. It always expresses the actor's interests, which in turn express the evolutionary state of a given system. The major actors may be classes, organized groups, MNCs, or the state when it represents a particular social configuration. Collaboration among units, or coordination of policy among them, takes place when interests converge and the incentive for coalition formation arises; it disappears when class or group interests diverge. Consciousness of one's interests dictates the amount and kind of collaboration, and participation in organizations follows from this. Organizations of all kinds (the U.N., the IMF, MNCs, or Third World producer associations) are merely temporary expressions of convergent interest, designed to confirm or challenge a particular structure of domination.

Clearly, egalitarians are more interested in criticizing existing regimes for failing to produce equitable outcomes than in prescribing for the creation of more efficient regimes. Hence the egalitarians' cost-benefit criteria supplement the indicators used in neoclassical economics. Evaluations are made so as to capture the externalities slighted in standard cost-benefit analyses, such as risks to population posed by nonredundant and centralized power facilities or the number of additional cases of death or ill-health associated with additional increments of energy, steel, or chemical fertilizers. Unlike the liberal, the egalitarian uses the theory of public goods not as a device for diagnosing when and where private control is suboptimal, but as a way of arguing for the socialization of the means of production or the creation of global commons. It is a rhetorical term that lacks the technical content the liberal mind-set associates with it.

Management also has a context-specific connotation. Managing a policy is supposed to change processes and therefore structures. Hence egalitarians pay a great deal of attention to the "policy instruments" appropriate for Third World countries. Management means undoing and reversing dominant processes, or at least manipulating them more intelligently. Learning must precede appropriate management. This "learning" is the unfolding of a new consciousness and an understanding of some historical dialectic; a redefinition of earlier interests as false consciousness is banished. History for the egalitarian, as for the eco-environmentalist and the eco-reformer, is the evolutionary unfolding of a higher state of morality. Though historical evolution looks like the secular equivalent of the religious idea of transcendence, the egalitarian image of evolution is far less literal than is true of the other organic mind-sets. Moreover, its indebtedness to science as a source of knowledge takes second place to its reliance on sociology and economics.

The superficiality of the evolutionary image held by egalitarians robs them of the ability to be specific about how regimes are to further equity. The mere unfolding of equality does not tell us *who* is going to be the equal of *whom*. Who are the favored clients: nations, states, people, all Third World nations, Fourth World nations, only "the poorest of the poor" in Fourth World nations, wheat farmers, workers, entrepreneurs, or electronics specialists? If equity is to define a regime there must be consensus on what constitutes a just social order, on its beneficiaries, on its place in time and in space. In the absence of such a consensus the affirmation of a specific egalitarian view is merely another input into a process of international negotiation, not an objective yardstick of diagnosis and prescription.

III. Regimes and the mechanical metaphor

A word of semantic reassurance is necessary: the adjectives organic and mechanical refer to the way theorists relate nature, culture, and politics; they are not synonyms for good and bad, intellectually dynamic and static. I call the three varieties of mechanical approaches to the study of regimes liberal, mercantilist, and mainstream. They differ from organic approaches because they have no commitment to an evolutionary logic of development corresponding to the views on nature and culture we encountered there. While the mechanical metaphor includes the notion that interdependence among states is becoming more complex, no particular organizational pattern or predetermined order is expected to emerge from increasing complexity.

Theorists adhering to the mechanical metaphor rely on economic and political knowledge to explain existing regimes and predict alternative ones. This reliance is symbolized by their use of the term "the world political economy" as an amalgam of the institutions of capitalism and the means of power politics. Their core idea is that differential state power over resources explains the regime governing those resources. Benefits derived and results obtained from the use of the resources are determined by the position in the power hierarchy of those who produce, sell, and consume the goods and services that make up international economic relations.

What makes this approach "mechanical"? Its fundamental image is the market. Relations among nations hinge on the production and exchange of goods and services, not merely those encountered in international trade and investment transactions but also those found in military security and milieu goals. The market may be oligopolistic; behavior will be similar to that of a firm in such a market. Each unit (firm) wishes to assure its own survival under the best conditions it can obtain, given a setting of conflict and competition in which survival is not assured by the character of the system in which the conflict occurs. In a market, prices are the indicators and measures of equilibrium; in the international system the role of price is played by quanta of power—military, economic, and organizational. A given distribution of these quanta defines equilibrium and disequilibrium. The norm is a steady state; disequilibria are seen as temporary deviations from that norm, to be restored by way of a rearrangement of the quanta of power, sometimes by means of regimes.

The central concept is *hegemony*, the relative position of a given state-actor in the international hierarchy of power. A hegemonial actor controls the resource and runs the regime; when control over resources is more diffuse, coalitions may be necessary to assert control or control cannot be exercised. Regimes may not be possible, be short-lived, or be fragmented in various ways.

Classical realism and the mechanical metaphor

How does this view differ from what we normally call the realist tradition in international studies, the tradition exemplified—for all their differences—by Hobbes, Morgenthau, Kissinger, and Waltz? These writers are not interested in regimes; they consider them, at most, temporary expedients for managing specific problems of disequilibrium, mere expressions of more basic problems of power. The structuring of power is what matters to them, not differential rates of industrial development, demographic trends, or changing modes of human problem-solving. Liberals, mercantilists, and mainstreamers see themselves as amending and adapting these postulates to the conditions they see prevailing in the modern world. But while many of them find their intellectual ancestry in classical realism, they are no longer at ease with it. Classical realism accepts a view of the world that Waltz has labeled the "third image." The mind-sets that concern us now sense that behavior patterns which fall into the "second image" may alter the intellectual force of the systemic view; they are attempting to link the two levels of analysis, though they differ on how to do this.

Classical realists consider the international system an entity with an independent existence that shapes and constrains the volitions and preferences of actors by forcing them to subordinate everything they may want to the knowledge that survival is not guaranteed. The system forces the actors to calculate the costs and benefits of actions much as the firm must make use of marginal utility functions to assure its survival. These calculations ought to be over the long run; short-run determinations of where one's interest lies, of the kind that make up the "second image," are not likely to aid in the enterprise of surviving. For the realist, the component units of the system are states, not totalitarian or democratic governments, ministries of trade or energy, trade associations or trade unions. The transnational and trans-governmental perspectives are irrelevant for the realist; sovereignty is alive and well as long as the structure of the international system remains "anarchic." Overall power relations form the measure of structure; as long as unrestrained self-help remains a prominent option in the armory of each major state, anarchy continues. Hegemony is an outgrowth of structure, not of command over one specific resource or another.

Liberals, mercantilists, and mainstreamers qualify every one of these postulates. The system does not wholly determine actor choices: causation can flow upward as well as downward. Military power is not freely used to settle every conflict that comes along, and this observation denies self-help a core conceptual role in every problem that engenders interstate conflict. Arrangements dealing with nuclear reactors, oil, wheat, footwear, steel, computers, convertible currencies, tariff preferences, ocean mining, or pollution-control devices have a different significance for differently endowed state-actors. Power is multidimensional; it is not only military or geopolitical. Hence different state-actors see matters differently, depending on what is being discussed. The international system is seen to result from state policies and preferences, an outcome produced by patterns of behavior and not exclusively an autonomous entity constraining actors in obedience to its "structure." A role is given to the independent play of domestic politics and policy. The overall structure of the system is replaced with the notion of "issue-specific" structure. In accepting the idea of complex interdependence, this view has stripped sovereignty of its absolute quality; sovereignty becomes porous.

Commonalities among theories

Liberals, mercantilists, and mainstreamers, despite important differences, all accept certain theoretical commitments that follow from their acceptance of the mechanical metaphor. These have to do with the conceptualization of process, particularly the process of social and economic change, and the standards for determining the costs and benefits of collaboration and noncollaboration.

These theorists may be ambivalent on whether the international system is altered qualitatively by the impact of changes at the domestic level; but they agree that these changes are *the* central process underlying the definition of actor interests and therefore trigger at least a quantitative change in the system. What are the constituents of the process? The variables of most interest have to do with investment, and the rate and kind of technological innovation. Countries remain competitive, acquire hegemony, or fall behind because of the rate and kind of innovation. Economists' cycles or regularities are used to describe the process, and each country is assigned its rank accordingly in the issue-specific structure of international life. Product cycles and other concepts for depicting the changing comparative advantage of national economies are important tools for mapping the process; so are demographic projections and assessments of changing consumer demands. Political choice—foreign economic policy in the context of overall macroeconomic policy—therefore is analyzed in this context. Regimes result from perceptions of interest derived by the actors and observers from these aspects of the economic process. Whether regimes remain intact depends on the permanence of these interests and the variable impact of the processes on specific members of the regime, on the hegemon as well as on the lesser partners.

The chief criterion of a regime's strength or stability is the idea of public goods. The balance of costs and benefits associated with a regime, for the hegemon and for the weaker members, determines whether they remain satisfied with the arrangement. Costs and benefits are determined, when possible, by some criterion that measures efficiency in the delivery of the good. What is efficient for the hegemon, however, may turn out to be seen as inequitable by some other member. In such cases, the perceived distribution of the good becomes important to the survival of the regime because those experiencing inequity will claim that the cost of membership exceeds the benefits. The concept of opportunity costs is therefore used to imagine the ratio of costs to benefits: in exchange for accepting the constraints of the regime rules, what other possible benefits does the member forego? If opportunity costs seem high, the weaker members will withdraw or the hegemon will abandon its management role. Sometimes the terms "weak" and "unstable" are used to describe regimes that frequently display these characteristics. Hence, "strong" and "stable" regimes must be characterized by the willingness of the hegemon so to construe its cost-benefit ratio as to be willing to suffer the presence of many free riders. Only powerful states can be expected to do so.

Managing a regime, therefore, means that the hegemon or the hegemonic coalition so calculates the opportunity costs as to make continued leadership seem profitable. Management means that the hegemon must present the convergence of interests among the members as a public good for all of them and must assume leadership by shouldering additional burdens of support or insurance when other members show signs of losing faith in the publicness of the good. That said, liberals, mercantilists, and mainstreamers part company.

Liberalism

The human situation addressed by the liberal explanation of regimes has to do with efficiency and stability and hierarchy. Liberalism is deeply enmeshed with neoclassical economics. It claims that international relations ought to be based on a division of labor that efficiently maximizes the welfare of all; but international life ought also to be stable and give satisfaction to those who might lose out in a pure liberal order. Third World dissatisfaction is incompatible with stability. While hierarchies are a fact of life, hegemonic leadership that is either ineffective or oppressive is incompatible with stability. Hence, liberals wish to fashion "strong" regimes, which maximize efficiency, stability, and the hierarchy appropriate to the issue to be regulated. The demise of Bretton Woods makes the current search for such regimes a matter of importance.

For the liberal, the international system is much like the neoclassical economist's perfect market. It tends toward equilibrium, or at least it ought to tend that way in the interest of attaining efficiency. The structure may be anarchical or hierarchical, depending on the issue; structure is hegemony as defined by the characteristics of each issue. The tendency toward equilibrium is maintained when hegemony is effectively exercised by a single state or a coalition. The exercise of this hegemony—or leadership, for liberals who happen to be actors in government—of course depends on how we understand the interests that motivate actors.

Here, the invisible hand of Adam Smith still rules. Optimal effects for the system are thought to come about as a result of short-run, selfish decisions of actors. Interests are defined in terms of the actors' short-run conception of welfare maximation (unlike the mercantilist approach to the same problem). Collaboration and coordination are practiced in proportion to the convergence of short-run perceived interests as they apply to a given resource or activity. Organizations follow from the same postulate. They are arrangements that states enter into in order to facilitate collaboration, if and when enough convergence among interests exists to make this useful, and only if the market proves inadequate to deliver efficient resource allocations with marginal respect for equity. Since convergences are time-bound, liberals do not expect organizations to develop a life of their own. In fact, organizations are a distinct second-best; they really become necessary only when hegemons decide that they do not wish to be solely responsible for running things and that the costs of control, compensation, support, or insurance are to be shared with others.

Nothing approaching the eco-reformer's or the egalitarian's notion of management and learning can be found in the liberal approach. Actors learn only that a given regime does not work because it fails to correspond to whatever notions of interest happen to prevail. Learning merely means solving the problems of imperfect markets more efficiently. "Managing the world economy" means no more than finding the right policy compromise to accommodate the value of efficiency and the separate interests of actors who recognize the existence of complex interdependence. Learning is devoid of historical direction. Management has no definable teleology.

Mercantilism

Today's mercantilists, unlike their ancestors in the seventeenth century, subscribe to the economics of the neoclassical school or to the variants applicable to "late developers" as formulated by Friedrich List in the nineteenth century and by Raul Prebisch in the twentieth. Mercantilists accept the logic of markets and, in principle, do not deny the virtues of an international division of labor based on comparative advantage. They differ from the liberal school in insisting that efficiency is not and should not be the determining criterion of order. They are concerned that economics should serve the end of state power-for-survival, not be considered only as the engine of welfare. The main practical and policy difference between liberals and mercantilists, now as in the eighteenth century, is the mercantilist refusal to worship free international trade and investment as the norm.

The system of interest to mercantilism is the balance of power. Its structure is anarchical, law-like, and ought to be the determinant of policy. It would be a mistake, however, to confine this dictum to the military aspect of international politics. Mercantilists are interested in welfare in its own right, not merely in the importance of economic prowess as a military and strategic resource. They think that the evaluative significance of efficiency ought to be qualified by considering who suffers costs and enjoys benefits. Mercantilists think that arguments about benefits in terms of aggregate welfare must be replaced by examinations of groups in society that are adversely affected by market operations; farmers, automobile workers, watch manufacturers, and aerospace firms may well qualify for nonmarket subsidies or other forms of protection at the expense of aggregate welfare, if such steps can be justified on the basis of the values of national survival and international stability in an anarchical system.

This calculus implies the replacement of the invisible hand as a definer of interest. The short-term calculations of actors are not considered good enough to assure the general welfare. Reliance on them triggers consequences such as the product cycle, which are likely to support neither the survival of the nation nor that of specific groups within it. What appears to be efficient for industry over one generation's time may well turn out to be inefficient in the longer term. Hence mercantilists use a definition of interest based on a long-run survival calculus, a definition that relies less on actor perceptions than on the prescriptions of theorists and observers. The national interest in survival and the international interest in stability are and ought to be the definers of regimes.

Organizations, therefore, are only institutionalized patterns of hegemony that reflect the calculations of long-run interests typical of their members. Collaboration can be no more than a continuing process of trading off among these interests. Institutionalized practices that reaffirm a norm by means of clear rules and routinized procedures are not to be anticipated. Mercantilists calculate costs and benefits in terms of the maintenance of systemic rules of hegemony or of balancing all kinds of power, not merely the economic variety. An acceptable regime for them is represented by an arrangement in which the costs of maintaining a given power position are bearable for the strong and for the weak. Benefits are assured if one succeeds in maintaining one's position relative to one's enemies or competitors, or gains a bit against them. Any regime that permits actors to do these things is adequately managed. Otherwise, decisive new management strategies, taking the place of automaticity, are prescribed to alter the ratio of costs and benefits in one's favor. The NIEO is a set of such alternative management strategies for the late developers; so are orderly marketing agreements and cartels for the fully industrialized.

Between liberalism and mercantilism: mainstream views

We now come to theorists about regimes who are united by the desire to explain and predict why and how regimes do come about and vanish, not why and how they ought to come about in the service of a normative principle of world order. The image of the market exercises a powerful hold on mainstream approaches. Eco-evolutionists, eco-reformers, egalitarians, liberals, and mercantilists make predictions about regimes based on their notions of process and of order. Mainstreamers confine their predictions to their understanding of process alone. *The process that interests them is the interaction between the ordering values derived from liberalism and mercantilism*. The empirical context in which the discussion takes place is the decay of the Bretton Woods regime and its replacement by arrangements tied to demands for a New International Economic Order and those designed to protect the industrial adjustment process in the North.

Therefore, mainstream views accept most of the verbal and semantic conventions that characterize liberals and mercantilists. Like their fellow adherents to the mechanical metaphor, mainstreamers are not interested in management, learning, and knowledge as teleological constructs for predicting changes in regimes. Complex interdependence is the main tool for testing the liberals' concern with market failure and the mercantilists' interest in hegemonic stability as explanations of regimes. However, propositions about market failure and eroding hegemony are hypotheses, not assumptions or verified truths. Mainstreamers want to understand why regimes change after granting that they originate for the reasons adduced by liberals and mercantilists. But since not all markets fail in the same manner and not all regimes decline in response to the hegemon's change of heart, a lot is left to be explored and understood. The correct identification and projection of the actors' interests is the core preoccupation. Such identification makes new norms, rules, and procedures predictable.

Mainstreamers, because they disaggregate power and issues, see causation running in both directions: the system constrains, but the room for judgment left to actors is broad enough to have the actors contribute substantially to the shaping of the system. Complex interdependence means, among other things, that there is no fixed hierarchy of preference orderings for single actors or among actors. It also means that "the state" is disaggregated because of the presence of important transnational and transgovernmental actors. Once we allow for these empirical phenomena and assign causative significance to them we can no longer insist on a closed system in which the actors behave according to structural laws. The "law" itself is too permissive. Thus, the structure of the mainstreamers' system contains some law-like constraining qualities (e.g., the role of market shares or the monopoly power of single firms), but it also sees structure as routinized bargaining behavior informed by relatively slowly changing perceptions of self-interest.

Interests remain the mainspring defining expectations and actions. Mainstreamers follow the liberals' practice of accepting the short-run, self-perceived interests of actors as the important element, not the national or global interest as defined by someone else. They rely on these interests to explain why markets fail and hegemony erodes. Market failure and declining hegemonic stability are ways of identifying actor-perceived costs and benefits of collaboration. Thus, regimes are arrangements to reduce the uncertainty engendered by such developments, to maximize actor-perceived benefits and minimize costs despite the change in conditions. One of the primary purposes of regimes is to provide and diffuse information to enable actors to reduce uncertainty. If reducing uncertainty were to be considered a value like equity or survival, it would be the mainstreamers' choice.

IV. Toward an evolutionary synthesis?

Mind-sets and prescriptions for regimes

Devotees of the organic metaphor show great concern for the future of mankind, but they make short shrift of the political arrangements necessary for assuring this future. Followers of the mechanical metaphor reverse the emphasis: they are sophisticated about politics and economics but they fail to show much interest in the substantive problématique to which politics and economics might be applied. What might a synthesis of the two attitudes do? Could it explain the origin of regimes, as well as predict regime change and prescribe the desired content of a future regime? To achieve this would require a conciliation of divergent principles of order as well as agreement on the nature of the system, process, management, interest, and perceived costs and benefits. I return to the Law of the Sea negotiations as a demonstration of what each mind-set has to say on a specific instance of regime creation.

Figure 2 lists the assumptions and predictions of each mind-set concerning the future rules governing these major ocean-related topics: (a) the width of the territorial sea; (b) the width of the continental shelf; (c) the width of special economic zones; (d) fishing and fisheries conservation; (e) passage through territorial waters; (f) prevention of pollution; (g) oceanographic research; (h) deep-sea mining. These are identified by means of the letters in the column "Issues Included." The entries in the cells represent the view of representatives of the various mind-sets, not necessarily the negotiating positions of governments. The numbers in the column "Organization/Collaboration" refer to these organizational solutions: (1) a global supranational authority, (2) issue-specific global arrangements, (3) regional inter-issue arrangements, (4) regional issue-specific arrangements, (5) bilateral agreements, (6) unilateral assertion.

Before attempting a synthesis of the views, it is worth noting that the attempt to reform the existing regime began in 1967 with the U.N.'s proclamation that the oceans are "the common heritage of mankind" and with the legitimation of this act in terms of arguments consistent with the eco-reformist mind-set. By 1981 the mercantilist view had won a smashing victory, though liberalism "won" on the navigation issue. Egalitarianism gained a few symbolic successes on deep-ocean mining and sharing underused capacity in the economic zone. Moreover, the mainstream explanation of why this occurred seems to be convincing. Why not simply rest the case and forget about the analyses associated with the organic metaphor? I answer with another question: why assume that 1981 represents that last turn in the screw of consciousness?

Two postulates inform my effort to fashion a synthesis: I accept the accuracy of the mainstream analysis of why the LOS negotiations ended as they did; but I also subscribe to the principle of order associated with the eco-reformist view. This poses a difficulty because the analysis of the outcome also confirms the principles of order embedded in mechanical views—efficiency and state survival—while equity is associated with that aspect of egalitarianism most like the mechanical mind-sets. Any synthesis must be able to suggest how the cognitive links between science, knowledge, and political choice can overcome the temporary victory of the mechanical views and yield, eventually, an outcome that conforms to the organic one.

The remainder of my argument will be as follows. The mainstream vocabulary and concepts are very useful in explaining the origin of any regime. They remain useful in explaining changes in the regime if the core notion of "interest" is understood to include the possibility that actors alter their perceptions in line with new knowledge, including the kind of knowledge found in the organic mind-sets. If we know which views enter the negotiating process we can fix a limited range of outcomes. The synthesis, however, cannot

Figure 2. Assumptions and predictions about LOS regime in each mind-set

Mind-Set and Principle of Order	Purpose of Management	Actors' Interests	Determination of Costs and Benefits	Membership	Issues Included[a]	Organization Collaboration[a]
Eco-Evolutionism Survival of species	substitute synoptic view and planning for incrementalism	should be concerned with role of ocean activities only in terms of collective survival	evolutionary principles of creative adaptation	global	all; considered as causally linked to achieve a rational survival strategy	none given; implies 1
Eco-Reformism Quality of life	as above with ecodevelopment	should be concerned with solving economic-ecological problématique	public goods analysis directed to identifying "commons"	global	concerned with d, f, h; keep b and c small	1 or 2 preferred, with participatory planning; 3 and 4 also acceptable
Egalitarianism Equity	redistribution of power and wealth	selfish, short-run, but interests of South are "progressive"	reverse the present pattern of benefits; increase those of South	global preferred; Southern-regional not precluded	a,b,c,e,g d,h,	to be solved by 5 + 6 to be solved by 1 (failing 1, 3 is acceptable)
Liberalism Efficiency	improve global division of labor	selfish, short-run	public goods analysis to identify issues characterized by market failure	to be determined issue by issue, according to actual interests	a,b,c,e d f,g,h	to be solved by 2 with minimal rules to be solved by 4 opposed to any regime
Mercantilism Survival and wealth of nations	increase national capacity	selfish, long-run	opportunity costs of access to resources	as above	a,e b,c,d,f,g h	restrict coastal jurisdiction broaden coastal jurisdiction via 5 + 6 if rich, oppose any regime if poor, solve via 1
Mainstream None	protect interests of hegemonic coalition	selfish, short-run	both of above	as above	as determined by tactical linkages among actors	

[a]For meanings of symbols, see text, p. 53.

predict a specific regime or a unique outcome. Finally, even if we open up the negotiating process to the possiblity of cognitive evolution we cannot successfully prescribe the ideal regime in a way that combines the competing principles of order. Effective prescription would presuppose that the survival of mankind or the definition of the problématique has become consensual knowledge. I now demonstrate why such a melding of views remains unlikely.

Science and moral commitment

I begin with the observation that it is possible to accept certain value commitments implicit in the teleology of regimes without having to accept the scientific, systemic, and structural apparatus that legitimates the teleology in most mind-sets. One can favor a more equitable regime for the high seas, for the management of food, or for limiting pollution, without being a full-blown eco-reformer or egalitarian. But one pays a price in so doing: purposes must then be deduced from the perceptions of the actors who build, maintain, and destroy regimes, not from the nature of nature and the place of choice in nature. Disaggregation then triumphs over a holistic perspective because actors tend to think incrementally, not synoptically (as the eco-reformer would prefer). Reaggregation of common purposes is reduced to watching how the actors learn to put the pieces together. We can never be certain that their learning approximates the system as understood by followers of the organic metaphor.

Therefore, moral and positive knowledge cannot be seen as always supporting one another. One may subscribe to meeting basic human needs as an ethical commitment, though little warrant for such a position can be found in biological evolution and genetics. One can argue for a clean environment on grounds of esthetics and health, but one cannot claim that the history of evolution or of the physical universe makes such choices imperative. Positive knowledge is linked to moral preference in the sense that the means for attaining a moral end are suggested by science. One can also find instances in which positive knowledge lays bare the causes for the nonattainment of some moral end. The match between the two types of knowledge is seldom satisfactory or final.

Hence, evolution can have no knowable political direction or purpose. Neither nature nor logic can tell us where we ought to head. How, then, can organic views be expected to alter mechanical truths?

I believe that growing human understanding of physical and biological laws or tendencies suggests policies and choices for the future that differ from those accepted in the past. We now think about policy by allowing for the impact of industrialism on the environment, on the gene pool, on health; we consider alternative developments that are ecologically preferable. The acceptance of long-linked chains of causation and their inclusion in the design of means to assure welfare-related ends constitute a cognitive evolution toward the recognition of increasing complexity. Knowledge about economics that goes beyond the customary variables of the discipline constitutes another type of cognitive change toward recognized complexity, though clearly less consensual than in the case of biology and chemistry. International behavior displays more and more instances of collaboration among states in recognition of growing complexity. But it continues to contain the opposite trend as well.

True evolutionists, however, assume that growing complexity in the inorganic, organic, and social realms is a *fact of nature;* nature commands that the survival of the species take the form of adaptation by specialization and by the discovery of new environmental niches. Politics is merely another arena where this must occur; the forms of collaboration among states are a type of adaptation demanded by functional specialization. Eco-evolutionists, eco-reformers, and some egalitarians therefore treat evolution as a direct determinant of regime construction. They infer human purpose from the nature of nature; they treat economic development and the maintenance of world peace as an aspect of evolution. They stipulate a direct causal relationship between changing social and political values and a new understanding of nature. Coping with complexity for them implies more complex organizational forms. Since I do not share these evolutionary assumptions I am really using the vocabulary of evolution as a metaphor. Nature and the computer do not provide the models for understanding regimes. But nature and the computer provide stimuli for thinking about how regimes might be altered so as to reflect changing human consciousness about needs, functions, and forms. My evolutionary perspective does not imply a belief in the obsolescence of politics, though it assumes that the content of politics is changed by the development of consensual knowledge about nature.

I have no single value to maximize and no specific order to promote. I want to understand how actors understand their predicament and how they cope with it. I want to show what rules tend to be adopted under varying conditions of interest convergence informed by notions of the problématique. Quality of life, equity, efficiency, and survival then become ideas for distinguishing how actors perceive the effects of norms, rules, procedures, and transactions, not criteria for advocating change. An evolutionary perspective leads to a range of conceivable future orders, not to a single utopia.

The words I prefer

If one rejects the determinative quality of the organic argument one should not use the basic concepts that go with it; if one wishes to be clear one should avoid metaphors that obscure; if one does not believe in fixed patterns of behavior but in an evolutionary epistemology, much of this vocabulary is unnecessary. I conclude by reviewing the extent to which my partial synthesis remains indebted to notions of system, structure, equilibrium, process, cost-benefit calculations, and management.

What matters is process. The actors' perceptions of reality result in policies that shape events; these effects create a new reality whose impact will then be perceived all over again, ad infinitum. As to mainstream views, I see processes as patterned behaviors of actors from which the analyst can draw summary conclusions about trends. These behaviors are not assumed to confirm any predetermined logic or tendency. Actors calculate their interests according to whatever values they—not the analyst—wish to maximize. Changing perceptions of values and interests among actors are thus associated with changed behavior, though not in obedience to any pattern of rationality imputed or imposed by the observer. There is no fixed "national interest" and no "optimal regime." Different perceptions of national interest, changeable in response to new information or altered values, will result in different processes and in a variety of regimes that will be considered rational by the actors—at least for a while. Collaboration among states, as in the mechanical views, expresses no more than the convergence of such interests. It declines or intensifies in proportion to the continuation of the initial, short-run interests.

But what about the long run? Here aspects of the organic view are reinserted into the synthesis: management and organization acquire a significance that is lacking in mechanical views. While organizations are created in response to converging actor perceptions of interests, these institutions are not therefore assumed to be merely fleeting manifestations of a short-lived consensus. Organizations, the cognitive evolutionist supposes, are capable of learning. They reflect more than the initial convergence of actor demands because actor interests themselves may change in response to new knowledge; organizations may autonomously feed the process of change by the information and ideas they are able to mobilize.

This view of management is consistent with eco-reformist and mainstream positions. Management involves the manipulation of knowledge so as to trigger patterns of regulation by the regime, patterns that are to cope with more ambitious understandings of cause and effect linkages. Management also calls for the use of political and economic bribery ("side-payments") to help persuade the less enthusiastic regime partners. The regime's leaders may have to forego their own short-term benefits to meet the short-term needs of their weaker partners. Management involves the frequent reassurance by the wealthy that the immediate needs of the poor partners will be met even if that trade-off calls for the suspension or the discriminatory application of regime rules. Management calls for the willingness of the wealthy to settle for less than perfect symmetry among interests, for temporary and sloppy convergences, in order to approximate improved management at a later point. This is conceivable only if the managers accept a version of their interests consistent with the view of the eco-reformers. The LOS regime, on this assumption, may yet evolve into a comprehensive resource management scheme.

But the organic view contains no warrant that this must happen. Being open to new knowledge does not predict the quality of knowledge or the political or organizational inference actors will draw. Choices are made in response to perceived—and changeable—interests, and in obedience to the rules of bargaining. The management doctrine of the eco-reformers is incorporated into bargaining only to the extent that hegemonic coalitions are persuaded of its importance. It follows that one of the most important functions of any regime is to allow for the collection and dissemination of information. Norms and rules cannot change without the inclusion of this function. Unlike adherents of the organic mind-sets, however, I make no assumption that this information *must* lead to the reduction of uncertainty by means of stronger and broader regimes. On the contrary, adaptive behavior may well take the form of reduced collaboration, the unlinking of issues, and withdrawal from the international arena. Coping with complexity may involve the rational effort to curb it. So the eco-reformist logic for the oceans may predict a more holistic regime for deep-sea mining and antipollution issues, but the mercantilist view may just as well prevail for fisheries and oil-drilling. And both projections are consistent with an evolutionary epistemology.

That said, do we still need the notions of system, structure, and public goods? Conceptions of the international system as a sharply constraining set of structural laws, whether derived from natural science, bargaining behavior, or state power, are inappropriate. At best the system could be viewed as the resultant of patterned actor behaviors; its structure would then involve the repetition of processes over a period sufficiently long to be experienced as a constraint on choice. Such a definition of structure is practically synonymous with process. Moreover, it suggests a finality that clashes with the openness built into my attempted synthesis. Hence, while I am prepared to accept the hypothesis that behavior may be patterned in a form to justify the use of the term structure, I am not willing to accept this notion as a given. The existence of structure must be demonstrated from the study of regimes, not be prespecified. The idea of system then falls by the wayside because an "open system" can be demonstrated to exist only if the structural regularities hypothesized are actually shown to prevail.

Therefore, a cognitive-evolutionary view cannot settle for a concept of hegemony imposed by the analyst. Whether states really calculate their participation in a regime on the basis of a concern for their overall rank in some international pecking order is a matter for empirical investigation, not definition. It is equally an empirical matter whether they do or do not tolerate free riders, or regard the oceans as a commons or as private property. Public goods theory as used in mechanical mind-sets seeks to predict the behavior of hegemons, hegemonic coalitions, and their opponents, by arguing that they ought to behave in some specified manner because of their place in the international system. The logic is compelling only if we also assume that we are dealing with uniform and homogeneous preference schedules, and that these schedules are consistent with the desire of states to retain or gain a certain rank in the international hierarchy. Yet the idea of complex interdependence argues against the existence of such schedules; it suggests the prevalence of several simultaneous mixed-motive games, some of which assume a zero-sum world (as in military relations) while others concede a variable-sum situation (as in trade). Costs and benefits result from complicated trade-off calculations made by each actor in deference to his own notions of interest. If actors define the "good" to be produced by the regime in idiosyncratic ways and do their best to make "private" whatever the benefit may be, the theory of public goods will describe behavior. But it will not permit a conceptualization of how calculations of costs and benefits may change in response to new knowledge.

In any event, the conversation will continue. It will feature all the words that cause trouble and the words will take their inspiration from the mind-sets we carry in our heads. I feel comfortable with cognitive evolutionism because it makes fewer claims about basic directions, purposes, laws, and trends than do other lines of thought. It is agnostic about the finality of social laws and about the links between scientific discovery and social design. While captivated by the language and imagery of evolution, it uses the idea only as a web of sound, not a blueprint. The web catches whatever key actors may be doing and thinking, whatever new knowledge is being turned out, and whatever policy is made incorporating it. The items caught are of importance to the arguments contained in all the mind-sets. The result is not a true synthesis, which would presuppose that the components are additive; it is like a "stereophonic record player; the *difference* in sound quality between the speakers enables you to hear the music three-dimensionally."[17] Awareness of this condition does not result in a consensual objective vision. But it increases our understanding of the tune produced by the speakers and thereby reduces extreme subjectivism. Knowing this, words will hurt a little less.

[17] Magoroh Maruyama, "Toward Cultural Symbiosis," in Erich Jantsch and Conrad H. Waddington, eds., *Evolution and Consciousness* (Reading, Mass.: Addison-Wesley, 1976), p. 209. Emphasis in original.

International regimes:
lessons from inductive analysis

Donald J. Puchala and Raymond F. Hopkins

Rising interest in the concept "international regime" in the 1970s is much like that accorded to "international system" in the 1950s. It has become intellectually fashionable to speak and write about regimes.[1] Current faddishness notwithstanding, the purpose of this article is to show that the notion of regime is analytically useful, and that the concept is therefore likely to become a lasting element in the theory of international relations. As realist and other paradigms prove too limited for explaining an increasingly complex, interdependent, and dangerous world, scholars are searching for new ways to organize intellectually and understand international activity. Using the term regime allows us to point to and comprehend sets of activities that might otherwise be organized or understood differently. Thinking in terms of regimes also alerts us to the subjective aspects of international behavior that might be overlooked altogether in more conventional inquiries.

A regime, as defined in this volume, is a set of principles, norms, rules,

---

[1] See Oran R. Young, "International Regimes: Problems of Conception Formation," *World Politics* (April 1980): 331–56; Ernst Haas, "Why Collaborate? Issue-Linkage and International Regimes," *World Politics* (April 1980): 357–405; Robert O. Keohane and Joseph S. Nye, *Power and Interdependence* (Boston: Little, Brown, 1977); S. Brown et al., *Regimes for the Ocean, Outer Space, and Weather* (Washington, D.C.: Brookings, 1977); Edward L. Morse, "The Global Commons," *Journal of International Affairs* (Spring/Summer 1977): 1–21; Raymond F. Hopkins and Donald J. Puchala, *Global Food Interdependence: Challenge to American Foreign Policy* (New York: Columbia University Press, 1980); Hopkins and Puchala, eds., *The Global Political Economy of Food* (Madison: University of Wisconsin Press, 1979); and Raymond F. Hopkins, "Global Management Networks: The Internationalization of Domestic Bureaucracies," *International Social Science Journal* (January 1978): 31–46. The major focus of the Council on Foreign Relations' 1980's Project on the construction of regimes is a good indicator of the importance the concept has achieved in both academic and practitioner circles.

International Organization 36, 2, Spring 1982
0020-8183/82/020245-31 $1.50

process for
regulation
in non-
crisis
periods

and procedures around which actors' expectations converge. These serve to channel political action within a system and give it meaning.[2] For every political system, be it the United Nations, the United States, New York City, or the American Political Science Association, there is a corresponding regime.[3] Regimes constrain and regularize the behavior of participants, affect which issues among protagonists move on and off agendas, determine which activities are legitimized or condemned, and influence whether, when, and how conflicts are resolved.

Several particular features of the phenomenon of regimes, as we conceive of it, are worth noting, since other authors do not stress or, in the case of some, accept these points. We stress five major features.

Ex's.

First, a regime is an attitudinal phenomenon. Behavior follows from adherence to principles, norms, and rules, which legal codes sometimes reflect. But *regimes themselves are subjective:* they exist primarily as participants' understandings, expectations or convictions about legitimate, appropriate or moral behavior. Such attitudes may exist in relation to systems of functionally interdependent activites centered in geographic regions, as in neutralization and arms control in Antarctica, or more consequentially, as in western European international economic affairs. Regimes may exist in relation to a mixture of geographic and functional concerns, as in the international air transport system or in the international regulation of the uses of the oceans. Or, again, regimes may exist in relation to largely functional concerns, such as the international regulation of drug trafficking or health systems generally.[4]

Second, an international regime includes tenets concerning appropriate procedures for making decisions. This feature, we suggest, compels us to identify a regime not only by a major substantive norm (as is done in characterizing exchange rate regimes as fixed or floating rate regimes) but also by the broad norms that establish procedures by which rules or policies—the detailed extensions of principles—are reached. Questions about the norms of a regime, then, include who participates, what interests dominate or are given priority, and what rules serve to protect and preserve the dominance in decision making.

Third, a description of a regime must include a characterization of the major principles it upholds (e.g., the sanctity of private property or the benefits of free markets) as well as the norms that prescribe orthodox and

---

[2] This definition draws upon a point made by David Easton, "An Approach to the Analysis of Political Systems," *World Politics* (April 1957): 383–400.

[3] For example, Lucy Mair finds that regimes exist to prescribe and proscribe behavior even in states with no formal government. See *Primitive Government* (Baltimore: Penguin, 1960).

[4] Young, "International Regimes," p. 340. In our sense, then, a regime is more specific than structure, such as the power relationship of the North to the South or the distribution of power in a particular issue-area, but is more enduring than mere historical case analysis of ongoing issues. The reality of a regime exists in the subjectivity of individuals who hold, communicate, reinforce or change the norms and authoritative expectations related to the set of activities and conduct in question.

proscribe deviant behavior. It is especially useful to estimate the hierarchies among principles and the prospects for norm enforcement. These bear upon the potential for change.

Fourth, each regime has a set of elites who are the practical actors within it. Governments of nation-states are the prime official members of most international regimes, although international, transnational, and sometimes subnational organizations may practically and legitimately participate. More concretely, however, regime participants are most often bureaucratic units or individuals who operate as parts of the "government" of an international subsystem by creating, enforcing or otherwise acting in compliance with norms. Individuals and bureaucratic roles are linked in international networks of activities and communication. These individuals and rules govern issue-areas by creating and maintaining regimes.

Finally, a regime exists in every substantive issue-area in international relations where there is discernibly patterned behavior. Wherever there is regularity in behavior some kinds of principles, norms or rules must exist to account for it. Such patterned behavior may reflect the dominance of a powerful actor or oligarchy rather than voluntary consensus among all participants. But a regime is present. Here, the tenets of the international regime come to match the values, objectives, and decision-making procedures of the pre-eminent participant or participants. A regime need not serve the common or separate interests of every participant very well or even at all. Slave states, as an extreme example, understand the norms and principles of a bondage regime, although they do not accept them voluntarily. On the other hand, a regime only weakly buttressed by participants' power or disputed among powerful actors may not consistently constrain behavior. Such a regime may be in a formative or transformative stage, but evidence of some normatively prescribed behavior would nonetheless confirm its existence, however tenuous.

Regime distinctions important for comparative study

Theorizing concerning regimes among political scientists is now in the "pigeonhole" stage (to put it more scientifically, we are currently "proliferating taxonomies"). After our initial excitement over discovering, or newly applying, the concept and after coming near to consensus on the concept's definition, we have moved to asking about analytic elements and dimensions that might become bases for comparative empirical studies. Are there, for example, varieties of international regimes, and, if so, how do we distinguish between or among them? If there are varieties of regimes and we are able to distinguish among them, what is the intellectual payoff in making such distinctions and comparisons?

Furthermore, how does one go about identifying regimes? Our methods differ from those adopted by some other contributors to this volume. In contrast to more deductive approaches, where regime tenets are derived from postulates of general theory in international relations or from modeled patterns in microeconomics, we induce principles and norms from evidence of participants' perceptions and find rules written in charters, treaties, and codes. Evidence of participants' perceptions comes from interviews, when these are possible, or from writings and recorded reflections. We do not, however, induce principles and norms from *behavior*, which would confuse dependent and independent variables and lead to circular reasoning.

Some theorists suggest that what is interesting about regimes is similar to what used to be interesting about "systems"—that is, their origins, their structure, their impact on participants, their durability, and their transformation. In addition, those who study regimes are also concerned with principles and norms, with their effect upon the patterns of behavior that constitute compliance and deviance, and, importantly, with the patterns of reward and punishment that result. "Who benefits, how and why" and, correspondingly, "who suffers" because of regime norms are also central questions. Categorizing regime participants as advantaged and disadvantaged, and explaining why they are favored or penalized by different regimes, are theoretically appropriate objectives. In raising this question we clearly assert that regimes are not benign with respect to all participants, and that regimes can be "imposed" as well as arising solely from voluntary agreement.

Our examination of several international regimes suggests four characteristics of theoretical importance.

1. Specific vs. diffuse regimes

Just as systems must be limited analytically before they can be examined, so too regimes must be intellectually mapped according to the activities and participants they include. Regimes can be differentiated according to function along a continuum ranging from specific, single-issue to diffuse, multi-issue. They may also be categorized by participants according to whether a few or a great many actors subscribe to their principles or at least adhere to their norms. No international regimes command universal adherence, though many approach it. More specific regimes often tend to be embedded in broader, more diffuse ones—the principles and norms of the more diffuse regimes are taken as givens in the more specific regimes. In this sense we may speak of normative *superstructures*, which are reflected in functionally or geographically specific normative substructures or regimes. For example, in the nineteenth century, principles concerning the rectitude of the balance of power among major actors (the normative superstructure) were reflected in norms legitimizing and regulating colonial expansion (a substructure), and in those regulating major-power warfare (another substructure). Current norms that legitimize national self-determination, sanctify sovereign equality, proscribe international intervention in domestic affairs, and permit international coercion, are all general principles of our world order. They are reflected in a variety of more specific regimes, such as that which governs the process of decolonization, and that which regulates the global food system.

If such relationships between normative superstructure and substructure are real, as we believe, some fascinating questions arise. What, for example, explains the origin of the normative superstructures that exist and persist at given periods in history? Why and how do principles of such diffuse regimes—the superstructures—change over time? Why and how are principles and norms from diffuse superstructures integrated into the normative and subjective features of narrower regimes? What is the relationship between regime change at this substructural level and change at the superstructural level?

2. Formal vs. informal regimes

Some regimes are legislated by international organizations, maintained by councils, congresses or other bodies, and monitored by international bureaucracies. We characterize these as "formal" regimes. The European Monetary System is one example. By contrast, other, more "informal" regimes are created and maintained by convergence or consensus in objectives among participants, enforced by mutual self-interest and "gentlemen's agreements," and monitored by mutual surveillance. For example, Soviet-American detente between 1970 and 1979 could be said to have been governed by a regime that constrained competitiveness and controlled conflict in the perceived mutual interests of the superpowers. Yet few rules of the relationship were ever formalized and few institutions other than the Hot Line and the Helsinki accords were created to monitor and enforce them.[5]

3. Evolutionary vs. revolutionary change

Regimes change substantively in at least two different ways: one preserves norms while changing principles; the other overturns norms in order to change principles. Regimes may change qualitatively because those who participate in them change their minds about interests and aims, usually because of changes in information available to elites or new knowledge otherwise attained.[6] We call this *evolutionary change*, because it occurs within the procedural norms of the regime, usually without major changes in the distribution of power among participants. Such change, undisturbing to the

---

[5] Ted Greenwood and Robert Haffa Jr., "Supply-Side Non Proliferation," *Foreign Policy* no. 42 (Spring 1981): 125–40.

[6] See Haas, "Why Collaborate," p. 397.

power structure and within the regime's "rules of the game," is rather exceptional and characteristic mainly of functionally specific regimes.

By contrast, *revolutionary* change is more common. Most regimes function to the advantage of some participants and to the disadvantage of others. The disadvantaged accept regime principles and norms (and diminished rewards or outright penalties) because the costs of noncompliance are understood to be higher than the costs of compliance. But disadvantaged participants tend to formulate and propagate counterregime norms, which either circulate in the realm of rhetoric or lie dormant as long as those who dominate the existing regime preserve their power and their consequent ability to reward compliance and punish deviance. However, if and when the power structure alters, the normative contents of a prevailing regime fall into jeopardy. Power transition ushers in regime transformation; previously disadvantaged but newly powerful participants ascend to dominance and impose new norms favoring their own interests. In extreme cases the advantaged and disadvantaged reverse status, and a new cycle begins with regime change contingent upon power change. Such revolutionary change is more characteristic of diffuse regimes, highly politicized functional regimes, or those where distributive bias is high.

4. Distributive bias

All regimes are biased. They establish hierarchies of values, emphasizing some and discounting others. They also distribute rewards to the advantage of some and the disadvantage of others, and in so doing they buttress, legitimize, and sometimes institutionalize international patterns of dominance, subordination, accumulation, and exploitation. In general, regimes favor the interests of the strong and, to the extent that they result in international governance, it is always appropriate to ask how such governance affects participants' interests. The degree of bias may make a considerable difference in a regime's durability, effectiveness, and mode of transformation. "Fairer" regimes are likely to last longer, as are those that call for side payments to disadvantaged participants. The food regime discussed below functions in this manner. Furthermore, it can make a difference whether the norms of a regime permit movement between the ranks of the advantaged and disadvantaged, as with the ascendance of some previously disadvantaged actors toward greater power over current issues in international finance. By contrast, some regimes institutionalize international caste systems, as under colonialism. We expect that regimes founded on more egalitarian norms, and those that prescribe sensitivity toward mobility for disadvantaged participants, would be more adhered to and less susceptible to revolutionary change. Many elitist, exploitative, and stratified regimes have, however, proven viable for extended periods, and theoretical generalizations must be carefully qualified.

In the next two sections, we use the regime framework to discuss international relations in two contrasting issue-areas, 19th century colonialism and mid-twentieth century food affairs. Readers will recognize that these two regimes differ significantly along each of the four analytical dimensions we have elaborated. The colonial regime was diffuse, largely informal, subject to revolutionary transformation, and distinctly biased in distributing rewards. By contrast, the food regime is more specific, more formalized, probably in the process of evolutionary transformation, and more generally rewarding to most participants. Our primary intention is to highlight and clarify our theoretical definitions and the variables we have identified as useful for comparative analysis. Conclusions will push toward generalizations concerning regime outcomes and patterns of stability and change.

Colonialism, 1870–1914

Though the subject of voluminous writing, colonialism, particularly European colonialism as practiced during the last decades of the 19th century, has not been approached as a regime. Therefore, one aim of our study was to seek new insights by subjecting an already familiar phenomenon to rather unconventional analysis. Our other goal was to select as a basis for comparison a diffuse, informal, highly biased regime that was transformed in a revolutionary manner.

The regime

Historians identify the years 1870 to 1914 as the heyday of European colonial expansion.[7] Our analysis reveals that during this period the international relations of the imperial powers were regulated by a regime that prescribed certain modes of behavior for metropolitan countries vis-à-vis each other and toward their respective colonial subjects. Save for the United States, which entered the colonial game rather late (and Japan, which entered later and never participated in the normative consensus until after it had come under challenge), all of the colonial powers were European. England, France, Germany, and Italy were most important, but the Netherlands, Belgium, Spain, Portugal, and Russia also behaved imperialistically, and characteristically as far as regime tenets were concerned. The "regime managers" by 1870 were the governments of major states, where ministries and ministers made the rules of the colonial game and diplomats, soldiers, businessmen, and settlers played accordingly. In addition, a variety of sub-

---

[7] See, for example, William L. Langer, *The Diplomacy of Imperialism*, 2d ed. (New York: Knopf, 1972); R. R. Palmer, *A History of the Modern World* (New York: Knopf, 1957), pp. 613–59.

national actors, including nebulous "publics" such as church societies, militarist lobbies, trade unions, and bankers, held opinions on issues of foreign policy and in some countries exercised substantial influence over the formulation of colonial policy.[8]

The international relations of colonialism were evident in distinctive patterns of political and economic transactions and interactions. Flows of trade and money were typically "imperial" in the sense implied by Hobson or Lenin: extracted raw materials flowed from colonies to metropoles, light manufactures flowed back, investment capital flowed outward from European centers, and profits and returns flowed back.[9] Elites also flowed outward as administrators, soldiers, entrepreneurs, and missionaries. They went abroad to rule new lands, make new fortunes, and win converts to their political, economic or religious causes. The flows of people were largely unidirectional. Transactions were discontinuous across empires and each—the British, French, German, Italian, etc.—became a political-economic system unto itself.

But much more important than the characteristic transaction flows of colonialism were the interaction patterns in relations among imperial powers and between them and their respective colonies. There was a pronounced competitiveness among metropoles as each country sought to establish, protect, and expand its colonial domains against rivals. Yet there was also a sense of limitation or constraint in major-power relations, a notion of imperial equity, evidenced in periodic diplomatic conferences summoned to sort out colonial issues by restraining the expansiveness of some and compensating others for their losses. Constraint and equity were also reflected in doctrines like "spheres of influence" and "open doors," which endorsed the notion that sharing and subdivision were in order.[10] Therefore, what we observe in international relations among metropolitan countries are numerous conflicts, frictions, and collisions at points where empires came geographically together, occasional armed skirmishes outside Europe, periodic conferences called to settle colonial issues, and countless bilateral treaties and agreements between colonial powers that defined borders on distant continents, transferred territories or populations, and codified the privileges and obligations of each colonial power with respect to the domains of others.[11] In inter-imperial relations, then, there were distinct elements of international management over selected parts of the non-European world.[12] This management rested upon implicit codes for managing colonies, rationales like

---

[8] Julius W. Pratt, *Expansionists of 1898* (New York: Peter Smith, 1951).

[9] John A. Hobson, *Imperialism* (London: Allen & Unwin, 1938); V. I. Lenin, *Imperialism: The Highest Stage of Capitalism* (New York: International Publishers, 1939).

[10] René Albrecht-Carrie, *A Diplomatic History of Europe since the Congress of Vienna* (New York: Harper & Row, 1958), pp. 207–226.

[11] The events surrounding the Fashoda Crisis well illustrate this point. Cf. Langer, *Diplomacy of Imperialism*, pp. 551ff.; Albrecht-Carrie, *Diplomatic History*, pp. 223–25.

[12] Louis L. Snyder, ed., *The Imperialism Reader* (Princeton, N.J.: Van Nostrand, 1962), pp. 206 & passim.

"civilizing mission," which were given credence, and growing willingness to agree on imperial borders by diplomatic conferences.

With regard to relations between the metropolitan powers and subject peoples, little equity prevailed. Commands, directives, and demands flowed from colonial ministries to colonial officers and then either to compliant local functionaries or directly to subjects. Deference and compliance flowed back. Defiance usually brought coercive sanctions, with success largely guaranteed by the technological superiority of European arms.[13] The pattern of colonization was typically characterized by initial economic exploitation (usually by private entrepreneurs) and the arrival of religious missionaries, followed by military expeditions and the imposition of political authority either by coopting local leaders and institutions or by eliminating them in favor of metropolitan administrators. The establishment of political authority was sometimes followed by immigration from the metropolitan country, though the European outflow was seldom substantial. Colonial expansion typically proceeded from established coastal settlements toward the interiors of Africa and Asia. It was hastened where rival colonial powers began simultaneous expansionist drives in geographically proximate regions.

Colonization resulted in a pattern of outcomes that were advantageous to metropolitan countries and especially to particular segments of their national elites, disadvantageous to colonial subjects or at least to the majority of them, and stabilizing to intra-European international politics. Colonies brought wealth and resources that enriched citizens, enlarged national treasuries, and enhanced national power. Overseas empires also brought international prestige. In the colonies collaborating local elites usually accumulated wealth and even power by supporting the colonizers.[14] But colonial peoples were generally exploited economically and certainly dominated politically (although it must be noted that ruler-subject relationships were in some areas less benign before European colonization). As for intra-European international relations, competition for empire became a surrogate for more direct confrontation in Europe and accounted in some measure for the absence of war on the continent for several decades after 1870. In addition, colonial expansion and the global subdivision that ensued were in themselves compensatory mechanisms that helped maintain the multipolar equilibrium among the major states. Above all, colonization skewed the global distribution of political autonomy and initiative as well as the distribution of wealth dramatically in Europe's favor.

All of this was surely pleasing to the colonial powers. While they bickered constantly over pieces of distant territory, none seriously questioned the rectitude or worth of the colonial system itself. In the thinking of foreign

[13] The Germans, for example, with their policy of *Schrecklichkeit* killed over 100,000 Hehe and Herreros in German East and West Africa.

[14] The Buganda, for example, expanded their territorial sphere within Uganda with British support, thanks to their collaboration. See David Apter, *The Political Kingdom in Uganda* (Princeton, N.J.: Princeton University Press, 1962).

and colonial offices throughout Europe, behavior directed toward acquiring, preserving, protecting, and expanding empire was eminently legitimate. The legitimacy of colonization was collectively endorsed by the metropolitan governments and, after 1870, by overwhelming cross-sections of national populations—including Americans.[15] It was this overriding sense of legitimacy, the convictions that imperialism and colonization were right, that all means toward colonial ends were justified, and that international management to preserve major-power imperialism was appropriate, that contributed to the durability of the system.

Norms of the colonial regime

The legitimacy in colonization was founded upon consensus in a number of norms that the governments of the major powers recognized and accepted. These subjective foundations of the international regime may be treated under six headings.

a. *The bifurcation of civilization.* Looking from the metropolitan capitals outward, the world was perceived as divided into two classes of states and peoples, civilized and uncivilized. Europe and northern North America occupied the civilized category, and all other areas were beyond the pale, save perhaps other "white-settled" dominions. Evidence of this genre of 19th and early 20th century thinking is readily gleaned from the popular literature and political rhetoric of statesmen of the day, where "we/they" distinctions abound and where "they" are continually referred to as "savages," "natives," "barbarians," "primitives," "children," or the like.[16] From this, it followed politically that inequality was an appropriate principle of international organization and that standards and modes of behavior displayed toward other international actors depended upon which category those others fell into. Toward the "uncivilized" it was reasonable to behave paternalistically, patronizingly, and dictatorially, and acceptable to behave brutally if the situation demanded.[17] Toward "civilized" countries normal behavior had to demonstrate restraint and respect: bargaining was an accepted mode of interaction, concession did not necessarily imply loss of face, humiliation was out of the question, and conquest for subjugation was not legitimate.

b. *The acceptability of alien rule.* The zenith of European imperialism occurred before the principle of national self-determination became a tenet

---

[15] Pratt, *Expansionists of 1898;* see also J.W. Pratt, *Expansionists of 1812* (New York: Peter Smith, 1949); and Langer, *Diplomacy of Imperialism,* pp. 67–96.

[16] Ibid.; Edward Salmon, "The Literature of Empire," in *The British Empire* vol. 11 (London, 1924).

[17] Even as late as 1939 Robert Delavignette could write a book, *Freedom and Authority in French West Africa* (New York: Oxford University Press, 1950 [original French version, 1939]) based on this paternalistic view. The book gives advice to colonial officers on how to deal with subject tribes and chiefs.

of world politics, and indeed before Europe itself had largely settled into the pattern of "one nation, one state."[18] Therefore, the idea and practice of elites and masses, government and governed, being of different ethnic or racial stock, speaking different languages, and espousing different religions and cultures were considered neither illegitimate nor particularly unorthodox. Ethnically alien rule was also common in the colonized regions prior to European penetration. Thus, the imposition of foreign rule and the superimposition of white elites on indigenous elites were approved as right and proper, especially when such behavior was also perceived as "civilizing" or "christianizing."

c. *The propriety of accumulating domain.* During the period 1870 to 1914 states' positions in the international status hierarchy were determined in considerable measure by expanses of territory (or numbers of inhabitants) under respective national jurisdictions. Domain was the key to prestige, prestige was an important ingredient in power, and power was the wherewithal to pursue a promising national destiny. The expansion of domain was therefore accepted by the European powers as a legitimate goal of imperial foreign policy and, indeed, reluctance to pursue such policies was considered unorthodox; it raised questions about the according of status. There were, of course, recognized limits upon imperial powers' expansiveness, as for instance in generally understood injunctions against expansion within Europe, into others' colonial empires, or into others' spheres of influence. States that stepped beyond these limits risked sanctions.[19] Also proscribed were colonial conquests of such magnitude or executed so suddenly as to threaten the balance of power among metropolitan states. Nonetheless, expansion by conquest through Africa and Asia was not considered internationally lawless activity. On the contrary, it was accepted as respectable and responsible behavior by major powers.

d. *The importance of balancing power.* Intra-European relations in the late 19th century were stabilized by principles of a multipolar balance of power (even though the bipolarization that would harden by the eve of World War I was already in evidence). There was a widespread recognition of the efficacy of the balance of power and a general consensus among foreign offices that it should be preserved and perfected. This principle also justified colonial expansion and it further supported the norm of compensation.[20] As a matter of right all colonial governments expected compensation for adjustments in the boundaries of colonial empires. In fact, the agendas of periodic international conferences on colonial matters directed discussion toward formulas for compensation, especially as European power pene-

[18] For a discussion of the principle of self-determination see Robert Emerson, *From Empire to Nation* (Boston: Beacon Press, 1960), pp. 295–362.

[19] Snyder, *Imperialism Reader*, pp. 209, 297, 368, 372, & passim.

[20] Richard Rosecrance, *Action and Reaction in World Politics* (Boston: Little, Brown, 1963), pp. 220–73.

trated the crumbling Ottoman realm and as imperialism extended into China and Africa.[21] Although often difficult to engineer, compensation was considered legitimate and appropriate.

e. *Legitimacy in neomercantilism.* Economic exclusivity was a norm of colonialism since, as we have noted, colonies were considered to be zones of economic exploitation. Hence metropolitan powers endorsed their rights to regulate the internal development and external commerce of their colonies for the benefit of the home country, and, when appropriate or necessary, to close their colonial regions to extra-empire transactions. Instances abound where powers complained strongly about the protective behavior of others in their empires, but as the latter decades of the 1800s wore on and free-trade principles faded from fashion and practice fewer questions were raised about the propriety of neomercantilism. It had become a behavioral norm of the colonial system before 1900.[22]

f. *Noninterference in others' colonial administration.* As colonial domains were considered to lie under the sovereign jurisdiction of metropolitan governments, external interference in "domestic" affairs was not countenanced. The colonial powers could, and did, chip away at each others' domains via strategic diplomacy and occasional military skirmishes. But seldom did any one power question the internal administration of another's colonies. This was a taboo; respect for it resulted in mutual tolerance for whatever modes of subjugation a power might choose to impose in its outlying domains. The slaughter of rebellious tribespeople in Tanganyika and South West Africa by Germans in 1904–1905 was largely ignored in Europe. We suppose, though we cannot actually prove, that one of the factors underlying this norm of noninterference was the fear of retaliation. No imperial country could claim a record of completely enlightened treatment of colonial subjects, since brutalities occurred everywhere, and exposing another's misdeeds might invite exposure of one's own. There was, then, a "glass house" effect in the collective restraints on both criticism and intervention in internal matters of empire. Although the extraordinary and continuing brutality of rule in King Leopold's Congo was exposed in 1909 by investigative journalism it was bankruptcy, not immorality, that led the Belgian government finally to assert control over Leopold's fiefdom. The details of life in the Congo shocked many and violated even the lower standards of human decency applied to "uncivilized" areas; but it was the breakdown of fiscal solvency that was decisive.

It is easy to see how these various tenets of the colonial regime affected international behavior. They abetted behavior directed toward establishing relationships of dominance and subordination, rationalized conquest and whatever brutalities it might involve, justified subjugation and exploitation, impelled a continuing major-power diplomacy concerning colonial matters,

[21] Snyder, *Imperialism Reader,* pp. 209, 304–324.
[22] Parker T. Moon, *Imperialism and World Politics* (New York: Macmillan, 1928).

and necessitated periodic conferences and continuing bureaucratic-level communication. Such communication was aimed at limiting overexpansiveness, providing compensation, and maintaining the balance of power, and it had the effect of insulating empires from extra-imperial scrutiny and intervention. In this normative setting, colonization was deemed right and legitimate. It flourished.

There is little mystery about the basis of the norms that underpinned colonization between 1870 and 1914. They followed from consensus in the preferences of the major powers of the period, preferences that fundamentally preserved a global system that awarded great benefits to the major powers. To deviate from the norms was to invite sanctions, imposed either unilaterally, by particularly offended metropolitan countries, or collectively, by the major powers in concert. For example, the collective suppression of the Boxer Rebellion in China, in 1898, was a response to the Chinese infraction of the "bifurcation" principle (the norm that endowed Europeans with the right to establish dominance-subordination relationships).[23] Conversely, to uphold the norms in one's actions was to preserve the flow of rewards from colonization, to preserve the European balance of power, and to preserve European ascendancy in the world.

The fundamental principles of the colonial regime were all challenged, even in their heyday, and eventually undermined during the years after 1920. By the 1970s dominance-subordination was considered an illegitimate mode of international relations, alien rule had become anathema, economic exploitation was condemned and attacked, territorial compensation was considered diplomatically ludicrous, and the internal affairs of empire (of which only small remnants remained) became matters of continuing international public disclosure and debate in the United Nations and elsewhere.[24] Colonization is no longer considered internationally legitimate, and current norms of international behavior prescribe decolonization just as emphatically as earlier norms prescribed colonization. Indeed, the U.N. Trusteeship Council was set up to terminate the colonial system. There has been a profound change in the international regime that governs relations between the weak and the strong.

Why did the regime change? First, and obviously, the power structure of the international system changed; western European power was drained in two world wars; the United States and the Soviet Union rose to fill the power vacuum; new elites had come to power in both the United States and Russia after World War I and their preferences were distinctly anticolonial (though for ideologically different reasons). After World War II, new power emerged to buttress new principles and to support new institutions like the United Nations, where anticolonialism, promoted by the Soviet Union and

---

[23] Albrecht-Carrie, *Diplomatic History,* pp. 243–44.
[24] David A. Kay, "The Politics of Decolonization: The New Nations and the United Nations Political Process," *International Organization* 21, 4 (Autumn 1967): 786–811.

acquiesced in by the United States, was taken up by smaller countries and proclaimed by excolonial states, whose ranks swelled yearly. A new global consensus was formed in the General Assembly under pressure from the Committee of Twenty-Four, and this held the tenets of the new anticolonial regime that prevails at present.

Some analytic characteristics of the colonial régime

The international regime that governed turn-of-the-century European colonialism was obviously diffuse, both geographically and functionally. Its tenets pertained to relations among metropolitan countries, and to relations between them and their subjects. Whatever the substance of relations among metropoles, principles of exclusivity, compensation, and power balancing applied. In metropolitan-colonial relations of whatever substance principles prescribing dominance-subordination and abetting exploitation applied. To the extent that there were also geographically or functionally specific sub-regimes operative during the imperial era, such as American hegemonism in the Caribbean, the antislavery system, or intracolonial trade, they tended to embody as givens the main tenets of the colonial regime. Interestingly, the colonial regime itself embodied some of the more general principles of 19th century international relations, as for example the central and explicit importance of power balancing, and the linkage between international stature and control over "domain." This suggests the hierarchical interrelationship of *superstructural* and *substructural* regimes discussed earlier.

Managing the colonial regime was a pluralistic exercise conducted largely by mutual monitoring and self-regulation practiced in national capitals. The regime was therefore, by and large, informal; there were few codified rules and no permanent organizations. Periodically, foreign ministers or heads of states would assemble to sort out colonial problems, as in Berlin in 1884–85. Terms of compensation and boundaries of political and economic jurisdiction were spelled out in treaties that concluded colonial conflicts, and the rights of colonizers and obligations of subjects were also elaborated from time to time in unequal treaties between metropolitan governments and local authorities in outlying areas, which established "protectorates." But this was the extent of formalization for the colonial regime. That the regime in its heyday lasted for nearly a half-century may be attributed in part to its informal structure and policy procedures. Formalization would have amounted to a spelling out of the rules, as for example those necessitating compensation, and would have jeopardized major-power relations by calling attention to constraints that rival governments could not admit to in public. The less said formally, the better, and the more durable the regime.

Little need be said about the distributive bias in the norms of the colonial regime. With regard to benefits among metropolitan rivals there was some sense of equity, born perhaps of the recognition that the regime could prevail only as long as major participants found it satisfactory; each, therefore, had to gain something from it. But with regard to intra-imperial relations, exploitation was the rule. More crucially, the rules of the game did not allow for changes in status, nor for legitimacy in side-payments in return for compliance. Unless they chose to grasp at occasional hints of "self-government someday" or unless they were white settlers or collaborating local elites, colonial subjects went unrewarded by the colonial regime. Yet they played by the rules anyway, deviating only intermittently, mainly because the costs of alternative behavior were kept prohibitively high by colonial authorities (or at least were so perceived by subjects). Nor was there much expectation of assistance from the outside world, where strong states accepted the legitimacy of colonialism and weak states would not challenge the status quo.

While our description of the colonial regime only hints at its transformation in the middle of the 20th century, the change was obviously of the revolutionary variety. There was little changing of minds or goals on the part of the colonial powers (save perhaps for the United States, whose government began to seek decolonialization almost as soon as the Pacific territories were annexed). Instead, counterregime norms took form in the European colonies in the 1920s and 1930s as nationalist elites emerged and movements were organized. The Russian Revolution created a formally anti-imperialistic state, thus breaking the European consensus that supported the principles of colonialism and modestly transferring power from the forces of imperialism to its challengers. Two world wars in the first half of the 20th century eclipsed European power and with it the capacity to retain great empires. After World War II the United States became aggressively anti-imperialistic for a time, thus shifting more power away from the supporters of the colonial regime. With the onset of the Cold War the United States subdued its anticolonialism in the interest of western unity (but Washington never admitted the legitimacy of empires). Meanwhile, counterregime norms prescribing decolonization had been legitimized and institutionalized by the United Nations General Assembly and its subsidiary bodies in the early 1960s. As the power to preserve the old regime waned, the power to replace it expanded. Personalities changed, norms changed, and power changed. As a result an international regime was discredited, eliminated, and replaced. The transformation was nothing less than a comprehensive change in the principles by which governments conducted their international relations.

Food, 1949–1980

The current international regime for food emerged in the aftermath of World War II as a result of several developments. The most important of these were the creation of international food organizations, the growth of North America as a major supplier of grains to the world market, and the creation and diffusion of more productive farming practices. We have already described the resulting regime at considerable length elsewhere.[25] The food regime regulates international activity affecting production, distribution, and consumption of food, and these effects are potent in nearly every country of the world.

Food constitutes a functionally rather specific regime, at least in comparison with diffuse regimes such as colonialism. Nonetheless, it conditions diverse policies and activity. Food trade, food aid, and international financing for rural development and agricultural research, for example, are all affected by the principles and norms of the international food regime. In contrast to the colonial regime, the food regime is more formal. Several organizations shape and spread regime norms and rules, and many rules are explicit and codified. Formal organizations include two specialized agencies of the United Nations, the Food and Agriculture Organization (FAO) and the World Food Program (WFP). Both legislate rules and enforce procedures. Other bodies, such as the International Wheat Council (IWC), the International Fund for Agricultural Development, and the Consultative Group on International Agricultural Research, also help to manage the world food system and uphold norms of the regime.

Many of the regime's principles and norms are codified in treaties, agreements, and conventions such as the FAO Charter, the International Grains Agreement, and the Food Aid Convention. The norms of the food regime are biased to favor developed and grain-trading countries, which have long enjoyed special weight in the IWC and FAO forums. Still, in contrast to the colonial regime, most participants in the food regime benefit to some extent from their compliance with norms. The regime is now in transition though, again in contrast to the colonial regime, change is taking place in evolutionary fashion.

We refer to and discuss an international *food* regime advisedly, because policy coordination among and within states is organized around food rather generally, not only around separate commodities. Formal organizations that regulate international trading in the agricultural sector do so as part of a broad focus on food, and many procedures are standardized across commodities. Much the same is true of trading in agricultural inputs and in other functional tasks related to food. Agronomic research, for example, is internationally channeled and coordinated by the Consultative Group on International Agricultural Research. Furthermore, most officials whose behavior is important to the regime tend to be professionally responsible for food affairs rather generally; they are not just commodity specialists. For example, the norms they accept relating to nutrition, hunger, and eligibility for aid are based on food needs broadly defined in terms of calories and protein; the

[25] Hopkins and Puchala, *Global Political Economy of Food,* pp. 18–27.

norms relating to prices are based on market needs as affected by total farm production, subsidies, and incentives.

For illustrative purposes we will focus on wheat as a key commodity in the international food regime, mainly because the international economics and politics of wheat have been thoroughly researched and we can therefore discuss regime influences with some confidence. Wheat is the most easily stored and substituted product in the world's basket of foods. It is the preferred grain of consumption among well-off people in most parts of the world (though rice is still preferred by many in Asia). Wheat is suitable for both livestock and human feeding, and, for its costs of production, compares favorably with other grains and food products in delivering calories, proteins, and other nutrients. For these reasons, not surprisingly, the management of the world's wheat supply is essential in adjusting the world's food supply through international mechanisms. Wheat constitutes a special sub-regime.[26]

The national actors dominating the international wheat market since World War II have been the United States and Canada. In 1934–38 these North American countries supplied 20 percent of the wheat, coarse grain, and rice traded, while in 1979 they supplied 70 percent.[27] These countries also held very large surpluses until 1972 (a byproduct of their domestic agricultural politics). Their common interests led them to operate as an informal duopoly. Together they controlled and stabilized international prices for two decades, though at the cost of allowing the price of internationally traded wheat to decline in constant terms by nearly one-half between 1950 and 1963–69.[28] Other important actors in the food regime, as reflected by their participation in the wheat sector, include 1) major producers and consumers such as members of the European Communities (EEC), eastern European countries, and the Soviet Union; 2) other principal exporters such as Australia and Argentina; 3) poor importers such as China, Bangladesh, and Egypt; and 4) various international bodies such as the World Food Council, the Committee on Surplus Disposal of the FAO, and the major grain-trading firms.[29] Some importers, notably Japan, import far larger proportions of their total consumption than many poor importers. Japan imports over 50 percent of its food grains, 80 percent of its feed grains, and 90 percent of its soybeans.[30] The economic strength of such industrial countries, or oil producers in the case of OPEC, gives these importers a strong position in

[26] For an elaboration of this point historically, see Wilfred Malenbaum, *The World Wheat Economy: 1885–1939* (Cambridge: Harvard University Press, 1953).

[27] See the figures in Hopkins and Puchala, *Global Food Interdependence*, p. 36. The U.S. share in this was about 80% and the Canadian about 12%.

[28] See Alex F. McCalla, "A Duopoly Model of World Wheat Pricing," *Journal of Farm Economics* 48, 3 (1968), pp. 711–17, and Hopkins and Puchala, *Global Food Interdependence*, chap. 2.

[29] Dan Morgan, *Merchants of Grain* (New York: Viking Press, 1979).

[30] Fred H. Sanderson, *Japan's Food Prospects and Policies* (Washington, D.C.: Brookings, 1978), pp. 1–2.

bargaining over food with major exporters. Poor importing countries, on the other hand, even those that are 80 to 90 percent self-reliant, remain the most vulnerable to international price changes and the least influential in shaping outcomes in the food system.[31] Of course, in more concrete terms the participants in the food regime are not really states and organizations but individuals, an international managerial elite of government officials who are responsible for food and agricultural policy within countries, and for bargaining about food affairs in international forums. Their network usually includes executives from the trading firms, some scientific experts, and occasionally representatives from public-interest organizations. But its core is a cluster of agricultural and trade officers. To take one example, the elites responsible for negotiating toward an international grain reserve agreement between 1974 and 1979, at least those most visible in London and Geneva, were senior officials in government ministries of agriculture and trade officials from the large grain-trading countries, along with delegation members from producers' associations and trading firms. The United States invited a representative from an organization concerned with hunger to serve in an advisory capacity, but the elites who determined the outcome were clearly representatives of large, concentrated economic interests.[32] The negotiations failed because consensus could not be mustered among the world's food managers.[33]

Carrying the grain reserve story a step further illustrates the central position of the United States in the world food system, and in shaping the regime that regulates it. In November 1980, after the breakdown of international negotiations on the grain reserve, the United States adopted a four-million-ton emergency reserve of wheat. This unilateral reserve resulted from a coalition of two interests. The first was the interest of wheat producers, whose anxieties were heightened by the embargo imposed on shipments of grain to the Soviet Union in response to the invasion of Afghanistan. The U.S. Department of Agriculture tried to prevent a drop in prices from the lost sales by using its reserve authority to buy up four million tons of wheat (and ten million tons of corn). But producers wanted assurances that this grain would not be later dumped on commercial markets. The second interest was that of the humanitarian hunger lobby. It was largely organized after

[31] Cheryl Christensen, "World Hunger: A Structural Approach," in Hopkins and Puchala, *Global Political Economy of Food,* pp. 171–200.

[32] The one exception was Brennon Jones of Bread for the World. Key talks at the negotiations involved American Agriculture Department negotiators who worked out their positions in consultation with Canadians and with representatives of American wheat farmers (the latter served on the United States delegation) and representatives of the EEC (where French officials played a leading role). Soviet Union trade officials also played an important contextual role through clarifying their intentions but declining to participate in reserve obligations.

[33] For some of this information we are indebted to Daniel Morrow. In 1978–79 he was Special Assistant to the Under Secretary for International Affairs and Commodity Programs, United States Department of Agriculture, and one of the principal negotiators working on the food aid convention.

the world food shortage of 1973–75 and had pressed for international reserves for five years. The coincidence of the two interests in 1980 resulted in
a food reserve that by law could be released to food-aid recipients but not to
commercial customers. The creation of this international reserve marked the
first time that a stockpile of food had been held for release *only* to poor
people overseas on concessional terms. Its creation represented a minor
change in the international food regime that was, ironically, engineered by
Americans playing at domestic politics.

Norms of the food regime

In regulating food affairs over the last several decades, regime managers
have been able to find consensus on a number of norms. Some of these reflect
the overarching principles or superstructure of the state system; others are
more specifically aimed at regulating food transfers. Eight norms in particular tend either to be embodied in the charters of food institutions, or to be
recognized as "standard operating procedures" by food managers.

Respect for a free international market. Most major participants in the
food trade of the post-World War II era adhered to the belief that a properly
functioning free market would be the most efficient allocator of globally
traded foodstuffs (and agricultural inputs). At the FAO and in other forums,
therefore, representatives of major trading countries advocated such a market, aspired towards it, at least in rhetoric, and assessed food affairs in terms
of free-market models. Communist countries did not accept this norm for
Soviet bloc trade, but abided by it nonetheless in East-West food trade. Actual practice often deviated rather markedly from free-trade ideals, as the
history of attempts at demand and supply controls testifies, but in deference
to the regime norm these were either rationalized as means toward a free
market or criticized for their unorthodox tenets. The Common Agricultural
Policy of the European Communities, certain United States policies with
regard to supported commodities, and Japanese rice pricing have been re-
lentlessly attacked as illegitimate and contraventions of free-trade norms.
Such practices are defended as "temporary," "unfortunate but necessary,"
"politically imperative," and the like, so that free-market principles tend to
be supported even in the breach.

National absorption of adjustments imposed by international markets.
This derives from norms worked out in the more diffuse trade and state-
system regimes. The relative price stability that prevailed in international
grain markets during much of the postwar era can be accounted for in large
measure by American and Canadian willingness to accumulate reserves in
times of market surplus and to release them, commercially and concession-
ally, in times of tightness. Of course, these practices occurred largely for
domestic reasons. Yet there was still the almost universal expectation that

North Americans could and would hold reserves for the world and would manipulate them in the interest of market stability. Hence this major norm—that each group dependent on the market should bear, through its own policies, burdens created by large price swings—was made easier to maintain as long as North American reserves acted to prevent large price variations.

Qualified acceptance of extramarket channels of food distribution. Food aid on a continuing basis and as an instrument of both national policy and international program became an accepted part of the postwar food regime. By 1954 it was institutionalized by national legislation in the United States and by international codes evolving through the FAO's Committee on Surplus Disposal. Concessional food trade was given major impetus by the United States' effort to legitimize its international disposal of grain surpluses. Yet in a system oriented toward free trade, participants' acquiescence in extramarket distribution could be obtained only on the stipulation that market distribution was to take precedence over extramarket distribution. Therefore, food aid was acceptable to American and foreign producers and exporters as long as aid did not dramatically reduce income from trade or distort market shares. Rules to this effect were explicitly codified in national and international law. One example is the "usual marketing requirement," which demands that a food-aid recipient must import commercially, in addition to food aid received, an amount equal to its average imports of the preceding five years.

Avoidance of starvation. The accepted international obligation to prevent starvation is not peculiar to the postwar period; it derives from more remote times. There has been and remains a consensus that famines are extraordinary situations and that they should be met by extraordinary and charitable means.

The free flow of scientific and crop information. Whereas most of the other norms of the international food regime (and, more specifically, the wheat regime) emerged during the postwar era largely because of American advocacy and practice, "free information" emerged in spite of U.S. misgivings. Freedom of information about the results of agricultural research was a notion nurtured by the FAO and welcomed by those seeking technology for development. With American acquiescence, especially after 1970, it became a norm of the food regime and has become nearly universal. The same is true of production information: even the Soviets now acquiesce to American and FAO reporting requirements on their current crops.

Low priority for national self-reliance. Partly because the global food system of the past thirty years was perceived by most participants as one of relative abundance and partly because of international divisions of labor implicit in free-trade philosophies, national self-reliance in food was not a norm of the international food regime. Indeed, food dependence was encouraged and becoming dependent upon external suppliers was accepted as legitimate and responsible international behavior. World Bank and World Food

Council efforts to conduct national food-sector studies in the most dependent food importers, begun in 1980, are explicit challenges to this norm.[34] Measures that reduce dependence in rich importers, such as the Common Agricultural Policy of the EEC and the subsidization of domestic rice production in Japan, also conflict with this norm implicitly. Such policies, however, reflect domestic political pressures rather than explicit goals of food self-reliance; hence they do not directly conflict with the emphasis on food trade *per se*.

National sovereignty and the illegitimacy of external penetration. The international food system of the last thirty years existed within the confines of the international political system, so that principles governing the latter necessarily conditioned norms of the food regime. Among them, the general acceptance of the principle of national sovereignty largely proscribed external interference or penetration into matters defined as "domestic" affairs. In practice this meant that food production, distribution, and consumption within countries, and the official policies that regulated them, remained beyond the legitimate reach of the international community; a "look the other way" ethic prevailed even in the face of officially perpetrated inhumanities in a number of countries. Relief for starving Ethiopians in 1973–74 was delayed a year, for example, by adherence to this norm.[35]

Low concern about chronic hunger. That international transactions in food should be addressed to alleviating hunger and malnutrition, or that these concerns should take priority over other goals such as profit maximization, market stability or political gains, were notions somewhat alien to the international food regime of the postwar era. It was simply not a rule of international food diplomacy that hunger questions should be given high priority, or, in some instances, it was not considered appropriate that they should even be raised when there was a danger of embarrassing or insulting a friendly country by exposing malnutrition among its citizens. President Carter, for example, established a World Hunger Commission, but its report was considered so unimportant that it took over three months in 1980 to secure an appointment to deliver it officially to the president.

Regime consequences

Some effects of the prevailing food regime upon the international food system during the postwar era are easily discernible. In setting and enforcing regime norms for commercial transactions, the United States worked out trading rules in conjunction with key importers and other exporters. The most formal expressions came in the series of international wheat agreements, beginning in 1949. Communist countries remained peripheral

[34] Other challenges to this norm may be found in the works of revisionists such as Frances Moore Lappé and Joseph Collins, *Food First* (Boston: Houghton Mifflin, 1977).
[35] See Jack Shephard, *The Politics of Starvation* (New York: Carnegie Endowment, 1975).

participants in these arrangements. They worked out their own rules within COMECON, although they occasionally interacted with "western" food traders, playing by western rules when they did. World trade in foodstuffs attained unprecedented absolute levels, and North Americans became grain merchants to the world to an unprecedented degree. Through concessional transactions the major problems of oversupply and instability in the commercial markets were resolved. Surpluses were disposed of in ways that enhanced the prospects for subsequent growth of commercial trade by the major food suppliers. Especially with respect to grain trading, adherence to regime norms enhanced the wealth and power (i.e., market share and control) of major exporters, most notably farmers and trading firms in the United States. The nutritional well-being and general standard of living of fairly broad cross-sections of populations were also enhanced within major grain-importing countries. Adhering to regime norms, however, also encouraged interdependence among exporters and importers, an interdependence that, over time, limited the international autonomy and flexibility of both. With regard to concessional food flows, regime norms facilitated global humanitarianism and enhanced survival during shortfalls and famines. In absolute terms no major famine has occurred in the world since the Bengal famine in 1943. The availability of food on a concessional basis also undoubtedly alleviated some miseries in a number of aided countries. On the other hand regime norms also contributed to huge gaps in living standards between richer and poorer countries; they helped to perpetuate large gaps between rich and poor within countries; and they failed to correct chronic nutritional inadequacies of poor people worldwide. By promoting transfers of certain types of production technology as well as foodstuffs, the food regime also contributed to the spread of more capital-intensive farming and specialized rather than self-reliant crop choices. Overall, the food regime reflected and probably reinforced the global political-economic status quo that prevailed from the late 1940s to the early 1970s. It was buttressed by, and in turn buttressed, the global power structure of American hegemony.

The period 1970–78 was one of substantial instability in markets and concern for food distribution, food insecurity, and malnutrition. In 1963, when crop failure led the Soviets to make large international purchases, resources in the form of large surplus stocks in the West were available to smooth adjustments. But in 1972 world grain production lagged and trade rose sharply, and such resources were not available in the 1973–75 period. Production actually declined worldwide and the traded tonnage expanded dramatically, and wheat prices tripled in the two years between the summer of 1972 and 1974. Sufficient concern was aroused both in and beyond the circle of elite regime managers that a World Food Conference was held in November 1974, to institute a series of reforms in the regime. Three substantive major defects in the world food system, as well as many minor ones, were identified at the Conference. The first was inadequate food reserves to assure reasonable stability in markets and security for consumers; second, the use of food aid in ways that reflected low priority for the food problems of less developed countries; and third, inadequate and inappropriate investment flows with respect to food production capacity in food-deficit areas.

These defects arose because behavior according to regime norms, which previously had not led to a conflict between domestic and international interests, now did so. The stockpiles that had guaranteed international price stability (though not the food security of those unable to buy food) had not been created or maintained with the purpose of providing international stability. No norm had been institutionalized that prescribed reserves for international purposes. Reserves, held mainly by the United States and Canada, had been largely a function of political and economic responses to the income demands of the politically significant farm populations in exporting countries. The norm held that adjustment to market conditions was a national responsibility. When reserves were no longer required for adjustment purposes in North America they were gladly, not cautiously, depleted. Similarly, for the most part food aid had been an attractive means of foreign assistance precisely because surplus stocks overhanging markets were thought undesirable. Food aid was a mechanism to reduce such stocks and to promote new markets. In addition, the largest donor, the United States, allocated the bulk of its food aid on the basis of political rather than nutritional criteria and in direct proportion to the size of American stocks. When food was no longer in surplus, nutritional and international welfare interests did not command enough influence to maintain food-aid levels or even to control allocations of diminished aid. Dietary adequacy in poorer countries was not prescribed by the regime. Thus, Egypt, South Korea, Taiwan, Israel, and even Chile got aid, while near-famine occurred in Bangladesh. Finally, investment in food production, especially in poor countries, was low because it was not seen as attractive by the dominant philosophy of economic development—import-substituting industrialization. Nor was it relevant to the largest motivation that shaped private capital flows, namely, the search for cheap sources of supply. As noted, agricultural development was not prescribed by the regime. These considerations abetted the transfer of existing rather than new technologies, and leaned against investment in rural areas and in food crops for local consumption (as opposed to fibers or tropical products such as coffee, tea, and pineapples). The outlook for managers of the food regime was shaped by their positions and the rewards for these positions. Food affairs were generally not decided in ministries of development, let alone ministries of health. Rather, they were managed by agriculture and trade officials, and served their understanding of interests and goals. The international arena, for them, was largely a means for solving domestic problems through market development or surplus disposal. Goals of public health, political stability, and general economic development were at best given lip service in the calculations and actions of the food regime's managers.

In the seven years since the World Food Conference, has the regime changed? The answer is "marginally," and by evolution. First, there has come to be a greater emphasis on rural development. Growing more food has received high priority at the World Bank and in the efforts of national foreign assistance agencies, especially in food-scarce countries. New norms emphasizing food in development planning have been codified by a special conference on rural development held in Rome in 1979 and by continuing World Food Council resolutions. Finally a new lending agency, the International Fund for Agricultural Development, has been established (1977). A second change is that greater security for food-aid recipients has been assured. This results from a new Food Aid Convention, agreed to in March 1980, which raised the minimum aid donor pledges from four-and-one-half to eight million tons, and from the four-million-ton emergency international wheat reserve of the United States signed into law in January 1981. New norms formalized by the WFP established the legitimacy and stressed the urgency of these steps. Such norms have also prompted policy changes in major countries. The United States adopted a Title III program—food aid for development—that increased its concessional aid. A violation of older, nonintervention norms is reflected in the way this aid intervenes in the domestic food policy of aid recipients. Another norm change is reflected in increased programming of food aid according to nutritional rather than political criteria, which has occurred in the food aid programs of the WFP, Australia, Canada, and Europe.

These changes constitute the evolution of new norms that challenge the priority of market principles and give higher priority to chronic hunger, food security, and food self-reliance. Such norms have been explicitly promoted by international conferences, by the Rockefeller and Ford Foundations, and by the Brandt and Carter Hunger Commissions.

In other respects the tenets of the old regime prevail, and priorities remain as they were in the early 1970s. National policies dominate international policies and "free market" mechanisms are still held to be ideal for the bulk of food allocations flowing in international channels. With respect to reserves to increase stability and security, progress has been limited. The total flow of food aid remains about one-half that of the mid 1960s in volume, and less than half on a per capita basis. A larger proportion, however, now goes to least-developed countries—85 percent, up from about 50 percent.

Food security remains tenuous. The internationally coordinated system of reserves for food security called for at the World Food Conference has not been created. World stocks, which have increased since 1974, are still less than half the average size of stocks in the 1950s and 1960s.

All current trends suggest that food deficits will grow in a number of regions of the world, particularly in Asia and Africa. Furthermore, the rising cost of production, ecological deterioration, and the decline of subsistence agriculture all point to increasing vulnerability in the relationship between food supplies and needy customers. Regime changes since 1974 to cope with this problem of maldistribution are almost certainly inadequate.

We expect that the higher degree of formalization of the food regime and its large number of voluntary participants will lead to continuing and accelerated efforts to change substantially the norms of the food regime. These efforts will occur within the frameworks of public and private organizations—United Nations agencies, special forums and secretariats, centers, councils, committees, conferences, and companies. Setting the rules of the game will remain the prerogative of powerful national governments, especially those whose foodstuffs dominate in trade and aid flows, and in particular the United States. To the extent that there has been incremental change in the global food regime, pressures from formal international institutions have been helpful. Periodic meetings of international organizations have compelled governments to think and rethink their policies, and to defend them. If goal change in the regime has been the result of learning, the institutions and organizations of the food regime have been the classrooms.

Otherwise, the food regime does not look very different or function very differently from other regimes. Its principles have legitimized unequal distributions of food and unequal distributions of benefits from buying and selling food. Its norms have given authority to the powerful, both informally and in formal international bodies. Interestingly, though, there has been little formulation or articulation of revolutionary norms. Suggestions of movement toward revolutionary change have been more prominent in American "hunger" groups than in speeches by leaders of the Group of 77. In short, there has been some evolutionary change but no major challenge to the central principles of the regime.

Conclusions

Regimes in the 1980s, nevertheless, seem more to be under construction (or perhaps reconstruction) than destruction. This is a consequence, we believe, of changing conditions in which either prevailing regime principles and norms have proved inadequate in serving the principles of powerful groups or norms themselves have come under challenge as wrong. The decline of U.S. hegemony and the attendant reduction in resources available for enforcing norms buttressed by American power have created challenges to existing regimes. Disagreements have arisen over appropriate norms in the areas of trade, oil, food, and even nuclear security. These disagreements could indicate the rise of a new anomie as a condition in international affairs or, as we believe, they could be ushering in new normative orders buttressed by new distributions of power and higher degrees of international organization.[36]

---

[36] Talcot Parsons, for example, argues that anomie is the absence of norms while its opposite, institutionalization, is marked by structured complementarity of norms. See *The Social System* (New York: Free Press, 1964), p. 39.

Six general conclusions

Our two cases, colonialism and food, suggest some conclusions. They are hardly definitive or universal, but they might be subject to broader generalization and further refinement.

Without intending to be trivial let us first underline that *regimes exist*. In international relations there are revered principles, explicit and implicit norms, and written and unwritten rules, that are recognized by actors and that govern their behavior. Adherence to regimes may impose a modicum of order on international interactions and transactions. Our two case studies demonstrate that actors are guided by norms in diverse issue-areas. We would suggest that regimes exist in all areas of international relations, even those, such as major-power rivalry, that are traditionally looked upon as clear-cut examples of anarchy. Statesmen nearly always perceive themselves as constrained by principles, norms, and rules that prescribe and proscribe varieties of behavior.

Second, taking regimes into account contributes to explaining international behavior by alerting students of international affairs to subjective and moral factors that they might otherwise overlook. Once this subjective dimension of international relations is included, explanations of international behavior can be pushed beyond factors such as goals, interests, and power. Our case study reveals that regimes mediate between goals, interests, and power on the one hand, and behavior on the other. Such normative mediation is most effective, and hence most theoretically significant, between two limiting sets of conditions. At one extreme, a regime may be an empty facade that rationalizes the rule of the powerful by elevating their preferences to the status of norms. Under such conditions a regime exists because subordinate actors recognize the rules and abide by them, but knowing this would not significantly improve upon our ability to explain behavior as all we would need to know are the identities of the powerful and their interests and goals. Under the colonial regime, for example, knowledge of norms contributed little to explaining the dominance of metropoles over colonies. Similarly, under the food regime, the knowledge that there were norms revering free markets does not contribute greatly to explaining major trends in the trading behavior of the major exporters. These actors pressed for free trade because it was in their interest. Promoting the liberal doctrine itself was largely incidental, and exceptions were made when this doctrine was countered by powerful national (domestic) interests.

At the other extreme are conditions where regimes are determinative, where codified international law or morality is the primary guide to behavior, and where the separate goals, interests or capabilities of actors are inconsequential. Such conditions are extraordinarily rare in international relations. Where they prevail (in narrow, highly technical issue-areas like smallpox control or international posts and telegrams) consequent international behavior is analytically uninteresting. One area where a regime could evolve to become determinative is the oceans; the Law of the Sea deserves close watching by regime analysts.

Between the limits of major-power hegemony and legal or moral order is a rather broad range of international relations where regimes mediate behavior largely by constraining unilateral adventurousness or obduracy. The case studies suggest conditions under which such normative mediation takes place. For example, it occurs in relations among powers of comparable capability, where the exertion of force cannot serve interests. Here, norms and rules tend to order oligarchies, establishing the terms of a stable and peaceful relationship, mediating and moderating conflict, and preserving collective status and prerogatives against outsiders. Relations among the colonial powers, for example, were obviously mediated by norms, and knowing this adds to our ability to explain behavior that had large consequences for colonial regions. Under the food regime, exporters' direct and indirect relations with each other were mediated by norms such as those proscribing concessional dealings until commercial markets were cleared. Knowing about these norms and their impacts helps to explain behavior that otherwise might be puzzling. Why, for example, did Americans or Canadians not fully push their competitive advantages when they held food supplies that could be sold at discount prices? Why also did they tacitly compensate for lost markets between them?

Regimes also mediate under conditions of diffused power, or under conditions where asymmetries in power are neutralized, as in one-state-one-vote international forums. Here, consensus about appropriate decision-making procedures and their legitimacy keeps pluralism from deteriorating into anarchy, and consensus about legitimate objectives makes policy possible. Artificial equalization of power in the United Nations General Assembly and the Committee of Twenty-Four was one of the factors that forced colonial powers to begin to comply with norms that eventually became components of a decolonization regime. Similar circumstances in FAO congresses helped to bring the United States to participate more fully in the international exchange of agronomic information, and to accept norms concerning the free flow of information and a higher floor for food aid.

Finally, regimes mediate during transitions of power. They tend to have inertia or functional autonomy and continue to influence behavior even though their norms have ceased either to reflect the preferences of powers or to be buttressed by their capabilities. This is one of the most fascinating and useful aspects of regime analysis, where compliance with norms explains why patterns of behavior continue long after reasoning in terms of power and interest suggests that they should have disappeared. For example, decolonization might have been a phenomenon of the 1930s instead of the 1960s had Asian and African nationalists dared sooner to challenge European imperialism with force. Similarly, French withdrawal from empire might have been less prolonged and less destabilizing within France had governments of the Fourth Republic less reverently espoused discredited norms of the colonial regime (and realized, as De Gaulle did, that most of the French had long since abandoned the colonial ethos). In the same vein, a lingering acceptance of the tenet that it is more appropriate to address food shortages by importing food than by growing it contributed to the severity of the global food crisis of the early 1970s. And a lingering endearment with the notion that the American and Canadian governments will duopolistically buffer grain prices in the interest of global stability may now be contributing to a new food crisis, even though neither government has either interest in or adequate capability for making domestic adjustments for global stability.

Our third conclusion is that functionally specific and functionally diffuse regimes differ importantly with regard to the locus of management and the nature of managers. Functionally specific regimes such as the food regime are directed by technical specialists and middle-echelon administrators in participating governments. Such officials are recruited for their expertise and skills, traits that are well dispersed internationally. As a result, specific regimes tend to follow rather democratic procedures, at least as concerns policies pursued by managers. By contrast, functionally diffuse regimes such as the colonial regime are more often managed by diplomatic generalists and higher-level political officers. Not only does this suggest that diffuse regimes are likely to be much more highly politicized than specific ones, but also that conflicts which arise in the contexts of various regimes will be different. Resistance to issue linkage, for example, will be more common in specific regimes, where managers will variously seek to insulate (or, alternatively, expand) their jurisdictional domains. On the other hand, difficulties in enforcing norms, and greater deviance and regime challenges, are likely in diffuse regimes.

Fourth, international regimes are formalized in varying degrees. Our analysis suggests that degrees of formality tend to have relatively little to do with the effectiveness of regimes measured in terms of the probabilities of participants' compliance. With the two regimes we considered, one formal and one informal, both predictably and consistently constrained most participants' behavior over considerable periods of time. The colonial case suggests that some of the most effective regimes are those that are quite informal. This would seem to be true especially for regimes that regulate the general political behavior of major powers. "Understandings," "gentlemen's agreements," expected reciprocities, expected restraints, and predicted reactions, largely informal and uncodified, are important determinants of major power behavior. It is not accidental, moreover, that major power behavior is more likely to be subject to informal instead of formal expressions of principles and norms. Low hierarchy among major states reduces authority based upon raw power among them. But part of the ethos of major-power status is that great states must appear to be able to act in an unrestrained manner. No government of a major power wishes to appear constrained, least of all by a rival power. Yet we observe in cases such as the colonial one that powers usually are constrained, and statesmen recognize this; but statesmen can behave "according to the rules" more readily when no one formalizes them.[37]

While there may be few differences in the effectiveness of formal and informal regimes, our analyses suggest that "formalization" itself may be a dynamic factor. Regimes tend to become more formal over time, as with the colonial regime, where multilateral diplomatic conferences became increasingly important in the latter years of the imperial system; or with the food regime, where organizations, institutions, and rules seem now to be proliferating to fill a void in management created by American reluctance to provide informal leadership. We believe that regimes formalize over time because maintenance often comes in one way or another to require explicitness. As those rewarded by a regime's functioning become either accustomed to or dependent upon such benefits, they tend to formalize interaction patterns in order to perpetuate them. As elites change, "understandings" and "gentlemen's agreements" have a way of getting confused or reinterpreted, and formalization becomes necessary to preserve established norms and procedures. As challenges to a status quo preserved by a regime arise, maintaining orthodoxy comes to require explicit doctrine and more formal commitment; or, contrariwise, as a new regime emerges to replace a discredited older one, proponents of change might press for formalization as a hedge against reaction. Formalization thus might represent the apogee of a regime's influence, the first symbol of its prevalence, or the beginning of its decline. In all these instances, changes in formality seem to be related to shifts in the capability of dominant actors to manage or control.

Fifth, effectiveness in terms of compliance with rules and procedures of any given regime depends largely upon the consensus or acquiescence of participants. Formal enforcement is extraordinary and coercive enforcement is rare despite its prevalence in relations between metropoles and colonies during the colonial era. Usually it is self-interest, broadly perceived, that motivates compliance.

Explaining why actors choose to exercise self-restraint and to behave compliantly, especially if such behavior differs from that prescribed by "purely selfish" interests, is rather involved. First, in most international regimes a certain degree of unorthodox behavior is tolerated and not taken as a challenge to the regime, since no international regime embodies enforcement mechanisms capable of controlling all deviance. Dumping and other questionable trading practices are intermittently engaged in by participants in the food regime, for example. Similarly, despite the "glass house" tenets of the colonial regime there was occasional "stone throwing"; King Leopold's Congo was one noteworthy target. Hence one answer to why actors comply with regime norms contrary to their selfish interest is simply that

---

[37] Michael Mandelbaum, for example, believes that important but informal principles and norms exist with respect to nuclear weapons. Our thanks for his comments at the Palm Springs Conference, 27 February 1981.

they do not always comply. But such deviance is usually inconsequential or short-lived.

On the other hand, those who customarily comply with regime norms do so sometimes because they value the regime itself. These participants have no wish to establish precedents that might cause unorthodox behavior to proliferate and eventually to destroy the regime. This is one of the reasons for compliance with norms of the food regime that assign low priority to nutritional questions and define starvation as a national problem until an affected government chooses to request international assistance.

But such "regime-mindedness" is probably a lesser reason for compliance. More common is compliance out of calculated self-interest. Most participants in international regimes, whether they are advantaged or disadvantaged under the regime's normative biases, usually comply because compliance is calculated to be more rewarding or less costly than deviance. Saying this is perhaps pushing the obvious. But what is intriguing is how regime participants calculate their benefits and costs, and especially how they assign weights to perceived "moral" benefits of acting in accord with norms, or perceived "moral" costs of acting against them. It is a tantalizing observation that patterns of compliance with regime norms, and hence the stability of regimes, may result from the faulty cost-benefit calculations of participants who exaggerate the importance of norms or the degree to which they are hallowed by actors who back them with power.

Sixth and finally, our comparative case studies of regimes suggest that regime change is closely linked to two classical political concepts—power and interest. Most regime change results from changes in the structure of international power. For diffuse regimes, the relevant power structure is the global political-strategic balance, as was the case with the colonial regime, which began to change when major powers such as Russia (the Soviet Union) and the United States defected from the normative consensus. On the other hand, for more functionally specific regimes, relevant power also must include command over specific resources within particular issue-areas, as with the oil companies during the 1930s and the oil states in the 1970s, and the food-supplying states in the food regime. Of course, principles such as sovereignty may extend from the diffuse state system to affect or be part of the features of these specific regimes as well.

Revolutionary change is the more frequent pattern of regime change, and such change most often comes after changes in the structure of power. On the other hand, regime change via cognitive learning and the recasting of goals among dominant elites also occurs. This evolutionary change seems less frequent than revolutionary change, perhaps because major wars, from the Thirty Years War to World War II, have preceded and been instrumental in regime change.

Regime change without significant changes in power structure occurs when leading elites seek to preserve their status and their control of the regime by eliminating "dysfunctional" behavior, either in the substantive performance or in the decision procedures of a regime. This results when learning and technology foster new or changed goals. Changes in interests and goals have arisen from expanding knowledge of the world and its environmental exigencies. New understanding and capability with respect to disease, food technology, and air travel are important instances of regime change and even regime creation. The norm that no one should be hungry is not accepted by the current food regime, but it has sparked major efforts at regime change, including the creation of international reserves and external aid to increase food production in areas of the world that are most chronically malnourished. Unfortunately, it is only rarely the case that controlling elites—especially the fragmented and oligarchic elites of the international system—learn enough in sufficient time to change from within.

★ important when considering CHANGE issue.

Regime dynamics: the rise
and fall of international regimes

Oran R. Young

Regimes are social institutions governing the actions of those interested in specifiable activities (or accepted sets of activities).[1] Like all social institutions, they are recognized patterns of behavior or practice around which expectations converge.[2] Accordingly, regimes are social structures; they should not be confused with functions, though the operation of regimes frequently contributes to the fulfillment of certain functions. As with other social institutions, regimes may be more or less formally articulated, and they may or may not be accompanied by explicit organizational arrangements.

International regimes are those pertaining to activities of interest to members of the international system. For the most part, these are activities taking place entirely outside the jurisdictional boundaries of sovereign states (for example, deep seabed mining), or cutting across international jurisdictional boundaries (for example, high-seas fishing), or involving actions with a direct impact on the interests of two or more members of the international community (for example, the management of exchange rates). In formal terms, the members of international regimes are always sovereign states, though the parties carrying out the actions governed by international regimes are often private entities (for example, fishing companies, banks, or private airlines). It follows that implementing the terms of international regimes will frequently involve a two-step procedure, a feature that is less characteristic of regimes at the domestic level.

[1] This definition conforms to my earlier formulation in Oran R. Young, "International Regimes: Problems of Concept Formation," *World Politics* 32 (1980): 331–56.
[2] This formulation is not identical to that in Stephen Krasner's introduction to this collection of essays. Nonetheless, I believe it to be compatible with the definition outlined there.

International Organization 36, 2, Spring 1982
0020-8183/82/020277-21 $1.50

The fact that international regimes are complex social institutions makes it tempting to approach them in static terms, abstracting them from the impact of time and social change. This practice, drastically simplifying the analysis of regimes, is justifiable in some contexts; for example, it is undoubtedly useful to understand the operation of any given social institution, even if its origins are obscure. But this orientation cannot provide the basis for any comprehensive analysis of regimes. Like other social institutions, international regimes develop or evolve over time. Consequently, it becomes important to think about the developmental patterns or life cycles of regimes. How can we account for the emergence of any given regime? What factors determine whether an existing regime will remain operative over time? Can we shed light on the rise of new regimes by analyzing the decline of their predecessors? Are there discernible patterns in these dynamic processes? Is it feasible to formulate nontrivial generalizations dealing with the dynamics of international regimes?

Regimes as human artifacts

The distinguishing feature of all social institutions, including international regimes, is the conjunction of convergent expectations and patterns of behavior or practice.[3] This is not to suggest that both these elements must crystallize simultaneously for a regime to arise: the occurrence of behavioral regularities sometimes gives rise to a convergence of expectations, and vice versa. Mutual reinforcement between these elements undoubtedly plays a role in the development and maintenance of many social institutions. The existence of such a conjunction, however, ordinarily produces conventionalized behavior or behavior based on recognizable social conventions. These are guides to action or behavioral standards, which actors treat as operative without making detailed calculations on a case-by-case basis.[4] Under the circumstances, the major features of international regimes, as of other social institutions, can be expected to acquire a life of their own in the form of operative social conventions. This does not mean that actors, even those who acknowledge the authoritative nature of social conventions, will always comply with the terms of these conventions. Deviance or nonconforming behavior is a common occurrence in connection with most social institutions.[5] Yet the rise of conventionalized behavior is apt to engender

---

[3] For a somewhat similar account of social institutions in conjunction with structures of property rights see A. Irving Hallowell, "The Nature and Function of Property as a Social Institution," *Journal of Legal and Political Sociology* 1 (1943): 115–38.

[4] For some suggestive thoughts on the nature and role of social conventions see Russell Hardin, "The Emergence of Norms," *Ethics* 90 (1980): 575–87 and Russell Hardin, *Collective Action* (forthcoming), chaps. 11–14.

[5] In other words, perfect compliance with social conventions is neither common nor necessary for conventions to play an influential role in human societies. For a broader study of problems of compliance see Oran R. Young, *Compliance and Public Authority: A Theory with International Applications* (Baltimore: Johns Hopkins University Press, 1979).

widespread feelings of legitimacy or propriety in conjunction with specific institutional arrangements. This is what observers ordinarily have in mind when they say that social institutions include sets of recognized norms or exhibit a normative element.[6]

Approached in this way, regimes can be differentiated from the broader field of international behavior and identified empirically through an analysis of social conventions. To be sure, this task will seldom be cut and dried. There is considerable variation in the density of networks of social conventions we will want to include under the rubric of regimes. While all regimes encompass sets of social conventions, there is little point in attempting to establish an arbitrary threshold regarding the number of interconnected conventions required to qualify for the status of regime. The occurrence of deviant behavior is common in connection with most social institutions and should not be treated as evidence of breakdown in the institutions in question. Additionally, social institutions change on a continuous basis, so that we will sometimes want to differentiate between established regimes and those that are either embryonic or decadent. On the other hand, actors commonly possess relatively accurate perceptions regarding the existence of social conventions. There is therefore considerable scope for the use of direct methods of inquiry (for example, survey research) in efforts to identify international regimes. Serious problems of identification will still arise, however, where actors have little conscious awareness of the social conventions that guide their activities. In such cases, it will be necessary to devise indirect approaches to the identification of regimes. While this should not be viewed as an impossible task, the history of modern utility theory and other similar lines of enquiry suggest that we must expect this task to be fraught with severe problems.[7]

This perspective on regimes emphasizes that they are human artifacts, having no existence or meaning apart from the behavior of individuals or groups of human beings. In this sense, they belong to the sphere of social systems rather than natural systems. For reasons I shall address shortly, this hardly means that regimes will be easy to construct or simple to reform on the basis of deliberate planning or social engineering. It does, however, have other important implications. International regimes do not exist as ideals or essences prior to their emergence as outgrowths of patterned human behavior. It is therefore pointless to think in terms of discovering regimes.[8] Simi-

---

[6] Here again my position differs from that of some of my collaborators in this collection. I do not regard norms as defining characteristics of international regimes. Rather, I take the position that social conventions typically acquire an aura of legitimacy or propriety, which is normative in character.

[7] On the problems of operationalizing modern utility theory see Ward Edwards and Amos Tversky, eds., *Decision Making* (Harmondsworth: Penguin, 1967).

[8] This view has much in common with the philosophical tenets of legal positivism as contrasted with natural law perspectives. See the well-known exchange on this distinction between H. L. A. Hart, "Positivism and the Separation of Law and Morals," *Harvard Law Review* 71 (1958): 593–629 and Lon L. Fuller, "Positivism and Fidelity to Law: A Reply to Professor Hart," *Harvard Law Review* 71 (1958): 630–71.

larly, there is no such thing as an unnatural regime; they are all responses to problems of coordination among groups of human beings and products of regularities in human behavior. But this is not to say that it is irrelevant or uninteresting to assess the performance of specific regimes or to strive for the articulation of more desirable regimes in concrete situations. Just as alternative language systems may yield more or less desirable results in terms of criteria like precision of communication or richness of description, international regimes will have a substantial impact on the achievement of allocative efficiency, equity, and so forth. Accordingly, it makes perfectly good sense to endeavor to modify existing regimes in the interests of promoting efficiency, equity, or any other desired outcome.

Note, however, that international regimes, like other social institutions, are commonly products of the behavior of large numbers of individuals or groups. While any given regime will reflect the behavior of all those participating in it, individual actors typically are unable to exercise much influence on their own over the character of the regime.[9] This does not mean, however, that regimes, as complex social institutions, never undergo rapid changes or transformations: consider, for example, the collapse of the old regime at the time of the French Revolution or the more recent disintegration of the Geneva system governing the use of the oceans.[10] Nonetheless, it is exceedingly difficult to bring about planned or guided changes in complex institutions of this sort. Social practices and convergent expectations frequently prove resistant to change, even when they produce outcomes that are widely understood to be undesirable or suboptimal. Existing institutional arrangements, such as the international agreements pertaining to coffee or Antarctica, are familiar constructs while new arrangements require actors to assimilate alternative procedures or patterns of behavior and to accept (initially) unknown outcomes. Additionally, planned changes in regimes require not only the destruction of existing institutions but also the coordination of expectations around new focal points.[11] Given the extent and severity of conflicts of interest in the international community, it is fair to assume that the convergence of expectations around new institutional arrangements will often be slow in coming. This problem is well known at the constitutional or legislative level (consider the law of the sea negotiations as a case in point), but it is apt to prove even more severe with respect to the behavior of individual actors who are expected to be subjects of any new or modified regime.

What is more, social institutions are complex entities, commonly en-

[9] This observation is of course a cornerstone of the analysis of competitive markets in neoclassical microeconomics. For a clear exposition that stresses this point see Francis M. Bator, "The Simple Analytics of Welfare Maximization," *American Economic Review* 47 (1957): 22–59.

[10] For the case of the French Revolution see Georges Lefebvre, *The Coming of the French Revolution*, trans. by Robert Palmer (Princeton: Princeton University Press, 1947).

[11] On the convergence of human expectations around focal points see Thomas C. Schelling, *The Strategy of Conflict* (Cambridge: Harvard University Press, 1960), esp. chap. 4.

compassing a range of informal as well as formal elements. Under the circumstances, deliberate efforts to modify or reform international regimes can easily produce disruptive consequences neither foreseen nor intended by those promoting specific changes, so that there is always some risk that ventures in social engineering will ultimately do more harm than good. The desire to engage in social engineering with respect to international regimes is understandably strong, and I do not mean to suggest that all efforts along these lines are doomed to failure.[12] Further, situations sometimes arise (for example, as a result of the collapse of some pre-existing order) in which it is difficult to avoid conscious efforts to create or reform specific regimes.[13] But these comments do suggest the observation that naive hopes concerning the efficacy of social engineering in the realm of international regimes constitute a common and serious failing among policy makers and students of international relations alike.[14]

Regime formation

What can we say about the origins of international regimes or the developmental processes through which these institutions arise? In a general way, social institutions and their constituent behavioral conventions constitute a response to coordination problems or situations in which the pursuit of interests defined in narrow individual terms characteristically leads to socially undesirable outcomes.[15] As the literature on prisoners' dilemmas, collective action problems, the tragedy of the commons, and security dilemmas clearly indicates, difficulties of this sort are pervasive at all levels of human organization.[16] Among other things, this helps to explain the common emphasis on the normative character of social conventions and the widespread desire to socialize actors to conform to the requirements of social institutions as a matter of course. But it tells us little about the actual processes through which international regimes arise. Is there a uniform de-

---

[12] For an analysis of the options available to individual actors seeking to bring about changes in prevailing institutional arrangements see Victor P. Goldberg, "Institutional Change and the Quasi-Invisible Hand," *Journal of Law and Economics* 17 (1974): 461–92.

[13] This is true, for example, of the situation with respect to international monetary arrangements in the aftermath of World War II.

[14] This point of view may seem conservative (in the Burkean sense), but surely it is more than that. There are similar themes in many of the anarchist critiques of Marxian or authoritarian socialism as well as in many contemporary expressions of libertarianism. Skepticism about the efficacy of social engineering, therefore, is not a good indicator of ideological orientation.

[15] Compare this formulation with the view articulated in Arthur Stein's contribution to this volume. I would argue that Stein, too, is concerned with coordination problems but that he focuses on only one of the three routes to solving such problems that I outline in this section.

[16] See, for example, Hardin, *Collective Action*, on prisoners' dilemmas; Mancur Olson Jr., *The Logic of Collective Action* (Cambridge: Harvard University Press, 1965) on collective action problems, and Garrett Hardin and John Baden, eds., *Managing the Commons* (San Francisco: W. H. Freeman, 1977) on the tragedy of the commons.

velopmental sequence for institutions of this type or is it necessary to differentiate several patterns pertinent to the emergence of international regimes?
Not surprisingly, it is impossible to formulate a definitive answer to this
question now. Nonetheless, my work on regimes has led me to conclude that
actual international regimes fall into three distinct categories.

Types of order

Some social institutions can be properly interpreted as *spontaneous* orders. They are, as Hayek puts it, ". . . the product of the action of many
men but . . . not the result of human design."[17] Such institutions are distinguished by the facts that they do not involve conscious coordination among
participants, do not require explicit consent on the part of subjects or prospective subjects, and are highly resistant to efforts at social engineering.
Though the term "spontaneous order" is Hayek's, Schelling evidently has a
similar phenomenon in mind in his discussion of interactive behavior,[18] and
Lewis covers some of the same ground in his study of social conventions.[19]
In fact, there are numerous cases in which subjects' expectations converge
to a remarkable degree in the absence of conscious design or even explicit
awareness. Natural markets constitute an important case in point well
known to most social scientists, and this is an appropriate interpretation of
many balance-of-power situations at the international level. But spontaneous orders relating to such things as language systems or mores are even
more striking in many societies. As those who have tried can attest, it is
extraordinarily difficult to create an effective language by design. Yet large
groups of individuals are perfectly capable of converging on relatively complex linguistic conventions and of using them proficiently without high levels
of awareness.

The processes through which spontaneous orders arise are not well understood.[20] The propositions associated with sociobiology can hardly provide a satisfactory account of social institutions that take such diverse forms
and change so rapidly.[21] As Schelling demonstrated some years ago, models
focusing on individual rationality and self-interested behavior are not adequate to account for the convergence of expectations around prominent or
salient outcomes.[22] And social psychology offers no comprehensive account

[17] Friedrich A. Hayek, *Rules and Order*, vol. 1 of *Law, Legislation, and Liberty* (Chicago:
Chicago University Press, 1973), p. 37.

[18] Thomas C. Schelling, *Micromotives and Macrobehavior* (New York: Norton, 1978).

[19] David K. Lewis, *Convention: A Philosophical Study* (Cambridge: Harvard University
Press, 1969).

[20] For some suggestive comments phrased in terms of the concept of social conventions,
however, see Hardin, *Collective Action*, chaps. 11–14.

[21] The seminal work on sociobiology is Edward O. Wilson, *Sociobiology: The New Synthesis*
(Cambridge: Harvard University Press, 1975).

[22] Schelling, *Strategy of Conflict*, chap. 4.

of interactive behavior or the emergence of social conventions.[23] At the same time, it is not hard to comprehend the attractions of spontaneous orders. They are capable of contributing significantly to the welfare of large groups in the absence of high transaction costs or formal restrictions on the liberty of the individual participants.[24] Additionally, they obviate the need to develop highly implausible arguments concerning the negotiation or articulation of social contracts.[25]

A strikingly different class of social institutions can be described under the rubric of *negotiated* orders. These are regimes characterized by conscious efforts to agree on their major provisions, explicit consent on the part of individual participants, and formal expression of the results.[26] At the outset, it is important to differentiate among several types of negotiated orders that occur in the international system. Such orders will take the form either of "constitutional" contracts or of legislative bargains. "Constitutional" contracts (for example, the arrangements for Antarctica) involve the development of regimes in which those expecting to be subject to a given regime are directly involved in the relevant negotiations.[27] Legislative bargains (for example, the various United Nations plans for the future of Palestine), by contrast, occur under conditions in which those likely to be subject to a regime do not participate directly but are only represented (more or less effectively) in the pertinent negotiations. Beyond this, it is useful to distinguish between comprehensive negotiated orders and those that can be thought of as partial or piecemeal. Comprehensive regimes (for example, the proposed comprehensive law of the sea convention) sometimes emerge from careful and orderly negotiations. Given the conflicts of interest prevalent in the international community, however, it is to be expected that negotiated orders will often exhibit a piecemeal quality, leaving many problems to be worked out on the basis of practice and precedent.[28] Negotiated orders are relatively common at the international level. In fact, there is some tendency to become so involved in thinking about negotiated orders in this domain that it is easy to forget that other types of order are also prominent in the international system.

[23] But see the work on the norm of reciprocity reported in Kenneth J. Gergen, *The Psychology of Behavior Exchange* (Reading, Mass.: Addison-Wesley, 1969).

[24] Note, however, that such orders may be characterized by effective (though informal) social pressures. On the generic phenomenon of social pressure consult C. A. Kiesler and Sara B. Kiesler, *Conformity* (Reading, Mass.: Addison-Wesley, 1969).

[25] For an elaborate effort to develop the concept of the social contract as a hypothetical construct see John Rawls, *A Theory of Justice* (Cambridge: Harvard University Press, 1971).

[26] For arguments that appear to associate the concept of "regime" exclusively with this type of order see Arthur Stein's and Robert O. Keohane's articles in this volume.

[27] On the idea of "constitutional" contracts see James M. Buchanan, *The Limits of Liberty* (Chicago: Chicago University Press, 1975), esp. chap. 4.

[28] This is, of course, an insight developed extensively in the literature on neofunctionalism. For a variety of assessments of this line of enquiry consult Leon Lindberg and Stuart Scheingold, eds., *Regional Integration: Theory and Practice* (Cambridge: Harvard University Press, 1971).

Any effort to understand the formation of negotiated orders requires a careful analysis of bargaining. This means that the existing theoretical and empirical work pertaining to bargaining can be brought to bear on the study of regime dynamics.[29] For example, the emergence of negotiated orders can be cast in terms of the theory of N-person, nonzero-sum, cooperative games[30] or in terms of the microeconomic models originating in the Edgeworth box situation and inspired by Zeuthen, Pen, and Cross.[31] While this work is helpful, it also serves to highlight some of the major problems in the study of regime dynamics. Theoretical models of bargaining are notorious for their tendency to yield conflicting results, and much of the empirical work on bargaining emphasizes the importance of somewhat specialized contextual factors. Additionally, the analytic literature on bargaining exhibits a marked tendency to abstract itself from a number of real-world factors that are important in the context of international regime formation (for example, incomplete information, unstable preferences). Among other things, this has produced a serious lack of emphasis on factors that can lead to a failure to reach agreement on the terms of a negotiated order despite the fact that striking a bargain of some sort would be required to satisfy the criterion of Pareto optimality. Thus, the disruptive potential of strategic moves, free riding, the absence of suitable enforcement mechanisms, and so forth is commonly overlooked or deemphasized in the general literature on bargaining.[32]

A third category of international regimes can be approached in terms of the concept of *imposed* orders. Imposed orders differ from spontaneous orders in the sense that they are fostered deliberately by dominant powers or consortia of dominant actors. At the same time, such orders typically do not involve explicit consent on the part of subordinate actors, and they often operate effectively in the absence of any formal expression. In short, imposed orders are deliberately established by dominant actors who succeed in getting others to conform to the requirements of these orders through some combination of coercion, cooptation, and the manipulation of incentives. Two types of imposed orders are worth differentiating in this discussion of international regime dynamics. Overt hegemony occurs when the dominant actor openly and explicitly articulates institutional arrangements and compels subordinate actors to conform to them. Classical feudal arrangements as well as many of the great imperial systems exemplify this pattern.[33] De facto imposition, on the other hand, refers to situations in which the dominant

[29] A comprehensive review of the major theories of bargaining can be found in Oran R. Young, editor and contributor, *Bargaining: Formal Theories of Negotiation* (Urbana: University of Illinois Press, 1975).

[30] See R. Duncan Luce and Howard Raiffa, *Games and Decisions* (New York: Wiley, 1957).

[31] These models are reviewed in Young, *Bargaining*, Part Two.

[32] For a discussion of these problems based on a detailed account of international bargaining see Oran R. Young, *The Politics of Force: Bargaining During International Crises* (Princeton: Princeton University Press, 1968).

[33] On imperialism in its classic forms see A. P. Thornton, *Doctrines of Imperialism* (New York: Wiley, 1965).

actor is able to promote institutional arrangements favorable to itself through various forms of leadership and the manipulation of incentives.[34] The role of price leader in an oligopolistic industry can be thought of in these terms. But similar observations are in order, for example, concerning the role of Britain in the nineteenth-century regime for the oceans or the role of the United States in the regime for the continental shelves that emerged in the aftermath of World War II.

It is clear that the dynamics of imposed orders must be understood in terms of power, despite the well-known conceptual problems afflicting efforts to come to terms with the phenomenon of power.[35] As regards international regimes, several observations about relevant relationships of power are worth emphasizing immediately. There is no reason to assume that dominant actors must continuously coerce subordinate actors to ensure conformity with the requirements of imposed orders. Habits of obedience on the part of subordinate actors can be cultivated over time.[36] Most forms of dependence have a strong ideational or cognitive component as well as some structural basis. And the recent literature on core-periphery relations has made it clear that the methods through which hegemonic powers acquire and exercise dominance in institutionalized relationships are apt to be highly complex.[37] Under the circumstances, it should come as no surprise that the most successful imposed orders have not been characterized by continuous exercises in overt coercion. Beyond this, it is worth observing that the role of hegemon carries with it limitations as well as advantages. Dominant actors will often find it difficult to avoid being thrust into leadership roles, and there are significant opportunity costs associated with the role of hegemon. For example, the United States could hardly have avoided playing a central role in shaping the structure of the international economic order that arose in the aftermath of World War II, even if it had wished to do so. Similarly, hegemonic actors will generally bear the burden of responsibility for the performance of imposed orders, and any actor assuming the role of hegemon will almost inevitably have to forego positions of moral or ethical leadership in the relevant society.

The route taken

How can we explain which of these tracks will be followed in the formation of specific international regimes? Why are serious efforts being made

[34] This theme is developed in an insightful fashion in Robert Gilpin, "The Politics of Transnational Economic Relations," *International Organization* 25 (1971): 398–419. It is also a major theme of the recent literature on *dependencia*.

[35] For a good recent review see David A. Baldwin, "Power Analysis and World Politics," *World Politics* 31 (1979): 161–94.

[36] On the idea of a habit of obedience see H. L. A. Hart, *The Concept of Law* (Oxford: Oxford University Press, 1961): 49–64.

[37] Consult Michael Hechter, *Internal Colonialism* (Berkeley: University of California Press, 1975).

to reach agreement on a negotiated order for the oceans today when regimes for marine resources have more often taken the form of imposed or
spontaneous orders in the past? Why have we come to rely increasingly on
negotiated commodity agreements when spontaneous orders (for example,
natural or unregulated markets) would have seemed perfectly adequate in
the past? The first thing to notice in reflecting on these questions is that the
three types of order I have identified need not be mutually exclusive, especially if we approach international regimes in dynamic terms. Thus, a spontaneous order is sometimes codified or legitimated in a formal, "constitutional" contract; the 1958 Geneva Convention on the Continental Shelf
offers a clear illustration of this phenomenon. The promulgation of a negotiated order will have little effect unless its concepts and requirements
are absorbed into the routine behavior of the participants. Efforts to translate the terms of regional fisheries arrangements into day-to-day management systems, for example, indicate clearly how difficult it may be to implement negotiated orders at the international level.[38] By the same token,
regimes that arise in the form of imposed orders are sometimes increasingly
accepted as legitimate with the passage of time, so that it becomes less necessary for the dominant actors to coerce others into conforming with their
requirements. A transition of this sort may well be occurring at present in
connection with the management authority of coastal states over marine
fisheries. Under the circumstances, any attempt to classify international regimes rigidly in terms of my three categories is apt to distort reality and to
produce confusion rather than increase understanding.

Nonetheless, we are still faced with the problem of identifying the factors that lead to the emergence of one type of order or another in connection
with activities of interest to the members of the international system. Without doubt, there is some tendency in this realm to exaggerate the importance
of negotiated orders in contrast to imposed orders and, especially, spontaneous orders. This emphasis on negotiated orders appeals to the conceptions of rationality and purposive choice that pervade the contemporary literature on public policy. Additionally, a focus on spontaneous orders seems
to connote an organic conception of society, an orientation that is often associated with illiberal political views.[39] Yet it is hard to escape the conclusion that spontaneous orders are of critical importance in the international
system just as they are in other realms. Even in cases where a new order is
articulated in a formal convention, formalization is often better understood
as a codification of behavioral patterns that have arisen spontaneously than
as the promulgation of a new order requiring dramatic changes in existing
behavioral patterns. Many of the major provisions under consideration for

---

[38] A number of regional fisheries arrangements are reviewed in J. A. Gulland, *The Management of Marine Fisheries* (Seattle: University of Washington Press, 1974), chap. 7.

[39] But notice that organic conceptions of society have also been articulated by radical
thinkers. To illustrate, see Peter Kropotkin, *Mutual Aid: A Factor of Revolution* (New York:
New York University Press, 1972).

inclusion in the proposed new law of the sea convention, for example, are properly understood as illustrations of this phenomenon.

Other things being equal, the incidence of negotiated orders will vary with the degree of centralization of power and authority in society. Thus, negotiated orders can be expected to be pervasive in societies in which the state is highly developed and not severely constrained in functional terms. This proposition would account for the lower incidence of negotiated orders in international society in contrast to domestic society[40] as well as for the growing role of negotiated orders in advanced industrialized societies. At the same time, the prominence of imposed orders will vary inversely with the level of interdependence in societies. As I have argued elsewhere, the growth of interdependence increases the capacity of all relevant actors to injure each other,[41] and this condition serves to blur (if not to eliminate) the distinction between dominant and subordinate actors. This would explain the higher incidence of imposed orders in international as opposed to domestic society, as well as in traditional societies, in contrast to advanced industrialized societies. Curiously, increases in the complexity of social systems will frequently operate to accentuate the role of spontaneous orders rather than imposed or negotiated orders. It is not surprising that the ability of dominant actors to impose order generally declines as a function of social complexity. But it is important to note that it will ordinarily become harder and harder for groups of actors to arrive at meaningful or coherent bargains as the issues at stake become increasingly complex.[42] Accordingly, spontaneous orders arising from interactive behavior loom large in modernized social settings, despite the fact that this runs counter to the widespread propensity to regard such orders as unsophisticated or irrational.[43] Beyond this, increases in the size of social systems will ordinarily operate against reliance on negotiated orders in contrast to spontaneous or imposed orders. In very large systems, it is hard for the participants to play a meaningful role in the negotiation of regimes, and eventually even the idea of explicit consent will begin to lose significance.[44] Of course, it is possible to offset these problems to some extent through the development of some form of representation. But the success of any system of representation is critically dependent not only on the presence of well-informed constituents but also on the maintenance of high standards of accountability in relationships between

[40] For further discussion see Hedley Bull, *The Anarchical Society* (New York: Columbia University Press, 1977).

[41] Oran R. Young, "Interdependencies in World Politics," *International Journal* 24 (1969): 726–50.

[42] Hayek, *Rules and Order*, chap. 2.

[43] For an account that stresses the pervasiveness of spontaneous orders see Schelling, *Micromotives*.

[44] Put in other language, the transaction costs of reaching negotiated settlements rise rapidly as a function of group size. See the comments on this phenomenon in E. J. Mishan, "The Postwar Literature on Externalities: An Interpretive Essay," *Journal of Economic Literature* 9 (1967), esp. pp. 21–24.

individual representatives and their constituents. It should come as no surprise, therefore, that international regimes exhibiting the superficial appearance of negotiated orders are sometimes better understood as imposed orders of the de facto type.

No doubt, there are other approaches to explaining the incidence of various types of order in the international system. Perhaps the ideas associated with sociobiology can be applied to this problem.[45] Some observers will certainly want to argue that there are cultural factors at work such that specific international regimes will be affected by the cultural backgrounds of their members.[46] Those familiar with the recent literature on social choice problems will have something to say about the difficulties of arriving at negotiated orders in constitutional or legislative settings in which voting plays an important part.[47] For my part, however, I am convinced that structural factors of the sort referred to in the preceding paragraph are of central importance in accounting for the incidence of different types of international regimes.[48] This is where I propose to place my bets in the search for understanding concerning this problem.

Does it make a difference?

In the light of this discussion, it is important to ask if it makes a difference whether an international regime takes the form of a spontaneous order, a negotiated order, or an imposed order. Unless the answer to this question is affirmative, the distinctions I have been developing might well be dismissed as being of no more than passing interest.

The obvious place to begin in thinking about this issue is with a consideration of outcomes or consequences. That is, is one type of order more likely than another to lead to peace, allocative efficiency, equity, and so forth in the governance of international activities? As it happens, this is a highly complex subject with respect to which we are not yet in a position to formulate definitive answers. Interestingly, however, there is much to be said for the virtues of spontaneous orders from this point of view.[49] Language systems arising spontaneously, for example, produce extraordinary social

---

[45] For various reviews and critiques of the major ideas of sociobiology consult Arthur L. Caplan, ed., *The Sociobiology Debate* (New York: Harper & Row, 1978).

[46] A well-known account stressing the role of culture in international relations is Adda B. Bozeman, *Politics and Culture in International History* (Princeton: Princeton University Press, 1960).

[47] For a survey of this literature consult Norman Frohlich and Joe A. Oppenheimer, *Modern Political Economy* (Englewood Cliffs, N.J.: Prentice-Hall, 1978), esp. chap. 1.

[48] The terms "structure" and "structuralism" have been given numerous conflicting meanings in the literature. My emphasis here is on the idea that social systems have properties (e.g., centralization, interdependence, complexity) that are attributes of these systems *per se* rather than of their constituent elements.

[49] For an interesting, though overly optimistic, account of these virtues see Hayek, *Rules and Order,* chap. 2.

benefits in a highly efficient fashion. Much the same can be said of unregulated markets, at least when certain conditions pertaining to information, competition, and externalities are met. Additionally, spontaneous orders produce these results in the absence of high transaction costs. They do not give rise to elaborate procedural requirements or armies of officials charged with implementing and enforcing the terms of specific regimes; the participants need not even be conscious of their existence. Nor do spontaneous orders lead to severe formal restrictions on the liberty of individual actors, though they ordinarily do give rise to effective forms of social pressure. Negotiated orders, by contrast, are typically accompanied by high transaction costs and the progressive introduction of more and more severe restrictions on individual liberty.[50] What is more, the articulation of a negotiated order can hardly be said to ensure the achievement of allocative efficiency. For their part, imposed orders are designed for the benefit of hegemonic powers, a condition that frequently leads to inefficient outcomes—as the history of mercantilism and guild arrangements attests. Moreover, an imposed order is apt to become expensive to maintain, unless the hegemon succeeds in persuading subordinate actors to accept the order as legitimate.[51]

normative

Of course, it is true that spontaneous orders may yield outcomes that are hard to justify in terms of any reasonable standard of equity. Unregulated markets certainly exemplify this proposition under a wide range of conditions. But unfortunately, negotiated orders and, especially, imposed orders cannot be counted on to produce outcomes more attractive by this criterion. This is obviously the case with respect to imposed orders, which are designed to advance the interests of one or a few dominant actors. But it is important to emphasize that negotiated orders frequently lead to results that are little better in terms of equity. The bargain struck initially will often be heavily influenced by an unequal distribution of bargaining power. And even if a negotiated order is fair in principle, there is generally considerable scope for implementing or administering it in an inequitable fashion.[52]

On the other hand, the situation strikes me as markedly different if we turn from the question of outcomes to a consideration of the stability of international regimes or their capacity to adjust to changing environmental conditions in an orderly fashion.[53] It is here that spontaneous orders typically run into more or less severe problems. As the cases of language sys-

---

[50] While this point has recently been taken up by the neoconservative movement, it is worth emphasizing that it has long been a major theme of the anarchist literature. See Daniel Guerin, *Anarchism: From Theory to Practice* (New York: Monthly Review Press, 1970).

[51] For a rich empirical account of this phenomenon see A. P. Thornton, *The Imperial Idea and Its Enemies* (New York: St. Martin's Press, 1967).

[52] This is a point largely overlooked by Rawls, who assumes perfect compliance with the principles of justice accepted by actors in the original position (see Rawls, *Theory of Justice,* p. 351).

[53] See also Oran R. Young, "On the Performance of the International Polity," *British Journal of International Studies* 4 (1978): 191–208.

tems and moral systems suggest, these orders are particularly well adapted to relatively settled social environments. The convergence of expectations takes time, especially in situations where a multiplicity of opinion leaders can be expected to direct attention toward conflicting focal points concerning behavioral standards. Rapid social change, therefore, is apt to undermine existing spontaneous orders without creating conditions conducive to the emergence of new orders. By contrast, negotiated orders and even imposed orders ordinarily stand up better in the face of social change. A flexible hegemon can succeed in adjusting the terms of an imposed order substantially, so long as its own position of dominance is not obviated by social change.[54] Even more to the point, negotiated orders can simply be modified or revised on a deliberate basis in response to the impact of social change. In the case of "constitutional" contracts, for example, there is ordinarily nothing to prevent the community from amending or even replacing major provisions of an existing regime. The ongoing negotiations aimed at modifying some of the provisions of the Antarctic regime exemplify this pattern.[55] Of course, it is true that this will sometimes promote incoherence in international regimes, since amendments to an existing convention are not always easy to square with its original provisions. Nonetheless, it is easy enough to see the attractions of negotiated orders in periods of rapid social change like the present.

All this suggests the existence of a dilemma of sorts. Negotiated orders are attractive in environments characterized by rapid social change, and they will appeal to those having faith in the efficacy of social engineering. Yet spontaneous orders have substantial advantages in terms of the outcomes they are likely to produce, at least as contrasted with negotiated orders and imposed orders. As a result, we find ourselves in an era featuring a growing emphasis on negotiated orders in the international realm, but we have yet to learn how to operate such orders in a cheap and efficient way, much less in a fashion likely to ensure equitable outcomes. It follows that we need to think much more systematically about the extent to which the problems of negotiated orders are endemic or, alternatively, subject to alleviation through the development of suitable management techniques.

Regime transformation

As I have already suggested, international regimes do not become static constructs even after they are fully articulated. Rather, they undergo continuous transformations in response to their own inner dynamics as well as

---

[54] A good argument can be made to the effect that many of America's current problems at the international level stem precisely from the fact that its position of dominance has eroded substantially. On this theme, see also George Liska, *Career of Empire* (Baltimore: Johns Hopkins University Press, 1978).

[55] See M. J. Peterson, "Antarctica: The Last Great Land Rush on Earth," *International Organization* 34 (1980): 377–403.

to changes in their political, economic, and social environments. In this connection, I use the term "transformation" to refer to significant alterations in a regime's structures of rights and rules, the character of its social choice mechanisms, and the nature of its compliance mechanisms.[56] How extensive must these alterations be to produce qualitative change in the sense that we would want to speak of one regime disappearing and another taking its place? Does a shift from unrestricted common property to a system of restricted common property for the high-seas fisheries, for example, constitute a case of regime transformation? Answers to these questions must ultimately be arbitrary,[57] and I shall not attempt to identify any general threshold of transformation for international regimes. Instead, I propose to focus on major alterations in existing regimes and to comment on the patterns of change leading to these alterations.

Patterns of change

As in the case of regime formation, my research to date suggests the importance of differentiating several types of processes leading toward regime transformation. To begin with, some regimes harbor *internal contradictions* that eventually lead to serious failures and mounting pressure for major alterations. Such contradictions may take the form of irreconcilable conflicts between central elements of a regime. To illustrate, a regime (like the one articulated in the Svalbard Treaty of 1920) that guarantees all participants unrestricted access to an area's resources while at the same time granting sovereignty over the area to one actor is bound to generate serious frictions.[58] On the other hand, internal contradictions will sometimes exhibit a developmental character, deepening over time as a result of the regime's normal operations. Of course, this is the perspective adopted in Marxian analyses of the capitalist world order.[59] At a somewhat more mundane level, however, much the same line of thought can be applied to the study of many international regimes. For example, it is quite easy to identify evolutionary contradictions in unrestricted common property regimes for high-seas fisheries during periods characterized by increasingly heavy usage of the resources.[60]

[56] Here again my point of view differs somewhat from that articulated in Krasner's introduction. In my judgment, this difference is attributable to the definitional issues to which I alluded at the outset.

[57] Compare the well-known query posed by philosophers: how many Chevrolet parts added to a Ford automobile would it take to transform the vehicle from a Ford into a Chevrolet?

[58] For a helpful discussion of conflicts among rights see Ronald Dworkin, *Taking Rights Seriously* (Cambridge: Harvard University Press, 1977), esp. chap. 4.

[59] To illustrate, consult Immanuel M. Wallerstein, *The Capitalist World Economy* (New York: Cambridge University Press, 1979).

[60] For a seminal argument along these lines consult H. Scott Gordon, "The Economic Theory of a Common Property Resource: The Fishery," *Journal of Political Economy* 62 (1954): 124–42.

Several approaches to the analysis of these internal contradictions are noteworthy. It is relatively straightforward to conceptualize such problems in terms of the stability conditions associated with equilibrium models. Treating an international regime as a system of action, we can ask how far its central elements can be pushed before they begin to blow up rather than moving back toward a point of equilibrium.[61] Perhaps the best known example of this approach at the international level involves the reaction process models devised by Richardson for the analysis of arms races.[62] Alternatively, it may be helpful to examine these internal contradictions in terms of the holistic perspective associated with dialectical reasoning.[63] Note that this approach need not take the form of dialectical materialism or of any particular variety of Marxism; rather, its hallmarks are the analysis of social orders as dynamic wholes coupled with the search for dialectical laws pertaining to patterns of change in these entities.[64] It is also worth pointing out that each of these approaches tends to direct attention toward the occurrence of crises in existing or old regimes, whether such crises are described in terms of systems going unstable or in terms of the collapse of old orders. And in fact, we are now becoming familiar with discussions of food crises, crises of common property in the fisheries, and pollution crises brought on by such practices as the use of the air mantle as a sink for the disposal of wastes.[65] This suggests that the recent literature on catastrophe theory is a likely source of insights in the pursuit of knowledge concerning regime transformation.

A second type of process leading to regime transformation arises from shifts in the *underlying structure of power* in the international system. It is perhaps obvious that imposed orders are unlikely to survive for long following major declines in the effective power of the dominant actor or actors.[66] This is undoubtedly why the postwar international economic order has begun to come apart in recent years. But it is important to notice that both negotiated orders and spontaneous orders also reflect the prevailing structure of power in society. Regimes are never neutral with respect to their impact on the interests of participating actors. Therefore, powerful actors

[61] For a relevant discussion of the stability conditions associated with equilibrium models see Anatol Rapoport, *Fights, Games, and Debates* (Ann Arbor: University of Michigan Press, 1960), Part 1.

[62] See the helpful discussion of these reaction process models in Kenneth Boulding, *Conflict and Defense* (New York: Harper & Row, 1962), esp. chap. 2.

[63] For a collection of perspectives on dialectical reasoning see John Mepham and David H. Rubin, eds., *Issues in Marxist Philosophy,* vol. 1 (Atlantic Highlands, N.J.: Humanities Press, 1979).

[64] Dialectical laws are discussed in an illuminating fashion in Bertell Ollman, *Alienation: Marx's Theory of Man in Capitalist Society,* 2d ed. (New York: Cambridge University Press, 1976).

[65] For an early, but still pertinent, account emphasizing the prospect of such crises see Richard A. Falk, *This Endangered Planet* (New York: Random House, 1971).

[66] See Reinhold Niebuhr, *The Structure of Nations and Empires* (New York: Scribner's, 1959).

will exert whatever pressure they can in the effort to devise "constitutional" contracts or legislative bargains favoring their interests.[67] And opinion leaders or pacesetters will move spontaneous orders in directions compatible with their own interests. Under the circumstances, it should come as no surprise that shifts in the distribution of power will be reflected, sometimes gradually rather than abruptly, in changes in social institutions like international regimes. In some cases, these changes are of a direct sort, involving power shifts in the immediate issue-area associated with a given regime. For example, there can be no doubt that the recent changes in the International North Pacific Fisheries Convention were a direct outgrowth of the expanding power of the United States over the major fisheries of the region. In other cases, the process is indirect in the sense that the character of an international regime is affected by much broader shifts in the power structure of the international system as a whole. To illustrate, it is difficult to comprehend many features of the ongoing efforts to transform the regime for the oceans without a sophisticated appreciation of broader shifts in the distribution of power in the international system during the recent past.[68]

The analysis of this process of regime transformation is hampered by both empirical and conceptual problems. The principal empirical limitation arises from the fact that we lack any satisfactory measure of power, despite numerous efforts to formulate a usable metric or index in this context.[69] Under the circumstances, while it is easy enough to recognize major shifts in power after the fact, it is exceedingly difficult to pin down the early stages of significant shifts or to monitor them closely as they unfold. Thus, there is no doubt that the ability of the United States to control the international monetary regime has declined in recent years, but it is hard to say just how rapidly this trend is progressing at present and how far it will go during the near future. On the conceptual front, the problem focuses on the lack of consensus with respect to the definition of power. This is partly attributable to the complex and elusive character of the phenomenon of power.[70] In part, however, it arises from the fact that the concept of power plays a significantly different role in various analytic perspectives in common use among social scientists. Compare, for example, the conceptions of power reflected in the views of those who think in terms of structural bases of dependence with those who focus on the behavior of individual actors and employ the language of interdependence.[71] It follows that this type of regime transforma-

[67] In other words, regimes are seldom developed under conditions approximating a Rawlsian "veil of ignorance." See Rawls, *Theory of Justice,* chap. 3 for an account of the nature and role of the "veil of ignorance."

[68] See also Joseph S. Nye Jr., "Ocean Rule-Making from a World Perspective," in Ocean Policy Project, *Perspectives on Ocean Policy* (Washington, 1974), pp. 221–44.

[69] For a critical review see David A. Baldwin, "Money and Power," *Journal of Politics* 33 (1971): 578–614.

[70] See also Baldwin, "Power Analysis."

[71] To illustrate, compare the ideas articulated in Johan Galtung, "A Structural Theory of Imperialism," *Journal of Peace Research* 2 (1971): 81–118 with those outlined in Robert O. Keohane and Joseph S. Nye Jr., *Power and Interdependence* (Boston: Little, Brown, 1977).

tion is not well understood at present. But this is hardly a sufficient reason to deemphasize the role of shifts in the structure of power in bringing about the transformation of specific international regimes. On the contrary, I would agree with those who argue that this situation calls for a renewed effort to come to terms systematically with power and changes in the distribution of power.

Beyond this, international regimes quite frequently fall victim to the impact of *exogenous forces*. That is, societal developments external to a specific regime (treated as one among many social institutions) may lead to alterations in human behavior that undermine the essential elements of the regime. Perhaps the most dramatic examples of this process occur in conjunction with changes in the nature and distribution of technology.[72] To illustrate, the advent of large stern trawlers and factory ships dealt a decisive blow to the unrestricted common property regime for the high-seas fisheries, which had yielded at least tolerable results for centuries. Similarly, the rapid growth of satellite communications technology has swamped earlier international arrangements for the use of the electromagnetic spectrum.[73] But other exogenous forces may produce equally striking effects with respect to the transformation of international regimes. Problems of heavy usage, for example, often arise as a consequence of overall population growth or of shifting tastes within existing populations.[74] This is surely a major factor underlying recent problems with regimes for high-seas fishing and the control of pollution in areas like the Mediterranean basin. Additionally, major changes in one international regime will sometimes lead to pressures for change in others. Thus, success in modifying the existing regime for whaling in such a way as to promote the growth of stocks of great whales would clearly have extensive implications for any regime governing the harvest of renewable resources in the Southern Ocean.[75] Without doubt, the impact of these exogenous forces is difficult to predict accurately. The course of technological development is discontinuous and hard to foresee in advance.[76] The processes through which human tastes develop and change are poorly understood. It is even difficult to make meaningful predictions concerning the growth of populations despite the availability of empirical projections based

[72] For a broad account of western history stressing the role of technological change see William H. McNeil, *The Rise of the West* (Chicago: Chicago University Press, 1963). For a more specific argument to the effect that technological change is the source of many contemporary environmental problems see Barry Commoner, *The Closing Circle* (New York: Knopf, 1971).

[73] See Seyom Brown et al., *Regimes for the Ocean, Outer Space, and Weather* (Washington, D.C.: Brookings, 1977), esp. chaps. 11–13.

[74] For relevant background on world population problems consult Paul R. Ehrlich, *The Population Bomb* (New York: Ballantine, 1968).

[75] On the natural resources of the Southern Ocean see G. L. Kesteven, "The Southern Ocean," in Elisabeth Mann Borgese and Norton Ginsburg, eds., *Ocean Yearbook* 1 (Chicago, 1978): 467–99.

[76] For an analysis of the assessment of technological change consult Lester B. Lave, *Technological Change: Its Conception and Measurement* (Englewood Cliffs, N.J.: Prentice-Hall, 1966).

on recent trends. And of course a clear understanding of the impact of changes in other regimes on any specific international regime presupposes the growth of knowledge pertaining to the whole issue of regime transformation. Nonetheless, it seems important to recognize the significance of exogenous forces in the analysis of regime transformation. If nothing else, this recognition reminds us of the dangers of thinking about specific social institutions in isolation from the broader social setting.

Paths to transformation

Which of these processes of transformation will occur most frequently in the realm of international regimes? How can we account for differences in the incidence of various processes of transformation? Once again, it is helpful to begin by observing that these processes are not mutually exclusive; several of them can occur simultaneously, interacting with each other to form a complex pattern. There is little doubt, for example, that technological developments severely exacerbated the internal contradictions built into the traditional regimes of unrestricted common property in the high-seas fisheries. And the emerging contradictions in common property arrangements governing the disposal of various effluents have provided a stimulus for the development of radically different technologies in this area, a sequence of events that can be expected to constitute a force for major changes in pollution control regimes. Under the circumstances, sophisticated analyses of the transformation of specific regimes will typically require examinations of several processes of transformation together with the interactions among them. For many purposes, it will not be particularly helpful to worry about the relative importance of individual processes of transformation.

At the same time, views concerning the relative importance of different processes of transformation will ordinarily correlate highly with broader philosophical or ideological perspectives. Thus, Marxists as well as others who think in dialectical terms can be expected to approach the problem of regime transformation primarily in terms of the impact of internal contradictions.[77] They will search for dialectical laws pertaining to regime dynamics and emphasize evolutionary developments leading toward the collapse of existing orders. Those whose outlook reflects geopolitical ideas, mercantilism, realism, or various forms of conservatism, by contrast, are apt to focus on structures of power and to attribute dramatic changes in international regimes to alterations in the distribution of power.[78] They will look at existing regimes as expressions of the structure of power in the international system

[77] For non-Marxian ideas along these lines see G. W. F. Hegel, *The Philosophy of History*, trans. by J. Sibree (New York: Dover, 1956) and Oswald Spengler, *The Decline of the West*, abridged trans. by Charles F. Atkinson (New York: Knopf, 1962).
[78] Consult Gilpin, "Politics of Transnational Relations," for a case in point.

as a whole, expecting specific institutions to change in the wake of shifts in this larger structure of power. Yet another orientation is characteristic of many liberals who emphasize rational behavior and the benefits of cooperation in contrast to dialectical laws or the central role of power.[79] They are inclined to approach the transformation of regimes as attempts to arrive at reasoned adjustments to exogenous forces like technological change or population growth.[80] Not surprisingly, those who exhibit this orientation generally prefer to work toward the articulation of negotiated orders, and they are among those most likely to exaggerate the scope for effective social engineering in this realm.

Efforts to determine which of these general orientations is correct seldom yield illuminating results. Not only does each point of view approach the problem of regime transformation from a fundamentally different direction, they also rest on incompatible first principles that are ultimately ontological in nature.[81] Nonetheless, it is useful to bear these differences in mind in exploring the problem of regime transformation. Doing so is likely to increase the sophistication of efforts to understand specific cases of regime transformation as well as to improve communication among those interested in the problem of regime transformation.

It is also tempting to argue that spontaneous orders, negotiated orders, and imposed orders will typically differ with respect to the processes of transformation they undergo. At first glance, it seems reasonable to expect spontaneous orders arising in the absence of human design to exhibit more internal contradictions than negotiated orders, which take the form of conscious agreements. Similarly, imposed orders, closely tied to the structure of power in the international system, would appear to be more sensitive to shifts in the distribution of power than spontaneous or negotiated orders. Yet this line of analysis has some serious flaws that are readily apparent on reflection. For example, major contradictions or elements of incoherence are commonplace in "constitutional" contracts, which are typically products of political compromise rather than coordinated planning.[82] Though it is undoubtedly true that imposed orders are sensitive to shifts in the distribution of power, much the same can also be said of negotiated orders and even spontaneous orders. To illustrate, what is more common than more or less drastic changes in interpretations of "constitutional" contracts in the wake of significant shifts in the structure of power in a social system?[83] This con-

[79] For a thoughtful account along these lines see Ernst B. Haas, "Why Collaborate? Issue-Linkage and International Regimes," *World Politics* 32 (1980): 357–405.

[80] See Falk, *This Endangered Planet,* for an argument that reflects this point of view.

[81] The seminal modern work on this problem is Thomas S. Kuhn, *The Structure of Scientific Revolutions,* 2d ed. (Chicago: Chicago University Press, 1970). But see also Graham Allison, *The Essence of Decision* (Boston: Little, Brown, 1971) for an analysis of similar issues with special reference to international politics.

[82] A variety of interesting observations on this phenomenon are articulated in Wolff's critique of Rawls. See Robert Paul Wolff, *Understanding Rawls* (Princeton: Princeton University Press, 1977).

[83] For an argument to the effect that such contracts are, in fact, nothing but interpretations

sideration does not lead me to rule out the formulation of nontrivial generalizations about regime transformation along these lines. But it does seem clear that such generalizations must await the development of more subtle distinctions among the types of order I have identified.

Conclusion

This essay proceeds from the proposition that international regimes constitute a proper subset of social institutions. They are therefore human artifacts whose distinguishing feature is the conjunction of convergent expectations and recognized patterns of behavior or practice. While such institutions are difficult to alter in a planned or guided fashion, they change continuously in response to their own inner dynamics as well as a variety of political, economic, and social factors in their environments. This suggests the relevance of two sets of questions concerning regime dynamics. How and why do regimes arise from the interactions of individual actors over time? The argument of this essay is that it is helpful to separate three developmental sequences for international regimes and that the resultant regimes can be labeled spontaneous orders, negotiated orders, and imposed orders. Beyond this, how do regimes change once they have become established in specific social settings? Here it is illuminating to distinguish several major types of pressures resulting in regime change. These can be described as internal contradictions, shifts in underlying power structures, and exogenous forces. If this perspective is adopted, the next task in the study of regime dynamics is to pursue a more sophisticated understanding of the factors determining the incidence of these developmental sequences and pressures for change.

---

arising from a flow of authoritative decisions see Myres S. McDougal and associates, *Studies in World Public Order* (New Haven: Yale University Press, 1960).

Coordination and collaboration: regimes in an anarchic world

Arthur A. Stein

Grappling with the problem of trying to describe and explain patterns of order in the anarchic world of international politics, scholars have fallen into using the term "regime" so disparately and with such little precision that it ranges from an umbrella for all international relations to little more than a synonym for international organizations. This article develops a conceptualization of regimes as serving to circumscribe national behavior and thus to shape international interactions. Because it is theoretically rooted, the formulation can be used to delineate the nature and workings of regimes and to explain why and under what conditions they arise, how they are maintained and transformed, and when they may be expected to break down or dissolve. Further, it helps us understand why there are many different regimes rather than a single overarching one.

At one extreme, regimes are defined so broadly as to constitute either all international relations or all international interactions within a given issue-area. In this sense, an international monetary regime is nothing more than all international relations involving money. Such use of the term regime does no more than signify a disaggregated issue-area approach to the study of international relations and, so defined, "regimes" have no conceptual status; they do not circumscribe normal patterns of international behavior. They do

I am grateful to Amy Davis, John Ferejohn, Robert Jervis, Robert Keohane, Stephen Krasner, and Thomas Willett for their comments, and to Valerie Melloff for research assistance. My thanks also to all the participants in the conferences held to discuss the articles in this volume. I would also like to acknowledge the financial assistance of the UCLA Committee on International and Comparative Studies, Center for International and Strategic Affairs, and Academic Senate.

International Organization 36, 2, Spring 1982
0020-8183/82/020299-26 $1.50

no more than delimit the issue domain under discussion. Similarly, a conceptual definition of regimes as, for example, "the rules of the game," in no way limits the range of international interactions to which it refers. We can, after all, describe even the most anarchic behavior in the international system as guided by the rules of self-interest or self-help.[1] To specify the rules of the international political game is to say that anything and everything goes. If this is all that we mean by regimes, then we have made no conceptual advance by using the term.

At the other extreme, regimes are defined as international institutions. In this sense, they equal the formal rules of behavior specified by the charters or constitutions of such institutions, and the study of regimes becomes the study of international organizations. This formulation reduces the new international political economy to the old study of international organizations and represents nothing more than an attempt to redress a tired and moribund field.

Anarchy and regimes

The conceptualization of regimes developed here is rooted in the classic characterization of international politics as relations between sovereign entities dedicated to their own self-preservation, ultimately able to depend only on themselves, and prepared to resort to force. Scholars often use anarchy as a metaphor to describe this state of affairs, providing an image of nation-states that consider every option available to them and make their choices independently in order to maximize their own returns. In this view, states are autonomous sovereign entities that "develop their own strategies, chart their own courses, make their own decisions."[2]

The outcomes that emerge from the interaction of states making independent decisions are a function of their interests and preferences. Depending on these interests, the outcome can range from pure conflict to no conflict at all and, depending on the actors' preference orderings, may or may not provide a stable equilibrium. Such independent behavior and the outcomes that result from it constitute the workings of normal international politics—not of regimes. An arms race, for example, is not a regime, even

---

[1] This is the basis of my disagreement with several of the other contributors to this volume. Donald J. Puchala and Raymond F. Hopkins, for example, treat international regimes as coextensive with international politics. Similarly, although Oran Young does not formally equate international politics with regimes, his definitions, both of regimes and of international relations, suggest such an equivalence. Also see his "International Regimes: Problems of Concept Formation," *World Politics* 32 (April 1980): 331–56, and *Compliance and Public Authority: A Theory with International Applications* (Baltimore: Johns Hopkins University Press, 1979). My concern is to develop a conceptualization of regimes that delineates a subset of international politics.

[2] Kenneth N. Waltz, *Theory of International Politics* (Reading, Mass.: Addison-Wesley, 1979), p. 96.

though each actor's decision is contingent on the other actor's immediately previous decision. As long as international state behavior results from unconstrained and independent decision making, there is no international regime.

A regime exists when the interaction between the parties is not unconstrained or is not based on independent decision making. Domestic society constitutes the most common regime. Even the freest and most open societies do not allow individualism and market forces full play; people are not free to choose from among every conceivable option—their choice set is constrained. The workings of a free market require a developed set of property rights, and economic competition is constrained to exclude predatory behavior.[3] Domestic society, characterized by the agreement of individuals to eschew the use of force in settling disputes, constitutes a regime precisely because it constrains the behavior of its citizens.

Some argue that the advent of complex interdependence in the international arena means that state actions are no longer unconstrained, that the use of force no longer remains a possible option. If the range of choice were indeed this circumscribed, we could, in fact, talk about the existence of an international regime similar to the domestic one. But if the international arena is one in which anything still goes, regimes will arise not because the actors' choices are circumscribed but because the actors eschew independent decision making.[4] International regimes exist when patterned state behavior results from joint rather than independent decision making.

International politics is typically characterized by independent self-interested decision making, and states often have no reason to eschew such individualistic behavior. There is no need for a regime when each state obtains its most preferred outcome by making independent decisions, for there is simply no conflict. Examples include barter and some forms of foreign aid (e.g., disaster relief aid). Figure 1 illustrates one such situation, a case in which actors A and B both agree on a most preferred outcome, A_1B_1. In addition, both actors have a dominant strategy—a course of action that maximizes an actor's returns no matter what the other chooses. A prefers A_1 whether B chooses B_1 or B_2, and B prefers B_1 regardless of A's decision. The

[3] On the importance of property rights, see Thomas M. Carroll, David H. Ciscil, and Roger K. Chisholm, "The Market as a Commons: An Unconventional View of Property Rights," *Journal of Economic Issues* 13 (June 1979): 605–627. On the constrained sense of economic competition, see J. Hirshleifer, "Competition, Cooperation, and Conflict in Economics and Biology," *American Economic Review* 68 (May 1978): 238–43; and J. Hirshleifer, "Economics From a Biological Viewpoint," *Journal of Law and Economics* 20 (April 1977): 1–52.

[4] The term "complex interdependence" is most fully presented in Robert O. Keohane and Joseph S. Nye, *Power and Interdependence: World Politics in Transition* (Boston: Little, Brown, 1977); yet it remains unclear, for example, if the use of force remains an option in the relations between advanced industrial societies but is dominated by other choices. Alternatively, it may be that nations sometimes prefer to threaten the use of force on a contingent basis, but recognize that the outcome resulting from the mutual *use* of force is the least preferred outcome for all actors.

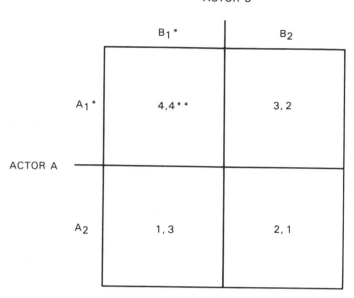

Figure 1. A no-conflict situation

In this and all following Figures, cell numerals refer to ordinally ranked preferences: 4 = best, 1 = worst. The first number in each cell refers to A's preference and the second number in each cell refers to B's preference.

*Actor's dominant strategy

**Equilibrium outcome

result of their independent choices, A_1B_1, is an equilibrium outcome, one from which neither actor can shift unilaterally to better its own position.[5] The equilibrium outcome leaves both actors satisfied. Because their interests are naturally harmonious and coincident, there is no conflict. The actors reach what is for both the optimal result from their independent choices.[6] No regime is needed.

There is also no need for a regime when the actors share a most preferred outcome but neither has a dominant strategy. In Figure 2, A prefers A_1 only if B chooses B_1, and B prefers B_1 only if A chooses A_1. The equilibrium outcome that emerges, A_1B_1, leaves both satisfied. There is, however, a second equilibrium outcome possible in this case, one that emerges from each actor's desire to maximize its minimum gain. Such a minimax decision rule would lead A to choose A_2 and B to choose B_2, the courses of action that would assure that, at the very least, they avoid their worst outcomes. Yet

---

[5] The A_1B_1 outcome is also a coordination equilibrium, which David K. Lewis defines as an outcome from which neither actor can shift and make *anyone* better off; see *Convention: A Philosophical Study* (Cambridge: Harvard University Press, 1969), p. 14.

[6] Individual accessibility is discussed by Jon Elster in *Ulysses and the Sirens: Studies in Rationality and Irrationality* (Cambridge: Cambridge University Press, 1979), p. 21.

ACTOR B

	B_1	B_2
A_1	4, 4**	1, 3
A_2	3, 1	2, 2**

ACTOR A

Figure 2. The assurance game

**Equilibrium outcome

the A_2B_2 outcome, although an equilibrium one, is mutually undesirable.[7] Thus, as long as both actors are aware of the other's preferences, they will converge on the A_1B_1 outcome that both most prefer. No regime is needed since both actors agree on a most preferred outcome, one that they can reach by acting autonomously.[8]

[7] Only A_1B_1, however, is a coordination equilibrium. The other equilibrium outcome, A_2B_2, is not a coordination equilibrium because each actor can shift from it and make the other better off by doing so. For Lewis this does not pose a coordination problem, which requires the existence of two or more coordination equilibria; see *Convention,* p. 24.

[8] For Elster, this case is individually inaccessible. Nonetheless, he expects convergence because the outcome is individually stable. I consider this case to be individually accessible precisely because there are convergent expectations. Note that if regimes are understood to include any devices that help actor expectations to converge, then regimes might arise even in this case, although solely to provide information. The proffered information would provide each actor with assurance about the others' preferences, as would be necessary for expectations to converge on the one of the two equilibria that all prefer.

I find a problem with Robert O. Keohane's treatment of the role of information in his article in this volume. He argues that, given a demand for international agreements, the more costly the information the greater the actual demand for international regimes (one of whose functions is to improve the information available to actors). It is unclear whether he means to suggest that all mechanisms which provide information are examples of regimes even when the actors' interests are harmonious, or that they are not regimes because there is no demand for agreements in such cases. Since he presents the demand for agreements as a given in his formulation, we do not know if the demand for information can be a basis for a demand for agreements or simply a basis for a demand for regimes which assumes a demand for agreements. His formulation is too imprecise to adduce the standing of assurance mechanisms and whether they do or do not constitute regimes.

The international extradition of criminals is an example of such an "assurance game." States began in the early nineteenth century unilaterally to adopt statutes stipulating extraditable offenses. Some states, such as the Federal Republic of Germany, are satisfied with assurances of reciprocity before they agree to extradite criminal fugitives. Other states, however, are unsatisfied with such informal arrangements because of the potential limitations that other nations may place on extradition. They require treaties to provide them with assurances that the other state will behave in a predictable fashion when questions of extradition arise.[9] It is important to understand, however, that these treaties only provide assurances and no more.

Nor will a regime arise when some actors obtain their most preferred outcome while others are left aggrieved. Figure 3 illustrates a situation in which both actors have dominant strategies leading to an equilibrium that is actor A's most preferred outcome but actor B's second-worst one. In such situations, the satisfied actors have no reason to eschew independent decision making and the aggrieved actors would only succeed in making themselves still worse off by being the only ones to forgo rational self-interested calculation. Voluntary export restraint is an example in which one actor gets its most preferred outcome while the other is left aggrieved by that equilibrium result.

In the foregoing examples, behavior and outcome result from the independent decisions of actors interacting in a context, prototypical of international relations, characterized by anarchy. There are situations, however, in which all the actors have an incentive to eschew independent decision making: situations, that is, in which individualistic self-interested calculation leads them to prefer joint decision making because independent self-interested behavior can result in undesirable or suboptimal outcomes. I refer to these situations as dilemmas of common interests and dilemmas of common aversions.[10]

Dilemmas of common interests

The dilemma of common interests arises when independent decision making leads to equilibrium outcomes that are Pareto-deficient—outcomes in which all actors prefer another given outcome to the equilibrium outcome. The classic example is, of course, the prisoners' dilemma, in which the actors' dominant strategies lead them to an equilibrium outcome that is

---

[9] In some cases, actors may require mechanisms for assurance, which extradition treaties exemplify. These treaties might thus be seen as "assurance regimes," regimes that arise when each actor's knowledge of others' preferences is enough to allow the actors' autonomous decisions to bring them to the outcome they all most prefer.

[10] The conceptualization of regimes presented here, that they arise to deal with the dilemmas of common interests and common aversions, is not, therefore, based on any inherent notion of "principles." Indeed, it is easy to conceive of unprincipled regimes, such as OPEC. Regimes may, but need not, have some principle underlying them.

ACTOR B

Figure 3. An equilibrium outcome that leaves one actor aggrieved

*Actor's dominant strategy

**Equilibrium outcome

Pareto-deficient. There is an alternative outcome that both actors prefer to the equilibrium one. Figure 4 illustrates the two-actor prisoners' dilemma in which both actors prefer the A_1B_1 outcome to the A_2B_2 equilibrium. But the preferred A_1B_1 outcome is neither individually accessible nor stable. To arrive at the Pareto-optimal outcome requires that all actors eschew their dominant strategy. In addition, they must not greedily attempt to obtain their most preferred outcome once they have settled at the unstable outcome they prefer to the stable equilibrium.[11]

The prisoners' dilemma is used as an allegory for a variety of situations. It is, for instance, the classic illustration of the failure of market forces always to result in optimal solutions—that is, of market rationality leading to suboptimal outcomes. Oligopolists, for example, prefer collusion to the deficient equilibrium that results from their competition.[12] Ironically, gov-

---

[11] The prisoners' dilemma is the only two-actor example of a Pareto-deficient equilibrium that occurs when both actors have dominant strategies. It is for this reason that it has received so much scholarly attention.

[12] The role of game models in analyzing oligopolistic relations is described by Jesse W. Markham, "Oligopoly," in *International Encyclopedia of the Social Sciences*, vol. 11 (New York: Macmillan, 1968): 283–88. F.M. Scherer discusses the prisoners' dilemma as a model for oligopolistic interaction in *Industrial Market Structure and Economic Performance* (Chicago: Rand McNally, 1970). The same observation is made by Lester G. Telser, who redubs the prisoners' dilemma as it applies to oligopolies the "cartel's dilemma"; see *Competition, Collusion, and Game Theory* (Chicago: Aldine-Atherton, 1972), p. 143.

ACTOR B

Figure 4. Prisoners' dilemma

*Actor's dominant strategy
**Equilibrium outcome

ernment intervenes in order to prevent collusion and enforce the outcome that is suboptimal for the oligopolists. There are other situations of suboptimality, such as problems of collective goods and externalities, that also require government intervention to insure collusion and collaboration and thus to insure avoidance of the suboptimal equilibrium outcome.[13]

Political theorists use the prisoners' dilemma to explain the contractarian-coercion conjunction at the root of the modern state, arguing that the state of nature is a prisoners' dilemma in which individuals have a dominant strategy of defecting from common action but in which the result of this mutual defection is deficient for all. Yet the outcome that results from mutual cooperation is not an equilibrium one since each actor can make itself immediately better off by cheating. It is for this reason, political theorists argue, that individuals came together to form the state by agreeing to coerce one another and thus insure the optimal outcome of mutual cooperation. In other words, they agreed to coerce one another in order to guarantee that no individual would take advantage of another's cooperation by defecting from the pact and refusing to cooperate. States are thus coercive institutions that allow individuals to eschew their dominant strategies—an individual actor's

[13] For a general discussion of suboptimality, see Jon Elster, *Logic and Society: Contradictions and Possible Worlds* (New York: Wiley, 1978), pp. 122–34.

rational course—as a matter of self-interest in order to insure an optimal rather than a Pareto-deficient equilibrium outcome.[14]

Put more simply, the argument is that individuals come together to form the state in order to solve the dilemma of common interests. The existence of a prisoners' dilemma preference ordering creates the likelihood that individual rationality will lead to suboptimal outcomes, a classic case of market failure. Individuals have a common interest in constraining the free rein of their individuality and independent rationality and form domestic political regimes to deal with the problem.

This view of the state is reinforced by the literature on collective goods, in which scholars argue that the suboptimal provision of collective goods stems from the individual's incentive to be a free rider, to enjoy the benefits of goods characterized by nonexcludability. Under certain conditions, the problem of collective goods is a classic prisoners' dilemma in which each individual is better off not contributing to the provision of a collective good, but in which the equilibrium outcome of everyone's deciding to be a free rider is a world in which all are worse off than if they had contributed equally to the provision of the good.[15] Some in fact argue that the state is formed to assure the provision of collective goods; the state coerces contributions from all individuals, each of whom would rather be a free rider but goes along because of the guarantee that all others will be similarly coerced. They form the state because the alternative outcome is a Pareto-deficient world in which collective goods are not provided. The most basic collective good provided by the state is, of course, security from outside attack. Thus, we have an explanation for the rise of states that also illuminates the anarchic character of relations between these states. The anarchy that engenders state formation is tamed only within domestic society. Individuals sacrifice a certain degree of autonomy—but the newly established nations do not do so. A world of vying individuals is replaced by a world of vying nations.

Regimes in the international arena are also created to deal with the collective suboptimality that can emerge from individual behavior.[16] There are,

---

[14] In one formulation, Jon Elster defines politics as "the study of ways of transcending the Prisoner's Dilemma"; see "Some Conceptual Problems in Political Theory," in *Power and Political Theory: Some European Perspectives,* ed. by Brian Barry (London: Wiley, 1976), pp. 248–49. Laurence S. Moss provides an assessment of modern and somewhat formal equivalents to the Hobbesian and Lockean views of state formation in "Optimal Jurisdictions and the Economic Theory of the State: Or, Anarchy and One-world Government Are Only Corner Solutions," *Public Choice* 35 (1980): 17–26. See also Michael Taylor, *Anarchy and Cooperation* (London: Wiley, 1976). Elster criticizes Taylor's alternative in *Logic and Society*, pp. 156–57, and *Ulysses and the Sirens*, pp. 64, 143, 146.

[15] Russell Hardin, "Collective Action as an Agreeable n-Prisoners' Dilemma," *Behavioral Science* 16 (September 1971): 472–81. Note Elster's distinction between counterfinality and suboptimality in explaining the behavior of free riders; *Logic and Society*, pp. 122–23.

[16] The dilemmas discussed in this article refer to specific actors and not necessarily to the system as a whole. In the prisoners' dilemma, for example, only the prisoners themselves face a Pareto-deficient outcome. The rest of society finds the outcome of their dilemma to be optimal. This is precisely analogous to the situation of oligopolists, who prefer collusion to competition. The rest of society, however, would prefer that they compete rather than collude. The collective suboptimality need not necessarily exist for all actors in the system.

for example, international collective goods whose optimal provision can only be assured if states eschew the independent decision making that would otherwise lead them to be free riders and would ultimately result in either the suboptimal provision or the nonprovision of the collective good. One such problem of international politics, that of collective security, was, in fact, the focus of some of the earliest studies of collective goods.[17]

Collective goods issues are not the only problems characterized by prisoners' dilemma preferences for which international regimes can provide a solution. The attempt to create an international trade regime after World War II was, for example, a reaction to the results of the beggar-thy-neighbor policies of the depression years. All nations would be wealthier in a world that allows goods to move unfettered across national borders. Yet any single nation, or group of nations, could improve its position by cheating—erecting trade barriers and restricting imports.[18] The state's position remains improved only as long as other nations do not respond in kind. Such a response is, however, the natural course for those other nations. When all nations pursue their dominant strategies and erect trade barriers, however, they can engender the collapse of international trade and depress all national incomes. That is what happened in the 1930s, and what nations wanted to avoid after World War II.[19]

[17] This literature was spawned by Mancur Olson Jr. and Richard Zeckhauser, "An Economic Theory of Alliances," *Review of Economics and Statistics* 48 (August 1966): 266–79. Other essays linking collective goods and international cooperation include Bruce M. Russett and John D. Sullivan, "Collective Goods and International Organization," *International Organization* 25 (Autumn 1971): 845–65; John Gerard Ruggie, "Collective Goods and Future International Collaboration," *American Political Science Review* 66 (September 1972): 874–93; and Todd Sandler and Jon Cauley, "The Design of Supranational Structures: An Economic Perspective," *International Studies Quarterly* 21 (June 1977): 251–76. More recent work stresses different institutional arrangements for international collective goods. See Todd M. Sandler, William Loehr, and Jon T. Cauley, "The Political Economy of Public Goods and International Cooperation," *Monograph Series in World Affairs* 15 (1978), and Duncan Snidal, "Public Goods, Property Rights, and Political Organizations," *International Studies Quarterly* 23 (December 1979): 532–66.

[18] Indeed, international trade regimes have historically exemplified the subsystemic character of many regimes. Scholars often characterize the mid 19th century, for example, as the era of free trade. Yet several major states, including the United States and Russia, did not take part. Similarly, the post-1945 era is now commonly referred to as the period of American economic hegemony. Ironically, this characterization is of a postwar economic system established by and within the sphere of only one pole of a bipolar international system—a bipolarity that has typically been offered as the most important characterization of the age. In other words, we should continually be reminded that references to "the" postwar economic system are, in fact, to a subsystem that excludes the Soviet bloc. See Arthur A. Stein, "The Hegemon's Dilemma: Great Britain, the United States, and the International Economic Order," paper presented at the annual meeting of the American Political Science Association, New York, 4 September 1981.

[19] A similar argument can sometimes be made about the decision to devalue a currency or maintain par value in a fixed exchange rate system when devaluation, although every nation's dominant strategy, results in the suboptimal outcome of mutual devaluation. Richard N. Cooper uses simple games in his discussion of the choice of an international monetary regime; see "Prolegomena to the Choice of an International Monetary System," *International Organization* 29 (Winter 1975): 63–97.

Dilemmas of common aversions

Regimes also provide solutions to dilemmas of common aversions. Unlike dilemmas of common interests, in which the actors have a common interest in *insuring* a particular outcome, the actors caught in the dilemma of common aversions have a common interest in *avoiding* a particular outcome. These situations occur when actors with contingent strategies do not most prefer the same outcome but do agree that there is at least one outcome that all want to avoid. These criteria define a set of situations with multiple equilibria (two equilibria if there are only two actors each with two choices) in which coordination is required if the actors are to avoid that least preferred outcome.[20] Thus, these dilemmas can also lead to the formation of regimes by providing the incentive for nations to eschew independent decision making.

Figure 5 provides one example of a dilemma of common aversions. Neither actor in this situation has a dominant strategy; nor does either most prefer a single given outcome. Rather, there exist two outcomes that both value equally and two outcomes that both wish to avoid. Thus, the situation has two equilibria, A_1B_1 and A_2B_2, but since the actors have contingent strategies, they cannot be certain that they will arrive at one of these outcomes if they act independently and simultaneously. Without coordination they may well end up with one of the outcomes that neither wants.[21]

This example of common aversions is relatively easy to deal with because the actors do not have divergent interests; neither cares which of the two equilibria emerges. Any procedure that allows for a convergence of their expectations makes coordination possible by allowing the actors to arrive at one of the equilibria. It is in such situations that conventions play an important role. Driving on the right is a simple coordination mechanism that allows for the smooth movement of traffic in opposite directions without collisions and bottlenecks. It is an arbitrary convention that allows actors' expectations to converge on one of the equilibrium outcomes. The alternative convention of driving on the left permits coordination by convergence on the other equilibrium. The actors are indifferent between the two equilibria.

There are times, however, when, although both still agree on the least preferable outcome or outcomes, each prefers a different one of the possible equilibria. In Figure 6, for example, there are two equilibria (A_2B_1 and A_1B_2), both of which the actors prefer to either of the other possible outcomes.

---

[20] In the dilemma of common interests, actors are averse to the suboptimal equilibrium outcome and resolution involves their arriving at the outcome they prefer to the equilibrium one. The dilemma is their inability individually to arrive at the outcome they prefer to the equilibrium one. In the dilemma of common aversions, on the other hand, the actors do have a common interest in avoiding a particular outcome but their dilemma is the possibility that they might arrive at a mutual aversion without some coordination. Beyond their desire to avoid that aversion, however, they disagree about which of the multiple equilibria they prefer.

[21] Both equilibria are also coordination equilibria. In this case, there is no minimax solution.

ACTOR B

	B$_1$	B$_2$
A$_1$	1, 1**	0, 0
A$_2$	0, 0	1, 1**

ACTOR A

Figure 5. Dilemma of common aversions and common indifference

In this example, 1 = most preferred, 0 = least preferred

**Equilibrium outcome

ACTOR B

	B$_1$	B$_2$
A$_1$	2, 2	3, 4**
A$_2$	4, 3**	1, 1

ACTOR A

Figure 6. Dilemma of common aversions and divergent interests

**Equilibrium outcome

Each does, however, most prefer one of the two equilibria—although they do not most prefer the same one. Actor A prefers A_1B_2, whereas B favors A_2B_1.[22]

When actors confront mutual aversions but diverge in their assessments of the equilibria, coordination can be accomplished in two different ways. In either case, the coordination regime establishes rules of behavior that allow actor expectations to converge whenever the dilemma arises. One means of insuring coordination is to specify behavior according to actor characteristics. Alternatively, the prearrangement can specify behavior by context. One example of this dilemma is provided by the simultaneous arrival of a north- or southbound and an east- or westbound car at an intersection. In this case, both drivers most want to avoid a collision. They would also prefer not to sit at their corners staring at one another. There are two ways for them to move through the intersection safely: either A goes first, or B does. The problem is that neither wants to be the one to wait. A coordination rule based on actor characteristics would specify, for example, that Cadillacs drive on while Volkswagens sit and wait. Under such a regime, more likely than not "coordination for the powerful," the same actor always gets the equilibrium that it prefers. Alternatively, the actors could adopt a contextual rule; one example is the specification that the actor on the right always gets the right of way. In this case, the context determines whether any actor gets its more preferred equilibrium; sometimes it does, and sometimes not. Ideally, this "fairness doctrine" would insure that all actors get their most preferred equilibrium half the time.

Collaboration and coordination

Regimes arise because actors forgo independent decision making in order to deal with the dilemmas of common interests and common aversions. They do so in their own self-interest, for, in both cases, jointly accessible outcomes are preferable to those that are or might be reached independently. It is in their interests mutually to establish arrangements to shape their subsequent behavior and allow expectations to converge, thus solving the dilemmas of independent decision making.[23] Yet, the need to solve the dilemmas of common interests and aversions provides two different bases

---

[22] If each of the actors chooses its minimax option, the A_1B_1 outcome results. This outcome is not their mutual aversion, but it is a Pareto-deficient nonequilibrium outcome because both prefer it less than either equilibrium.

[23] Precommitment has been variously described as the power to bind, as imperfect rationality, and as egonomics; see Thomas C. Schelling, *The Strategy of Conflict* (Cambridge: Harvard University Press, 1960), pp. 22–28; Elster, *Ulysses and the Sirens*, pp. 36–111; and T. C. Schelling, "Egonomics, or the Art of Self-Management," *American Economic Review* 68 (May 1978): 290–94. Such a formulation of prior agreement on principles does not require John Rawls's veil of ignorance; see *A Theory of Justice* (Cambridge: Harvard University Press, 1971). Thinking ahead without agreement in strategic interaction, however, is no solution; see Frederic Schick, "Some Notes on Thinking Ahead," *Social Research* 44 (Winter 1977): 786–800.

for international regimes, which helps to explain the differences between regimes that have often confused analysts. Regimes established to deal with the dilemma of common interests differ from those created to solve the dilemma of common aversions. The former require *collaboration,* the latter *coordination.*

The dilemma of common interests occurs when there is only one equilibrium outcome that is deficient for the involved actors. In other words, this dilemma arises when the Pareto-optimal outcome that the actors mutually desire is not an equilibrium outcome. In order to solve such dilemmas and assure the Pareto-optimal outcome, the parties must collaborate, and all regimes intended to deal with dilemmas of common interests must specify strict patterns of behavior and insure that no one cheats.[24] Because each actor requires assurances that the other will also eschew its rational choice, such collaboration requires a degree of formalization. The regime must specify what constitutes cooperation and what constitutes cheating, and each actor must be assured of its own ability to spot others' cheating immediately.

The various SALT agreements provide examples of the institutionalized collaboration required in a regime intended to deal with the dilemma of common interests, for the security dilemma is an example of a prisoners' dilemma situation in which all actors arm themselves even though they prefer mutual disarmament to mutual armament. Yet international disarmament agreements are notoriously problematic. Indeed, the decision to comply

---

[24] The prisoners' dilemma is the only situation with a Pareto-deficient equilibrium in which all the actors have dominant strategies. There are other cases of Pareto-deficient equilibria in which some have dominant strategies and some contingent strategies. These too are dilemmas of common interests and require regimes for solution; in these cases, however, only those actors with dominant strategies must eschew independent decision making. Thus, the regime formed to insure collaboration in this case is likely to have stipulations and requirements that apply asymmetrically to those who must eschew independent decision making to achieve optimality and to those who must be assured that the others have actually done so and will continue to do so.

Some argue that the cooperative nonequilibrium outcome of the prisoners' dilemma can emerge spontaneously—without collaborative agreement. Social psychologists have done extensive experiments on the emergence of cooperation in repeated plays of the prisoners' dilemma game; the most recent review is by Dean G. Pruitt and Melvin J. Kimmel, "Twenty Years of Experimental Gaming: Critique, Synthesis, and Suggestions for the Future," *Annual Review of Psychology* 28 (1977): 163–92. See also Anatol Rapoport, Melvin J. Guyer, and David G. Gordon, *The 2 × 2 Game* (Ann Arbor: University of Michigan Press, 1976). For a mathematician's deductive assessment of the prospects for the emergence of such cooperation, see Steve Smale, "The Prisoner's Dilemma and Dynamical Systems Associated to Non-Cooperative Games," *Econometrica* 48 (November 1980): 1617–1634. See also Robert Axelrod, "The Emergence of Cooperation Among Egoists," *American Political Science Review* 75 (June 1981): 306–318.

The conditions for this are rarely met in international politics, however. The first such requirement is that play be repeated indefinitely. Because states can disappear, and because they are therefore concerned with their own survival, international politics must be seen as a finite game by the actors. Moreover, the stakes in international politics are typically so high that fear of exploitation will *insure* that states follow their dominant strategy, to defect, in the absence of a collaborative agreement.

with or cheat on an arms control agreement is also a prisoners' dilemma situation in which each actor's dominant strategy is to cheat. Thus, it is not surprising that arms control agreements are highly institutionalized, for these regimes are continually concerned with compliance and policing. They must define cheating quite explicitly, insure that it be observable, and specify verification and monitoring procedures.

Oligopolists also confront the dilemma of common interests, and their collusion represents the collaboration necessary for them to move from the suboptimal equilibrium that would otherwise result. Such collusive arrangements require policing and monitoring because of the individual's incentive to cheat. International market sharing arrangements exemplify this collusive form of collaboration and require the same sort of monitoring provisions. Not surprisingly, such successful market sharing regimes as the International Coffee Agreement have extensive enforcement provisions and elaborate institutional structures for monitoring compliance.[25]

"The tragedy of the commons" exemplifies the dilemma of common interests. The commons were pasture and grazing grounds open to all and the tragedy was the overgrazing that resulted from unrestrained individual use. This is not, as it may seem at first, a dilemma of common aversions in which the actors' least preferred outcome is the depletion of a valuable common resource. Rather, each actor most prefers to be the only user of a common resource, next prefers joint restraint in the mutual use of the good, then prefers joint unrestrained use even if it leads to depletion, and least prefers a situation in which its own restraint is met by the other actors' lack of restraint. Each actor would rather share in such use of the resource that leads to depletion than to see its own restraint allow either the continued existence of the resource for others' use or the disappearance of the resource because the others show no restraint. The actors have a common interest in moving from their suboptimal (but not least preferred) outcome to one in which they exercise mutual restraint by collaboratively managing the resource. The commons thus represent a class of dilemmas of common interests in which individually rational behavior leads to a collectively suboptimal outcome.[26] Current international commons problems, such as the overfishing of a common sea, are all international manifestations of this dilemma of common interests.

By contrast, regimes intended to deal with the dilemma of common aversions need only facilitate coordination. Such situations have multiple equilibria, and these regimes must assure neither a particular outcome nor

[25] Bart S. Fisher, *The International Coffee Agreement: A Study in Coffee Diplomacy* (New York: Praeger, 1972), and Richard B. Bilder, "The International Coffee Agreement: A Case History in Negotiation," *Law and Contemporary Problems* 28 (Spring 1963): 328–91. The latter appeared in a special issue devoted to "International Commodity Agreements."
[26] Garrett Hardin, "The Tragedy of the Commons," *Science* 162 (13 December 1968): 1243–1248; Thomas C. Schelling characterizes the commons as a prisoners' dilemma in *Micromotives and Macrobehavior* (New York: W.W. Norton, 1978), pp. 110–15.

compliance with any particular course of action, for they are created only to insure that particular outcomes be avoided.[27] Nevertheless, such coordination is difficult to achieve when, although both actors least prefer the same outcome, they disagree in the choice of preferred equilibrium. The greater this conflict of interest, the harder it is for them to coordinate their actions. Yet once established, the regime that makes expectations converge and allows the actors to coordinate their actions is self-enforcing; any actor that departs from it hurts only itself.[28] Thus, there is no problem here of policing and compliance. Defections do not represent cheating for immediate self-aggrandizement, but are expressions of relative dissatisfaction with the coordination outcome. An actor will *threaten* to defect before actually doing so; it may choose to go through with its threat only if the other actor does not accede to its demands. Again, such defection is never surreptitious cheating; it is a public attempt, made at some cost, to force the other actor into a different equilibrium outcome. Departures from regime-specified behavior thus represent a fundamentally different problem in coordination regimes than in collaboration ones.

There are many international regimes that serve to facilitate coordination and thus solve the dilemma of common aversions. These solutions provide mechanisms that allow actor expectations to converge on one of the possible equilibria. Conventions alone are adequate in these situations; institutions are not required. Not surprisingly, many involve standardization. The adoption of a common gauge for railroad tracks throughout western Europe is one example.[29]

Traffic conventions are also examples of international regimes.[30] Under the rules of the International Civil Aviation Organization, for example, every

[27] The following authors all discuss coordination, although they do not agree fully on a definition: Schelling, *Strategy of Conflict;* Lewis, *Conventions;* Philip B. Heymann, "The Problem of Coordination: Bargaining and Rules," *Harvard Law Review* 86 (March 1973): 797–877; and Robert E. Goodin, *The Politics of Rational Man* (London: Wiley, 1976), pp. 26–46. The distinction between collaboration and coordination made here can be compared to distinctions between negative and positive *coordination* and between negative and positive *cooperation* made by the following: Marina v. N. Whitman, "Coordination and Management of the International Economy: A Search for Organizing Principles," in *Contemporary Economic Problems 1977,* ed. by William Fellner (Washington, D.C.: American Enterprise Institute for Public Policy Research, 1977), p. 321; and Jacques Pelkmans, "Economic Cooperation Among Western Countries," in *Challenges to Interdependent Economies: The Industrial West in the Coming Decade,* ed. by Robert J. Gordon and Jacques Pelkmans (New York: McGraw-Hill, 1979), pp. 97–123.

[28] This notion of self-enforcement differs from that developed by L.G. Telser, "A Theory of Self-enforcing Agreements," *Journal of Business* 53 (January 1980): 27–44. For Telser, an arrangement is self-enforcing if the actor calculates that defection may bring future costs. Thus, even if cheating brings immediate rewards, an actor will not cheat if others' responses cause it to bear a net loss. For me, regimes are self-enforcing only if the cost that an actor bears for defecting is immediate rather than potential and is brought about by its own defection rather than by the response of others to that defection.

[29] Standardization may reflect harmonious interests rather than coordination solutions to dilemmas of common aversions. This may, for example, explain the adoption of a common calendar.

[30] Schelling provides an interesting discussion of the traffic light as a self-enforcing convention in *Micromotives and Macrobehavior,* pp. 119–21.

flight control center must always have enough English-speakers on duty to direct all those pilots who do not happen to speak the native language of the country whose airspace they happen to be crossing.[31] Communication between ground and aircraft may be in any mutually convenient language, but there must be a guarantee that communication is indeed possible; finding a language matchup cannot be left to chance. Thus, English is recognized as the international language of air traffic control, and all pilots who fly between nations must speak enough English to talk to the ground. The pilot who never leaves French airspace is perfectly safe knowing only French, and should a Mexicana Airlines pilot wish to speak Spanish to the ground in Madrid, that is also acceptible. But if no one on the ground speaks the pilot's language, the parties can always converse in English. The mutual aversion, an air disaster, is avoided and a safe equilibrium is assured.[32]

Preemption provides still another solution to dilemmas of common aversions. In these situations with multiple equilibria and a mutually least preferred outcome, an actor's incentive is often to preempt the other because it knows that the other must then go along. If it is wrong, of course, assuming, for example, that an oncoming car will swerve if it keeps going, the attempted preemption leads directly to the common aversion. Often, however, preemption is based on firm knowledge or safe assumptions and is therefore successful. In these cases, preemption forms the basis of coordination, and it works well when it involves the exercise of squatters' rights in an area where they are traditionally respected or are likely to be so. One striking example has been the preemption of radio frequencies within accepted constraints. International meetings have allocated various portions of the radio spectrum for specific uses, and countries have then been free to broadcast appropriately along whatever frequency is available. They are required to register the frequencies they have claimed with the International Frequency Registration Board, but even then, other nations sometimes broadcast on the same wavelength when it is available. This practice is not permitted, but it is accepted. It has been without challenge that the Soviet Union prowls the shortwave band for unused frequencies on which it then broadcasts its own propaganda. The result is a system of allocation that allows all nations the

---

[31] The organization is the governing body for almost all international civil air traffic.

[32] There does exist a dilemma of common aversions that can be solved by coordination *or* by collaboration. Like other situations characterized as dilemmas of common aversions, the actors in the game of chicken have contingent strategies, do not agree on a most-preferred outcome, but do share a mutual aversion. In this case, the actors diverge in their assessment of the two equilibria. Unlike those of other dilemmas of common aversions, the two equilibria in chicken are not coordination equilibria. In chicken, the nonequilibrium minimax outcome is the second choice of both actors and is not Pareto-deficient. Thus, the situation is not merely one of deadlock avoidance, but one that can be solved either by coordination to arrive at one of the two equilibria or by collaboration to accept second-best. Here, too, the collaboration is not self-enforcing and requires mutual assurances about defection from a particular outcome. No-fault insurance agreements are one example of a collaboration regime to resolve a dilemma of common aversions. Note that Lewis would not consider chicken to be a coordination problem because the two equilibria in chicken are not coordination equilibria. I believe that it *is* a coordination problem, but one that collaboration can also solve.

use of an adequate number of frequencies for broadcast with minimal international interference.

As the number of nations in the world has increased, however, the radio band has become more crowded, and Third World nations have demanded greater access to radio frequencies.[33] To some, the allocation of frequencies has now become a dilemma of common interests, for their worst outcome is to fail to get on the radio at all. In other words, they actually prefer the radio traffic jam that previously constituted the dilemma of common aversions in the hope that the other broadcaster will eventually give up and leave them an unimpeded signal. No longer willing to accept what has become in practice a form of coordination for the powerful, they are calling for "planning" (i.e., collaboration) to replace the current system. Broadcasting has long been a traffic problem requiring only coordination in order to facilitate access to the airwaves. With greater congestion, however, it is rapidly becoming a dilemma of the commons, which requires a *collaborative* allocation of a scarce resource.

Regimes and interests

This conceptualization of regimes is interest-based. It suggests that the same forces of autonomously calculated self-interest that lie at the root of the anarchic international system also lay the foundation for international regimes as a form of international order. The same forces that lead individuals to bind themselves together to escape the state of nature also lead states to coordinate their actions, even to collaborate with one another. Quite simply, there are times when rational self-interested calculation leads actors to abandon independent decision making in favor of joint decision making.

This formulation presumes the existence of interdependence—that an actor's returns are a function of others' choices as well as its own. If actors were independent in the sense that their choices affected only their own returns and not others', then there would be no basis for international regimes.[34] Interdependence in the international arena, especially given the relatively small size of the system, makes mutual expectations (and therefore perceptions) very important.[35] An analogy from economics is often used to make this point. There are so many firms in a perfectly competitive market

[33] For background and analysis of the most recent World Administrative Radio Conference of 1979, see the articles in *Foreign Policy* no. 34 (Spring 1979): 139–64; and those in *Journal of Communication* 29 (Winter 1979): 143–207. See also "Scramble for the Waves," *Economist,* 1 September 1979, p. 37; "The Struggle Over the World's Radio Waves Will Continue," *Economist,* 8 December 1979, p. 83; and "Policing the Radio," *New Statesman,* 14 December 1979, p. 924.

[34] The absence of regimes does not mean, however, that the actors are independent of one another.

[35] The conditions in which misperception matters, and the ways in which it matters, are delineated in Arthur A. Stein, "When Misperception Matters," *World Politics* 34 (July 1982).

that each firm is assumed to have a dominant strategy and to make decisions without taking into account expectations of others' potential behavior or responses. Oligopolistic or imperfect competition is distinguished precisely by the small number of actors, which makes necessary and possible the incorporation of expectations in the context of interdependence.

This conceptualization also explains why the same behavior that sometimes results from independent decision making can also occur under regimes. Arms buildups provide one example. On one hand, an arms race is not a regime, despite the existence of interaction and although each actor's decisions are contingent on the other's. An arms race is not a regime because the behavior, although patterned, is the result of independent decision making. On the other hand, arms increases can result from an arms control agreement that *is* a regime because the arms buildup results from mutual arrangements that shape subsequent decisions. Indeed, most arms control agreements have not been arms reduction agreements, but agreements of controlled escalation. By arriving at such an agreement, both actors thus participate in shaping their subsequent actions.[36]

This conceptualization of regimes also clarifies the role of international institutions, which many equate with regimes. Even those who recognize that regimes need not be institutionalized still suggest that institutionalization is one of their major dimensions. Indeed, one scholar refers to noninstitutionalized regimes as quasi-regimes.[37] But the conceptualization I have presented here suggests that international organizations and regimes are independent of one another; each can exist without the other. Regimes can be noninstitutionalized as well as institutionalized, and international organizations need not be regimes, although they certainly can be.[38] The United Nations is an example of an international organization that is not a — regime, for mere membership in no way constrains independent decision making. The UN provides a forum for formal and informal interaction and

[36] Goodin, in *Politics of Rational Man,* p. 26, puts it this way: "Joint decision making is said to occur when all actors participate in determining the decisions of each actor. It implies that there was interaction between all the actors prior to the decisions and that this interaction shaped the decision of each actor." It is not surprising, then, that two recent formulations both stress the importance of agreement as part of their definition of regimes: see Young, "International Regimes"; and Ernst B. Haas, "Why Collaborate? Issue-Linkage and International Regimes," *World Politics* 32 (April 1980), p. 358. For interesting delineations of the range of decision-making procedures, see Knut Midgaard, "Co-operative Negotiations and Bargaining: Some Notes on Power and Powerlessness," in Barry, *Power and Political Theory;* and I. William Zartman, "Negotiations as a Joint Decision-Making Process," *Journal of Conflict Resolution* 21 (December 1977): 620–23. Both of these authors, however, heavily emphasize the bargaining process. Various forms of international cooperation can also be seen as forms of decision making; see Jan Tinbergen, "Alternative Forms of International Co-operation: Comparing Their Efficiency," *International Social Science Journal* 30 (1978): 224–25.

[37] Hayward R. Alker Jr., "A Methodology for Design Research on Interdependence Alternatives," *International Organization* 31 (Winter 1977), pp. 37–38.

[38] Although I do not define regimes by reference to their degree of institutionalization, it is the case that collaboration regimes are more likely to be institutionalized than coordination regimes, because of the requirements of enforcement.

discussion, but it is not a regime because membership generates no convergent expectations that constrain and shape subsequent actions.

The presumption of the existence of dilemmas of common interests and common aversions that give rise to regimes assumes that self-interested actors do indeed have things in common. This is very much a liberal, not mercantilist, view of self-interest; it suggests that actors focus on their own returns and compare different outcomes with an eye to maximizing their own gains.

An alternative conception of competitive self-interest is that actors seek to maximize the difference between their own returns and those of others. This decision rule, that of difference maximization, is competitive, whereas a decision-criterion of self-maximization is individualistic. When applied by any actor, it transforms a situation into one of pure conflict in which the actors have no mutual interests or common aversions; it implies a constant-sum world in which an improvement in one actor's returns can only come at the expense of another's.[39]

Actors who are competitors rather than individualists do not confront dilemmas of common interests or common aversions. Out for relative gain, they have nothing in "common." The prisoners' dilemma is an interesting illustration of this point. When both actors apply a difference-maximization decision rule to the preference ordering that defines a prisoners' dilemma, the situation that results is one in which the actors' dominant strategies are the same. They no longer find the equilibrium outcome deficient and do not prefer an alternative one. The situation no longer provides them with a rational incentive to eschew independent decision making in order to create and maintain a regime. Thus, to see the existence of international regimes composed of sovereign entities who voluntarily eschew independent decision making in certain cases is to see the world in nonconstant-sum terms, a world in which actors can have common interests and common aversions.[40] It is self-interested actors who find a common interest in eschewing individuality to form international regimes.

This conceptualization of regimes also explains why there are many regimes and why they vary in character, why they exist in some issue-areas

[39] Difference maximization is discussed by Charles G. McClintock, "Game Behavior and Social Motivation in Interpersonal Settings," in *Experimental Social Psychology*, ed. by Charles Graham McClintock (New York: Holt, Rinehart and Winston, 1972), pp. 271–92. Taylor calls them pure difference games and designates them a subtype of games of difference generally; see *Anarchy and Cooperation*, pp. 73–74. See also Martin Shubik, "Games of Status," *Behavioral Science* 16 (March 1971): 117–29.

[40] Those who argue that world politics constitutes a zero-sum game cannot, of course, sustain their position at the extremes. After all, it is impossible for all dyadic relationships to be zero-sum or constant-sum in a world of more than two actors. Thus, even if some relationships in international politics are zero- or constant-sum, there must also exist some subset of relationships that are nonconstant-sum and therefore provide a basis for regime formation among this subset of nations. Yet Robert Gilpin still claims "that in power terms, international relations is a zero-sum game." See *U.S. Power and the Multinational Corporation: The Political Economy of Foreign Direct Investment* (New York: Basic Books, 1975).

and not in others, and why states will form regimes with one another in one domain while they are in conflict in another. The existence or nonexistence of regimes to deal with given issues, indeed the very need to distinguish them by issue, can be attributed to the existence of different constellations of interests in different contexts.

Structural bases of regime formation

In this formulation, the factors that others argue to be the bases of regime formation, whatever they may be, should be understood instead as constituting the determinants of those different patterns of interests that underlie the regimes themselves. More specifically, I argue here that behavior is best explained by constellations of preferences that are in turn rooted in other factors. Many of these foundations are structural. The view most widely held among international relations theorists, for example, is that the global distribution of power is the structural characteristic that determines the nature of global order. One currently popular proposition links global predominance to stability; more specifically, it links a hegemonic distribution of power to open international economic regimes.[41] Most blithely tie the distribution of power to the nature of the economic order, but few make the explicit causal argument that depends on deducing a set of interests from a particular distribution of power and then ascertaining what order will emerge given power and interests.[42] The argument here is that interests determine regimes, and that the distribution of power should be viewed as one determinant of interests. In other words, a state's degree of power in the international system is one of the things that explains its preferences, and the distribution of power between states determines the context of interaction and the preference orderings of the interacting states and thus determines the incentives and prospects for international regimes. Structural arguments should be recognized as constituting the determinants of those different patterns of interest that underlie the regimes themselves.

A similar structural argument can be used to explain subsystemic regimes, for the extraregional context or structure can determine the constellation of preferences among intraregional actors. Great powers can often structure the choices and preferences of minor powers and thus shape regional outcomes. Many of the cooperative arrangements between western

---

[41] Recent exponents of the predominance model of stability, as opposed to the classical balance-of-power model of stability, include A. F. K. Organski, *World Politics,* 2nd ed. (New York: Knopf, 1968), pp. 338–76, and George Modelski, "The Long Cycle of Global Politics and the Nation-State," *Comparative Studies in Society and History* 20 (April 1978): 214–35. The international political economy variant of the argument is provided by Stephen D. Krasner, "State Power and the Structure of International Trade," *World Politics* 28 (April 1976): 317–47; see also Stein, "The Hegemon's Dilemma."

[42] Note that this is precisely the way in which Krasner develops his argument in "State Power."

European states immediately following the Second World War can be said to reflect the way in which, through carrot and stick, the United States structured the choices and preferences of those states. The prisoners' dilemma also illustrates this, for the dilemma can be seen as a parable of domination in which the district attorney structures the situation to be a dilemma for the prisoners.[43] Divide-and-conquer is one strategy by which the powerful can structure the interactions between others by determining for them their preferences among a given set of choices.

There are other structural factors, such as the nature of knowledge and the nature of technology, that also determine actor preferences and thus the prospects for regimes. The nature of technology, for example, is critically important to a state's decision whether or not to procure weapons. Typically, scholars have argued that states confront a security dilemma in which they have prisoners' dilemma preferences. All states have a dominant strategy of arming themselves, yet all find the armed world that results less preferable than a totally disarmed one. Yet the security dilemma presumes either that offensive weapons exist and are superior to defensive ones, or that weapons systems are not easily distinguishable.[44] If only defensive weapons existed, however, then no security dilemma could arise. The actors would no longer have dominant strategies of arming themselves, for the arms could not be used to exploit those who had not armed, and procurement would not be a required defense against exploitation at the hands of others' defensive weapons. The interaction between states would no longer lead to a Pareto-deficient equilibrium outcome, therefore, and there would be no need for an arms regime. Thus, the different constellations of preferences that exist in different areas and create different incentives and prospects for international regimes are in part a function of the nature of technology.

Changes in the nature of human understanding about how the world works, knowledge, can also transform state interests and therefore the prospects for international cooperation and regime formation. As late as the middle of the last century there was enormous variation in national quarantine regulations, for example. As long as there was no agreed body of validated knowledge about the causes of communicable disease and the nature of its transmission and cure, then state policy could and did reflect political concerns. Regulations to exclude or isolate goods and individuals, ostensibly for health reasons, were used as instruments of international competition and became the basis of conflict. But new scientific discoveries transformed this situation. There were medical discoveries about the microbes that caused cholera and leprosy among other diseases; discoveries of the transmission of yellow fever by mosquitoes and plague by rat fleas; and discoveries of preventive vaccines such as the one for cholera. "The numerous international

<hr />

[43] Tom Burns and Walter Buckley, "The Prisoners' Dilemma Game as a System of Social Domination," *Journal of Peace Research* 11 (1974): 221–28.

[44] Robert Jervis, "Cooperation Under the Security Dilemma," *World Politics* 30 (January 1978): 167–214.

sanitary conferences, from 1851 up to the Constitution of the World Health Organization in 1946, clearly expressed the various milestones of medical insight."[45] International agreements on quarantine rules grew on this foundation. New knowledge thus changed state preferences and provided the basis for international cooperation and the depoliticization of health care policy.[46]

Just as structural factors underpin actor preferences, so do internal national characteristics. The interests of domestic economic sectors, for example, can be the basis for national interests.[47] Even if a state's interests do not reflect those of any specific sector or class, they may emerge from a state's attributes. Large populations and high technology generate demands that will require that a state go abroad for resources if domestic access to resources is inadequate.[48] Yet needed resources can be obtained by exchange as well as by plunder. One cannot, therefore, move from a delineation of internal characteristics to state behavior without incorporating some aspect of a state's relations and interactions with others. Internal characteristics may determine a single actor's preferences but, in order to ascertain outcomes, it is also necessary to know the interests of other actors and to have a sense of the likely pattern of strategic interaction.[49]

Regime change

The same factors that explain regime formation also explain regime maintenance, change, and dissolution. Regimes are maintained as long as the patterns of interest that gave rise to them remain. When these shift, the character of a regime may change; a regime may even dissolve entirely. In-

[45] The quotation and the substantive discussion are from Charles O. Pannenberg, *A New International Health Order: An Inquiry into the International Relations of World Health and Medical Care* (Germantown, Maryland: Sijthoff and Noordhoff, 1979), pp. 179–80.

[46] Regulations founded on health reasons and scientifically based can still become the basis of political disagreement, as the Japanese response to the California medfly spraying in 1981 demonstrates.

[47] See, for example, Peter Alexis Gourevitch, "International Trade, Domestic Coalitions, and Liberty: The Crisis of 1873–1896," *Journal of Interdisciplinary History* 8 (Autumn 1977): 281–313; and James R. Kurth, "The Creation and Destruction of International Regimes: The Impact of the World Market," paper delivered at the American Political Science Association Meeting, Washington, D.C., August 1980.

[48] Robert C. North, "Toward a Framework for the Analysis of Scarcity and Conflict," *International Studies Quarterly* 21 (December 1977): 569–91.

[49] Note that this clearly distinguishes domestic sectoral from international structural approaches. Although both approaches can be seen as delineating the determinants of actor preferences, the international structural perspective can be claimed to determine the constellation of all actors' preferences. Thus, the existence of offensive weapons creates a prisoners' dilemma situation for any pair of nations. On the other hand, the sectoral approach explains one actor's preferences at a time, and thus must be linked with an analysis of the interaction between actors to explain outcome. This is, of course, why the analysis of foreign policy is not equivalent to the analysis of international relations. Thus, the works of Allison, Gourevitch, Katzenstein, and Kurth, among others, which explain foreign policy by reference to domestic economic or bureaucratic interests, remain incomplete precisely because they do not incorporate relations *between* nations.

corporating the determinants of interests leads one to argue that regimes are maintained only as long as the distribution of power (or the nature of technology, or knowledge, etc.) that determines a given constellation of interests remains. When the international distribution of power shifts, affecting, in turn, the preferences of actors, then the regime will change. Those who make a direct link between structure and regimes necessarily conclude that changes in the distribution of power lead to regime change. The argument here is more subtle. If interests intervene between structure and regimes, then only those structural changes that affect patterns of interest will affect regimes. Further, since other factors also affect interests, it may be that the impact of changing power distributions on actor preferences can be negated by other structural changes, such as those in technology. Or, changes in the other factors, such as knowledge, can lead to regime change without a change in the distribution of power. This describes the history of quarantine regulations, for example. Together, these might explain why some changes in the distribution of power have clearly been linked with regime changes whereas others have not.[50]

Regimes may be maintained even after shifts in the interests that gave rise to them, however. There are a number of reasons why. First, nations do not continually calculate their interactions and transactions. That is, nations only periodically reassess interests and power or the institutional arrangements that have been created to deal with a particular configuration of them. Once in place, the institutions serve to guide patterned behavior, and the costs of continual recalculation are avoided. Decision costs are high, and once paid in the context of creating institutions, they are not continually borne.[51]

An alternative argument is that the legitimacy of international institutions does not emerge from any waiving of national interest, but from an interest developed in the institutions themselves. Any shift in interest does not automatically lead to changes in the regime or to its destruction, because there may well be uncertainty about the permanence of the observed changes. The institutions may be required again in the future, and their destruction for short-term changes may be very costly in the long run. Institutional maintenance is not, then, a function of a waiving of calculation; it becomes a factor in the decision calculus that keeps short-term calculations from becoming decisive. There are sunk costs involved in international institutions and thus they are not lightly to be changed or destroyed. The costs of reconstruction are likely to be much higher once regimes are consciously

---

[50] The recognition of the multiple determination of actor interests also makes possible an issue approach to international politics that is not necessarily issue-structural.

[51] One can, of course, expect there to be lags between changes in interests and actor behavior; see Michael Nicholson, *Oligopoly and Conflict: A Dynamic Approach* (Liverpool: Liverpool University Press, 1972). Schick distinguishes realization lags from adaptation lags in "Some Notes on Thinking Ahead," p. 790.

destroyed. Their very existence changes actors' incentives and opportunities.[52]

There is, however, an alternative to the explanation that regime maintenance is merely a perpetuation of the exogenous factors that occasioned
their rise. It may be that neither sunk costs nor delays in recalculation or
reassessment are responsible for the maintenance of regimes. Max Weber
argues that tradition provides legitimacy and is one basis for the maintenance of a political order, and this argument can be extended to international
relations. International regimes can be maintained and sustained by tradition
and legitimacy. Even those international institutions that exist in an anarchic
environment can attain a legitimacy that maintains patterned international
behavior long after the original basis for those institutions has disappeared.
Thus, even though the constellations of interest that give rise to regimes may
change, the regimes themselves may remain. This can be explained by
means of interests by arguing that actors attach some value to reputation and
that they damage their reputations by breaking with customary behavior.[53]
An actor that no longer prefers the regime to independent decision making
may nevertheless choose not to defect from it because it values an undi-
minished reputation more than whatever it believes it would gain by depart-
ing from the established order.

Finally, there is a possibility that the creation of international regimes
leads not to the abandonment of national calculation but to a shift in the
criteria by which decisions are made. Institutions created to assure international coordination or collaboration can themselves serve to shift decision
criteria and thus lead nations to consider others' interests in addition to their
own when they make decisions. Once nations begin to coordinate their behavior and, even more so, once they have collaborated, they may become
joint-maximizers rather than self-maximizers. The institutionalization of
coordination and collaboration can become a restraint on individualism and
lead actors to recognize the importance of joint maximization. Those who
previously agreed to bind themselves out of self-interest may come to accept
joint interests as an imperative. This may be especially true of collaboration
regimes, which require that actors trust one another not to cheat since they
all have an incentive to do so. In these situations, one nation's leaders may
come to have an interest in maintaining another nation's leaders in power,
for they have worked together to achieve the optimal nonequilibrium outcome and they trust one another not to cheat. Recognition of the importance

[52] One can argue that regimes actually change actor preferences. The property rights argument about dealing with externalities through changes in liability rules is an example of a situation in which prearranged agreements are specifically devised in order to change utilities in
subsequent interaction; see John A. C. Conybeare, "International Organization and the Theory
of Property Rights," *International Organization* 34 (Summer 1980): 307–334.

[53] George A. Akerlof, "A Theory of Social Custom, of Which Unemployment May Be One
Consequence," *Quarterly Journal of Economics* 94 (June 1980): 749–75.

of maintaining the position of others may become the basis for the emergence of joint maximization as a decision criterion for actors.

Conclusion

The problems of analyzing regime formation, maintenance, and dissolution demonstrate the clear necessity for a strategic interaction approach to international politics. State behavior does not derive solely from structural factors like the distribution of power; neither can state behavior be explained solely by reference to domestic sectors and interests. Structure and sectors play a role in determining the constellation of actor preferences, but structural and sectoral approaches are both incomplete and must be supplemented by an emphasis on strategic interaction between states. It is the combination of actor preferences and the interactions that result from them that determine outcome, and only by understanding both is it possible to analyze and understand the nature of regimes in an anarchic world.

We have long understood that anarchy in the international arena does not entail continual chaos; cooperative international arrangements do exist. This article differentiates the independent decision making that characterizes "anarchic" international politics from the joint decision making that constitutes regimes. In doing so, it distinguishes the natural cooperation that results from harmonious interests from those particular forms of collective decision making that define regimes. Sovereign nations have a rational incentive to develop processes for making joint decisions when confronting dilemmas of common interests or common aversions. In these contexts, self-interested actors rationally forgo independent decision making and construct regimes.

The existence of regimes is fully consistent with a realist view of international politics, in which states are seen as sovereign and self-reliant. Yet it is the very autonomy of states and their self-interests that lead them to create regimes when confronting dilemmas.

The demand for
international regimes

Robert O. Keohane

We study international regimes because we are interested in understanding order in world politics. Conflict may be the rule; if so, institutionalized patterns of cooperation are particularly in need of explanation. The theoretical analysis of international regimes begins with what is at least an apparent anomaly from the standpoint of Realist theory: the existence of many "sets of implicit or explicit principles, norms, rules, and decision-making procedures around which actor expectations converge," in a variety of areas of international relations.

This article constitutes an attempt to improve our understanding of international order, and international cooperation, through an interpretation of international regime-formation that relies heavily on rational-choice analysis in the utilitarian social contract tradition. I explore why self-interested actors in world politics should seek, under certain circumstances, to establish international regimes through mutual agreement; and how we can account

The original idea for this paper germinated in discussions at a National Science Foundation-sponsored conference on International Politics and International Economics held in Minneapolis, Minnesota, in June 1978.

I am indebted to Robert Holt and Anne Krueger for organizing and to the NSF for funding that meeting. Several knowledgeable friends, particularly Charles Kindleberger, Timothy J. McKeown, James N. Rosse, and Laura Tyson, provided bibliographical suggestions that helped me think about the issues discussed here. For written comments on earlier versions of this article I am especially grateful to Robert Bates, John Chubb, John Conybeare, Colin Day, Alex Field, Albert Fishlow, Alexander George, Ernst B. Haas, Gerald Helleiner, Harold K. Jacobson, Robert Jervis, Stephen D. Krasner, Helen Milner, Timothy J. McKeown, Robert C. North, John Ruggie, Ken Shepsle, Arthur Stein, Susan Strange, Harrison Wagner, and David Yoffie. I also benefited from discussions of earlier drafts at meetings held at Los Angeles in October 1980 and at Palm Springs in February 1981, and from colloquia in Berkeley, California, and Cambridge, Massachusetts.

International Organization 36, 2, Spring 1982
0020-8183/82/020325-31 $1.50

for fluctuations over time in the number, extent, and strength of international regimes, on the basis of rational calculation under varying circumstances.

Previous work on this subject in the rational-choice tradition has emphasized the "theory of hegemonic stability": that is, the view that concentration of power in one dominant state facilitates the development of strong regimes, and that fragmentation of power is associated with regime collapse.[1] This theory, however, fails to explain lags between changes in power structures and changes in international regimes; does not account well for the differential durability of different institutions within a given issue-area; and avoids addressing the question of why international regimes seem so much more extensive now in world politics than during earlier periods (such as the late 19th century) of supposed hegemonic leadership.[2]

The argument of this article seeks to correct some of these faults of the hegemonic stability theory by incorporating it within a supply-demand approach that borrows extensively from microeconomic theory. The theory of hegemonic stability can be viewed as focusing only on the supply of international regimes: according to the theory, the more concentrated power is in an international system, the greater the supply of international regimes at any level of demand.[3] But fluctuations in demand for international regimes are not taken into account by the theory; thus it is necessarily incomplete. This article focuses principally on the demand for international regimes in order to provide the basis for a more comprehensive and balanced interpretation.

Emphasizing the demand for international regimes focuses our attention on why we should want them in the first place, rather than taking their desirability as a given. I do not assume that "demand" and "supply" can be specified independently and operationalized as in microeconomics. The same actors are likely to be the "demanders" and the "suppliers." Furthermore, factors affecting the demand for international regimes are likely simultaneously to affect their supply as well. Yet supply and demand language allows us to make a distinction that is useful in distinguishing phenomena that, in the first instance, affect the desire for regimes, on the one hand, or the ease of supplying them, on the other. "Supply and de-

---

[1] See especially Robert O. Keohane, "The Theory of Hegemonic Stability and Changes in International Economic Regimes, 1967–1977," in Ole R. Holsti, Randolph Siverson, and Alexander George, eds., *Changes in the International System* (Boulder: Westview, 1980); and Linda Cahn, "National Power and International Regimes: The United States and International Commodity Markets," Ph.D. diss., Stanford University, 1980.

[2] Current research on the nineteenth century is beginning to question the assumption that Britain was hegemonic in a meaningful sense. See Timothy J. McKeown, "Hegemony Theory and Trade in the Nineteenth Century," paper presented to the International Studies Association convention, Philadelphia, 18–21 March 1981; and Arthur A. Stein, "The Hegemon's Dilemma: Great Britain, the United States, and the International Economic Order," paper presented to the American Political Science Association annual meeting, New York, 3–6 September 1981.

[3] The essential reason for this (discussed below) is that actors that are large relative to the whole set of actors have greater incentives both to provide collective goods themselves and to organize their provision, than do actors that are small relative to the whole set. The classic discussion of this phenomenon appears in Mancur Olson Jr., *The Logic of Collective Action: Political Goods and the Theory of Groups* (Cambridge: Harvard University Press, 1965).

mand'' should be seen in this analysis as a metaphor, rather than an attempt artificially to separate, or to reify, different aspects of an interrelated process.[4]

Before proceeding to the argument, two caveats are in order. First, the focus of this article is principally on the *strength* and *extent* of international regimes, rather than on their *content* or *effects*. I hope to contribute to understanding why international regimes wax and wane, leaving to others (in this volume and elsewhere) the analysis of what ideologies they encompass or how much they affect ultimate, value-laden outcomes. The only significant exception to this avoidance of questions of content comes in Section 5, which distinguishes between control-oriented and insurance-oriented regimes. Second, no claim is made here that rational-choice analysis is the only valid way to understand international regimes, or even that it is preferable to others. On the contrary, I view rational-choice analysis as one way to generate an insightful interpretation of international regimes that complements interpretations derived from analyses of conventions and of learning (illustrated in the articles in this volume by Young and Haas). My analysis is designed to be neither comprehensive nor exclusive: I suggest hypotheses and try to make what we know more intelligible, rather than seeking to put forward a definitive theory of international regimes.

The major arguments of this article are grouped in five sections. First, I outline the analytical approach by discussing the virtues and limitations of "systemic constraint-choice analysis." Section 2 lays the basis for the development of a constraint-choice theory of international regimes by specifying the context within which international regimes operate and the functions they perform. In Section 3 elements of a theory of the demand for international regimes are presented, emphasizing the role of regimes in reducing transactions costs and coping with uncertainty. In Section 4, I use insights from theories of information and uncertainty to discuss issues of closure and communication. Section 5 suggests that control-oriented regimes are likely to be increasingly supplemented in the 1980s by insurance regimes as the dominance of the advanced industrial countries in the world political economy declines.

1. Systemic constraint-choice analysis: virtues and limitations

The argument developed here is deliberately limited to the *systemic* level of analysis. In a systemic theory, the actors' characteristics are given by assumption, rather than treated as variables; changes in outcomes are explained not on the basis of variations in these actor characteristics, but on the basis of changes in the attributes of the system itself. Microeconomic theory, for instance, posits the existence of business firms, with given utility

[4] I am indebted to Albert Fishlow for clarifying this point for me.

functions, and attempts to explain their behavior on the basis of environmental factors such as the competitiveness of markets. It is therefore a systemic theory, unlike the so-called "behavioral theory of the firm," which examines the actors for internal variations that could account for behavior not predicted by microeconomic theory.

A systemic focus permits a limitation of the number of variables that need to be considered. In the initial steps of theory-building, this is a great advantage: attempting to take into account at the outset factors at the foreign policy as well as the systemic level would lead quickly to descriptive complexity and theoretical anarchy. Beginning the analysis at the systemic level establishes a baseline for future work. By seeing how well a simple model accounts for behavior, we understand better the value of introducing more variables and greater complexity into the analysis. Without the systemic microeconomic theory of the firm, for instance, it would not have been clear what puzzles needed to be solved by an actor-oriented behavioral theory.

A systems-level examination of changes in the strength and extent of international regimes over time could proceed through historical description. We could examine a large number of cases, attempting to extract generalizations about patterns from the data. Our analysis could be explicitly comparative, analyzing different regimes within a common analytical framework, employing a methodology such as George's "focused comparison."[5] Such a systematic comparative description could be quite useful, but it would not provide a theoretical framework for posing questions of why, and under what conditions, regimes should be expected to develop or become stronger. Posing such fundamental issues is greatly facilitated by *a priori* reasoning that makes specific predictions to be compared with empirical findings. Such reasoning helps us to reinterpret previously observed patterns of behavior as well as suggesting new questions about behavior or distinctions that have been ignored: it has the potential of "discovering new facts."[6] This can be useful even in a subject such as international politics, where the variety of relevant variables is likely to confound any comprehensive effort to build deductive theory. Deductive analysis can thus be used in interpretation as well as in a traditional strategy of theory-building and hypothesis-testing.

This analysis follows the tradition of microeconomic theory by focusing on constraints and incentives that affect the choices made by actors.[7] We

[5] Alexander L. George, "Case Studies and Theory Development: The Method of Structured, Focused Comparison," in Paul Lauren, ed., *Diplomacy: New Approaches in History, Theory, and Policy* (New York: Free Press, 1979).

[6] Imre Lakatos, "Falsification and the Methodology of Scientific Research Programmes," in Lakatos and Alan Musgrave, eds., *Criticism and the Growth of Scientific Knowledge* (Cambridge: Cambridge University Press, 1970).

[7] Stimulating discussions of microeconomic theory can be found in Martin Shubik, "A Curmudgeon's Guide to Microeconomics," *Journal of Economic Literature* 8 (1970): 405–434; and Spiro J. Latsis, "A Research Programme in Economics," in Latsis, ed., *Method and Appraisal in Economics* (Cambridge: Cambridge University Press, 1976).

assume that, in general, actors in world politics tend to respond rationally to constraints and incentives. Changes in the characteristics of the international system will alter the opportunity costs to actors of various courses of action, and will therefore lead to changes in behavior. In particular, decisions about creating or joining international regimes will be affected by system-level changes in this way; in this model the demand for international regimes is a function of system characteristics.

This article therefore employs a form of rational-choice analysis, which I prefer to term "constraint-choice" analysis to indicate that I do not make some of the extreme assumptions often found in the relevant literature. I assume a prior context of power, expectations, values, and conventions; I do not argue that rational-choice analysis can derive international regimes from a "state of nature" through logic alone.[8] This paper also eschews deterministic claims, or the *hubris* of believing that a complete explanation can be developed through resort to deductive models. To believe this would commit one to a narrowly rationalistic form of analysis in which expectations of gain provide both necessary and sufficient explanations of behavior.[9] Such beliefs in the power of Benthamite calculation have been undermined by the insufficiency of microeconomic theories of the firm—despite their great value as initial approximations—as shown by the work of organization theorists such as Simon, Cyert, and March.[10]

see critiques of these models (AJPS)

Rational-choice theory is not advanced here as a magic key to unlock the secrets of international regime change, much less as a comprehensive way of interpreting reality. Nor do I employ it as a means of explaining particular actions of specific actors. Rather, I use rational-choice theory to develop models that help to explain trends or tendencies toward which patterns of behavior tend to converge. That is, I seek to account for typical, or modal, behavior. This analysis will not accurately predict the decisions of all actors, or what will happen to all regimes; but it should help to account for overall trends in the formation, growth, decay, and dissolution of regimes. The deductive logic of this approach makes it possible to generate hypotheses about international regime change on an *a priori* basis. In this article several such hypotheses will be suggested, although their testing will have to await further specification. We shall therefore be drawing on microeconomic theories and rational-choice approaches heuristically, to help us con-

[8] I am indebted to Alexander J. Field for making the importance of this point clear to me. See his paper, "The Problem with Neoclassical Institutional Economics: A Critique with Special Reference to the North/Thomas Model of Pre–1500 Europe," *Explorations in Economic History* 18 (April 1981).

[9] Lance E. Davis and Douglass C. North adopt this strong form of rationalistic explanation when they argue that "an institutional arrangement will be innovated if the expected net gains exceed the expected costs." See their volume, *Institutional Change and American Economic Growth* (Cambridge: Cambridge University Press, 1971).

[10] Two of the classic works are James March and Herbert Simon, *Organizations* (New York: Wiley, 1958); and Richard Cyert and James March, *The Behavioral Theory of the Firm* (Englewood Cliffs, N.J.: Prentice-Hall, 1963).

struct nontrivial hypotheses about international regime change that can guide future research.

The use of rational-choice theory implies that we must view decisions involving international regimes as in some meaningful sense voluntary. Yet we know that world politics is a realm in which power is exercised regularly and in which inequalities are great. How, then, can we analyze international regimes with a voluntaristic mode of analysis?

My answer is to distinguish two aspects of the process by which international regimes come into being: the imposition of constraints, and decision making. Constraints are dictated not only by environmental factors but also by powerful actors. Thus when we speak of an "imposed regime," we are speaking (in my terminology) of a regime agreed upon within constraints that are mandated by powerful actors.[11] Any agreement that results from bargaining will be affected by the opportunity costs of alternatives faced by the various actors: that is, by which party has the greater need for agreement with the other.[12] Relationships of power and dependence in world politics will therefore be important determinants of the characteristics of international regimes. Actor choices will be constrained in such a way that the preferences of more powerful actors will be accorded greater weight. Thus in applying rational-choice theory to the formation and maintenance of international regimes, we have to be continually sensitive to the structural context within which agreements are made. Voluntary choice does not imply equality of situation or outcome.

We do not necessarily sacrifice realism when we analyze international regimes as the products of voluntary agreements among independent actors within the context of prior constraints. Constraint-choice analysis effectively captures the nonhierarchical nature of world politics without ignoring the role played by power and inequality. Within this analytical framework, a systemic analysis that emphasizes constraints on choice and effects of system characteristics on collective outcomes provides an appropriate way to address the question of regime formation.

Constraint-choice analysis emphasizes that international regimes should not be seen as quasi-governments—imperfect attempts to institutionalize centralized authority relationships in world politics. Regimes are more like contracts, when these involve actors with long-term objectives who seek to structure their relationships in stable and mutually beneficial ways.[13] In

[11] For a discussion of "spontaneous," "negotiated," and "imposed" regimes, see Oran Young's contribution to this volume.

[12] For a lucid and original discussion based on this obvious but important point, see John Harsanyi, "Measurement of Social Power, Opportunity Costs and the Theory of Two-Person Bargaining Games," *Behavioral Science* 7, 1 (1962): 67–80. See also Albert O. Hirschman, *National Power and the Structure of Foreign Trade* (1945; Berkeley: University of California Press, 1980), especially pp. 45–48.

[13] S. Todd Lowry, "Bargain and Contract Theory in Law and Economics," in Warren J. Samuels, ed., *The Economy as a System of Power* (New Brunswick, N.J.: Transaction Books, 1979), p. 276.

some respects, regimes resemble the "quasi-agreements" that Fellner discusses when analyzing the behavior of oligopolistic firms.[14] In both contracts and quasi-agreements, there may be specific rules having to do with prices, quantities, delivery dates, and the like; for contracts, some of these rules may be legally enforceable. The most important functions of these arrangements, however, are not to preclude further negotiations, but to establish stable mutual expectations about others' patterns of behavior and to develop working relationships that will allow the parties to adapt their practices to new situations. Rules of international regimes are frequently changed, bent, or broken to meet the exigencies of the moment. They are rarely enforced automatically, and they are not self-executing. Indeed, they are often matters for negotiation and renegotiation; as Puchala has argued, "attempts to enforce EEC regulations open political cleavages up and down the supranational-to-local continuum and spark intense politicking along the cleavage lines."[15]

This lack of binding authority associated with international regimes has important implications for our selection of analytical approaches within a constraint-choice framework: it leads us to rely more heavily on microeconomic, market-oriented theory than on theories of public choice. Most public-choice theory is not applicable to international regime change because it focuses on the processes by which authoritative, binding decisions are made within states.[16] Yet in international politics, binding decisions, arrived at through highly institutionalized, rule-oriented processes, are relatively rare and unimportant, and such decisions do not constitute the essence of international regimes. Traditional microeconomic supply and demand analysis, by contrast, assumes a situation in which choices are made continuously over a period of time by actors for whom "exit"—refusal to purchase goods or services that are offered—is an ever-present option. This conforms more closely to the situation faced by states contemplating whether to create, join, remain members of, or leave international regimes. Since no binding decisions can be made, it is possible to imagine a market for international regimes as one thinks of an economic market: on the basis of an analysis of relative prices and cost-benefit calculations, actors decide which regimes to "buy." In general, we expect states to join those regimes in which they expect the benefits of membership to outweigh the costs. In such an analysis, observed changes in the extent and strength of international

[14] William Fellner, *Competition among the Few* (New York: Knopf, 1949).

[15] Donald J. Puchala, "Domestic Politics and Regional Harmonization in the European Communities," *World Politics* 27,4 (July 1975), p. 509.

[16] There are exceptions to this generalization, such as Tiebout's "voting with the feet" models of population movements among communities. Yet only one chapter of fourteen in a recent survey of the public-choice literature is devoted to such models, which do not focus on authoritative decision-making processes. See Dennis C. Mueller, *Public Choice* (Cambridge: Cambridge University Press, 1980). For a brilliantly innovative work on "exit" versus "voice" processes, see Albert O. Hirschman, *Exit, Voice, and Loyalty* (Cambridge: Harvard University Press, 1970).

regimes may be explained by reference to changes either in the characteristics of the international system (the context within which actors make choices) or of the international regimes themselves (about which the choices are made).

This constraint-choice approach draws attention to the question of why disadvantaged actors join international regimes even when they receive fewer benefits than other members—an issue ignored by arguments that regard certain regimes as simply imposed. Weak actors as well as more powerful actors make choices, even if they make them within more severe constraints. (Whether such choices, made under severe constraint, imply obligations for the future is another question, one not addressed here.)[17]

2. The context and functions of international regimes

Analysis of international regime-formation within a constraint-choice framework requires that one specify the nature of the context within which actors make choices and the functions of the institutions whose patterns of growth and decay are being explained. Two features of the international context are particularly important: world politics lacks authoritative governmental institutions, and is characterized by pervasive uncertainty. Within this setting, a major function of international regimes is to facilitate the making of mutually beneficial agreements among governments, so that the structural condition of anarchy does not lead to a complete "war of all against all."

The actors in our model operate within what Waltz has called a "self-help system," in which they cannot call on higher authority to resolve difficulties or provide protection.[18] Negative externalities are common: states are forever impinging on one another's interests.[19] In the absence of authoritative global institutions, these conflicts of interest produce uncertainty and risk: possible future evils are often even more terrifying than present ones. All too obvious with respect to matters of war and peace, this is also characteristic of the international economic environment.

Actors in world politics may seek to reduce conflicts of interest and risk

[17] Anyone who has thought about Hobbes's tendentious discussion of "voluntary" agreements in *Leviathan* realizes the dangers of casuistry entailed in applying voluntaristic analysis to politics, especially when obligations are inferred from choices. This article follows Hobbes's distinction between the structure of constraints in a situation, on the one hand, and actor choices, on the other; but it does not adopt his view that even severely constrained choices ("your freedom or your life") create moral or political obligations.

[18] Kenneth N. Waltz, *Theory of International Politics* (Reading, Mass.: Addison-Wesley, 1979).

[19] Externalities exist whenever an acting unit does not bear all of the costs, or fails to reap all of the benefits, that result from its behavior. See Davis and North, *Institutional Change and American Economic Growth*, p. 16.

by coordinating their behavior. Yet coordination has many of the characteristics of a public good, which leads us to expect that its production will be too low.[20] That is, increased production of these goods, which would yield net benefits, is not undertaken. This insight is the basis of the major "supply-side" argument about international regimes, epitomized by the theory of hegemonic stability. According to this line of argument, hegemonic international systems should be characterized by levels of public goods production higher than in fragmented systems; and, if international regimes provide public goods, by stronger and more extensive international regimes.[21]

This argument, important though it is, ignores what I have called the "demand" side of the problem of international regimes: why should governments desire to institute international regimes in the first place, and how much will they be willing to contribute to maintain them? Addressing these issues will help to correct some of the deficiencies of the theory of hegemonic stability, which derive from its one-sidedness, and will contribute to a more comprehensive interpretation of international regime change. The familiar context of world politics—its competitiveness, uncertainty, and conflicts of interest—not only sets limits on the supply of international regimes, but provides a basis for understanding why they are demanded.

Before we can understand why regimes are demanded, however, it is necessary to establish what the functions of international regimes, from the perspective of states, might be.[22]

At the most specific level, students of international cooperation are interested in myriads of particular agreements made by governments: to

[20] Olson, *The Logic of Collection Action;* Bruce M. Russett and John D. Sullivan, "Collective Goods and International Organization," with a comment by Mancur Olson Jr., *International Organization* 25,4 (Autumn 1971); John Gerard Ruggie, "Collective Goods and Future International Collaboration," *American Political Science Review* 66,3 (September 1972); Duncan Snidal, "Public Goods, Property Rights, and Political Organization," *International Studies Quarterly* 23,4 (December 1979), p. 544.

[21] Keohane, "The Theory of Hegemonic Stability"; Charles P. Kindleberger, *The World in Depression, 1929–1939* (Berkeley: University of California Press, 1974); Mancur Olson and Richard Zeckhauser, "An Economic Theory of Alliances," *Review of Economics and Statistics* 48,3 (August 1966), reprinted in Bruce M. Russett, ed., *Economic Theories of International Politics* (Chicago: Markham, 1968). For a critical appraisal of work placing emphasis on public goods as a rationale for forming international organizations, see John A. C. Conybeare, "International Organizations and the Theory of Property Rights," *International Organization* 34,3 (Summer 1980), especially pp. 329–32.

[22] My use of the word "functions" here is meant to designate consequences of a certain pattern of activity, particularly in terms of the utility of the activity; it is not to be interpreted as an explanation of the behavior in question, since there is no teleological premise, or assumption that necessity is involved. Understanding the function of international regimes helps, however, to explain why actors have an incentive to create them, and may therefore help to make behavior intelligible within a rational-choice mode of analysis that emphasizes the role of incentives and constraints. For useful distinctions on functionalism, see Ernest Nagel, *The Structure of Scientific Explanation* (New York: Harcourt, Brace, 1961), especially "Functionalism and Social Science," pp. 520–35. I am grateful to Robert Packenham for this reference and discussions of this point.

maintain their exchange rates within certain limits, to refrain from trade discrimination, to reduce their imports of petroleum, or progressively to reduce tariffs. These agreements are made despite the fact that, compared to domestic political institutions, the institutions of world politics are extremely weak: an authoritative legal framework is lacking and regularized institutions for conducting transactions (such as markets backed by state authority or binding procedures for making and enforcing contracts) are often poorly developed.

Investigation of the sources of specific agreements reveals that they are not, in general, made on an *ad hoc* basis, nor do they follow a random pattern. Instead, they are "nested" within more comprehensive agreements, covering more issues. An agreement among the United States, Japan, and the European Community in the Multilateral Trade Negotiations to reduce a particular tariff is affected by the rules, norms, principles, and procedures of the General Agreement on Tariffs and Trade (GATT)—that is, by the trade regime. The trade regime, in turn, is nested within a set of other arrangements—including those for monetary relations, energy, foreign investment, aid to developing countries, and other issues—that together constitute a complex and interlinked pattern of relations among the advanced market-economy countries. These, in turn, are related to military-security relations among the major states.[23]

Within this multilayered system, a major function of international regimes is to facilitate the making of specific agreements on matters of substantive significance within the issue-area covered by the regime. International regimes help to make governments' expectations consistent with one another. Regimes are developed in part because actors in world politics believe that with such arrangements they will be able to make mutually beneficial agreements that would otherwise be difficult or impossible to attain. In other words, regimes are valuable to governments where, in their absence, certain mutually beneficial agreements would be impossible to consummate. In such situations, *ad hoc* joint action would be inferior to results of negotiation within a regime context.

Yet this characterization of regimes immediately suggests an explanatory puzzle. Why should it be worthwhile to construct regimes (themselves requiring agreement) in order to make specific agreements within the regime frameworks? Why is it not more efficient simply to avoid the regime stage and make the agreements on an *ad hoc* basis? In short, why is there any demand for international regimes apart from a demand for international agreements on particular questions?

An answer to this question is suggested by theories of "market failure" in economics. Market failure refers to situations in which the outcomes of

---

[23] Vinod Aggarwal has developed the concept of "nesting" in his work on international regimes in textiles since World War II. I am indebted to him for this idea, which has been elaborated in his "Hanging by a Thread: International Regime Change in the Textile/Apparel System, 1950–1979," Ph.D. diss., Stanford University, 1981.

market-mediated interaction are suboptimal (given the utility functions of actors and the resources at their disposal). Agreements that would be beneficial to all parties are not made. In situations of market failure, economic activities uncoordinated by hierarchical authority lead to *in*efficient results, rather than to the efficient outcomes expected under conditions of perfect competition. In the theory of market failure, the problems are attributed not to inadequacies of the actors themselves (who are presumed to be rational utility-maximizers) but rather to the structure of the system and the institutions, or lack thereof, that characterize it.[24] Specific attributes of the system impose transactions costs (including information costs) that create barriers to effective cooperation among the actors. Thus institutional defects are responsible for failures of coordination. To correct these defects, conscious institutional innovation may be necessary, although a good economist will always compare the costs of institutional innovation with the costs of market failure before recommending tampering with the market.

Like imperfect markets, world politics is characterized by institutional deficiencies that inhibit mutually advantageous coordination. Some of the deficiencies revolve around problems of transactions costs and uncertainty that have been cogently analyzed by students of market failure. Theories of market failure specify types of institutional imperfections that may inhibit agreement; international regimes may be interpreted as helping to correct similar institutional defects in world politics. Insofar as regimes are established through voluntary agreement among a number of states, we can interpret them, at least in part, as devices to overcome the barriers to more efficient coordination identified by theories of market failure.[25]

The analysis that follows is based on two theoretical assumptions. First, the actors whose behavior we analyze act, in general, as rational utility-maximizers in that they display consistent tendencies to adjust to external changes in ways that are calculated to increase the expected value of outcomes to them. Second, the international regimes with which we are concerned are devices to facilitate the making of agreements among these actors. From these assumptions it follows that the demand for international regimes

[24] Of particular value for understanding market failure is Kenneth J. Arrow, *Essays in the Theory of Risk-Bearing* (New York: North Holland/American Elsevier, 1974).

[25] Helen Milner suggested to me that international regimes were in this respect like credit markets, and that the history of the development of credit markets could be informative for students of international regimes. The analogy seems to hold. Richard Ehrenberg reports that the development of credit arrangements in medieval European Bourses reduced transaction costs (since money did not need to be transported in the form of specie) and provided high-quality information in the form of merchants' newsletters and exchanges of information at fairs: "during the Middle Ages the best information as to the course of events in the world was regularly to be obtained in the fairs and the Bourses" (p. 317). The Bourses also provided credit ratings, which provided information but also served as a crude substitute for effective systems of legal liability. Although the descriptions of credit market development in works such as that by Ehrenberg are fascinating, I have not been able to find a historically-grounded theory of these events. See Richard Ehrenberg, *Capital and Finance in the Age of the Renaissance: A Study of the Fuggers and Their Connections,* translated from the German by H. M. Lucas (New York: Harcourt, Brace, no date), especially chap. 3 (pp. 307–333).

at any given price will vary directly with the desirability of agreements to states and with the ability of international regimes actually to facilitate the making of such agreements. The condition for the theory's operation (that is, for regimes to be formed) is that sufficient complementary or common interests exist so that agreements benefiting all essential regime members can be made.

The value of theories of market failure for this analysis rests on the fact that they allow us to identify more precisely barriers to agreements. They therefore suggest insights into how international regimes help to reduce those barriers, and they provide richer interpretations of previously observed, but unexplained, phenomena associated with international regimes and international policy coordination. In addition, concepts of market failure help to explain the strength and extent of international regimes by identifying characteristics of international systems, or of international regimes themselves, that affect the demand for such regimes and therefore, given a supply schedule, their quantity. Insights from the market-failure literature therefore take us beyond the trivial cost-benefit or supply-demand propositions with which we began, to hypotheses about relationships that are less familiar.

The emphasis on efficiency in the market-failure literature is consistent with our constraint-choice analysis of the decision-making processes leading to the formation and maintenance of international regimes. Each actor must be as well or better off with the regime than without it—given the prior structure of constraints. This does not imply, of course, that the whole process leading to the formation of a new international regime will yield overall welfare benefits. Outsiders may suffer; indeed, some international regimes (such as alliances or cartel-type regimes) are specifically designed to impose costs on them. These costs to outsiders may well outweigh the benefits to members. In addition, powerful actors may manipulate constraints prior to the formation of a new regime. In that case, although the regime *per se* may achieve overall welfare improvements compared to the immediately preceding situation, the results of the joint process may be inferior to those that existed before the constraints were imposed.

3. Elements of a theory of the demand for international regimes

We are now in a position to address our central puzzle—why is there any demand for international regimes?—and to outline a theory to explain why this demand exists. First, it is necessary to use our distinction between "agreements" and "regimes" to pose the issue precisely: given a certain level of demand for international agreements, what will affect the demand for international regimes? The Coase theorem, from the market-failure literature, will then be used to develop a list of conditions under which international regimes are of potential value for facilitating agreements in world politics. This typological analysis turns our attention toward two central problems, *transactions cost* and *informational imperfections*. Questions of information, involving uncertainty and risk, will receive particular attention, since their exploration has rich implications for interpretation and future research.

The demand for agreements and the demand for regimes

It is crucial to distinguish clearly between international regimes, on the one hand, and mere *ad hoc* substantive agreements, on the other. Regimes, as argued above, facilitate the making of substantive agreements by providing a framework of rules, norms, principles, and procedures for negotiation. A theory of international regimes must explain why these intermediate arrangements are necessary.

In our analysis, the demand for agreements will be regarded as exogenous. It may be influenced by many factors, particularly by the perceptions that leaders of governments have about their interests in agreement or nonagreement. These perceptions will, in turn, be influenced by domestic politics, ideology, and other factors not encompassed by a systemic, constraint-choice approach. In the United States, "internationalists" have been attracted to international agreements and international organizations as useful devices for implementing American foreign policy; "isolationists" and "nationalists" have not. Clearly, such differences cannot be accounted for by our theory. We therefore assume a given desire for agreements and ask: under these conditions, what will be the demand for international regimes?

Under certain circumstances defining the demand and supply of agreements, there will be no need for regimes and we should expect none to form. This will be the situation in two extreme cases, where demand for agreements is nil and where the supply of agreements is infinitely elastic and free (so that all conceivable agreements can be made costlessly). But where the demand for agreements is positive at some level of feasible cost, and the supply of agreements is not infinitely elastic and free, there may be a demand for international regimes *if* they actually make possible agreements yielding net benefits that would not be possible on an *ad hoc* basis. In such a situation regimes can be regarded as "efficient." We can now ask: under what specific conditions will international regimes be efficient?

One way to address this question is to pose its converse. To ask about the conditions under which international regimes will be *worthless* enables us to draw on work in social choice, particularly by Ronald Coase. Coase was able to show that the presence of externalities alone does not necessarily prevent Pareto-optimal coordination among independent actors: under certain conditions, bargaining among these actors could lead to Pareto-optimal solutions. The key conditions isolated by Coase were (a) a legal framework establishing liability for actions, presumably supported by governmental authority; (b) perfect information; and (c) zero transactions costs (including organization costs and costs of making side-payments).[26] If all these conditions were met in world politics, *ad hoc* agreements would be costless and regimes unnecessary. *At least one of them must not be fulfilled if international regimes are to be of value, as facilitators of agreement, to independent utility-maximizing actors in world politics.* Inverting the Coase theorem provides us, therefore, with a list of conditions, at least one of which must apply if regimes are to be of value in facilitating agreements among governments:[27]

(a) lack of a clear legal framework establishing liability for actions;
(b) information imperfections (information is costly);
(c) positive transactions costs.[28]

In world politics, of course, *all* of these conditions are met all of the time: world government does not exist; information is extremely costly and often impossible to obtain; transactions costs, including costs of organization and side-payments, are often very high. Yet the Coase theorem is useful not merely as a way of categorizing these familiar problems, but because it suggests how international regimes can improve actors' abilities to make mutually beneficial agreements. Regimes can make agreement easier if they provide frameworks for establishing legal liability (even if these are not perfect); improve the quantity and quality of information available to actors; or reduce other transactions costs, such as costs of organization or of making side-payments. This typology allows us to specify regime functions—as devices to make agreements possible—more precisely, and therefore to understand demand for international regimes. Insofar as international regimes can correct institutional defects in world politics along any of these three dimensions (liability, information, transactions costs), they may become efficient devices for the achievement of state purposes.

Regimes do not establish binding and enforceable legal liabilities in any strict or ultimately reliable sense, although the lack of a hierarchical struc-

---

[26] Ronald Coase, "The Problem of Social Cost," *Journal of Law and Economics* 3 (October 1960). For a discussion, see James Buchanan and Gordon Tullock, *The Calculus of Consent: Logical Foundations of Constitutional Democracy* (Ann Arbor: University of Michigan Press, 1962), p. 186.

[27] If we were to drop the assumption that actors are strictly self-interested utility-maximizers, regimes could be important in another way: they would help to develop norms that are internalized by actors as part of their own utility functions. This is important in real-world political-economic systems, as works by Schumpeter, Polanyi, and Hirsch on the moral underpinnings of a market system indicate. It is likely to be important in many international systems as well. But it is outside the scope of the analytical approach taken in this article—which is designed to illuminate some issues, but not to provide a comprehensive account of international regime change. See Joseph Schumpeter, *Capitalism, Socialism, and Democracy* (New York: Harper & Row, 1942), especially Part II, "Can Capitalism Survive?"; Karl Polanyi, *The Great Transformation: The Political and Economic Origins of Our Time* (1944; Boston: Beacon Press, 1957); and Fred Hirsch, *Social Limits to Growth* (Cambridge: Harvard University Press, 1976).

[28] Information costs could be considered under the category of transaction costs, but they are so important that I categorize them separately in order to give them special attention.

ture does not prevent the development of bits and pieces of law.[29] Regimes are much more important in providing established negotiating frameworks (reducing transactions costs) and in helping to coordinate actor expectations (improving the quality and quantity of information available to states). An explanation of these two functions of international regimes, with the help of microeconomic analysis, will lead to hypotheses about how the demand for international regimes should be expected to vary with changes in the nature of the international system (in the case of transactions costs) and about effects of characteristics of the international regime itself (in the case of information).

International regimes and transactions costs

Neither international agreements nor international regimes are created spontaneously. Political entrepreneurs must exist who see a potential profit in organizing collaboration. For entrepreneurship to develop, not only must there be a potential social gain to be derived from the formation of an international arrangement, but the entrepreneur (usually, in world politics, a government) must expect to be able to gain more itself from the regime than it invests in organizing the activity. Thus organizational costs to the entrepreneur must be lower than the net discounted value of the benefits that the entrepreneur expects to capture for itself.[30] As a result, international cooperation that would have a positive social payoff may not be initiated unless a potential entrepreneur would profit sufficiently. This leads us back into questions of supply and the theory of hegemonic stability, since such a situation is most likely to exist where no potential entrepreneur is large relative to the whole set of potential beneficiaries, and where "free riders" cannot be prevented from benefiting from cooperation without paying proportionately.

Our attention here, however, is on the demand side: we focus on the efficiency of constructing international regimes, as opposed simply to making *ad hoc* agreements. We only expect regimes to develop where the costs of making *ad hoc* agreements on particular substantive matters are higher than the sum of the costs of making such agreements within a regime framework and the costs of establishing that framework.

With respect to transactions costs, where do we expect these conditions to be met? To answer this question, it is useful to introduce the concept of *issue density* to refer to the number and importance of issues arising within a given policy space. The denser the policy space, the more highly interdependent are the different issues, and therefore the agreements made about

[29] For a discussion of "the varieties of international law," see Louis Henkin, *How Nations Behave: Law and Foreign Policy*, 2d ed. (New York: Columbia University Press for the Council on Foreign Relations, 1979), pp. 13–22.

[30] Davis and North, *Institutional Change and American Economic Growth*, especially pp. 51–57.

them. Where issue density is low, *ad hoc* agreements are quite likely to be adequate: different agreements will not impinge on one another significantly, and there will be few economies of scale associated with establishing international regimes (each of which would encompass only one or a few agreements). Where issue density is high, on the other hand, one substantive objective may well impinge on another and regimes will achieve economies of scale, for instance in establishing negotiating procedures that are applicable to a variety of potential agreements within similar substantive areas of activity.[31]

Furthermore, in dense policy spaces, complex linkages will develop among substantive issues. Reducing industrial tariffs without damaging one's own economy may depend on agricultural tariff reductions from others; obtaining passage through straits for one's own warships may depend on wider decisions taken about territorial waters; the sale of food to one country may be more or less advantageous depending on other food-supply contracts being made at the same time. As linkages such as these develop, the organizational costs involved in reconciling distinct objectives will rise and demands for overall frameworks of rules, norms, principles, and procedures to cover certain clusters of issues—that is, for international regimes—will increase.

International regimes therefore seem often to facilitate side-payments among actors within issue-areas covered by comprehensive regimes, since they bring together negotiators to consider a whole complex of issues. Side-payments in general are difficult in world politics and raise serious issues of transaction costs: in the absence of a price system for the exchange of favors, these institutional imperfections will hinder cooperation.[32] International regimes may provide a partial corrective.[33] The well-known literature on "spillover" in bargaining, relating to the European Community and other integration schemes, can also be interpreted as being concerned with side-

[31] The concept of issue density bears some relationship to Herbert Simon's notion of "decomposability," in *The Sciences of the Artificial* (Cambridge: MIT Press, 1969). In both cases, problems that can be conceived of as separate are closely linked to one another functionally, so that it is difficult to affect one without also affecting others. Issue density is difficult to operationalize, since the universe (the "issue-area" or "policy space") whose area forms the denominator of the term cannot easily be specified precisely. But given a certain definition of the issue-area, it is possible to trace the increasing density of issues within it over time. See, for example, Robert O. Keohane and Joseph S. Nye, *Power and Interdependence: World Politics in Transition* (Boston: Little, Brown, 1977), chap. 4.

[32] On questions of linkage, see Arthur A. Stein, "The Politics of Linkage," *World Politics* 33,1 (October 1980): 62–81; Kenneth Oye, "The Domain of Choice," in Oye et al., *Eagle Entangled: U.S. Foreign Policy in a Complex World* (New York: Longmans, 1979), pp. 3–33; and Robert D. Tollison and Thomas D. Willett, "An Economic Theory of Mutually Advantageous Issue Linkage in International Negotiations," *International Organization* 33,4 (Autumn 1979).

[33] GATT negotiations and deliberations on the international monetary system have been characterized by extensive bargaining over side-payments and complex politics of issue-linkage. For a discussion see Nicholas Hutton, "The Salience of Linkage in International Economic Negotiations," *Journal of Common Market Studies* 13, 1–2 (1975): 136–60.

payments. In this literature, expectations that an integration arrangement can be expanded to new issue-areas permit the broadening of potential side-payments, thus facilitating agreement.[34]

It should be noted, however, that regimes may make it more difficult to link issues that are clustered separately. Governments tend to organize themselves consistently with how issues are treated internationally, as well as vice versa; issues considered by different regimes are often dealt with by different bureaucracies at home. Linkages and side-payments become difficult under these conditions, since they always involve losses as well as gains. Organizational subunits that would lose, on issues that matter to them, from a proposed side-payment are unlikely to support it on the basis of another agency's claim that it is in the national interest. Insofar as the dividing lines between international regimes place related issues in different jurisdictions, they may well make side-payments and linkages between these issues less feasible.

The crucial point about regimes to be derived from this discussion of transactions costs can be stated succinctly: the optimal size of a regime will increase if there are increasing rather than diminishing returns to regime-scale (reflecting the high costs of making separate agreements in a dense policy space), or if the marginal costs of organization decline as regime size grows. The point about increasing returns suggests an analogy with the theory of imperfect competition among firms. As Samuelson notes, "increasing returns is the prime case of deviations from perfect competition."[35] In world politics, increasing returns to scale lead to more extensive international regimes.

The research hypothesis to be derived from this analysis is that increased issue density will lead to greater demand for international regimes and to more extensive regimes. Since greater issue density is likely to be a feature of situations of high interdependence, this forges a link between interdependence and international regimes: increases in the former can be expected to lead to increases in demand for the latter.[36]

The demand for principles and norms

The definition of international regimes provided in the introduction to this volume stipulates that regimes must embody principles ("beliefs of fact, causation, and rectitude") and norms ("standards of behavior defined in

[34] Ernst B. Haas, *The Uniting of Europe* (Stanford: Stanford University Press, 1958).

[35] Paul A. Samuelson, "The Monopolistic Competition Revolution," in R. E. Kuenne, ed., *Monopolistic Competition Theory* (New York: Wiley, 1967), p. 117.

[36] Increases in issue density could make it more difficult to supply regimes; the costs of providing regimes could grow, for instance, as a result of multiple linkages across issues. The 1970s Law of the Sea negotiations illustrate this problem. As a result, it will not necessarily be the case that increases in interdependence will lead to increases in the number, extensiveness, and strength of international regimes.

terms of rights and obligations'') as well as rules and decision-making procedures.[37] Otherwise, international regimes would be difficult to distinguish from any regular patterns of action in world politics that create common expectations about behavior: even hostile patterns of interactions could be seen as embodying regimes if the observer could infer implied rules and decision-making procedures from behavior.

Arguments about definitions are often tedious. What is important is not whether this definition is "correct," but that principles and norms are integral parts of many, if not all, of the arrangements that we regard as international regimes. This raises the question of why, in interactions (such as those of world politics) characterized by conflict arising from self-interest, norms and principles should play any role at all.

The constraint-choice framework used in this article is not the best approach for describing how principles and norms of state behavior evolve over time. The legal and sociological approaches discussed in this volume by Young are better adapted to the task of historical interpretation of norm-development. Nevertheless, a brief analysis of the function of principles and norms in an uncertain environment will suggest why they are important for fulfilling the overall function of international regimes: to facilitate mutually advantageous international agreements.

An important principle that is shared by most, if not all, international regimes is what Jervis calls "reciprocation": the belief that if one helps others or fails to hurt them, even at some opportunity cost to oneself, they will reciprocate when the tables are turned. In the Concert of Europe, this became a norm specific to the regime, a standard of behavior providing that statesmen should avoid maximizing their interests in the short term for the sake of expected long-run gains.[38]

This norm requires action that does not reflect specific calculations of self-interest: the actor making a short-run sacrifice does not know that future benefits will flow from comparable restraint by others, and can hardly be regarded as making precise calculations of expected utility. What Jervis calls the norm of reciprocation—or (to avoid confusion with the concept of reciprocity in international law) what I shall call a norm of generalized commitment—precisely forbids specific interest calculations. It rests on the premise that a veil of ignorance stands between us and the future, but that we should nevertheless assume that regime-supporting behavior will be beneficial to us even though we have no convincing evidence to that effect.

At first glance, it may seem puzzling that governments ever subscribe either to the principle of generalized commitment (that regime-supporting behavior will yield better results than self-help in the long run) or to the corresponding norm in a given regime (that they should act in a regime-supporting fashion). But if we think about international regimes as devices to

[37] Stephen D. Krasner, article in this volume, p. 2.
[38] Robert Jervis, article in this volume, p. 180.

facilitate mutually beneficial agreements the puzzle can be readily resolved. Without such a norm, each agreement would have to provide net gains for every essential actor, or side-payments would have to be arranged so that the net gains of the package were positive for all. Yet as we have seen, side-payments are difficult to organize. Thus, packages of agreements will usually be difficult if not impossible to construct, particularly when time is short, as in a balance of payments crisis or a sudden military threat. The principle of generalized commitment, however, removes the necessity for specific clusters of agreements, each of which is mutually beneficial. Within the context of a regime, help can be extended by those in a position to do so, on the assumption that such regime-supporting behavior will be reciprocated in the future. States may demand that others follow the norm of generalized commitment even if they are thereby required to supply it themselves, because the result will facilitate agreements that in the long run can be expected to be beneficial for all concerned.

The demand for specific information

The problems of organization costs discussed earlier arise even in situations where actors have entirely consistent interests (pure coordination games with stable equilibria). In such situations, however, severe information problems are not embedded in the structure of relationships, since actors have incentives to reveal information and their own preferences fully to one another. In these games the problem is to reach some agreement point; but it may not matter much which of several is chosen.[39] Conventions are important and ingenuity may be required, but serious systemic impediments to the acquisition and exchange of information are lacking.[40]

The norm of generalized commitment can be seen as a device for coping with the conflictual implications of uncertainty by imposing favorable assumptions about others' future behavior. The norm of generalized commitment requires that one accept the veil of ignorance but act *as if* one will benefit from others' behavior in the future if one behaves now in a regime-supporting way. Thus it creates a coordination game by ruling out potentially antagonistic calculations.

Yet in many situations in world politics, specific and calculable conflicts of interest exist among the actors. In such situations, they all have an interest in agreement (the situation is not zero-sum), but they prefer different types of agreement or different patterns of behavior (e.g., one may prefer to

[39] The classic discussion is in Thomas C. Schelling, *The Strategy of Conflict* (1960; Cambridge: Harvard University Press, 1980), chap. 4, "Toward a Theory of Interdependent Decision." See also Schelling, *Micromotives and Macrobehavior* (New York: Norton, 1978).

[40] For an interesting discussion of regimes in these terms, see the paper in this volume by Oran R. Young. On conventions, see David K. Lewis, *Convention: A Philosophical Study* (Cambridge: Cambridge University Press, 1969).

cheat without the other being allowed to do so). As Stein points out in this volume, these situations are characterized typically by unstable equilibria. Without enforcement, actors have incentives to deviate from the agreement point:

> [Each] actor requires assurances that the other will also eschew its rational choice [and will not cheat, and] such collaboration requires a degree of formalization. The regime must specify what constitutes cooperation and what constitutes cheating.[41]

In such situations of strategic interaction, as in oligopolistic competition and world politics, systemic constraint-choice theory yields no determinate results or stable equilibria. Indeed, discussions of "blackmailing" or games such as "prisoners' dilemma" indicate that, under certain conditions, suboptimal equilibria are quite likely to appear. Game theory, as Simon has commented, only illustrates the severity of the problem; it does not solve it.[42]

Under these circumstances, power factors are important. They are particularly relevant to the supply of international regimes: regimes involving enforcement can only be supplied if there is authority backed by coercive resources. As we have seen, regimes themselves do not possess such resources. For the means necessary to uphold sanctions, one has to look to the states belonging to the regime.

Yet even under conditions of strategic interaction and unstable equilibria, regimes may be of value to actors by providing information. Since high-quality information reduces uncertainty, we can expect that there will be a demand for international regimes that provide such information.

Firms that consider relying on the behavior of other firms within a context of strategic interaction—for instance, in oligopolistic competition—face similar information problems. They also do not understand reality fully. Students of market failure have pointed out that risk-averse firms will make fewer and less far-reaching agreements than they would under conditions of perfect information. Indeed, they will eschew agreements that would produce mutual benefits. Three specific problems facing firms in such a context are also serious for governments in world politics and give rise to demands for international regimes to ameliorate them.

(1) Asymmetric information. Some actors may have more information about a situation than others. Expecting that the resulting bargains would be unfair, "outsiders" may therefore be reluctant to make agreements with "insiders."[43] One aspect of this in the microeconomic literature is "quality uncertainty," in which a buyer is uncertain about the real value of goods

---

[41] Arthur A. Stein, article in this volume, p. 128.

[42] Herbert Simon, "From Substantive to Procedural Rationality," in Latsis, ed., *Method and Appraisal in Economics;* Spiro J. Latsis, "A Research Programme in Economics," in ibid.; and on blackmailing, Oye, "The Domain of Choice."

[43] Oliver E. Williamson, *Markets and Hierarchies: Analysis and Anti-Trust Implications* (New York: Free Press, 1975).

being offered. In such a situation (typified by the market for used cars when sellers are seen as unscrupulous), no exchange may take place despite the fact that with perfect information, there would be extensive trading.[44]

(2) Moral hazard. Agreements may alter incentives in such a way as to encourage less cooperative behavior. Insurance companies face this problem of "moral hazard." Property insurance, for instance, may make people less careful with their property and therefore increase the risk of loss.[45]

(3) Deception and irresponsibility. Some actors may be dishonest, and enter into agreements that they have no intention of fulfilling. Others may be "irresponsible," and make commitments that they are unlikely to be able to carry out. Governments or firms may enter into agreements that they intend to keep, assuming that the environment will continue to be benign; if adversity sets in, they may be unable to keep their commitments. Banks regularly face this problem, leading them to devise standards of "creditworthiness." Large governments trying to gain adherents to international agreements may face similar difficulties: countries that are enthusiastic about cooperation are likely to be those that expect to gain more, proportionately, than they contribute. This is analogous to problems of self-selection in the market-failure literature. For instance, if rates are not properly adjusted, people with high risks of heart attack will seek life insurance more avidly than those with longer life expectancies; people who purchased "lemons" will tend to sell them earlier on the used-car market than people with "creampuffs."[46] In international politics, self-selection means that for certain types of activities—for example, sharing research and development information—weak states (with much to gain but little to give) may have greater incentives to participate than strong ones. But without the strong states, the enterprise as a whole will fail. From the perspective of the outside observer, irresponsibility is an aspect of the problem of public goods and free-riding;[47] but from the standpoint of the actor trying to determine whether to rely on a potentially irresponsible partner, it is a problem of uncertainty and risk. Either way, information costs may prevent mutually beneficial agreement, and the presence of these costs will provide incentives to states to demand international regimes (either new regimes or the maintenance of existing ones) that will ameliorate problems of uncertainty and risk.

4. Information, openness, and communication in international regimes

International regimes, and the institutions and procedures that develop in conjunction with them, perform the function of reducing uncertainty and

---

[44] George A. Ackerlof, "The Market for 'Lemons': Qualitative Uncertainty and the Market Mechanism," *Quarterly Journal of Economics* 84,3 (August 1970).

[45] Arrow, *Essays in the Theory of Risk-Bearing.*

[46] Ackerlof, "The Market for 'Lemons' "; Arrow, *Essays in the Theory of Risk-Bearing.*

[47] For an analysis along these lines, see Davis B. Bobrow and Robert T. Kudrle, "Energy R&D: In Tepid Pursuit of Collective Goods," *International Organization* 33,2 (Spring 1979): 149–76.

risk by linking discrete issues to one another and by improving the quantity and quality of information available to participants. Linking issues is important as a way to deal with potential deception. Deception is less profitable in a continuing "game," involving many issues, in which the cheater's behavior is closely monitored by others and in which those actors retaliate for deception with actions in other areas, than in a "single-shot" game. The larger the number of issues in a regime, or linked to it, and the less important each issue is in proportion to the whole, the less serious is the problem of deception likely to be.

Another means of reducing problems of uncertainty is to increase the quantity and quality of communication, thus alleviating the information problems that create risk and uncertainty in the first place. Williamson argues on the basis of the organization theory literature that communication tends to increase adherence to group goals: "Although the precise statement of the relation varies slightly, the general proposition that intragroup communication promotes shared goals appears to be a well-established empirical finding."[48] Yet not all communication is of equal value: after all, communication may lead to asymmetrical or unfair bargaining outcomes, deception, or agreements entered into irresponsibly. And in world politics, governmental officials and diplomats are carefully trained to communicate precisely what they wish to convey rather than fully to reveal their preferences and evaluations. Effective communication is not measured well by the amount of talking that used-car salespersons do to customers or that governmental officials do to one another in negotiating international regimes. Strange has commented, perhaps with some exaggeration:

> One of the paradoxes of international economic relations in the 1970s has been that the soft words exchanged in trade organizations have coexisted with hard deeds perpetuated by national governments. The reversion to economic nationalism has been accompanied by constant reiterations of continued commitment to international cooperation and consultation. The international bureaucracies of Geneva, New York, Paris and Brussels have been kept busier than ever exchanging papers and proposals and patiently concocting endless draft documents to which, it is hoped, even deeply divided states might subscribe. But the reality has increasingly been one of unilateral action, even where policy is supposedly subject to multilateral agreement.[49]

The information that is required in entering into an international regime is not merely information about other governments' resources and formal negotiating positions, but rather knowledge of their internal evaluations of the situation, their intentions, the intensity of their preferences, and their

---

[48] Oliver E. Williamson, "A Dynamic Theory of Interfirm Behavior," *Quarterly Journal of Economics* 79 (1965), p. 584.

[49] Susan Strange, "The Management of Surplus Capacity: or How Does Theory Stand Up to Protectionism 1970s Style?", *International Organization* 33,3 (Summer 1979): 303–334.

willingness to adhere to an agreement even in adverse future circumstances. As Hirsch points out with respect to the "Bagehot Problem" in banking, lenders need to know the moral as well as the financial character of borrowers.[50] Likewise, governments contemplating international cooperation need to *know* their partners, not merely know *about* them.

This line of argument suggests that governments that successfully maintain "closure," protecting the autonomy of their decision-making processes from outside penetration, will have more difficulty participating in international regimes than more open, apparently disorganized governments. "Closed" governments will be viewed with more skepticism by potential partners, who will anticipate more serious problems of bounded rationality in relations with these closed governments than toward their more open counterparts. Similarly, among given governments, politicization of issues and increases in the power of political appointees are likely to reduce the quality of information and will therefore tend to reduce cooperation. Thus as an issue gains salience in domestic politics, other governments will begin to anticipate more problems of bounded rationality and will therefore perceive greater risks in cooperation. International cooperation may therefore decline quite apart from the real intentions or objectives of the policy makers involved.

This conclusion is important: international policy coordination and the development of international regimes depend not merely on interests and power, or on the negotiating skills of diplomats, but also on expectations and information, which themselves are in part functions of the political structures of governments and their openness to one another. Intergovernmental relationships that are characterized by ongoing communication among working-level officials, "unauthorized" as well as authorized, are inherently more conducive to information-exchange and agreements than are traditional relationships between internally coherent bureaucracies that effectively control their communications with the external world.[51]

Focusing on information and risk can help us to understand the performance of international regimes over time, and therefore to comprehend better the sources of demands for such regimes. Again, reference to theories of oligopoly, as in Williamson's work, is helpful. Williamson assumes that cooperation—which he refers to as "adherence to group goals"—will be a function both of communication and of the past performance of the oligopoly; reciprocally, communication levels will be a function of cooperation. In addition, performance will be affected by the condition of the environment. Using these assumptions, Williamson derives a model that has two points of equilibrium, one at high levels and one at low levels of cooperation.

---

[50] Fred Hirsch, "The Bagehot Problem," *The Manchester School* 45,3 (1977): 241–57.

[51] Notice that here, through a functional logic, a systemic analysis has implications for the performance of different governmental structures at the level of the actor. The value of high-quality information in making agreements does not force governments to become more open, but it gives advantages to those that do.

His oligopolies are characterized by substantial inertia. Once a given equilibrium has been reached, substantial environmental changes are necessary to alter it:

> If the system is operating at a low level of adherence and communication (i.e., the competitive solution), a substantial improvement in the environment will be necessary before the system will shift to a high level of adherence and communication. *Indeed, the condition of the environment required to drive the system to the collusive solution is much higher than the level required to maintain it once it has achieved this position. Similarly, a much more unfavorable condition of the environment is required to move the system from a high to a low level equilibrium than is required to maintain it there.* [52]

It seems reasonable to suppose that Williamson's assumptions about relationships among communication, cooperation or adherence, and performance have considerable validity for international regimes as well as for cartels. If so, his emphasis on the role of information, for explaining persistent behavior (competitive or oligopolistic) by groups of firms, helps us to understand the lags between structural change and regime change that are so puzzling to students of international regimes. In our earlier work, Nye and I observed discrepancies between the predictions of structural models (such as what I later called the "theory of hegemonic stability") and actual patterns of change; in particular, changes in international regimes tend to lag behind changes in structure. [53] But our explanation for this phenomenon was essentially *ad hoc*: we simply posited the existence of inertia, assuming that "a set of networks, norms, and institutions, once established, will be difficult either to eradicate or drastically to rearrange." [54] Understanding the role of communication and information in the formation and maintenance of international regimes helps locate this observation in a theoretical context. The institutions and procedures that develop around international regimes acquire value as arrangements permitting communication, and therefore facilitating the exchange of information. As they prove themselves in this way, demand for them increases. Thus, even if the structure of a system becomes more fragmented—presumably increasing the costs of providing regime-related collective goods (as suggested by public goods theory)—increased demand for a particular, well-established, information-providing international regime may, at least for a time, outweigh the effects of increasing costs on supply.

These arguments about information suggest two novel interpretations of puzzling contemporary phenomena in world politics, as well as providing the

---

[52] Williamson, "A Dynamic Theory of Interfirm Behavior," p. 592, original italics.

[53] *Power and Interdependence*, especially pp. 54–58 and 146–53. Linda Cahn also found lags, particularly in the wheat regime; see "National Power and International Regimes."

[54] *Power and Interdependence*, p. 55.

basis for hypotheses that could guide research on fluctuations in the strength and extent of international regimes.

Understanding the value of governmental openness for making mutually beneficial agreements helps to account for the often-observed fact that effective international regimes—such as the GATT in its heyday, or the Bretton Woods international monetary regime[55]—are often associated with a great deal of informal contact and communication among officials. Governments no longer act within such regimes as unitary, self-contained actors. "Transgovernmental" networks of acquaintance and friendship develop, with the consequences that supposedly confidential internal documents of one government may be seen by officials of another; informal coalitions of like-minded officials develop to achieve common purposes; and critical discussions by professionals probe the assumptions and assertions of state policies.[56] These transgovernmental relationships increase opportunities for cooperation in world politics by providing policy makers with high-quality information about what their counterparts are likely to do. Insofar as they are valued by policy makers, they help to generate demand for international regimes.

The information-producing "technology" that becomes embedded in a particular international regime also helps us to understand why the erosion of American hegemony during the 1970s has not been accompanied by an immediate collapse of international regimes, as a theory based entirely on supply-side public goods analysis would have predicted. Since the level of institutionalization of postwar regimes was exceptionally high, with intricate and extensive networks of communication among working-level officials, we should expect the lag between the decline of American hegemony and the disruption of international regimes to be quite long and the "inertia" of the existing regimes relatively great.

The major hypothesis to be derived from this discussion of information is that demand for international regimes should be in part a function of the effectiveness of the regimes themselves in providing high-quality information to policy makers. The success of the institutions associated with a regime in providing such information will itself be a source of regime persistence.

Three inferences can be made from this hypothesis. First, regimes accompanied by highly regularized procedures and rules will provide more information to participants than less regularized regimes and will therefore, on

---

[55] On the GATT, see Gardner Patterson, *Discrimination in International Trade: The Policy Issues* (Princeton: Princeton University Press, 1966); on the international monetary regime, see Robert W. Russell, "Transgovernmental Interaction in the International Monetary System, 1960–1972," *International Organization* 27,4 (Autumn 1973) and Fred Hirsch, *Money International,* rev. ed. (Harmondsworth, England: Pelican Books, 1969), especially chap. 11, "Central Bankers International."

[56] Robert O. Keohane and Joseph S. Nye, "Transgovernmental Relations and International Organizations," *World Politics* 27,1 (October 1974): 39–62.

information grounds, be in greater demand. Thus, considerations of high-quality information will help to counteract the normal tendencies of states to create vague rules and poorly specified procedures as a way of preventing conflict or maintaining freedom of action where interests differ.

Second, regimes that develop norms internalized by participants—in particular, norms of honesty and straightforwardness—will be in greater demand and will be valued more than regimes that fail to develop such norms.

Third, regimes that are accompanied by open governmental arrangements and are characterized by extensive transgovernmental relations will be in greater demand and will be valued more than regimes whose relationships are limited to traditional state-to-state ties.[57]

Perhaps other nontrivial inferences can also be drawn from the basic hypothesis linking a regime's information-provision with actors' demands for it. In any event, this emphasis on information turns our attention back toward the regime, and the process of institutionalization that accompanies regime formation, and away from an exclusive concern with the power structure of world politics. The extent to which institutionalized cooperation has been developed will be an important determinant, along with power-structural conditions and issue density, of the extent and strength of international regimes.

From a future-oriented or policy perspective, this argument introduces the question of whether governments (particularly those of the advanced industrial countries) could compensate for the increasing fragmentation of power among them by building communication-facilitating institutions that are rich in information. The answer depends in part on whether hegemony is really a necessary condition for effective international cooperation or only a facilitative one. Kindleberger claims the former, but the evidence is inconclusive.[58] Analysis of the demand for international regimes, focusing on questions of information and transactions costs, suggests the possibility that international institutions could help to compensate for eroding hegemony. International regimes could not only reduce the organization costs and other transactions costs associated with international negotiations; they could also provide information that would make bargains easier to strike.

How effectively international regimes could compensate for the erosion of hegemony is unknown. Neither the development of a theory of international regimes nor the testing of hypotheses derived from such a theory is likely to resolve the question in definitive terms. But from a contemporary policy standpoint, both theory development and theory testing would at least

---

[57] These first three inferences focus only on the *demand* side. To understand the degree to which norms, for example, will develop, one needs also to look at supply considerations. Problems of organization, such as those discussed in the public goods literature and the theory of hegemonic stability, may prevent even strongly desired regimes from materializing.

[58] Kindleberger has asserted that "for the world economy to be stabilized, there has to be a stabilizer, one stabilizer." *The World in Depression*, p. 305.

help to define the dimensions of the problem and provide some guidance for thinking about the future consequences of present actions.

5. Coping with uncertainties: insurance regimes

Creating international regimes hardly disposes of risks or uncertainty. Indeed, participating in schemes for international cooperation entails risk for the cooperating state. If others fail to carry out their commitments, it may suffer. If (as part of an international growth scheme) it reflates its economy and others do not, it may run a larger-than-desired current-account deficit; if it liberalizes trade in particular sectors and its partners fail to reciprocate, import-competing industries may become less competitive without compensation being received elsewhere; if it curbs bribery by its multinational corporations without comparable action by others, its firms may lose markets abroad. In world politics, therefore, governments frequently find themselves comparing the risks they would run from lack of regulation of particular issue-areas (i.e., the absence of international regimes) with the risks of entering into such regimes. International regimes are designed to mitigate the effects on individual states of uncertainty deriving from rapid and often unpredictable changes in world politics. Yet they create another kind of uncertainty, uncertainty about whether other governments will keep their commitments.

In one sense, this is simply the old question of dependence: dependence on an international regime may expose one to risks, just as dependence on any given state may. Governments always need to compare the risks they run by being outside a regime with the risks they run by being within one. If the price of achieving short-term stability by constructing a regime is increasing one's dependence on the future decisions of others, that price may be too high.

Yet the question of coping with risk also suggests the possibility of different types of international regimes. Most international regimes are *control-oriented.* Through a set of more or less institutionalized arrangements, members maintain some degree of control over each other's behavior, thus decreasing harmful externalities arising from independent action as well as reducing uncertainty stemming from uncoordinated activity. A necessary condition for this type of regime is that the benefits of the regularity achieved thereby must exceed the organizational and autonomy costs of submitting to the rules, both for the membership as a whole and for each necessary member.

Control-oriented regimes typically seek to ensure two kinds of regularity, internal and environmental. Internal regularity refers to orderly patterns of behavior among members of the regime. The Bretton Woods international monetary regime and the GATT trade regime have focused, first of all, on members' obligations, assuming that, if members behaved according to the rules, the international monetary and trade systems would be orderly. Where all significant actors within an issue-area are members of the regime, this assumption is warranted and mutual-control regimes tend to be effective.

Yet there are probably few, if any, pure cases of mutual-control regimes. Typically, an international regime is established to regularize behavior not only among the members but also between them and outsiders. This is a side-benefit of stable international monetary regimes involving convertible currencies.[59] It was an explicit purpose of the nonproliferation regime of the 1970s, in particular the "suppliers' club," designed to keep nuclear material and knowledge from diffusing rapidly to potential nuclear powers. Military alliances can be viewed as an extreme case of attempts at environmental control, in which the crucial benefits of collaboration stem not from the direct results of cooperation but from their effects on the behavior of outsiders. Alliances seek to induce particular states of minds in nonmembers, to deter or to intimidate.

Observers of world politics have often assumed implicitly that all significant international regimes are control-oriented. The economic literature, however, suggests another approach to the problem of risk. Instead of expanding to control the market, firms or individuals may diversify to reduce risk or may attempt to purchase insurance against unlikely but costly contingencies. Portfolio diversification and insurance thus compensate for deficiencies in markets that lack these institutions. Insurance and diversification are appropriate strategies where actors cannot exercise control over their environment at reasonable cost, but where, in the absence of such strategies, economic activity would be suboptimal.[60]

In world politics, such strategies are appropriate under similar conditions. The group of states forming the insurance or diversification "pool" is only likely to resort to this course of action if it cannot control its environment effectively. Second, for insurance regimes to make sense, the risks insured against must be specific to individual members of the group. If the catastrophic events against which one wishes to insure are likely (should they occur at all) to affect all members simultaneously and with equal severity, risk sharing will make little sense.[61]

[59] Charles P. Kindleberger, "Systems of International Economic Organization," in David P. Calleo, ed., *Money and the Coming World Order* (New York: New York University Press for the Lehrman Institute, 1978); Ronald McKinnon, *Money in International Exchange: The Convertible Currency System* (New York: Oxford University Press, 1979).

[60] Arrow, *Essays in the Theory of Risk-Bearing,* pp. 134–43.

[61] In personal correspondence, Robert Jervis has suggested an interesting qualification to this argument. He writes: "If we look at relations that involve at least the potential for high conflict, then schemes that tie the fates of all the actors together may have utility even if the actors are concerned about catastrophic events which will affect them all. They can worry that if some states are not affected, the latter will be much stronger than the ones who have been injured. So it would make sense for them to work out a scheme which would insure that a disaster would not affect their relative positions, even though this would not mean that they would all not be worse off in absolute terms." The point is certainly well taken, although one may wonder whether such an agreement would in fact be implemented by the states that would make large relative gains in the absence of insurance payments.

International regimes designed to share risks are less common than those designed to control events, but three examples from the 1970s can be cited that contain elements of this sort of regime:

(1) The STABEX scheme of the Lomé Convention, concluded between the European Community and forty-six African, Caribbean, and Pacific states in 1975. "Under the STABEX scheme, any of the 46 ACP countries dependent for more than 7.5 percent (2.5 percent for the poorest members of the ACP) of their export earnings on one of a list of commodities, such as tea, cocoa, coffee, bananas, cotton, and iron ore, will be eligible for financial help if these earnings fall below a certain level."[62] STABEX, of course, is not a genuine mutual-insurance regime because the guarantee is made by one set of actors to another set.

(2) The emergency sharing arrangements of the International Energy Agency, which provide for the mandatory sharing of oil supplies in emergencies, under allocation rules devised and administered by the IEA.[63]

(3) The Financial Support Fund of the OECD, agreed on in April 1975 but never put into effect, which would have provided a "lender of last resort" at the international level, so that risks on loans to particular countries in difficulty would have been "shared among all members, in proportion to their quotas and subject to the limits of their quotas, however the loans are financed."[64]

Control-oriented and insurance strategies for coping with risk and uncertainty have different advantages and liabilities. Control-oriented approaches are more ambitious; when effective, they may eliminate adversity rather than simply spread risks around. After all, it is more satisfactory to prevent floods than merely to insure against them; likewise, it would be preferable for consumers to be able to forestall commodity embargoes rather than simply to share their meager supplies fairly if such an embargo should take place.

Yet the conditions for an effective control-oriented regime are more stringent than those for insurance arrangements. An effective control-oriented regime must be supported by a coalition that has effective power in the issue-area being regulated, and whose members have sufficient incentives to exercise such power.[65] Where these conditions are not met, insurance regimes may be "second-best" strategies, but they are better than no strategies at all. Under conditions of eroding hegemony, one can expect the increasing emergence of insurance regimes, in some cases as a result of the

[62] Isebill V. Gruhn, "The Lomé Convention: Inching toward Interdependence," *International Organization* 30,2 (Spring 1976), pp. 255–56.

[63] Robert O. Keohane, "The International Energy Agency: State Influence and Transgovernmental Politics," *International Organization* 32,4 (Autumn 1978): 929–52.

[64] OECD *Observer*, no. 74 (March–April 1975), pp. 9–13.

[65] The optimal condition under which such a coalition may emerge could be called the "paper tiger condition": a potential external threat to the coalition exists but is too weak to frighten or persuade coalition members to defect or to desist from effective action. OPEC has been viewed by western policy makers since 1973 as a real rather than paper tiger, although some observers keep insisting that there is less to the organization than meets the eye.

unwillingness of powerful states to adopt control-oriented strategies (as in the case of STABEX), in other cases as replacements for control-oriented regimes that have collapsed (as in the cases of the IEA emergency sharing arrangements and the OECD Financial Support Fund or "safety net"). Economic theories of risk and uncertainty suggest that as power conditions shift, so will strategies to manage risk, and therefore the nature of international regimes.

6. Conclusions

The argument of this paper can be summarized under six headings. First, international regimes can be interpreted, in part, as devices to facilitate the making of substantive agreements in world politics, particularly among states. Regimes facilitate agreements by providing rules, norms, principles, and procedures that help actors to overcome barriers to agreement identified by economic theories of market failure. That is, regimes make it easier for actors to realize their interests collectively.

Second, public goods problems affect the supply of international regimes, as the "theory of hegemonic stability" suggests. But they also give rise to demand for international regimes, which can ameliorate problems of transactions costs and information imperfections that hinder effective decentralized responses to problems of providing public goods.

Third, two major research hypotheses are suggested by the demand-side analysis of this article.

(a) Increased issue density will lead to increased demand for international regimes.
(b) The demand for international regimes will be in part a function of the effectiveness of the regimes themselves in developing norms of generalized commitment and in providing high-quality information to policymakers.

Fourth, our analysis helps us to interpret certain otherwise puzzling phenomena, since our constraint-choice approach allows us to see how demands for such behavior would be generated. We can better understand transgovernmental relations, as well as the lags observed between structural change and regime change in general, and between the decline of the United States' hegemony and regime disruption in particular.

Fifth, in the light of our analysis, several assertions of structural theories appear problematic. In particular, it is less clear that hegemony is a necessary condition for stable international regimes under all circumstances. Past patterns of institutionalized cooperation may be able to compensate, to some extent, for increasing fragmentation of power.

Sixth, distinguishing between conventional control-oriented international regimes, on the one hand, and insurance regimes, on the other, may help us to understand emerging adaptations of advanced industrialized countries to a global situation in which their capacity for control over events is much less than it was during the postwar quarter-century.

None of these observations implies an underlying harmony of interests in world politics. Regimes can be used to pursue particularistic and parochial interests, as well as more widely shared objectives. They do not necessarily increase overall levels of welfare. Even when they do, conflicts among units will continue. States will attempt to force the burdens of adapting to change onto one another. Nevertheless, as long as the situations involved are not constant-sum, actors will have incentives to coordinate their behavior, implicitly or explicitly, in order to achieve greater collective benefits without reducing the utility of any unit. When such incentives exist, and when sufficient interdependence exists that *ad hoc* agreements are insufficient, opportunities will arise for the development of international regimes. If international regimes did not exist, they would surely have to be invented.

Security regimes

Robert Jervis

Can the concept of regime be fruitfully applied to issues of national security? As Viotti and Murray have pointed out, it is anomalous to have a concept that explains phenomena in some parts of the field but lacks utility in others.[1] At the very least, we should be able to understand the differences among various aspects of international politics that account for this discrepancy.

By a security regime I mean, in parallel with the other discussions in this volume, those principles, rules, and norms that permit nations to be restrained in their behavior in the belief that others will reciprocate. This concept implies not only norms and expectations that facilitate cooperation, but a form of cooperation that is more than the following of short-run self-interest. To comply with a robber's demand to surrender money is not to participate in a regime even if the interaction occurs repeatedly and all participants share the same expectations. Similarly, the fact that neither superpower attacks the other is a form of cooperation, but not a regime. The links between the states' restraint and their immediate self-interest are too direct and unproblematic to invoke the concept.

I would like to thank the participants at the meeting to discuss this volume, held in Palm Springs, California, in February 1981, for their comments on an earlier draft.

[1] Paul Viotti and Douglas Murray, "International Security Regimes: On the Applicability of a Concept," paper delivered at the August 1980 meeting of the American Political Science Association. For other attempts to apply the concept of security regimes, see Randy Rydell and Athanassios Platias, "International Security Regimes: The Case of a Balkan Nuclear Weapon Free Zone," paper delivered at the March 1981 meeting of the International Studies Association, and Dan Caldwell, "Inter-State Security Regimes: The Soviet-American Case," paper presented at the September 1981 meeting of the American Political Science Association.

International Organization 36, 2, Spring 1982
0020-8183/82/020357-22 $1.50

Why security is different

If patterns of international relations can be explained by the distribution of military and economic power among the states, then the concept of regime will not be useful. But if the connections between outcomes and national power are indirect and mediated, there is more room for choice, creativity, and institutions to restrain and regulate behavior, and to produce a regime. Although the research in both security and nonsecurity areas on these points is far from definitive, it appears that the connections are less direct in nonsecurity areas.

Prisoners' dilemma dynamics in security and nonsecurity areas

This is not to say that the politics of security is completely different from the politics of trade, sea-bed exploitation, or international communication. In all these areas a frequent problem is that unrestrained competition can harm all the actors. The obvious model is the prisoners' dilemma, in which the rational pursuit of self-interest leads to a solution that is not Pareto-optimal. When this model applies, states will benefit by setting up rules and institutions to control the competition among them.

Both the incentives for establishing such regimes and the obstacles to so doing are especially great in the security arena because of the "security dilemma." As Herz and Butterfield have pointed out,[2] many of the policies that are designed to increase a state's security automatically and inadvertently decrease the security of others. Security regimes are thus both especially valuable and especially difficult to achieve—valuable, because individualistic actions are not only costly but dangerous; difficult to achieve, because the fear that the other is violating or will violate the common understanding is a potent incentive for each state to strike out on its own even if it would prefer the regime to prosper.

These dynamics, of course, can be present in nonsecurity areas. Tariff wars can be seen as analogous to arms races, beggar-thy-neighbor trade policies look like attempts to gain short-run security, the despoiling of the global commons resembles a war that both sides hoped to avoid. But four differences remain. First, security issues often involve greater competitiveness than do those involving economics.[3] If one state cheats or is a free rider

---

[2] John Herz, "Idealist Internationalism and the Security Dilemma," *World Politics* 2 (January 1950): 157–80; Herbert Butterfield, *History and Human Relations* (London: Collins, 1950), pp. 19–20. For elaboration see Robert Jervis, *Perception and Misperception in International Politics* (Princeton: Princeton University Press, 1976), pp. 62–83, and Jervis, "Cooperation under the Security Dilemma," *World Politics* 30 (January 1978): 167–214.

[3] This line of argument suggests that the crucial variable is the degree of conflict of interest, not the content of the issue. Some security issues engender less conflict than some economic issues, and an examination of such cases might prove fruitful. When we study security, however, our attention is usually drawn to areas of high conflict.

in an economic regime, it may be better off, and the others worse off, than would have been the case had it cooperated. But the very fact that one state is better off does not make the others worse off. When the security dilemma operates, however, the conflicts between states' security can be inherent. Because military power meets its test in clashes between states, it is relative, not absolute.[4] The second difference is linked to this problem: offensive and defensive security motives often lead to the same behavior. Whether wanting to ensure that the status quo is not altered to its detriment or wanting to change it in its favor, the state may seek arms that threaten others. The problem is often less severe in nonsecurity questions, where the state can usually prepare for the danger that others will seek to take advantage of its restraint without automatically impinging on others. Here protection, like the purchasing of insurance, is costly, but it does not necessarily harm or menace others, as it usually does in the security area.

A third difference in the operation of prisoners' dilemma dynamics in the security and nonsecurity areas is that the stakes are higher in the former. Not only is security the most highly valued goal because it is a prerequisite for so many things, but the security area is unforgiving. Small errors can have big consequences, and so the costs of living up to the rules of a regime while others are not are great. Temporarily falling behind others can produce permanent harm. *information / outcomes*

Fourth, detecting what others are doing and measuring one's own security are difficult. Tariff increases, monetary manipulations, and illegal fishing activities can sometimes be disguised, but they are usually more transparent than are military laboratories. Similarly, while the effects of actions in nonsecurity areas are not entirely clear, they are usually clearer than analogous military activities. No one knows exactly what will happen to the stock of fish under various agreements, or knows the consequences of cheating. The relationship between tariffs and the health of countries' economies is also uncertain. But uncertainty is greater in the security area. In many cases the state does not know in advance who its allies and enemies will be. Even if it does know this, it can rarely predict with confidence the outcome of war. The surprising course of the Iran-Iraq war is just the latest case in which observers and at least some participants made strikingly incorrect assessments. Of course, not all wars have surprising outcomes. But enough do to make statesmen realize that what looks an adequate guarantee of their security may not prove to be so if it is put to the test, thus increasing the pressures on statesmen to be less restrained in the pursuit of additional protection.

The primacy of security, its competitive nature, the unforgiving nature of the arena, and the uncertainty of how much security the state needs and has, all compound the prisoners' dilemma and make it sharper than the problems that arise in most other areas. Furthermore, decision makers usu-

---

[4] Nuclear weapons have changed this.

ally react by relying on unilateral and competitive modes of behavior rather than by seeking cooperative solutions. Both courses of action are dangerous; each of these strategies has worked in some cases and failed in others. But statesmen usually think they should "play it safe" by building positions of greater strength; rarely do they consider seriously the possibility that such a policy will increase the danger of war instead of lessening it. The result is that security regimes, with their call for mutual restraint and limitations on unilateral actions, rarely seem attractive to decision makers.

One interesting question is raised but not answered by this analysis. To what extent do we need to examine decision-making variables to account for the difficulties of regime formation? The security dilemma creates the main impediment to effective security regimes, but what is the impact of the beliefs outlined above? Can they be altered without a change in the structure of the international system? Do decision makers misunderstand international politics—perhaps because of the teachings of Realist scholars—and so follow less than optimal policies? Some decision makers seem oblivious to the fact that increasing their arms can have undesired and unintended consequences. If such leaders are in power, the chances for developing a security regime will be decreased, not by the structure of the situation but by the ignorance of the actors. Furthermore, even sophisticated statesmen tend to underestimate the degree to which their actions harm others, and so they both take actions they might not have taken had they understood the consequences and also misinterpret others' reactions as evidence of unprovoked hostility.[5] These errors reinforce reliance on unilateral actions rather than cooperative arrangements and could, in principle, be altered by a better understanding of international politics. But given the range of statesmen who have opted for relatively unrestrained policies, one must wonder whether in practice it would be possible to alter their beliefs in a way that would produce greater cooperation.

Conditions for forming a security regime

What conditions are most propitious for the formation and maintenance of a security regime? First, the great powers must want to establish it—that is, they must prefer a more regulated environment to one in which all states behave individualistically. This means that all must be reasonably satisfied with the status quo and whatever alterations can be gained without resort to the use or threat of unlimited war, as compared with the risks and costs of less restrained competition. One could not have formed a security regime with Hitler's Germany, a state that sought objectives incompatible with those of the other important states and that would not have been willing to

[5] Jervis, *Perception and Misperception,* pp. 69–72, 88–89, 95–96, 352–55.

sacrifice those objectives for a guarantee that the others would leave it secure in the borders it had attained.

Second, the actors must also believe that others share the value they place on mutual security and cooperation—if a state believes it is confronted by a Hitler, it will not seek a regime. In principle this is simple enough; in practice, determining whether others are willing to forgo the chance of forcible expansion is rarely easy. Indeed, decision makers probably overestimate more than underestimate others' aggressiveness.[6] This second condition is not trivial: in several cases security regimes may have been ruled out not by the fact that a major power was an aggressor but by the fact that others incorrectly perceived it as an aggressor.

Third, and even more troublesome, even if all major actors would settle for the status quo, security regimes cannot form when one or more actors believe that security is best provided for by expansion. Statesmen may deny that moderate and cooperative policies can protect them. This belief may be rooted in a general analysis of politics that is common in energetic powers: "That which stops growing begins to rot," in the words of a minister of Catherine the Great.[7] Similarly, in 1812 an American politician argued: "I should not wish to extend the boundary of the United States by war if Great Britain would leave us the quiet enjoyment of independence; but considering her deadly and implacable enmity, and her continued hostilities, I shall never die contented until I see her expulsion from North America."[8] This perspective may be a reflection of something close to paranoia, perhaps brought about by long experience with strong enemies. In the interwar period France did not believe that Germany could be conciliated. The belief was less the product of an analysis of specific German governments and leaders than it was the result of the historically-induced fear that Germany was ineradicably hostile and that French security therefore depended on having clear military superiority.

Thus France could only be secure if Germany were insecure. The security dilemma here operated not as the unintended consequence of policy but rather as its object.

Again, the question of the extent to which decision makers' beliefs are independent and autonomous causes of the problem can be raised but not answered. In some cases beliefs are rooted in an accurate appreciation of the effects of military technology, as we will discuss shortly. But in other cases the roots are less easy to trace and may be susceptible to alteration without basic changes in the domestic or external environment.

The fourth condition for the formation of a regime is a truism today: war

---

[6] Ibid., pp. 73–75, 218–20, 340–41, 350–51.

[7] Quoted in Adam Ulam, *Expansion and Coexistence* (New York: Praeger, 1968), p. 5.

[8] Robert Remini, *Andrew Jackson and the Course of American Empire 1767–1821* (New York: Harper & Row, 1977), p. 166. See ibid., p. 389, for a similar justification for pushing the Spanish out of Florida.

WAR
not
an option

and the individualistic pursuit of security must be seen as costly. If states believe that war is a good in itself (e.g., because it weeds out the less fit individuals and nations), they will not form a regime to prevent it, although it would still be possible for them to seek one that would impose certain limits on fighting. If states think that building arms is a positive good (e.g., because it supports domestic industries), there will be no incentives to cooperate to keep arms spending down. If states think that arms procurement and security policies can be designed carefully enough so that there is little chance of unnecessary wars, then a major reason to avoid individualistic policies disappears. If hostility in the security area is not believed to spill over into hostility in economic issues, or if decreased cooperation in that sphere is not viewed as a cost, then an important incentive for cooperation will be absent. While it is rare for all these conditions to be met, in some eras the major ones are, thus reducing the pressures to form security regimes.

The possibility for regimes is also influenced by variables that directly bear on the security dilemma. As I have discussed elsewhere,[9] it is not always true that individualistic measures which increase one state's security decrease that of others. It depends on whether offensive measures differ from defensive ones and on the relative potency of offensive and defensive policies. If defensive measures are both distinct and potent, individualistic security policies will be relatively cheap, safe, and effective and there will be less need for regimes. When the opposite is the case—when offensive and defensive weapons and policies are indistinguishable and when attacking is more effective than defending—status quo powers have a great need for a regime, but forming one will be especially difficult because of the strong fear of being taken advantage of. The most propitious conditions for regime formation, then, are the cases in which offensive and defensive weapons and policies are distinguishable but the former are cheaper and more effective than the latter, or in which they cannot be told apart but it is easier to defend than attack. In either of these worlds the costs or risks of individualistic security policies are great enough to provide status quo powers with incentives to seek security through cooperative means, but the dangers of being taken by surprise by an aggressor are not so great as to discourage the states from placing reliance on joint measures.

The Concert of Europe as a security regime

An analysis of the best example of a security regime—the Concert of Europe that prevailed from 1815 to 1823 and, in attenuated form, until the Crimean War—should provide a complementary perspective to this theoretical discussion. In this era the great powers behaved in ways that sharply diverged from normal "power politics." They did not seek to

---

[9] Jervis, "Cooperation under the Security Dilemma."

maximize their individual power positions, they did not always take advantage of others' temporary weaknesses and vulnerabilities, they made more concessions than they needed to, and they did not prepare for war or quickly threaten to use force when others were recalcitrant. In short, they moderated their demands and behavior as they took each other's interests into account in setting their own policies. As one scholar notes, "nineteenth-century diplomatic history furnishes several examples of states forgoing gains which they could probably have gotten. . . . Few similar instances can be cited in the eighteenth or the twentieth centuries."[10]

Of course the Concert did not banish conflict. But it did regulate it. War was not thought to be likely and states rarely threatened to use this ultimate sanction. The actors were aware of the shift; a Prussian scholar and diplomat described the system, albeit in exaggerated terms, as follows:

> The five great powers, closely united among themselves and with the others, for a system of solidarity, by which one stands for all and all for one; in which power appears only as protection for everybody's possessions and rights; in which the maintenance of the whole and the parts within legal bounds, for the sake of the peace of the world, has become the only aim of political activity; in which one deals openly, deliberates over everything collectively and acts jointly.[11]

Castlereagh, perhaps the most articulate exponent of the Concert, employed his circular dispatch of 1816 to instruct his representatives abroad to work for a new diplomacy in both substance and procedure:

> You will invite [the sovereigns to which you are accredited] in the spirit which has so happily carried the Alliance through so many difficulties, to adopt an open and direct mode of intercourse in the conduct of business, and to repress on all sides, as much as possible, the spirit of local intrigue in which diplomatic policy is so falsely considered to consist, and which so frequently creates the very evil which it is intended to avert. . . .
>
> His [Royal Highness'] only desire is, and must be, to employ all His influence to preserve the peace, which in concert with His Allies he has won.
>
> To this great end you may declare that all His Royal Highness' efforts will be directed; to this purpose all minor considerations will be made subordinate; wherever His voice can be heard, it will be raised to discourage the pursuit of secondary and separate interests at the hazard of that general peace and goodwill, which, after so long a period of suf-

[10] Richard Elrod, "The Concert of Europe," *World Politics* 28 (January 1976), p. 168. Elrod attributes this to the damage that lack of restraint would have done to the states' "moral position." I think this is too narrow a focus. Paul Schroeder argues that while most statesmen of this period, even Czar Alexander, were willing to eschew policies of narrow national interest in favor of maintaining the Concert, Metternich generally manipulated the latter to serve the former. See his *Metternich's Diplomacy at Its Zenith* (New York: Greenwood Press, 1968), pp. 238, 251–52, 256, 265.

[11] Quoted in Carsten Holbrad, *The Concert of Europe* (London: Longman, 1970), p. 37.

fering it should be the object of all the Sovereigns of Europe to preserve to their people.

To effectuate this, it ought to be the study of every public servant abroad, more especially of the Greater States, whose example must have the most extensive influence, to discourage that spirit of petty intrigue and perpetual propagation of alarm, upon slight evidence and antient jealousies, which too frequently disgrace the diplomatic profession, and often render the residence of Foreign ministers the means of disturbing rather than preserving harmony between their respective Sovereigns.[12]

When Canning, Castlereagh's successor as Foreign Secretary, broke with the Concert in 1822 over intervention to suppress the Spanish revolution, he noted the contrast: "Things are getting back to a wholesome state again. Every nation for itself and God for us all!"[13]

This is not to deny that each state in the Concert placed primary value on its own security and welfare and did not care much about others' well-being as an end in itself. What is crucial, however, is that "self-interest" was broader than usual, in that statesmen believed that they would be more secure if the other major powers were also more secure. Others were seen as partners in a joint endeavor as well as rivals, and unless there were strong reasons to act to the contrary their important interests were to be respected. Indeed it was not only the individual states that were treated with some respect, but the collectivity of Europe as a whole. There was a sense that the fates of the major powers were linked, that Europe would thrive or suffer together.

The self-interest followed was also longer-run than usual. Much of the restraint adopted was dependent on each statesman's belief that if he moderated his demands or forebore to take advantage of others' temporary weakness, they would reciprocate. For this system to work, each state had to believe that its current sacrifices would in fact yield a long-run return, that others would not renege on their implicit commitments when they found themselves in tempting positions. This implies the belief that conflicts of interest could be limited and contained by shared interests, including the interest in maintaining the regime.

Because cooperation was much greater than usual, diplomatic procedures involved more consultation and openness and less duplicity than usual.[14] The power of these norms is shown in the reaction to their being broken, as Metternich broke them when he ended a stalemate at the Confer-

---

[12] Quoted in Charles Webster, *The Foreign Policy of Castlereagh, 1812–1822* (London: G. Bell, 1963), 2: 510–11.

[13] Quoted in Walter Alison Phillips, *The Confederation of Europe* (New York: Fertig, 1966), p. 183.

[14] For a good discussion of the mutual reinforcing relationships between cooperative processes and cooperation as a substantive outcome, see Morton Deutsch, "Fifty Years of Conflict," in *Retrospections on Social Psychology,* ed. by Leon Festinger (New York: Oxford University Press, 1980).

ence of Troppau by presenting Britain and France with a *fait accompli* in the form of an agreement with Russia and Prussia on intervention in Italy. Metternich's was a standard tactic of normal diplomacy—Britain and France had been blocking his policy and he simply moved to line up support for his position behind their backs. But in the context of the Concert, such deception was not expected. When the British ambassador discovered what was happening "his amazement and indignation were therefore immense," and Castlereagh shared his anger.[15]

The Concert was supported by the shared stake that the major powers had in avoiding war. They had just lived through an enormously destructive series of wars and were acutely aware of the costs of armed conflict, which not only destroyed men and wealth but also undermined the social fabric. Conservatives feared that wars would lead to revolution; liberals associated war and preparations for it with autocracy. All feared that high levels of conflict would destroy their security, not enhance it.

Controlling internal instability was another important shared value— although the states differed on how much instability was tolerable and how it should be kept within bounds. The previous era had taught statesmen that revolutions spread abroad and caused wars, two evils that endangered them all. Even Castlereagh argued that an important object of British diplomacy was to make other statesmen "feel that the existing concert is their only perfect security against the revolutionary embers more or less existing in every State of Europe; and that their true wisdom is to keep down the petty contentions of ordinary times, and to stand together in support of the established principles of social order."[16]

Each state, then, had a stake in seeing that none underwent a revolution; as a result the destabilizing of other governments, an unpleasant but not unusual tool of statecraft, was ruled out and states were not likely to desert the Concert when they feared that embarking on an isolated course of action might lead to unrest.[17] Furthermore, to the extent that revolutions were believed to be caused by foreign setbacks, statesmen had reason to see that no major power suffered too serious a diplomatic defeat. To bring one country low could bring them all down. Only in a world in which moderate policies were pursued could statesmen enjoy the fruits of their triumphs.

The regime as a cause of national behavior

Although these conditions and common interests explain why the Concert was formed, what is more important here is that the regime influenced the behavior of the states in ways that made its continuation possible even

---

[15] Webster, *Foreign Policy of Castlereagh*, 2: 294 and 301.
[16] Quoted in Holbrad, *Concert of Europe*, p. 119.
[17] Schroeder, *Metternich's Diplomacy at Its Zenith*, p. 174.

Concept of
Europe
regime

after the initial conditions had become attenuated. The regime was more than a reflection of causally prior variables; it was a force in its own right, exerting influence through four paths. First, the expectation that the Concert could continue to function helped maintain it through the operation of familiar self-fulfilling dynamics. If an actor thinks the regime will disintegrate—or thinks others hold this view—he will be more likely to defect from the cooperative coalition himself. On the other hand, if he believes the regime is likely to last, he will be more willing to "invest" in it (in the sense of accepting larger short-run risks and sacrifices) in the expectation of reaping larger gains in the future. Important here is the expectation that peace could be maintained. For if war were seen as likely, states would have to concentrate on building up their short-run power to prepare for the coming conflict.

Thus part of the explanation for the Concert's success was that its health was generally seen as quite good. There were no "runs on the bank," as each state stopped being restrained in the belief that the system would not last long enough for moderation to be reciprocated. We can, to some extent, trace this belief back to the actors' common interest in continuing cooperation. Although no states were completely satisfied with the Concert, all felt that it was better than the likely alternative arrangements and so placed a high priority on maintaining it. To equate outcomes with intentions usually violates a basic tenet of systems theory; to talk of the goal of systems maintenance often commits the teleological fallacy. But these actors consciously sought the continuation of the Concert and, partly for this reason, it survived many stresses and shocks. Valuing the Concert did not ensure its survival; however, it was important that the participants expected it to survive.

A second way in which the regime perpetuated itself was the greater opposition it was expected to foster against attempts forcibly to change the status quo. In contrast to eras that lacked security regimes, opposition would not be limited to those states immediately affected. Even if the short-run self-interest of a third party called for neutrality or even aid to the aggressor, there were strong incentives for the third party to uphold the Concert. Since others would be joining in the coalition, the third party would not be isolated or forced to carry an excessive share of the burden and, by strengthening the Concert, it would increase the chance that others would come to its aid if it were to become the target of predation. Under the Concert, then, states were discouraged from expansionist moves that would have looked attractive if others were expected to follow individualistic security policies.

The Concert pattern also strengthened itself through the operation of the norm of reciprocity. This norm did more than codify cooperative relationships; it allowed states to cooperate in circumstances under which they would not have been able to do so had the norm been absent. This in turn increased the value of the Concert to the states. Because reciprocity was expected to guide actors' behavior, statesmen did not fear that if they made concessions in one case, others would see them as weak and expect further concessions. This is a major obstacle to cooperation, for statesmen are often less concerned with the substance of the issue they are facing than they are with the inferences about them that others will draw from their behavior. If it is believed that states moderate their demands only when they are forced to, then not only are there no positive incentives to be reasonable in the form of expectations of reciprocal moderation but the costs of not pushing as hard as one can extend beyond the loss of position on the issue at stake and encompass the danger that others will see the state as unable to stand up for its interests. Losses then will tend to snowball. Fearing this, states will be reluctant to make concessions, even if doing so would yield to the other benefits that are significantly greater than the short-run costs the state would pay. Under the Concert, by contrast, reasonableness was expected and so making concessions did not lead others to think the state was weak and would retreat in the future. This drastically lowered the risks and costs of cooperative behavior.

This stress on reciprocation may seem to some to be misplaced. After all, even when there is no security regime states often exchange concessions to arrive at an agreement. But in these cases what the states do is make a bargain—the deal is relatively explicit, it is struck only because each side believes it has driven as hard a bargain as it can, the exchange is between identifiable partners, and it is carried out quite swiftly. Under the Concert calculation was less fine and states would support others without knowing exactly when or even from whom their repayment would come. It was expected that others would not take advantage of their temporary problems just as they would not take advantage of others. This pattern greatly widens the opportunities for cooperation. In normally competitive international politics, trades cannot occur unless they are even, direct, and immediate. The possibilities in normal times are much more limited than they were under the Concert, when states would assist others in the expectation that any one of a number of other states would support them over the next several years.

Finally, the regime became an independent factor by developing at least a limited degree of institutionalization. In an age of limited communication and travel, the opportunities for direct conversations among national leaders were rare. When they occurred, they were seized on not only to conduct important business but also to develop an understanding of the personalities and interests driving other states. Formal machinery was lacking, no supranational secretariat was formed, and all decisions and their implementation remained in the hands of national leaders. But coordination was facilitated, and information and expectations were fairly quickly and effectively shared. Furthermore, the representatives to the conferences worked together long and frequently enough to develop "a common outlook distinct from their governments."[18] Thus the Prussian Foreign Minister noted that the confer-

[18] Charles Webster, *The Art and Practice of Diplomacy* (New York: Barnes and Noble, 1962), p. 67.

ence which established the new state of Belgium "had grown into a sort of European power of itself, the plenipotentiaries who composed it deliberating and acting without instructions and frequently in opposition to the views of their governments."[19]

Demise of the regime

The Concert, of course, did not last forever. By 1823 it had begun to decay, although an unusual degree of concern for others' important interests remained for another quarter-century. I have neither the space nor the expertise for a full discussion of the demise of the regime, but several causes can at least be noted.

The memories of the ravages of the Napoleonic Wars faded, and with them the main incentives to avoid confrontations. Similarly, the fear of domestic unrest, its links to war, and its contagion also diminished. Although the revolutions of 1848 revived these concerns, they also cut old ties and brought unsocialized leaders to power. Conflicts among the great powers, never far beneath the surface even during the high points of the Concert, came increasingly to the fore. Controlling revolutions, a shared interest, produced conflict because two powers (Britain and France) had much more tolerance for domestic liberty than did the others (Russia, Austria, and Prussia). Furthermore, the former suspected that the latter were using the excuse of suppressing dangerous revolutions as a cover for expanding their own influence. It was thus felt that the Concert was being used to serve narrow and competitive national interests.

It was not only Britain and France that felt aggrieved. Each state was more sharply aware of the sacrifices it had made than it was of others' restraint. The gains forgone were painfully clear; the losses that others might have inflicted were ambiguous and hypothetical. Each state thought it was paying more than others and more than it was receiving. This was especially troubling since the possibility that it would have to rely on its own resources to protect itself in the future loomed larger as frictions increased. (This difference in countries' perspectives weakens most regimes, and an obvious question, parallel to the one we have raised previously, is whether it can be ameliorated by greater understanding of the situation.)

Finally, by controlling the risk of war and yet not becoming institutionalized and developing supranational loyalties, the Concert may have contained the seeds of its own destruction. Since world politics did not seem so dangerous, pushing harder seemed sensible to individual states. The structure appeared stable enough to permit states to impose a greater strain on it. But seeking individualistic gains raised doubts in others' minds as to whether moderation and reciprocation would last, thus giving all states greater incentives to take a narrower and shorter-run perspective.

[19] Quoted in ibid.

The balance of power

The balance of power is clearly different from the Concert. Is it also a regime? The answer turns on whether the restraints on state action it involves are norms internalized by the actors or arise from the blocking actions of others and the anticipation of such counteractions.[20] Some of the debate between Waltz and Kaplan can be seen in these terms. For Waltz each actor in the balance of power may try to maximize his power; each fails because of the similar efforts of others. The system restrains the actors rather than the actors being self-restrained. Moderation is an unintended result of the clash of narrow self-interests.[21] Although patterns recur, actors share expectations, and aberrant behavior is curbed by the international system, states do not hold back in the belief that others will do likewise and they do not seek to maintain the system when doing so would be contrary to their immediate interests. It is hard to see how the concept of regime helps explain the behavior that results.

Kaplan's view is different. The kind of balance of power that Waltz describes, Kaplan sees as unstable. As one of his students has put it, "A system containing merely growth-seeking actors will obviously be unstable; there would be no provision for balance or restraint."[22] Similarly, Kaplan points out that in his computer model, "if actors do not take system stability requirements into account, a 'balance of power' system will be stable only if some extrasystemic factor. . . . prevents a roll-up of the system."[23] For Kaplan, if the system is to be moderate, the actors must also be moderate (a remarkably antisystemic view). Thus two of Kaplan's six rules call for self-restraint: "Stop fighting rather than eliminate an essential national actor," and "Permit defeated or constrained essential national actors to re-enter the system as acceptable role partners. . . ."[24] Of most interest here is that for Kaplan these propositions not only describe how states behave, they are rules that consciously guide statesmen's actions: states exercise self-restraint. In one interpretation—and we will discuss another in the next

[20] For a different approach to this question, see Richard Ashley, "Balance of Power as a Political-Economic Regime," paper presented at the August 1980 meeting of the American Political Science Association.

[21] Kenneth Waltz, *Theory of International Politics* (Reading, Mass.: Addison-Wesley, 1979). This corresponds to Claude's "automatic" version of the balance of power (Inis L. Claude Jr., *Power and International Relations* [New York: Random House, 1962], pp. 43–47). Kaplan also expresses this view in one paragraph of his "Balance of Power, Bipolarity, and Other Models of International Systems" (*American Political Science Review* 51 [September 1957], p. 690), but this paragraph is not repeated in *System and Process in International Politics* (New York: Wiley, 1957) and, as we shall discuss below, is inconsistent with his analysis there.

[22] Donald Reinken, "Computer Explorations of the 'Balance of Power,'" in *New Approaches to International Relations*, ed. by Morton Kaplan (New York: St. Martin's, 1968), p. 469. This corresponds to Claude's "manually operated" balance of power (Claude, *Power and International Relations*, pp. 48–50).

[23] Morton Kaplan, *Towards Professionalism in International Theory* (New York: Free Press, 1979), p. 136.

[24] Kaplan, *System and Process*, p. 23.

paragraph—they do so because they seek to preserve the system.[25] This would certainly be a regime, indeed one not so different from the Concert.

If restraint follows from the ability to predict that immoderate behavior will call up counterbalancing actions by others, does the resulting pattern form a regime? A state may forgo taking advantage of another not because it expects reciprocation, but because it fears that unless it exercises self-restraint others will see it as a menace, increase their arms, and coalesce against it. This is a possible interpretation of Kaplan's rules. He says that states obey them because, by accepting the restraints that they embody, each state is better off than it would be if it broke them: "Under the governing assumptions, states would follow these rules in order to optimize their own security. Thus there is motivation to observe the rules. . . . There is in this system a general, although not necessarily implacable, identity between short-term and long-term interests."[26]

This formulation of the rules is a happy and therefore an odd one. It posits no conflict between the narrow self-interest of each state and the maintenance of the regime.[27] The rules are self-enforcing. This is a logical possibility and can be illustrated by the incentives to follow traffic laws when traffic is heavy. Here it is to one's advantage to keep to the right and to stop when the light turns red. To do otherwise is to get hit; cheating simply does not pay irrespective of whether others cheat.[28] The matter is different when traffic is lighter and cars have more room to maneuver. Then, running a red light or cutting in front of another car does not bring automatic sanctions. Aggressive drivers want others to obey the law while they cut corners. The generally orderly and predictable pattern that facilitates driving is maintained, but they are able to get through a bit faster than the others.

In this interpretation of Kaplan's rules, the states are operating in an environment that resembles heavy traffic.[29] They do not have incentives to

---

[25] Kaplan, *Towards Professionalism*, pp. 39, 73, 86. Since states rarely fight wars to the finish and eliminate defeated actors, Kaplan's arguments seem plausible. But this is to confuse result with intent. The desire to maximize power can limit wars and save fallen states. As long as each state views all the others as potential rivals, each will have to be concerned about the power of its current allies. And as long as each views current enemies as potentially acceptable alliance partners in a future war, each will have incentives to court and safeguard the power of states on the other side. To destroy another state may be to deprive oneself of an ally in the future; to carve up a defeated power is to risk adding more strength to potential adversaries than to oneself. Of the Ottoman Empire in the early nineteenth century, a Russian diplomat said: "If the cake could not be saved, it must be fairly divided" (quoted in Edward Gulick, *Europe's Classical Balance of Power* [New York: Norton, 1967], p. 72). This has it backwards: it was because the cake could not be divided evenly that it had to be preserved. Also see Kaplan, *System and Process*, p. 28.

[26] Kaplan, *Towards Professionalism*, p. 139; see also pp. 67, 135.

[27] This is partly true because Kaplan excludes some of the main problems when he says that his system assumes that none of the major powers seeks to dominate the system (ibid., p. 136).

[28] Thomas Schelling, *Micromotives and Macrobehavior* (New York: Norton, 1978), pp. 120–21.

[29] This would seem to contradict Kaplan's argument that the international system is subsystem dominant—i.e., that the environment is not so compelling as to foreclose meaningful national choice (Kaplan, *System and Process*, p. 17).

take advantage of others' restraint nor do they have to be unrestrained out of the fear that if they are not, others will try to take advantage of them. The dynamics of the security dilemma, the prisoners' dilemma, and public goods, which are so troublesome in situations lacking central authority, are absent. This makes for an unusual systems theory, since these dynamics are a major element in most conceptions of a system. Such a formulation blots out the possibility that all states could be best off if all were moderate, but that each would suffer badly if any of the others were not. It also denies the more likely situation in which each actor prefers taking advantage of others' restraint to mutual cooperation, but perfers mutual cooperation to unrestrained competition. A regime of mutual cooperation is then better for all than no regime, but each actor is constantly tempted to cheat, both to make competitive gains and to protect against others doing so. This is the central problem for most regimes, and indeed for the development of many forms of cooperation. Kaplan has disposed of it in a formula of words, but it is hard to see what arrangement of interests and perceptions could so easily dissolve the difficulties in actual world politics.

Security in the postwar era

It is not clear whether a security regime regulates superpower relations today. Patterns of behavior exist (although it is hard to trace them), but the question is whether they are far enough removed from immediate, narrow self-interest to involve a regime. I think the answer is no, but the subject is so complex that I lack confidence in this judgment. Because of the difficulties involved, I will examine the subject from several directions.

Rules of conduct

Does the fact that a form of cooperation must have been present to have kept the peace between America and Russia for thirty-five years mean that there is a security regime? I think the answer is no because narrow and quite short-run self-interest can account for most of the restraints. To launch a war is to invite one's own destruction; to challenge the other's vital interests is to risk a confrontation one is likely to lose (as the Russians did in Cuba), not to mention the chance of blundering into a war. That each side has more or less respected the other's sphere of influence does not mean that each side has developed the stake in the other's security or the expectation of reciprocity that was found in the Concert. It merely means that each is able to protect what it values most and that each can see that menacing the other's most important concerns entails costs that far outrun the likely gains.

At the May 1972 summit conference in Moscow, the U.S. and Soviet Union agreed to a set of rules that look like the foundations for a regime. The text sounded all the right notes: "mutually advantageous development of their relations," "exercise restraint," "reciprocity, mutual accommodation and mutual benefit," forgoing "efforts to obtain unilateral advantage at the expense of the other."[30] But it seems likely that from the beginning each side had a different conception of the sort of cooperation that might arise. In any case, the use of regime-like language did not yield a regime.

A greater semblance of agreement on rules is manifest in the way superpowers have fought limited wars. In Korea, the U.S. forces did not attack China, while the Communists not only left Japan as a sanctuary but also spared the port of Pusan, which the U.S. used around the clock for its build-up in September 1950. The Communists also used mines only once, when they blocked the port of Wonsan as they evacuated it. It took the U.S. a month to clear the harbor, an unpleasant reminder of what the Communists could do (perhaps designed to help the Americans avoid the common trap of believing that only they were restraining their conduct). In Vietnam, the U.S. refrained from ground attacks against the North, carefully controlled its bombing of the North, respected the Chinese sanctuary, and only toward the end of the war cut maritime supply lines. Whether there was much the North Vietnamese could have done but chose not to do is hard to determine, but the Russians exercised restraint in limiting the weapons they provided to the North.

The implicit rules established in one conflict seem to have some influence as precedent in the next. In Vietnam, the U.S. bombed the North but for most of the war did not interdict supplies coming into that country. Furthermore, both sides treated this situation as expected and almost "natural." This seems to have affected at least the western perceptions of the guerilla war in Afghanistan. The West seems to have understood that the sanctuaries in Pakistan would be respected as long as the military aid being funneled through that country was sharply limited. But if this restraint were loosened, so probably would be that on attacking the bases in Pakistan.

These sorts of arrangements do not constitute a regime. First, most of them are too directly linked to immediate self-interest. Just as neither side launches a war because of fear of retaliation, so most of the outlines if not the details of restraints in a limited war derive from the ability of each state to punish the other if it steps too far out of bounds, and from each's ability to see that the other's restraint depends on its own moderation.

Second, the precedents are neither unambiguous nor binding; they do not specify what aid, activities, and sanctuaries are permitted. China was a sanctuary in the Korean War; why was North Vietnam not a sanctuary during the war in the South? Indeed, one does not have to accept the argument that the North had a legitimate right to aid the Viet Cong because North and South were part of one country to say that the North's participation was less of a violation of norms than was the entry of China into the Korean war. Yet the sanctions levied against her were greater than those inflicted on China.

[30] *Historic Documents, 1972* (Washington, D.C.: Congressional Quarterly, 1973), pp. 442–48.

The direct role of interests and power is apparent. North Vietnam was a small country, fully engaged in the South. There was little it could do in response to American bombing; there was little it was willing to refrain from doing in order to induce the U.S. not to bomb. China, on the other hand, was more powerful and had more options, requiring the U.S. to be more restrained.

A third reason these limits do not constitute a regime is related to the two previous points. States change or break the rules as their power and interests change. Some attention is paid to the way in which these actions break or set precedents, but these concerns rarely dominate when short-run incentives are strong. Thus, after a decade of respecting the Soviet right to supply North Vietnam by sea, the U.S. finally mined Northern harbors in the spring of 1972. This was doubly striking—it both altered a quite well-established rule, and set what might be seen as a dangerous precedent, for it is the U.S., not the Soviet Union, that relies more heavily on keeping the shipping lanes open. But what was most important was defeating the North Vietnamese offensive, even at the cost of potential problems later; and it is far from clear that this cost would be significant. For the Russians ever to block U.S. shipping would be to run very high risks. The precedent set by the American action would matter only if others believed that because the U.S. had interfered with Russian shipping in Vietnam (and, earlier, in the Cuban missile crisis), it would be more likely to permit others to interfere with its ships. This is improbable; the American response—and others' predictions of it—would be largely determined by the degree to which the situation differentially involved the superpowers' important interests. Double standards may be morally uncomfortable, but they are hardly unusual in international politics.

Different conceptions of security

As we noted earlier, a necessary condition for the formation of a security regime is that major actors prefer the status quo—with the potential for modification by uncoerced political changes—to the world of possible gains and possible losses that they expect to flow from the individualistic pursuit of security policies.[31] It is far from clear that this condition is now met. Do the Russians value the chance of expansionism so much that they would be unwilling to forgo it in order to gain greater peace, stability, and reduced defense budgets? Even if they mainly want security, do they believe it can be provided by cooperation with capitalist powers? As Kennan remarked, the U.S. feels menaced by what the Soviet does; the Soviets feel menaced by

---

[31] It is not enough that both sides want to prevent all-out war. Because this outcome can be avoided by the cooperation of only one side, this common interest opens the door to unilateral exploitation as well as to mutual cooperation.

what that U.S. is.[32] Can any country that is unable to live with independent trade unions in Poland live with another superpower with a different political and economic system? If the Russians feel secure only to the extent that the U.S. is weak and insecure, the prospects for a security regime are dim. Similar questions can be posed about the United States. Is the U.S. willing to continue to permit changes in the Third World that erode the unprecedented dominance it achieved in the 1950s and 1960s? Do revolutionary changes make it so insecure that it feels it must respond in a way that is likely to create conflict with the Soviets? If it is menaced by a weak Communist state within its sphere of influence, can it accept the Soviet Union as a superpower with legitimate worldwide interests?

Even if both sides' conceptions of their security interests are compatible in principle, military technology and military doctrine may present formidable impediments to the formation of a regime. As mentioned earlier, the security dilemma is compounded when offensive and defensive weapons are indistinguishable and offense is more efficacious. The dilemma is decreased, and even disappears, when the reverse is true. Leaving aside as only a theoretical but not a real possibility a world in which antiballistic missile systems protect cities, American declaratory policy holds that mutual security results from both sides' having second-strike capability. Mutual Assured Destruction (MAD is the telling acronym) escapes from the security dilemma as each side gains security not from its ability to protect itself, but from its ability to retaliate and so to deter the other from launching an attack. If both sides followed this doctrine neither would need to expand its nuclear arsenal beyond the point where it could absorb the other's strike and still destroy the other's cities; neither would need to react if the other were to purchase excessive forces. A security regime in the realm of strategic weapons would be easy to obtain, but might not be necessary. Restraint would be easy because the states gain nothing by larger stockpiles, but for this very reason a regime would not be necessary—mutual restraint will result even if the superpowers do not take account of each other's security requirements, look to the long run, or develop rules and expectations of restraint. It would therefore be possible for states to escape from the security dilemma without developing the sorts of cooperative understandings that help ameliorate political conflicts across a broad range of issues. But even if competitive policies were pursued in many areas, and indeed were made safer by the stability of the strategic balance,[33] the achievement of a high degree of mutual security from attack would be no mean feat.

There are, however, two problems with applying this argument to contemporary world politics. First, American procurement and targeting poli-

---

[32] George Kennan, *Russia and the West Under Lenin and Stalin* (New York: Mentor, 1962), p. 181.

[33] This is what Glenn Snyder calls the "stability-instability paradox." Snyder, "The Balance of Power and the Balance of Terror," in *The Balance of Power*, ed. by Paul Seabury (San Francisco: Chandler, 1965).

cies have never followed the strictures of Mutual Assured Destruction. Instead the U.S. has not consistently shunned postures that provided at least some capabilities for defense. Similarly, American weapons have always been aimed at a wide range of Soviet military targets as well as at Soviet cities.[34] President Carter's Presidential Directive 59 of July 1980, which took the position that the U.S. would not target the Soviet population *per se*, was not a change of policy. As early as January 1950 the Joint Chiefs of Staff were arguing that the U.S. did not seek "to destroy large cities *per se*," but "only to attack such targets as are necessary in war in order to impose the national objections of the United States upon the enemy."[35] The second problem is more familiar—Russian declaratory policy as well as its military posture seem to reject the logic of MAD. Instead it appears that the Soviets hold more traditional military views, which deny the conflict between deterrence and defense and argue that both are reached through the same posture (being able to do as well as possible in a war). They thus see mutual security as a myth and thereby present us with the military counterpart to the problem discussed above, that a state may believe that its security requires making others insecure. If the Soviets believe that in order to deter American expansionism or cope with an American attack they need the capability to come as close as possible to military victory, then, even if they do not think that their security requires infringing on U.S. vital interests, forming a security regime will be extremely difficult.

This raises two issues. First is the familiar question of the scope for the independent role of beliefs. Can cooperation be increased by persuading the Russians to alter their military doctrine? The U.S. tried in the 1960s. Epitomizing these efforts was Secretary of Defense McNamara's attempt at Glassboro to explain to Prime Minister Kosygin the destabilizing nature of ballistic missile defenses. Similarly, much of the American energy at the start of the SALT negotiations went not into bargaining but into trying to show the Russians that certain outcomes should be seen as the solution to common problems, which would aid both sides. That these efforts failed does not prove that the task is beyond reach, but at this point the burden of proof rests with those who are optimistic. Successful persuasion depends not only on the validity of the logic of the U.S. position but also on how deeply rooted the Russians' views are, and whether the American posture can be seen as a cover for competitive policy. At this writing, the Russians seem closer to persuading the Americans to adopt their views. If they do, both

---

[34] David Rosenberg, "American Atomic Strategy and the Hydrogen Bomb Decision," *Journal of American History* 66 (June 1979): 62–87; Aaron Friedberg, "A History of the U.S. Strategic 'Doctrine'—1945 to 1960," *Journal of Strategic Studies* 3 (December 1980): 37–71; Gregg Herken, *The Winning Weapon* (New York: Knopf, 1980); Desmond Ball, "The Role of Strategic Concepts and Doctrine in U.S. Strategic Nuclear Force Development," in *National Security and International Stability*, ed. by Michael Intriligator and Roman Kolkowicz (forthcoming).

[35] Quoted in Herken, *The Winning Weapon*, p. 317.

sides would have the same doctrine, but this cognitive agreement would not pave the way for coordinated policies.

The second issue is whether a security regime is possible if the super-powers hold contrasting military doctrines. The rules of any regime formed under such circumstances could not be symmetrical, and an element of un-usual complexity would be introduced. But this would not automatically rule out the possibility of a degree of harmonization of policies aimed at increas-ing mutual security. The specific content of Soviet doctrine may have this effect, however, since it argues that security is inherently competitive, being produced by pulling as far ahead of the adversary as possible. Of course this modifier hints at a possible solution. The costs of arms, coupled with the competition from the U.S., could lead the Soviets to settle for arrangements that, although far from optimal in their eyes, still are more attractive than unrestrained individualistic policies. Another possibility would be for each side to follow quite different paths. The U.S. would not match Soviet arms increases, but would only maintain its second-strike capability. There would be no formal agreements codifying this, but common expectations would still be possible. The states would have different outlooks and policies, but at least they would understand these differences. This argument, however, is currently rejected by American opinion on the grounds that it would permit the Soviets to infringe on important western interests.

Different perspectives

Even if both sides were to adopt MAD, the theoretical possibility for mutual security could be defeated by the tendency for adversaries to see the strategic balance and international events very differently. American, and presumably Soviet, leaders make their calculations of the nuclear balance very conservatively. That is, they assume that their own systems will work badly and that the other's will work well. It is highly likely that each side's calculation of its own fate in the event of war is more pessimistic than that found in the other's estimate. Each side may fear that it is "behind" the other or even open to a successful first strike when the balance is actually even, thus making it extremely hard to find force levels that are mutually satisfactory.

Furthermore, neither side fully understands this difference in perspec-tive. To each, the other's alarm at its arms procurement seems hypocritical if not a cover for aggressive designs. Each not only underestimates the degree to which its programs disturb the other, but rarely devotes much attention to this danger. For example, U.S. declaratory policy respects Soviet second-strike capability, but one wonders if the U.S. analyzed whether a conserva-tive Russian planner might not see the MX, with its ten accurate warheads, as a threat to Soviet retaliatory capability. Similarly, for several years U.S. officials have argued that stability would be increased if the Russians put a higher proportion of their strategic forces into submarine-launched missiles, but it is not clear that they made due allowance for how the Russians would interpret this argument in light of the U.S.'s increasingly effective antisubmarine warfare capability.

The problem is magnified because both sides view the strategic balance within the context of world events, a context they also see from different perspectives. Each usually magnifies dangers, concentrates on the gains made by the other side, and overlooks its own threatening behavior. Thus as most American statesmen look back on the past few years, they see increasing Soviet assertiveness and confidence—for example, a buildup of strategic forces, the modernization of the armies in East Europe, the use of Cuban troops in Angola and Ethiopia, the consolidation of Soviet power in Vietnam, the sponsorship of the invasion of Cambodia, and their take-over of Afghanistan. But to the Russians things may look different. It would not be surprising if they were less optimistic than U.S. leaders think they are, paying more attention to defeats and threats than to what may be transient victories. To them, what may loom large are American strategic programs (the MX, the cruise missile, and the "stealth" technology for a new generation of bombers); the long-range tactical nuclear modernization program for NATO, which will significantly increase western capability for destroying targets in western Russia; the setting aside of the SALT II treaty; and increasing western ties with China.[36]

These measures probably take on a particularly suspicious hue when combined with what the Russians must see as the American habit of suddenly denouncing the Soviet Union for unacceptably altering established patterns when it is American actions that contravene the implicit understandings which have helped bring predictability to the world scene. Three examples probably stand out in the Soviet mind. First, the U.S. discovered the Soviet "combat brigade" in Cuba and threatened to overturn SALT II unless it was disbanded. But these troops had been there for a long time and were not doing anything new. Second, the U.S. did not protest when a coup installed a Communist government in Afghanistan in April 1978, but raised a furious storm when Soviet troops were needed to finish the job off eighteen months later. It was the former move that changed the status quo, although it was not very different in kind from many American actions. The latter move merely consolidated the earlier gain and should hardly have been expected to provide the occasion for cries of outrage, attempts to humiliate Russia, and the final blow to SALT II. Finally, the U.S. tried to deter the Soviet Union from invading Poland, thus upsetting the well-established understanding that East Europe was within the Russian sphere. It is hard to think of anything that could have shown so clearly that the U.S. was not concerned about the growth of Soviet power but instead was seeking to take

[36] For a good discussion, see Richards Heuer Jr., "Analyzing the Soviet Invasion of Afghanistan," *Studies in Comparative Communism* 13 (Winter 1980): 347–55.

advantage of Soviet difficulties to undermine its security. In Russian eyes, the U.S. stance probably undercut the credibility of its grounds for objecting to the invasion of Afghanistan—that it was a unilateral change in the status quo showing that Russia had no interest in equitable cooperation and mutual security—since the U.S. had strongly objected to the Soviet attempt to maintain the status quo in East Europe.

Conclusion

The demand for a security regime is decreased by the apparent stability of the strategic balance. The dangers of Russian expansion and nuclear war are contained by the current posture in such a way that drastic change is not seen as needed. Two kinds of people dissent from this judgment—those who fear that the Soviets are gaining usable military superiority and those who fear some sort of accidental war. The former, most of whom see only limited scope for Soviet-American cooperation, far outnumber the latter. Indeed, it may be doubted whether there will ever be strong political pressures in favor of a regime unless there is dramatic evidence that individualistic security policies are leading to disaster. Of course the strongest possible evidence—an all-out war—would render the project irrelevant. Perhaps a regime could be formed only in the wake of a limited nuclear exchange or the accidental firing of a weapon. Interestingly enough, it was Herman Kahn who saw the effect that such a crisis might have:

> I can even imagine something as extreme as the following occurring. There is a well-known book on possible constitutional forms for world government, *World Peace Through World Law*. At this point, the President of the United States might send a copy of this book to [the Soviet] Premier saying, "There's no point in your reading this book; you will not like it any more than I did. I merely suggest you sign it, right after my signature. This is the only plan which has been even roughly thought through; let us therefore accept it. We surely do not wish to set up a commission to study other methods of organizing the world, because within weeks both of us will be trying to exploit our common danger for unilateral advantages. If we are to have a settlement, we must have it now, before the dead are buried." I can even imagine [the Soviet] Premier accepting the offer and signing.[37]

I grant that this is a bizarre chain of events, but it is hard to think of a more plausible shock that could provide the basis for the formation of a regime.

[37] Herman Kahn, *Thinking About the Unthinkable* (New York: Horizon Press, 1962), pp. 148–49.

International regimes, transactions, and change: embedded liberalism in the postwar economic order

> A philosopher is someone who goes into a dark room at night, to look for a black cat that isn't there. A theologian does the same thing, but comes out claiming he found the cat.
>
> Nick Philips, "The Case of the Naked Quark,"
> *TWA Ambassador Magazine,* October 1980.

One of our major purposes in this volume is to establish whether we, as students of international regimes, most resemble the philosopher, the theologian or, as most of us would like to believe, the social scientist— suspecting from the beginning that there is a black cat in there somewhere, and emerging from the room with scratches on the forearm as vindication. This article consists of another set of scratches, together with what I hope will be persuasive reasoning and demonstration that a black cat put them there.

My focus is on how the regimes for money and trade have reflected and affected the evolution of the international economic order since World War II. Let me state my basic approach to this issue at the outset, for, as Krasner shows in the Introduction, a good deal of the disagreement and confusion

I have benefited from the comments and suggestions of a large number of friends, colleagues, and fellow travelers, and am particularly indebted to the detailed written remarks of Catherine Gwin, Ernst Haas, Robert Keohane, Stephen Krasner, and Susan Strange, as well as to Albert Fishlow's constructive criticism at the Palm Springs conference. Research for this article was made possible by financial support from the Rockefeller Foundation and the Ira D. Wallach Chair of World Order Studies at Columbia University.

International Organization 36, 2, Spring 1982
0020-8183/82/020379-37 $1.50

about international regimes stems from deeper epistemological and even ontological differences among observers.

International regimes have been defined as social institutions around which actor expectations converge in a given area of international relations.[1] Accordingly, as is true of any social institution, international regimes limit the discretion of their constituent units to decide and act on issues that fall within the regime's domain. And, as is also true of any social institution, ultimate expression in converging expectations and delimited discretion gives international regimes an intersubjective quality. To this extent, international regimes are akin to language—we may think of them as part of "the language of state action."[2] The constituent units of a regime, like speakers of a common language, generally have little difficulty in determining what even an entirely new usage signifies. Should it be technically inappropriate or incorrect, they nevertheless may still "understand" it—in the dual sense of being able to comprehend it and willing to acquiesce in it. In sum, we know international regimes not simply by some descriptive inventory of their concrete elements, but by their generative grammar, the underlying principles of order and meaning that shape the manner of their formation and transformation. Likewise, we know deviations from regimes not simply by acts that are undertaken, but by the intentionality and acceptability attributed to those acts in the context of an intersubjective framework of meaning.[3]

The analytical components of international regimes we take to consist of principles, norms, rules, and procedures. As the content for each of these terms is specified, international regimes diverge from social institutions like language, for we do not normally attribute to language any specific "consummatory" as opposed to "instrumental" values.[4] Insofar as international regimes embody principles about fact, causation, and rectitude, as well as political rights and obligations that are regarded as legitimate, they fall closer to the consummatory end of the spectrum, into the realm of political authority. Thus, the formation and transformation of international regimes may be said to represent a concrete manifestation of the internationalization of political authority.[5]

[1] Oran R. Young, "International Regimes: Problems of Concept Formation," *World Politics* 32 (April 1980); and Stephen D. Krasner's introduction to this volume.

[2] This phrase is taken from Bruce Andrews's application of the linguistic metaphor to the study of foreign policy: "The Language of State Action," *International Interactions* 6 (November 1979).

[3] Cf. Noam Chomsky, *Current Issues in Linguistic Theory* (The Hague: Mouton, 1964), chap. 1.

[4] These are derived from the standard Weberian distinction between *Wert-* and *Zweckrational*. Max Weber, *Economy and Society*, ed. by Guenther Roth and Claus Wittich (Berkeley: University of California Press, 1978), pp. 24–26.

[5] Discussions of political authority often fuse the very meaning of the concept with one of its specific institutional manifestations, that expressed in super-subordinate relations. But, as demonstrated repeatedly in organization theory and recognized by Weber, authority rests on a form of legitimacy that ultimately can derive only from a community of interests. Chester Barnard has carried this line of reasoning the furthest: "Authority is another name for the willingness and capacity of individuals to submit to the necessities of cooperative systems." *The*

What is the "generative grammar" that shapes the internationalization of political authority? The most common interpretation has been stated succinctly by Kenneth Waltz: the elements of international authority, he maintains, "are barely once removed from the capability that provides [their] foundation. . . ."[6] On this interpretation others, in turn, have built what now amounts to a prevalent model of the formation and transformation of international economic regimes. In its simplest form, the model makes this prediction: if economic capabilities are so concentrated that a hegemon exists, as in the case of Great Britain in the late 19th century and the U.S.A. after World War II, an "open" or "liberal" international economic order will come into being.[7] In the organization of a liberal order, pride of place is given to market rationality. This is not to say that authority is absent from such an order. It is to say that authority relations are constructed in such a way as to give maximum scope to market forces rather than to constrain them. Specific regimes that serve such an order, in the areas of money and trade, for example, limit the discretion of states to intervene in the functioning of self-regulating currency and commodity markets. These may be termed "strong" regimes, because they restrain self-seeking states in a competitive international political system from meddling directly in domestic and international economic affairs in the name of their national interests. And the strength of these regimes, of course, is backed by the capabilities of the hegemon. If and as such a concentration of economic capabilities erodes, the liberal order is expected to unravel and its regimes to become weaker, ultimately being replaced by mercantilist arrangements, that is, by arrangements under which the constituent units reassert national political authority over transnational economic forces. If the order established by British economic supremacy in the 19th century and that reflecting the supremacy of the United States after World War II illustrate liberal orders with strong regimes, the interwar period illustrates the darker corollary of the axiom.

I do not claim that this model is fundamentally wrong. But it does not take us very far in understanding international economic regimes, and, by extension, the formation and transformation of international regimes in gen-

Functions of the Executive (Cambridge: Harvard University Press, 1968), p. 184. See also the important statement by Peter Blau, "Critical Remarks on Weber's Theory of Authority," *American Political Science Review* 57 (June 1963). An illustration (though unintended) of how *not* to think of authority if the concept is to be at all useful in a discussion of international relations is provided by Harry Eckstein, "Authority Patterns: A Structural Basis for Political Inquiry," *American Political Science Review* 67 (December 1973). More elaborate typologies of forms of authority relations in international regimes may be found in my papers, "International Responses to Technology: Concepts and Trends," *International Organization* 29 (Summer 1975), and "Changing Frameworks of International Collective Behavior: On the Complementarity of Contradictory Tendencies," in Nazli Choucri and Thomas Robinson, eds., *Forecasting in International Relations* (San Francisco: W. H. Freeman, 1978).

  [6] *Theory of International Politics* (Reading, Mass.: Addison-Wesley, 1979), p. 88.

  [7] The relevant literature is cited in Robert O. Keohane, "The Theory of Hegemonic Stability and Changes in International Economic Regimes, 1967–1977," in Ole Holsti et al., eds., *Change in the International System* (Boulder, Col.: Westview Press, 1980).

eral.[8] This is so precisely because it does not encompass the phenomenological dimensions of international regimes.

From this vantage point, I develop three theoretical arguments; each yields an interpretation of central features of the postwar international economic order that is distinct from the prevailing view.

The first concerns the "generative grammar" or what I shall call the "structure" of the internationalization of political authority. Whatever its institutional manifestations, political authority represents a fusion of power with legitimate social purpose. The prevailing interpretation of international authority focuses on power only; it ignores the dimension of social purpose.[9] The problem with this formulation is that power may predict the *form* of the international order, but not its *content*. For example, in the era of the third hegemon in the complex of modern state-system and capitalist-world-economy, the Dutch in the 17th century, the condition of hegemony coexisted with mercantilist behavior,[10] and it would be straining credulity to attribute this difference solely or even mainly to differences in the relative economic supremacy of the three hegemons without discussing differences in social purpose. Moreover, had the Germans succeeded in their quest to establish a "New International Order" after World War II, the designs Hjalmar Schacht would have instituted were the very mirror image of Bretton Woods[11]—obviously, differences in social purpose again provide the key. Lastly, the common tendency to equate the 19th century liberal international economic order and its post–World War II counterpart itself obscures exceedingly important differences in their domestic and international organization, differences that stem from the fact that the one represented laissez-faire liberalism and the other did not. In sum, to say anything sensible about the *content* of international economic orders and about the regimes that serve them, it is necessary to look at how power and legitimate social purpose become fused to project political authority into the international system. Applied to the post–World War II context, this argument leads me to characterize the international economic order by the term "em-

---

[8] Nor should it be expected to. As Waltz makes clear, his is a theory intended to predict that certain conditioning and constraining forces will take effect within the international system as a whole depending upon variation in its structure, not to account for such "process-level" outcomes as international regimes. Some of the literature cited by Keohane attempts to do more than this, however, though Keohane himself reaches a conclusion that is not at variance with my own.

[9] More accurately, it either assumes social purpose (as in Waltz, *Theory of International Politics*), or seeks to deduce it from state power (as in Krasner, "State Power and the Structure of International Trade," *World Politics* 28 [April 1976]).

[10] To my knowledge, the case of Dutch supremacy in the world economy has not been addressed in the "hegemonic stability" literature; but see Immanuel Wallerstein, *The Modern World System*, vol. 2 (New York: Academic Press, 1980), chap. 2.

[11] A brief description may be found in Armand Van Dormael, *Bretton Woods: Birth of a Monetary System* (London: Macmillan, 1978), chap. 1. The classic statement of how it actually worked remains Albert O. Hirschman, *National Power and the Structure of Foreign Trade*, expanded ed. (Berkeley: University of California Press, 1980).

bedded liberalism,'' which I show to differ from both its classical ancestor and its ignominious predecessor even as it has systematically combined central features of both.

My second theoretical argument concerns the relationship between international economic regimes and developments in the international economy, particularly at the level of private transaction flows.[12] Conventional structural arguments, whether Realist or Marxist, see transnationalization as a direct reflection of hegemony: high levels of trade and capital flows obtain under the *pax Britannica* and the *pax Americana*. The regimes for trade and money are largely epiphenomenal adjuncts that may be invoked to legitimate this outcome, but they have little or no real bearing on it. Conventional liberals, on the other hand, hold that high levels of trade and capital flows will obtain only if there is strict adherence to open international economic regimes, so that these become virtually determinative. Neither formulation is satisfactory.

The relationship between economic regimes and international transaction flows is inherently problematical, because the domain of international regimes consists of the behavior of states, vis-à-vis one another and vis-à-vis the market-place, *not* the market-place itself. Nevertheless, simply on *a priori* grounds we may argue that because there is no direct relationship, it is highly unlikely that the character of international regimes would have a determinative impact on international transaction flows; and yet, because international regimes do encompass the behavior of states vis-à-vis the market-place, it stands to reason that they would have some effect on international transaction flows. I contend that the nature of this relationship, at least in the first instance, is one of complementarity. That is to say, international economic regimes provide a permissive environment for the emergence of *specific kinds* of international transaction flows that actors take to be complementary to the particular fusion of power and purpose that is embodied within those regimes.[13] The contextual specificity of this complementarity makes equations of the variety ''pax Britannica is equal to pax Americana,'' as well as insistence on universal regime formulae to achieve a given outcome, extremely dubious propositions.

Applying this argument to the postwar international economic order, I conclude that the emergence of several specific developments in transnational economic activities can be accounted for at least in part by their perceived first-order contribution to the regimes for trade and money.[14] These regimes, then, are neither determinative nor irrelevant, but provide part of the context that shapes the character of transnationalization.

---

[12] In this connection, see also Charles Lipson's chapter in this volume.

[13] This is not to ignore the possibility that the same developments may have second-order consequences or long-term effects that pose stresses or even contradictions for international economic regimes, a problem which I take up in a later section.

[14] The present formulation of this conclusion owes much to Albert Fishlow's commentary on an earlier version at the Palm Springs Conference, for which I am obliged to him.

My third theoretical argument concerns the occurrence of change in and of regimes. The prevailing model postulates one source of regime change, the ascendancy or decline of economic hegemons, and two directions of regime change, greater openness or closure. If, however, we allow for the possibility that power and purpose do not necessarily covary, then we have two potential sources of change and no longer any simple one-to-one correspondence between source and direction of change. For example, we could have a situation in which there exists a predominant economic power whose economic program differs fundamentally from that of its leading rivals (e.g., Dutch supremacy in the 17th century). Or, we could have a situation in which power and purpose covary negatively, that is, in which neither a hegemon nor a congruence of social purpose exists among the leading economic powers (the interwar period approximates this case). We could have a situation in which power and purpose covary positively (e.g., Bretton Woods). There remains the situation of no hegemon but a congruence of social purpose among the leading economic powers (albeit imperfectly, the post–1971 international economic order illustrates this possibility).

It is the last possibility that interests me most. It suggests the need for a more nuanced formulation of regime change than is currently available. If and as the concentration of economic power erodes, and the "strength" of international regimes is sapped thereby, we may be sure that the *instruments* of regimes also will have to change.[15] However, as long as purpose is held constant, there is no reason to suppose that the *normative framework* of regimes must change as well. In other words, referring back to our analytical components of international regimes, rules and procedures (instruments) would change but principles and norms (normative frameworks) would not. Presumably, the new instruments that would emerge would be better adapted to the new power situation in the international economic order. But insofar as they continued to reflect the same sense of purpose, they would represent a case of norm-governed as opposed to norm-transforming change.

Applying this argument to the post–1971 period leads me to suggest that many of the changes that have occurred in the regimes for money and trade have been norm-governed changes rather than, as is often maintained, reflecting the collapse of Bretton Woods and a headlong rush into mercantilism. Indeed, in certain cases earlier acts by the hegemon had violated the normative frameworks of these regimes, so that some post–1971 changes may be viewed as adaptive restorations of prior sets of norms in the context of a new and different international economic environment. Both occurrences may to taken to demonstrate what we might call "the relative autonomy" of international regimes (with due apologies to the appropriate quarters).

The various parts of my argument clearly stand or fall together. Ulti-

---

[15] The "hegemonic stability" school effectively demonstrates why this is so. See Keohane, "Theory of Hegemonic Stability."

mately, they lead back to my depiction of international authority as reflecting a fusion of power and legitimate social purpose. An historical illustration of this interpretation of the "structure" of international authority therefore serves as my point of departure.

1. The structure of international authority

Karl Polanyi's magisterial work, *The Great Transformation*, was first published in 1944. In it, he developed a distinction between "embedded" and "disembedded" economic orders: "normally, the economic order is merely a function of the social, in which it is contained. Under neither tribal, nor feudal, nor mercantile conditions was there, as we have shown, a separate economic system in society. Nineteenth century society, in which economic activity was isolated and imputed to a distinctive economic motive, was, indeed, a singular departure."[16] The best known international forms taken by this "singular departure" were, of course, the regimes of free trade and the gold standard. What were their bases?

The internationalization of domestic authority relations

Charles Kindleberger, who is justly accorded a leading role in having established the efficacy of the "hegemonic stability" model in his book on the Great Depression,[17] subsequently managed to write an account of the rise of free trade in western Europe without even mentioning British economic supremacy as a possible source of explanation.[18] He focused instead on a fundamental reordering of the relationships between domestic political authority and economic processes. Free trade, he reminds us, was due first of all to the general breakdown of the manor and guild system and the so-called policy of supply, through which a complex structure of social regulations rather than market exchange determined the organization of economic activity at home and abroad. Indeed, the earliest measures undertaken in order to free trade were to dismantle prohibitions on exports, prohibitions that had restricted the outward movement of materials, machinery, and artisans. The bulk of these prohibitions was not removed until well into the 1820s and 1830s, and in some instances even later. A second part of the stimulus "came from the direct self-interest of particular dominant groups.

[16] Boston: Beacon Press, 1944, p. 71. The historical claims are backed up in Polanyi et al., eds., *Trade and Markets in the Early Empires* (Glencoe, Ill.: Free Press, 1957).

[17] Charles P. Kindleberger, *The World in Depression, 1929–1939* (Berkeley: University of California Press, 1973), esp. chaps. 1 and 14.

[18] "The Rise of Free Trade in Western Europe, 1820–1875," *Journal of Economic History* 35 (March 1975): 20–55.

. . ."[19] In the Netherlands, these were merchants, shipowners, and bankers; in Great Britain, the manufacturing sectors backed by the intellectual hegemony established by the Manchester School; in France, largely industrial interests employing imported materials and equipment in production, though they would not have succeeded against the weight of countervailing interests had not Louis Napoleon imposed free trade for unrelated reasons of international diplomacy; in Prussia, grain and timber exporters, though Bismarck was not adverse to using trade treaties in the pursuit of broader objectives and free trade treaties seemed to be *au courant;* in Italy, the efforts of Cavour, which prevailed over disorganized opposition. Equally particularistic factors were at work in Belgium, Denmark, Norway, Sweden, Spain, and Portugal. But how did such diverse forces come to converge on the single policy response of free trade? In a certain sense, Kindleberger contends, Europe in this period should be viewed not as a collection of separate economies, but "as a *single entity* which moved to free trade for ideological or perhaps better doctrinal reasons."[20] The image of the market became an increasingly captivating social metaphor and served to focus diverse responses on the outcome of free trade. And unless one holds that ideology and doctrine exist in a social vacuum, this ascendancy of market rationality in turn must be related to the political and cultural ascendance of the middle classes. In Polanyi's inimitable phrase, *"Laissez-faire* was planned. . . ."[21]

In sum, this shift in what we might call the balance between "authority" and "market" fundamentally transformed state-society relations, by redefining the legitimate social purposes in pursuit of which state power was expected to be employed in the domestic economy. The role of the state became to institute and safeguard the self-regulating market. To be sure, this shift occurred unequally throughout western Europe, and at uneven tempos. And of course nowhere did it take hold so deeply and for so long a period as in Great Britain. Great Britain's supremacy in the world economy had much to do with the global expansion of this new economic order, and even more with its stability and longevity. But the authority relations that were instituted in the international regimes for money and trade reflected a new balance of state-society relations that expressed a *collective* reality.

These expectations about the proper scope of political authority in economic relations did not survive World War I. Despite attempts at restoration, by the end of the interwar period there remained little doubt about how thoroughly they had eroded. Polanyi looked back over the period of the "twenty years' crisis" from the vantage point of the Second World War—at the emergence of mass movements from the Left and the Right throughout Europe, the revolutionary and counterrevolutionary upheavals in central

[19] Ibid., p. 50.
[20] Ibid., p. 51, italics added.
[21] Polanyi describes the parallel movements, in the case of Great Britain, of the middle class into the political arena and the state out of the economic arena.

and eastern Europe in the 1917–20 period, the General Strike of 1926 in Great Britain, and, above all, the rapid succession of the abandonment of the gold standard by Britain, the instituting of the Five Year Plans in the Soviet Union, the launching of the New Deal in the United States, unorthodox budgetary policies in Sweden, *corporativismo* in Fascist Italy, and *Wirkschaftslenkung* followed by the creation of both domestic and international variants of the "new economic order" by the Nazis in Germany. Running throughout these otherwise diverse events and developments, he saw the common thread of social reaction against market rationality. State-society relations again had undergone a profound—indeed, the *great*—transformation, as land, labor, and capital had all seized upon the state in the attempt to reimpose broader and more direct social control over market forces. Once this domestic transformation began, late in the 19th century, international liberalism of the orthodox kind was doomed. Thus, it was the singular tragedy of the interwar period, Polanyi felt, to have attempted to restore internationally, in the form of the gold-exchange standard in particular, that which no longer had a corresponding social base domestically. The new international economic order that would emerge from World War II, Polanyi concluded, on the one hand would mark the end of "capitalist internationalism," as governments learned the lesson that international automaticity stands in fundamental and potentially explosive contradiction to an active state domestically, and, on the other hand, the emergence of deliberate management of international economic transactions by means of collaboration among governments.[22]

Some of Polanyi's thoughts about the future had already been entertained by the individuals who would come to be directly responsible for negotiating the monetary component of the postwar international economic order. In the depth of the Depression, Harry Dexter White had pondered the problem of how to buffer national economies from external disturbances without, at the same time, sacrificing the benefits of international economic relations. "The path, I suspect, may lie in the direction of centralized control over foreign exchanges and trade."[23] Indeed, in 1934 White had applied for a fellowship to study planning techniques at the Institute of Economic Investigations of Gosplan in Moscow. Instead, he accepted an offer to go to Washington and work in the New Deal. For his part, one of the first assignments that Keynes undertook after he joined the British Treasury in 1940 was to draft the text of a radio broadcast designed to discredit recent propaganda proclamations by Walther Funk, minister for economic affairs and president of the Reichsbank in Berlin, on the economic and social benefits that the "New Order" would bring to Europe and the world. Keynes was instructed to stress the traditional virtues of free trade and the gold standard. But this, he felt, "will not have much propaganda value." Britain would have to offer

---

[22] *The Great Transformation*, esp. chaps. 2 and 19–21.
[23] Quoted in Van Dormael, *Bretton Woods*, p. 41.

"the same as what Dr. Funk offers, except that we shall do it better and more honestly."[24] He had reached the conclusion that only a refinement and improvement of the Schachtian device would restore equilibrium after the war. "To suppose that there exists some smoothly functioning automatic mechanism of adjustment which preserves equilibrium if only we trust to methods of *laissez-faire* is a doctrinaire delusion which disregards the lessons of historical experience without having behind it the support of sound theory."[25]

Polanyi's prediction of the end of capitalist internationalism does not stand up well against the subsequent internationalization of production and finance; White's views were altered considerably over the years as a result of negotiations within the bureaucracy and the adversarial process with Congress, before he was driven from Washington altogether in an anticommunist witch-hunt; and American resistance scaled down even the multilateral variants of Keynes's ambitious vision. Yet each had been correct in the essential fact that a new threshold had been crossed in the balance between "market" and "authority," with governments assuming much more direct responsibility for domestic social security and economic stability. The extension of the suffrage and the emergence of working-class political constituencies, parties, and even governments was responsible in part; but demands for social protection were very nearly universal, coming from all sides of the political spectrum and from all ranks of the social hierarchy (with the possible exception of orthodox financial circles). Polanyi, White, and Keynes were also correct in their premise that, somehow, the postwar international economic order would have to reflect this change in state-society relations if the calamities of the interwar period were not to recur.

Transformations in power versus purpose

Changes in the distribution of power and in the structure of social purpose covaried from the pre–World War I era through to the interwar period, so that we cannot say with any degree of certainty what might have happened had only one changed. However, by looking at the relationship between the two in greater detail in a single, circumscribed domain, we may get closer to a firm answer. I focus on the monetary regime under the gold standard before World War I, and its attempted approximation in the gold-exchange standard of the interwar period.

I begin with the domestic side of things, though this distinction itself would barely apply to currencies under a "gold specie" standard[26] where

---

[24] Quoted in ibid., p. 7.

[25] Quoted in ibid., p. 32.

[26] Unless otherwise noted, this paragraph is based on League of Nations [Ragnar Nurkse], *International Currency Experience: Lessons of the Inter-War Period* (League of Nations, Economic, Financial and Transit Department, 1944), chap. 4. (Hereafter referred to as Nurkse.)

both domestic circulation and international means of settlement took the form largely of gold, and the domestic money supply therefore was determined directly and immediately by the balance of payments. Under the more familiar "gold bullion" standard prior to World War I, where the bulk of domestic money took the form of bank notes and deposits, backed by and fixed in value in terms of gold, there still existed a strong relationship between domestic money supply and the balance of payments, but it was more indirect. In theory, it worked via the effects of gold movements on the domestic credit supply: an expansion of credit in the gold-receiving country, and a contraction in the gold-losing country, affected prices and incomes in such a way as to close the balance of payments discrepancy that had triggered the gold movement in the first place. This was reinforced by an attending change in money rates, which would set off equilibrating movements in short-term private funds. In practice, gold movements among the major economies were relatively infrequent and small. Temporary gaps to a large extent were filled by short-term capital movements, responding to interest differentials or slight variations within the gold points.[27] More fundamental adjustments were produced by the impact of the balance of payments not only on domestic money stock and the volume of credit, but also through the direct effects of export earnings on domestic income and effective demand.

In sum, even in its less than pristine form, the pre–World War I gold standard was predicated upon particular assumptions concerning the fundamental purpose of domestic monetary policy and the role of the state in the process of adjusting imbalances in the level of external and internal economic activity. With respect to the first, in Bloomfield's words, the "dominant and overriding" objective of monetary policy was the maintenance of gold parity. "The view, so widely recognized and accepted in recent decades, of central banking policy as a means of facilitating the achievement and maintenance of reasonable stability in the level of economic activity and prices was scarcely thought about before 1914, and certainly not accepted, as a formal objective of policy."[28] Second, insofar as the adjustment process ultimately was geared to securing external stability, state abstinence was prescribed so as not to undermine the equilibrating linkages between the balance of payments, changes in gold reserves and in domestic credit supply,

---

[27] Note, however, Bloomfield's cautionary remark: "While this picture is broadly accurate, the nature and role of private short-term capital movements before 1914 have usually been oversimplified and their degree of sensitivity to interest rates and exchange rates exaggerated. At the same time these movements have been endowed with a benign character that they did not always possess." Arthur I. Bloomfield, "Short-Term Capital Movements Under the Pre-1914 Gold Standard," *Princeton Studies in International Finance* 11 (1963), p. 34. Bloomfield presents a more complex and balanced picture, which, however, does not contradict the basic generalization.

[28] Arthur I. Bloomfield, *Monetary Policy Under the International Gold Standard* (New York: Federal Reserve Bank of New York, 1959), p. 23. Bloomfield shows that central banks did attempt partially to "sterilize" the effects of gold flows.

income, and demand. This was not incompatible with partial efforts at sterilization. As Nurkse put it, "all that was required for this purpose was that countries should not attempt to control their national income and outlay by deliberate measures—a requirement which in the age of laissez-faire was generally fulfilled."[29]

It is impossible to say precisely when these assumptions ceased to be operative and their contraries took hold. But it is clear that after World War I there was a growing tendency "to make international monetary policy conform to domestic social and economic policy and not the other way round."[30] The proportion of currency reserves held in the form of foreign exchange more than doubled between 1913 and 1925, to 27 percent; in 1928, it stood at 42 percent. And international reserves increasingly came to serve as a "buffer" against external economic forces rather than as their "transmitter"; Nurkse found that throughout the interwar period the international and domestic assets of central banks moved in opposite directions far more often than in the same direction.[31] After the collapse of the gold-exchange standard in 1931, exchange stabilization funds were established in the attempt to provide more of a cushion than "neutralization" had afforded. Mere stabilization was followed by direct exchange controls in many instances, with the gold bloc countries attempting to achieve analogous insulation through import quotas. Governments everywhere had developed increasingly active forms of intervention in the domestic economy in order to affect the level of prices and employment, and to protect them against external sources of dislocation.[32] The international monetary order disintegrated into five more or less distinct blocs, each with its own prevailing currency arrangement.

On the international side, there is little doubt that the pre–World War I gold standard functioned as it did because of the central part Great Britain played in it. In general terms, "if keeping a free market for imports, maintaining a flow of investment capital, and acting as lender of last resort are the marks of an 'underwriter' of an international system, then Britain certainly fulfilled this role in the nineteenth-century international economy."[33] More specifically, in the domain of monetary policy it was the role of sterling as the major vehicle currency, held by foreign business, banks, and even central banks, that gave the Bank of England the influence to shape international monetary conditions consistent with the fundamental commitments and

[29] Nurkse, *International Currency Experience*, p. 213.

[30] Ibid., p. 230.

[31] Ibid., pp. 68–88.

[32] For a good global overview of these policy shifts, see Asa Briggs, "The World Economy: Interdependence and Planning," in C. L. Mowat, ed., *The New Cambridge Modern History*, vol. 12 (Cambridge: Cambridge University Press, 1968).

[33] Robert J. A. Skidelsky, "Retreat from Leadership: The Evolution of British Economic Foreign Policy, 1870–1939," in Benjamin M. Rowland, ed., *Balance of Power or Hegemony: The Interwar Monetary System* (New York: New York University Press, 1976), p. 163. Cf. Kindleberger, *The World in Depression*, chap. 1.

dynamics of the regime. And yet, the critical issue in the stability of this regime was not simply some measure of material "supremacy" on the part of Britain, but that "national monetary authorities were inclined to *'follow the market'* —and indirectly the Bank of England—rather than to assert independent national objectives of their own."[34] Thus, the international gold standard rested on both the special position of Great Britain and prevailing attitudes concerning the role of the state in the conduct of national monetary policy. It reflected a true "hegemony," as Gramsci used the term.

What of the interwar period? Counterfactual historiography is little better than a parlor game under ideal circumstances; it should be especially suspect when an outcome is as overdetermined as institutional failure in the international economy between the wars.[35] It seems reasonable to assume, though, that with the end of monetary laissez-faire, "the monetary leader would need to dispose of more monetary influence and political authority than Britain ever possessed, except within its own imperial system."[36] And where British hegemony lingered on, as in the Financial Committee of the League of Nations, the outcome was not salutary. For example, the eastern European countries that had their currencies stabilized by the League and were put under the gold-exchange standard before the major countries had fixed their currency rates did so at considerable domestic social cost.[37] And virtually every effort at constructing a viable international monetary regime in the interwar period, in which Britain took a leading role, did little more than decry the newly prevailing social objectives of state policy while pleading for a speedy return to the principles of "sound finance."[38] The consequences of course were counterproductive: just as the rhetoric of the

[34] Harold van B. Cleveland, "The International Monetary System in the Interwar Period," in Rowland, *Balance of Power*, p. 57, emphasis added. Note, in addition, that major primary-producing countries, who may well have borne more than their share of the international adjustment process under the gold standard, by and large did not establish their own central banks until the 1930s—this includes Argentina, Canada, India, New Zealand, and Venezuela. The argument that the adjustment process worked disproportionately on primary-producing countries is made by Robert Triffin, "National Central Banking and the International Economy," in Lloyd A. Metzler et al., eds., *International Monetary Policies* (Washington, D.C.: Board of Governors of the Federal Reserve System, 1947).

[35] There is almost no end to the number of dislocating features of the post–World War I international economy that can be adduced as part of the explanation for its institutional failure. Kindleberger, *The World in Depression*, chap. 1, briefly recounts most of them.

[36] Cleveland, "International Monetary System," p. 57.

[37] "The deflationist's ideal came to be 'a free economy under a strong government'; but while the phrase on government meant what it said, namely, emergency powers and suspension of public liberties, 'free economy' meant in practice the opposite of what it said: . . . while the inflationary governments condemned by Geneva subordinated the stability of the currency to stability of incomes and employment, the deflationary governments put in power by Geneva used no fewer interventions in order to subordinate the stability of incomes and employment to the stability of the currency." Polanyi, *The Great Transformation,* p. 233. For French skepticism concerning the "dogma of Geneva," see Judith L. Kooker, "French Financial Diplomacy: The Interwar Years," in Rowland, *Balance of Power*.

[38] For summary descriptions of the major conferences, see Dean E. Traynor, *International Monetary and Financial Conferences in the Interwar Period* (Washington, D.C.: Catholic Universities Press of America, 1949).

League concerning collective security and disarmament sought and in some measure served morally to undermine the balance of power system, without providing a viable alternative, so too did the League and successive international gatherings in the monetary sphere seek to undermine the legitimacy of domestic stabilization policies while offering only the unacceptable gold-exchange standard in their place.[39]

It is hardly surprising, therefore, that apart from Britain, seized by its own ideology and institutional past and willing to pay the domestic social cost, there were few takers among the major countries.[40] In sum, efforts to construct international economic regimes in the interwar period failed not because of the lack of a hegemon. They failed because, even had there been a hegemon, they stood in contradiction to the transformation in the mediating role of the state between market and society, which altered fundamentally the social purpose of domestic and international authority. As Ragnar Nurkse observed in 1944,

> There was a growing tendency during the inter-war period to make international monetary policy conform to domestic social and economic policy and not the other way round. Yet the world was still economically interdependent; and an international currency mechanism for the multilateral exchange of goods and services, instead of primitive bilateral barter, was still a fundamental necessity for the great majority of countries. The problem was to find a system of international currency relations compatible with the requirements of domestic stability. Had the period been more than a truce between two world wars, the solution that would have evolved would no doubt have been in the nature of a compromise.[41]

Ultimately, it was. The liberalism that was restored after World War II differed in kind from that which had been known previously. My term for it is "embedded liberalism."

[39] The most trenchant critique of the moral failure of the League remains that of Edward Hallett Carr, *The Twenty Years' Crisis, 1919–1939* (1939, 1946; New York: Harper Torchbooks, 1964).

[40] For example, France decided in 1928 to accept only gold in settlement of the enormous surplus it was accruing; and in 1929 the U.S. "went off on a restrictive monetary frolic of its own" even though it was in surplus" (Cleveland, "International Monetary System," p. 6). Four years later, in his inaugural address, President Roosevelt proclaimed the primacy of domestic stabilization, as he did again a few months later when, on the eve of the World Economic Conference of 1933, he took the U.S. off gold.

[41] *International Currency Experience*, p. 230. Note that Nurkse was speaking of "the great majority of countries." Those who chose bilateralism as an instrument of economic warfare and imperialism were unlikely to be accommodated within any multilateral regime. However, mere state trading or even the participation of centrally planned economies, while posing special problems, were not seen to be insuperable obstacles to multilateralism; see Herbert Feis, "The Conflict Over Trade Ideologies," *Foreign Affairs* 25 (July 1947), and Raymond F. Mikesell, "The Role of the International Monetary Agreements in a World of Planned Economies," *Journal of Political Economy* 55 (December 1947). I think it is fair to say, though, that reconciling the many variants and depths of state intervention would have been a difficult task in the best of times, which the 1930s of course weren't. We are justified, therefore, in "coding" the interwar period as "no hegemon, no agreement on purpose."

2. The compromise of embedded liberalism

Liberal internationalist orthodoxy, most prominent in New York financial circles, proposed to reform the old order simply by shifting its locus from the pound to the dollar and by ending discriminatory trade and exchange practices.[42] Opposition to economic liberalism, nearly universal outside the United States, differed in substance and intensity depending upon whether it came from the Left, Right, or Center, but was united in its rejection of unimpeded multilateralism.[43] The task of postwar institutional reconstruction, as Nurkse sensed, was to maneuver between these two extremes and to devise a framework which would safeguard and even aid the quest for domestic stability without, at the same time, triggering the mutually destructive external consequences that had plagued the interwar period. This was the essence of the embedded liberalism compromise: unlike the economic nationalism of the thirties, it would be multilateral in character; unlike the liberalism of the gold standard and free trade, its multilateralism would be predicated upon domestic interventionism.

If this was the objective of postwar institutional reconstruction for the international economy, there remained enormous differences among countries over precisely what it meant and what sorts of policies and institutional arrangements, domestic and international, the objective necessitated or was compatible with. This was the stuff of the negotiations on the postwar international economic order. The story of these negotiations has been told by others, in detail and very ably.[44] I make no attempt to repeat it here. I simply summarize the conjunction of the two themes that constitutes the story's plot. The first, which we tend to remember more vividly today, concerned

[42] Professor John H. Williams, vice-president of the Federal Reserve Bank of New York, was a leading spokesman for the New York financial community, which resented having lost control over international monetary affairs when authority shifted from the FRBNY to the U.S. Treasury under Secretary Morgenthau. Their plan, which had some support in Congress, called simply for a resurrection of the gold-exchange standard, with the dollar performing the role that sterling had played previously. They opposed the New Deal "gimmickry" of the White Plan, and of course they liked Keynes's Clearing Union even less. See Van Dormael, *Bretton Woods*, chap. 9.

[43] In the case of Britain, the other major actor in the negotiations concerning postwar economic arrangements, opposition from the Left was based on the desire to systematize national economic planning, which would necessarily entail discriminatory instruments for foreign economic policy. Opposition from the Right stemmed from a commitment to imperial preferences and the imperial alternative to a universal economic order. Speaking for many moderates, Hubert Henderson was opposed because he doubted the viability of a "freely working economic system," that is, of laissez-faire. "To attempt this would be not to learn from experience but to fly in its face. It would be to repeat the mistakes made last time in the name of avoiding them. It would be to invite the same failure, and the same disillusionment; the same economic chaos and the same shock to social and political stability; the same discredit for the international idea." (Richard N. Gardner, *Sterling-Dollar Diplomacy in Current Perspective* [New York: Columbia University Press, 1980], chap. 1; the quotation is from a memorandum prepared by Henderson in December 1943, while serving in the British Treasury; reproduced in Gardner, p. 30.)

[44] The following account draws heavily on Gardner's classic study, as supplemented by the greater detail on the monetary side presented in Van Dormael.

multilateralism versus discrimination. It was an achievement of historic proportions for the United States to win adherence to the principle of multilateralism, particularly in trade. It required the expenditure of enormous resources. Still, it would not have succeeded but for an acceptable resolution of the dilemma between internal and external stability, the story's second theme. Here, history seemed not to require any special agent. True, the United States from the start of the negotiations was far less "Keynesian" in its positions than Great Britain. Within the United States, the social and economic reforms of the New Deal had lacked ideological consistency and programmatic coherence, and opposition had remained firmly entrenched. The transformation of the full-employment bill into the Employment Act of 1946 demonstrated the country's continuing ambivalence toward state intervention. This, of course, affected the outcome of the negotiations. Indeed, the United States would come to use its influence abroad in the immediate postwar years, through the Marshall Plan, the Occupation Authorities in Germany and Japan, and its access to transnational labor organizations, for example, to shape outcomes much more directly, by seeking to moderate the structure and political direction of labor movements, to encourage the exclusion of Communist Parties from participation in governments, and generally to discourage collectivist arrangements where possible or at least contain them within acceptable Center-Left bounds.[45] But these differences among the industrialized countries concerned the forms and depth of state intervention to secure domestic stability, not the legitimacy of the objective.[46]

In the event, on the list of Anglo-American postwar economic objectives, multilateralism was joined by collaboration to assure domestic economic growth and social security as early as the Atlantic Charter, issued in August 1941. Indeed, progress on multilateralism seemed to be made contingent upon progress in expanding domestic production, employment, and the exchange and consumption of goods in Article VII of the Mutual Aid Agreement (Lend Lease), which was signed in February 1942.

On the monetary side, however different White's Stabilization Fund may have been from Keynes's Clearing Union (and there were considerable differences on instrumentalities), they shared a common purpose: intergov-

---

[45] Charles S. Maier, "The Politics of Productivity: Foundations of American International Economic Policy After World War II," *International Organization* 31 (Autumn 1977), and Robert W. Cox, "Labor and Hegemony," *International Organization* 31 (Summer 1977).

[46] Interesting in this regard is the role played by Leon Keyserling, appointed in 1949 as the first Keynesian on the Council of Economic Advisers, in helping to undermine the previous "economy-in-defense" policy by providing economic support for the proposed rearmament program contained in NSC-68 (Fred M. Kaplan, "Our Cold-War Policy, Circa '50," *New York Times Magazine*, 18 May 1980). Radicals have implied that "military Keynesianism" was the only kind of Keynesianism acceptable in the U.S. at that time (cf. Fred L. Block, *The Origins of International Economic Disorder* [Berkeley: University of California Press, 1977], pp. 102–8). But this interpretation slights the substantial state involvement in the U.S. in the postwar years in infrastructural investment (interstate highways, for example), agricultural price supports, and even in social expenditures, well before the full impact of Keynesian thinking was felt on monetary and fiscal policy in the 1960s.

ernmental collaboration to facilitate balance-of-payments equilibrium, in an international environment of multilateralism and a domestic context of full employment. Early in 1943, Adolf Berle foresaw that the compromise on the means to achieve these ends would have to "free the British people from their fear that they might have to subordinate their internal social policy to external financial policy, and to assure the United States that a share of its production was not claimable by tender of a new, 'trick' currency, and that the economic power represented by the US gold reserves would not be substantially diminished."[47] By the time of the Anglo-American "Joint Statement of Principles," issued not long before the Bretton Woods Conference, the consensus that had emerged provided for free and stable exchanges, on the one hand, and, on the other, the erection of a "double screen," in Cooper's words,[48] to cushion the domestic economy against the strictures of the balance of payments. Free exchanges would be assured by the abolition of all forms of exchange controls and restrictions on current transactions. Stable exchanges would be secured by setting and maintaining official par values, expressed in terms of gold. The "double screen" would consist of short-term assistance to finance payments deficits on current account, provided by an International Monetary Fund, and, so as to correct "fundamental disequilibrium," the ability to change exchange rates with Fund concurrence. Governments would be permitted to maintain capital controls.

In devising the instruments of the monetary regime, the most intense negotiations were occasioned by the functioning of the "double screen." On the question of the Fund, Keynes had argued for an international overdraft facility. This would have created some $25 billion to $30 billion in new liquidity, with the overall balance of credits and debits in the Fund being expressed in an international unit of account, which was to be monetized. The arrangement would have been self-clearing unless a country were out of balance with the system as a whole, in which case corrective measures were called for on the part of creditors and debtors alike. The White plan originally called for a $5 billion Fund, though the U.S. ultimately agreed to $8.8 billion. However, these funds would have to be paid in by subscription. Access to the Fund as well as total liability were strictly limited by quotas, which in turn reflected paid-in subscriptions—the initial U.S. contribution was $3.175 billion. And a country that sought to draw on the Fund had to make "representations" that the particular currency was needed for making payments on current account. Thus, with the United States, the sole major creditor country, seeking to limit its liabilities, the first part of the "double screen" was both more modest and more rigid than the United Kingdom and other potential debtor countries would have liked. But there was no question about its being provided. On the second part, exchange rate changes, the

[47] Paraphrased by Van Dormael, *Bretton Woods*, p. 103.
[48] Richard N. Cooper, "Prolegomena to the Choice of an International Monetary System," *International Organization* 29 (Winter 1975), p. 85.

U.K. was more successful in assuring automaticity and limiting intrusions into the domain of domestic policy. The Fund was required to concur in any change necessary to correct a "fundamental disequilibrium," and if the change was less than 10 percent the Fund was given no power even to raise objections. Most important, the Fund could not oppose *any* exchange rate change on the grounds that the domestic social or political policies of the country requesting the change had led to the disequilibrium that made the change necessary. Lastly, the final agreement did include a provision to shift at least some of the burden of adjustment onto creditor countries. This was by means of the "scarce currency" clause, which Keynes, in the end, thought to be quite important. It empowered the Fund, by decision of the Executive Directors, to ration its supply of any currency that had become scarce in the Fund and authorized members to impose exchange restrictions on that currency.

Once negotiations on postwar commercial arrangements got under way seriously, in the context of preparations for an International Conference on Trade *and* Employment, the principles of multilateralism and tariff reductions were affirmed, but so were safeguards, exemptions, exceptions, and restrictions—all designed to protect the balance of payments and a variety of domestic social policies. The U.S. found some of these abhorrent and sought to limit them, but even on so extraordinary an issue as making full employment an international obligation of governments it could do no better than to gain a compromise. The U.S. Senate subsequently refused to ratify the Charter of the International Trade Organization (ITO), as a result of which a far smaller domain of commercial relations became subject to the authority of an international regime than would have been the case otherwise. The regulation of commodity markets, restrictive business practices, and international investments were the most important areas thereby excluded.[49] But within this smaller domain, consisting of the more traditional subjects of commercial policy, the conjunction of multilateralism and safeguarding domestic stability that had evolved over the course of the ITO negotiations remained intact.[50]

Jacob Viner summarized the prevailing consensus in 1947, at the time of the negotiations for a General Agreement on Tariffs and Trade (GATT): "There are few free traders in the present-day world, no one pays any attention to their views, and no person in authority anywhere advocates free trade."[51] The United States, particularly the State Department, was the

[49] The provisions of the ITO Charter became internally so inconsistent that it is difficult to say just what sort of a regime it would have given rise to. See William Diebold Jr., "The End of the ITO," *Princeton Essays in International Finance* 16 (Princeton, N.J., October 1952).

[50] The following account draws heavily on Gardner, *Sterling-Dollar Diplomacy,* and on Gerard and Victoria Curzon, "The Management of Trade Relations in the GATT," in Andrew Shonfield, ed., *International Economic Relations of the Western World, 1959–1971,* vol. I (London: Oxford University Press for the Royal Institute of International Affairs, 1976).

[51] Jacob Viner, "Conflicts of Principle in Drafting a Trade Charter," *Foreign Affairs* 25 (January 1947), p. 613.

prime mover behind multilateralism in trade. But this meant nondiscrimina-tion above all. The reduction of barriers to trade of course also played a role in American thinking, but here too the concern was more with barriers that were difficult to apply in a nondiscriminatory manner. Tariff reduction was subject to much greater domestic constraint. For their part, the British made it clear from the beginning that they would countenance no dismantling of imperial preferences unless the U.S. agreed to deep and linear tariff cuts. The proposed Commercial Union, put forward by James Meade on behalf of Britain, contained such a formula, together with an intergovernmental code of conduct for trade and machinery to safeguard the balance of payments. But the U.S. Congress could not be expected to accept linear tariff cuts.[52]

The General Agreement on Tariffs and Trade made obligatory the most-favored-nation rule, but a blanket exception was allowed for all exist-ing preferential arrangements, and countries were permitted to form customs unions and free trade areas. Moreover, quantitative restrictions were pro-hibited, but were deemed suitable measures for safeguarding the balance of payments—*explicitly* including payments difficulties that resulted from domestic policies designed to secure full employment. They could also be invoked in agricultural trade if they were used in conjunction with a domes-tic price support program. The substantial reduction of tariffs and other bar-riers to trade was called for; but it was not made obligatory and it was coupled with appropriate emergency actions, which were allowed if a domestic producer was threatened with injury from import competition that was due to past tariff concessions. The Agreement also offered a blanket escape from any of its obligations, provided that two-thirds of the contract-ing parties approved. Lastly, procedures were provided to settle disputes arising under the Agreement and for the multilateral surveillance of the invo-cation of most (though not all) of its escape clauses. The principle of reci-procity was enshrined as a code of conduct, to guide both tariff reductions and the determination of compensation for injuries suffered.

To repeat my central point: that a multilateral order gained acceptance reflected the extraordinary power and perseverance of the United States.[53]

---

[52] In the spring of 1947, the U.S. delegation arrived in Geneva armed with congressional authorization for an overall tariff reduction to 50% of their 1945 levels (which, however, would still have left U.S. tariffs relatively high), in return for elimination of preferences. But, at the same time, the United States entered into preferential trade agreements with Cuba and the Philippines. Though mutual concessions on several important items were made in Geneva, in the end some 70% of existing British preferences remained intact (Gardner, *Sterling-Dollar Diplomacy*, chap. 17).

[53] At the Palm Springs Conference, Peter Kenen argued that this is true more for trade than for money. He maintains that, with the exception of the particulars of the credit arrangement (and the future role of the dollar, which I take up below), the general outlines of Bretton Woods would not have differed appreciably had there not been an American hegemon present. This is so because the basic design rested on a widely shared consensus. However, in trade, Kenen suggests, it is unlikely that nondiscrimination would have been accepted as a guiding principle had it not been for American "muscle." Keep in mind that even here the U.S. was forced to accept the indefinite continuation of all existing preferential trade agreements.

But that multilateralism and the quest for domestic stability were coupled and even conditioned by one another reflected the shared legitimacy of a set of social objectives to which the industrial world had moved, unevenly but "as a single entity." Therefore, the common tendency to view the postwar regimes as liberal regimes, but with lots of cheating taking place on the domestic side, fails to capture the full complexity of the embedded liberalism compromise.[54]

3. Complementary transaction flows

The postwar regimes for trade and money got off to a slow start. The early GATT rounds of tariff negotiations were modest in their effects. As a lending institution, the IMF remained dormant well into the 1950s. Meanwhile, bilateral currency arrangements in the late 1940s and early 1950s became far more extensive than they had ever been in the 1930s, doubling to some four hundred between 1947 and 1954.[55] But by the late 1950s, the Europeans had "the worst of their post-war problems behind them—and new ones had not yet come to take their place." Both Europe and the United States were poised "on the brink of a decade of phenomenal expansion which imperiously demanded wider markets through freer trade."[56] This in turn demanded the elimination of exchange restrictions on current account. Liberalization in trade and money soon followed.

Preoccupation with the fact of subsequent liberalization has tended to detract from consideration of its precise characteristics, at least on the part of political scientists.[57] The questions that have dominated discussion concern the impact of liberalization on the expansion of international economic transactions, or the effects on both of U.S. hegemony (with a time lag), operating directly by means of the exercise of American state power or indi-

---

[54] The third panel of the Bretton Woods triptych was the World Bank, which to some extent may also be said to reflect this conjunction of objectives. True, the grandiose concept of an international bank to engage in countercyclical lending and to help stabilize raw materials prices, which both White and Keynes had entertained at one point, was shelved due to opposition on both sides of the Atlantic. Nevertheless, for the first time, international *public* responsibility was acknowledged for the provision of investment capital, supplementing the market mechanism. For Secretary Morgenthau's strong views on this subject, see Gardner, *Sterling-Dollar Diplomacy*, p. 76.

[55] Of the 1954 total, 235 existed in Europe. Margaret G. De Vries and J. Keith Horsefield, *The IMF, 1945–1965*, vol. 2 (Washington, D.C.: International Monetary Fund, 1969), chap. 14.

[56] Curzon and Curzon, "Management of Trade," pp. 149–50.

[57] A notable exception is Kenneth N. Waltz, "The Myth of National Interdependence," in Charles P. Kindleberger, ed., *The International Corporation* (Cambridge: MIT Press, 1970). However, Waltz considers the characteristics of an international division of labor at any given point in time to be a product solely of international polarity. And this, in turn, requires that he consider Great Britain in the 19th century to have been but one among several coequal members of a plural system. He concludes that the international division of labor in the present era has been less extensive in kind and degree than in the pre–World War I setting *because of* bipolarity today and multipolarity then.

rectly through the internationalization of American capital. These of course are interesting questions, but they are not the questions that concern me here. Having argued that the postwar regimes for trade and money institutionalized the normative framework of embedded liberalism, I now examine whether and how this framework is reflected in the character of the international economic transactions that emerged when imminent expansion "imperiously" demanded liberalization.

I proceed by way of hypothesis. Imagine a world of governments seized by the compelling logic of David Ricardo; following a bout with mercantilism, this world is poised "on the brink" of liberalization. What kinds of international economic transactions are governments likely to encourage?

> Under a system of perfectly free trade each country naturally devotes its capital and labour to such employments as are most beneficial to each. This pursuit of individual advantage is admirably connected with the universal good of the whole. By stimulating industry, by rewarding ingenuity, and by using most efficaciously the peculiar powers bestowed by nature, it distributes labour most effectively and most economically; while, by increasing the general mass of productions, it diffuses general benefit, and binds together, by one common tie of interest and intercourse, the universal society of nations throughout the civilised world. It is this principle which determines that wine shall be made in France and Portugal, that corn shall be grown in America and Poland, and that hardware and other goods shall be manufactured in England.[58]

In short, our governments are likely to encourage an international division of labor based on the functional differentiation of countries that reflects their comparative advantage. Trade among them therefore would be socially highly profitable.

Now imagine the same governments under similar circumstances, the only difference being that they are committed to embedded liberalism rather than to laissez-faire. What sorts of international economic transactions would we expect them to favor? The essence of embedded liberalism, it will be recalled, is to devise a form of multilateralism that is compatible with the requirements of domestic stability. Presumably, then, governments so committed would seek to encourage an international division of labor which, while multilateral in form and reflecting *some* notion of comparative advantage (and therefore gains from trade), *also* promised to minimize socially disruptive domestic adjustment costs as well as any national economic and political vulnerabilities that might accrue from international functional differentiation. They will measure collective welfare by the extent to which these objectives are achieved. However, as neoclassical trade theory defines the term, the overall social profitability of this division of labor will be lower than of the one produced by laissez-faire.

[58] David Ricardo, *Works*, ed. by Piero Sraffa (Cambridge: Cambridge University Press, 1955), 1:133–34.

Let us return from the world of hypothesis and review briefly the character of postwar transaction flows.[59]

The great bulk of international economic transactions since the 1950s shows very definite patterns of concentration. The growth in trade has exceeded the growth in world output, and the most rapidly growing sector of trade has been in manufactured products among the industrialized countries. Within this general category, some two-thirds of the increase in trade from 1955 to 1973 is accounted for by "intracontinental" trade, that is, trade within western Europe and within North America.[60] What is more, it appears that trade in products originating in the same sector, or "intra-industry" trade, is growing far more rapidly than trade involving products of different sectors.[61] This in turn reflects a secular decline of specialization in different sectors of manufacturing activity among the industrialized countries.[62] Lastly, there is evidence to suggest that trade among related corporate parties, or "intrafirm" trade, accounts for an ever-larger portion of total world trade.[63] On the financial side, international investments have been rising even more rapidly than world trade, and they conform roughly to the same pattern of geographical, sectoral, and institutional concentration.[64] This is also true of international transfers of short-term funds.[65]

What kind of division of labor among the industrialized countries do these patterns portray? It is, in Cooper's words, one characterized by a

[59] The facts are well enough known, but not enough is made of them. For example, I find that much of what I have to say is implied in if not anticipated by the *locus classicus* of liberal interdependence theorists: Richard N. Cooper, *The Economics of Interdependence* (1968; New York: Columbia University Press, 1980). However, Cooper was concerned with telling a different story, so he chose not to take up issues and conclusions that, from the present vantage point, appear more scintillating. To cite but one illustration, Cooper demonstrates a converging cost structure among the industrialized countries. His major concern is to argue that this contributes to the increasing marginal price sensitivity of rapidly growing foreign trade—that is, to interdependence as he defines the term. In passing, he mentions another implication of this convergence, but one "which will not much concern us here." It is "that international trade becomes less valuable from the viewpoint of increasing economic welfare" (pp. 75–76). This striking departure from the textbook case for free trade, amidst an explosion in world trade, is left unexplored.

[60] Richard Blackhurst, Nicolas Marian, and Jan Tumlir, "Trade Liberalization, Protectionism and Interdependence," *GATT Studies in International Trade* 5 (November 1977), pp. 18–19.

[61] Ibid., pp. 10–11, 15–16; and Charles Lipson's article in this volume.

[62] Richard Cooper has traced this back to 1938, and finds that ten of thirteen manufacturing sectors show declines in variation among countries, and none shows a sharp increase. Cooper, *Economics of Interdependence*, pp. 74–78. In a further refinement, Blackhurst, Marian, and Tumlir, "Trade Liberalization," add that the proportion of imports and exports consisting of intermediate manufactured goods, as opposed to goods destined for final use, is rising rapidly, particularly in the category of engineering products. This reflects, among other things, "the growth in intra-branch specialization, foreign processing and sub-contracting" (pp. 15–16).

[63] Gerald K. Helleiner, "Transnational Corporations and Trade Structure: The Role of Intra-Firm Trade," in Herbert Giersch, ed., *Intra-Industry Trade* (Tübingen: J. C. B. Mohr, Paul Siebeck, 1979).

[64] For a historical overview, see John H. Dunning, *Studies in International Investments* (London: Allen & Unwin, 1970).

[65] A recent survey may be found in Joan Edelman Spero, *The Failure of the Franklin National Bank* (New York: Columbia University Press, 1980), chap. 2.

"narrowing of the economic basis" on which international transactions rest.[66] By this he means that international economic transactions increasingly reflect the effects of marginal cost and price differentials of similar activities and products, rather than the mutual benefits of divergent investment, production, and export structures. Moreover, within this division of labor there is a critical shift in functional differentiation *from* the level of country and sector *to* the level of product and firm. And the economic gains from trade are correspondingly smaller.[67]

All of this stands in stark contrast to the half-century prior to 1914. Intercontinental trade was higher.[68] Intersectoral trade dominated.[69] Long-term capital movements favored capital-deficient areas, and were concentrated overwhelmingly in the social-overhead capital sector of the borrowing countries.[70] Marginal cost and price differentials appear to have had only limited bearing on the pattern of trade and investment flows;[71] the requirements of international functional differentiation and, later, absorptive capacity, account for much more of the variance.[72] Lastly, the large dif-

---

[66] *Economics of Interdependence*, p. 68.

[67] Ibid., p. 76. Cooper adds that both product differentiation and economies of scale may modify this conclusion, "but several of the countries under consideration have sufficiently large domestic markets to reap most benefits likely to flow from large scale production even without trade."

[68] A. G. Kenwood and A. L. Lougheed, *The Growth of the International Economy, 1820–1960* (London: Allen & Unwin, 1971), chap. 5.

[69] For example, in 1913 Great Britain imported 87% of the raw materials it consumed (excluding coal), and virtually as much of its foodstuffs. Moreover, the share of primary products in world trade from 1876–1913 remained steady at about 62%, even though total world trade trebled. And right up to World War I, Germany, Great Britain's main industrial rival, remained a major source of supply of manufactured materials for Great Britain, including chemicals and dyestuffs. Kenwood and Lougheed, *Growth of International Economy*, chap. 5, and Briggs, "World Economy," p. 43.

[70] During the fifty years preceding 1914, the Americas received 51% of British portfolio foreign investment (North America 34%, South America 17%); overall, some 69% of British portfolio foreign investment went into transportation, public utilities, and other public works; 12% into extractive industries; and only 4% into manufacturing. Matthew Simon, "The Pattern of New British Portfolio Foreign Investment, 1865–1914," in A. R. Hall, ed., *The Export of Capital from Britain* (London: Methuen, 1968), p. 23; cf. A. K. Cairncross, *Home and Foreign Investment, 1870–1913* (Cambridge: Cambridge University Press, 1953). A broader survey of the various forms of investment from all sources may be found in Kenwood and Lougheed, *Growth of International Economy*, chap. 2.

[71] For trade, see ibid., chap. 5; for investment, A. I. Bloomfield, "Patterns of Fluctuations in International Investment Before 1914," *Princeton Studies in International Finance* 21 (1968), esp. pp. 35–40. Cooper (*Economics of Interdependence*, pp. 151–52), concerned to show that interdependence in the pre-1914 world economy "was something of an illusion," argues that despite the freedom of capital to move, "it did not in fact move in sufficient volume *even* to erase differences in short-term interest rates." (Emphasis added, to underscore his looking at the pre-1914 world through post-1960 lenses).

[72] "The industrialization of Europe and the growth of its population created a steadily growing demand for raw materials and foodstuffs, much of which had to be imported. At the same time, important advances in technical knowledge, especially in transportation and communications, and the existence of underpopulated and land-rich countries in other continents provided the means whereby these demands could be met. The greater part of the foreign investment undertaken during the nineteenth century was concerned with promoting this international specialization between an industrial centre located in Europe (and, later, in the United States) and a

ferences in comparative cost structures meant that trade was socially very profitable.[73]

To explain fully the differences between the pre–1914 and the post–1950s international division of labor would require linking them to a number of potentially causal factors. Among these, the most frequently invoked are differences in the relative levels of economic and technological development of the major countries concerned;[74] the evolution of the global organization of capital over the course of the past century;[75] the effects of differences in the configuration of interstate power in the two eras;[76] and the respective external consequences of shifts in domestic state-society relations.[77] International regimes thus do not determine these outcomes. At the same time, however, the close similarity between our hypothesized expectations of laissez-faire liberalism and embedded liberalism and actual patterns of transaction flows suggests that regimes do play a mediating role.

This mediating role of the postwar regimes for trade and money, and the complementary transaction flows to which they gave rise, have come to be recognized even by those most consistently espousing conventional liberal orthodoxies. As Charles Lipson points out, GATT negotiations have strongly favored intra-industry specialization.[78] And a recent GATT study notes that liberalization has produced "surprisingly few adjustment problems" among the industrialized countries because there has been "no abandonment of whole industrial sectors." Instead, specialization is "achieved mainly by individual firms narrowing their product range. . . ."[79] As a result, national export structures among the industrialized countries are becoming ever more alike.[80] On reflection, however, this outcome should not cause surprise. For governments pursuing domestic stabilization, it is quite safe to liberalize this kind of trade. Adjustment costs are low. It poses none of the vulnerabilities that a true Ricardian specialization among sectors would pose. Whatever political vulnerabilities might arise from it are more or less shared by all parties to it, so that it is unlikely to lead to a contest for political

---

periphery of primary producing countries." Kenwood and Lougheed, *Growth of International Economy*, p. 48.

[73] Cooper, *Economics of Interdependence*, p. 152.

[74] This is generally considered to be the driving force by liberal economists, as exemplified by Cooper, ibid.

[75] Marxists have tended to stress this factor; see, for example, Christian Palloix, "The Self-Expansion of Capital on a World Scale," *Review of Radical Political Economy* 9 (Summer 1977), which is drawn from his larger work, *L'internationalisation du capital* (Paris: Maspero, 1975).

[76] This is the realists' explanandum, as developed in Waltz, "Myth of National Interdependence," though most realists, unlike Waltz, would characterize the distribution of power in the pre–1914 world political economy as having been hegemonic. Cf. Robert Gilpin, *U.S. Power and the Multinational Corporation* (New York: Basic Books, 1975).

[77] See Polanyi's *Great Transformation* for one expression of this social-organicist position; for another, from a different location on the political spectrum, see Gunnar Myrdal, *Beyond the Welfare State* (New Haven: Yale University Press, 1960).

[78] His article in this volume.

[79] Blackhurst, Marian, and Tumlir, "Trade Liberalization," p. 11.

[80] See Lipson's article in this volume, and the references he cites.

advantage among them. And all the while it offers gains from trade. In contrast, there has been no progress in liberalizing agricultural trade. Furthermore, where trade in industrial products is based on a more classical notion of comparative advantage, as it is with imports from the so-called newly industrializing countries, the trade regime has encountered difficulty.[81] Apart from oil, North-South raw materials trade has posed few problems for the industrialized countries, both because of their overall domination of world trade and because of the characteristics of the raw materials sector.[82]

International financial flows may be expected to follow closely the evolving patterns of production and trade. Since the liberalization of payments facilities at the end of the 1950s and the loosening of capital controls in the early 1960s, they have done so. Two additional features of international financial transactions bear on my argument. First, international investments in social overhead capital, which provided the great bulk of private flows in the 1865–1914 period, now are almost the exclusive domain of national and international public institutions, acting alone or in cofinancing arrangements with private capital.[83] This has meant a welcome supplement to the vagaries of the market mechanism for recipient countries, and for donor countries as well, though in a different sense. For the donor countries, it has meant an ability to exercise far greater discretion over patterns of investment decisions in this leading sector than governments in the 19th century either enjoyed or sought. Second, the international financial markets that emerged in the 1960s, above all the Euromarkets, offered governments an important supplement to the monetary regime. Under Keynes's Clearing Union, capital controls were combined with generous overdraft allowances and parity changes as needed. In their absence or, more accurately, under the more modest forms of each that came to prevail in the 1960s, these markets offered the prospect of an adjustment mechanism to cushion both surplus and deficit countries (at least in the short run). Accordingly, governments did little to control and much to encourage the formation and growth of these markets.[84] Today, they constitute the main source of balance-of-payments financing.[85]

[81] This is not to suggest that the trade regime has encountered no other difficulties. One of the more serious is surplus capacity, which shows that the apparent ease with which liberalization has been accommodated was also dependent upon unprecedented rates of economic growth.

[82] Paul Bairoch, *The Economic Development of the Third World since 1900* (Berkeley: University of California Press, 1975), chap. 5.

[83] Dunning, *International Investments*, chap. 1. Governmental loans were largely confined to Continental Europe in the 19th century, and were small in comparison with private loans. Today, the situation is reversed in each respect.

[84] A good discussion of the role of governments in triggering the expansion of these markets may be found in Susan Strange, *International Monetary Relations*, vol. 2 of Shonfield, ed., *International Economic Relations of the Western World*, esp. chap. 6. Strange's primary concern is to show how the Euromarkets transformed from "good servant" to "bad master," by making difficult the conduct of domestic monetary policy and generally eroding national monetary sovereignty. The good servant role received rather more attention again in the mid to late 1970s, following the enormous payments imbalances produced by oil price increases. More on this general problem below.

[85] Benjamin J. Cohen's article in this volume.

In sum, international economic regimes do not determine international economic transactions. For determinants we have to look deeper into basic structural features of the world political economy. But, as we have seen, nor are international economic regimes irrelevant to international economic transactions. They play a mediating role, by providing a permissive environment for the emergence of certain kinds of transactions, specifically transactions that are perceived to be complementary to the normative frameworks of the regimes having a bearing on them. This conclusion does not imply that perceptions are never mistaken, that "good servants" never go on to become "bad masters," that complementarity is never condemned to coexist with contradiction—or, indeed, that international regimes have a bearing on the entire range of international transactions. Nor does it suggest that the effectiveness of international regimes may not become undermined by such disjunctions. The question of possible responses to second-order consequences of this sort takes us into a different analytical realm, that of regime change.

4. Norm-governed change

The 1970s witnessed important changes in central features of the post-war regimes for money and trade. Among political scientists and some economists, the decline of U.S. hegemony is most often adduced as the *causa causans* of these changes. Terms such as "erosion" and even "collapse" are most often invoked to describe them. Triffin depicted the Jamaica Accords as "slapstick comedy" rather than monetary reform, while for a former U.S. trade official the Tokyo Round "performed the coup de grace" on liberal trade.[86] The sense of discontinuity is pervasive. Is it justified?

Once again I take temporary refuge in hypothesis. If we allow that international regimes are not simply emanations of the underlying distribution of interstate power, but represent a fusion of power and legitimate social purpose, our cause and effect reasoning becomes more complex. For then the decline of hegemony would not necessarily lead to the collapse of regimes, provided that shared purposes are held constant. Instead, one ought to find changes in the instrumentalities of regimes, which, under hegemony, are likely to have relied on disproportionate contributions by and therefore reflected the preferences of the hegemon.[87] At the same time, one ought to find continuity in the normative frameworks of regimes, which would still

[86] Robert Triffin, "Jamaica: 'Major Revision' or Fiasco," in Edward M. Bernstein et al., "Reflections on Jamaica," *Princeton Essays in International Finance* 115 (Princeton, N.J., 1976), as cited in Benjamin J. Cohen, *Organizing the World's Money* (New York: Basic Books, 1977), chap. 4, fn. 24; and Thomas Graham, "Revolution in Trade Politics," *Foreign Policy* 36 (Fall 1979), p. 49.

[87] Supporters of the hegemonic stability position speak of "burdens of leadership"; critics, of "exorbitant privileges." The empirical referents are the same.

reflect shared purposes. And the new instrumentalities ought to be more appropriate to the new power distribution while remaining compatible with the existing normative framework. In short, the result would be "norm-governed" change.

Let us turn back to the post–1971 changes in the regimes for money and trade. On the monetary side, the major changes at issue are the end of the dollar's convertibility into gold and the adoption of floating rates of exchange, both in violation of the original Articles of Agreement. On the trade side, no discrete event fully symbolizes the perceived discontinuities, though they are characterized generally as "the new protectionism" and include the proliferation of nontariff barriers to trade and violations of the principle of nondiscrimination, in the form of domestic interventions as well as internationally negotiated export restraints. In both cases a weakening of the central institutions, the IMF and the GATT, is taken to reflect the same syndrome.

It is my contention that, on balance, the hypothesis of norm-governed change accounts for more of the variance than claims of fundamental discontinuity.

Base-line

The base-line against which change is here to be compared consists of two parts. First, if we compare changes in the monetary and trade regimes against some ideal of orthodox liberalism, then we are bound to be disappointed if not shocked by recent trends. But we are also bound to be misled. For orthodox liberalism has not governed international economic relations at any time during the postwar period. My starting point, of course, is the institutional nexus of embedded liberalism. Within this framework, it will be recalled, multilateralism and domestic stability are linked to and conditioned by one another. Thus, movement toward greater openness in the international economy is likely to be coupled with measures designed to cushion the domestic economy from external disruptions. At the same time, measures adopted to effect such domestic cushioning should be commensurate with the degree of external disturbance and compatible with the long-term expansion of international transactions. Moreover, what constitutes a deviation from this base-line cannot be determined simply by the "objective" examination of individual acts in reference to specific texts. Rather, deviation will be determined by the "intersubjective" evaluation of the intentionality and consequences of acts within the broader normative framework and prevailing circumstances.

The second component of my base-line is the peculiar relation of the United States to the institutionalization of embedded liberalism immediately after the war. The United States was, at one and the same time, the paramount economic power *and* the country in which the domestic state-society shift remained the most ambivalent. This had several complex consequences, with differential effects on the two regimes. The United States would have to provide the bulk of the material resources required to translate the negotiated compromises into institutional reality. This would give the U.S. influence that it could be expected to exercise in keeping not only with its own interests, but also with its preferred interpretations of both the compromises and how they were to be realized. The impact on the institutionalization of the trade agreement, once the ITO was abandoned, on the whole supported the basic design and need not detain us. But the institutionalization of the monetary agreement was profoundly skewed by the asymmetrical position of the U.S.[88] At Bretton Woods, through a combination of stealth and inevitability, the dollar had become equated with gold and was recognized officially but apparently without the knowledge of Keynes as the key currency.[89] Once the IMF came into existence, the U.S. insisted on terms of reference and a series of "interpretations" of the Articles, as well as decisions of the Executive Directors, that had the effect of launching what would come to be known as "IMF orthodoxy" and, inadvertently or otherwise, guaranteeing that there would be no intergovernmental alternative to U.S. payments deficits as the major instrument of international liquidity creation.[90] Thus, the monetary regime that emerged in the 1950s already differed in several important respects from the intent of Bretton Woods.

It is against this starting point that subsequent developments must be assessed.

[88] The differential impact on the two regimes is explained largely by the total asymmetry that prevailed in the monetary domain and the relatively more balanced configuration in trade. In the case of money, the U.S. possessed the fungible resources that everyone required, including some two-thirds of the world's monetary gold supply, which it acquired as an unbalanced creditor country before World War II. At the same time, the U.S. saw no situation in which it might become dependent upon the regime as a debtor. The case of trade is inherently somewhat more symmetrical, since the mutual granting of access to markets is the key resource. It is also a domain in which the domestic constraints within the United States differed little from domestic constraints elsewhere.

[89] Harry Dexter White and his staff had complete control over the organization of meetings, scheduling of subjects, rules of procedure, and drafting of all official documentation including daily minutes and the Final Act. In addition, White headed the so-called special committee, which resolved ambiguities and elaborated operational details. According to Van Dormael, on whose account I draw here, this committee "prepared for inclusion in the Final Act a number of provisions that were never discussed nor even brought up" (*Bretton Woods*, pp. 202–3). Even senior members of the American delegation were not always fully aware of what White was up to; Dean Acheson, normally no slouch, expressed confusion, and what he suspected he didn't much care for (ibid., pp. 200–203). In any case, Van Dormael attributes several features of the Fund to these organizational and procedural manipulations, the most important of which was an equation that no one else became aware of until after the fact, between gold and the U.S. dollar. This was in clear violation of the Joint Statement of Principles. Keynes had rejected any special role for the dollar; he favored the monetization of an international unit of account, and he assumed a multiple-currency reserve system. But in the final analysis, the major consequence of White's maneuverings on this issue was simply to give *de jure* expression to what surely would have occurred *de facto* and have been sanctified by subsequent practice.

[90] At the inaugural meeting of the Boards of Governors of the IMF and IBRD, held in Savannah, Georgia, the United States succeeded in having both institutions located in Washington, which could be expected to amplify day-to-day influence by Congress and the Administration,

The evolving monetary regime

The post–1971 inconvertibility of the dollar into gold may be usefully framed within the broader rubric of liquidity problems and floating rates of exchange within adjustment problems. I take up each in turn, and conclude with a comment on the IMF.

As noted, the liquidity provisions of Bretton Woods proved inadequate, even though, as Cohen points out elsewhere in this volume, an adequate supply of international liquidity was one of its cardinal principles. The growing volume of international trade increased liquidity requirements, as did the growing magnitude of speculative pressure on exchange rates. The dollar exchange standard, which had "solved" this problem in the short run, was already in trouble when the monetary regime first began to function without the protective shield of the postwar transitional arrangements. In 1958, just as the Europeans were resuming full convertibility of their currencies, U.S. gold reserves fell permanently below U.S. overseas liabilities. And before the next year was out, Professor Triffin had articulated his famous dilemma.[91] Throughout the 1960s, a seemingly endless series of stopgap measures was tried in an effort to devise what Robert Roosa, former

---

and in having the Executive Directors be full-time and highly paid officials, which was seen by the British as assuring greater Fund meddling in the affairs of members when they applied for assistance. They were not mistaken. In May 1947, the United States pushed through a meeting of the Executive Directors an "interpretation" of the Articles of Agreement, to the effect that the Fund could "challenge" the representations made by governments that a currency was presently needed for balance-of-payments purposes, *and* that the Fund had the authority to "postpone or reject the request, *or accept it subject to conditions*. . . ." (Reproduced in Horsefield, *The IMF*, 3: 227, emphasis added.) This interpretation was confirmed by decision of the Executive Directors in 1948. And thus was IMF conditionality born. In a further decision, taken in 1952, conditionality was elaborated to include "policies the member will pursue" to overcome payments deficits. (Ibid., 3: 228.) In the meantime, once the Marshall Plan went into effect, the United States secured further agreement that recipients of Marshall Plan aid could not also draw on the Fund. With the Europeans effectively excluded from the Fund, its only clients were developing countries. And it was during this period, on initiatives by the United States and in response to requests for assistance by developing countries, that the Fund developed its program of "stabilization" measures: exchange depreciation, domestic austerity measures, reduced public spending, rigid conditionality. Total drawings from the Fund dropped to zero in 1950, and did not exceed 1947 levels again until 1956. With respect to liquidity, the provisions of Bretton Woods were modest and proved inadequate. The European Reconstruction Program took care of Europe's needs. But the IMF repeatedly turned aside requests for new measures to increase its own capacity to supply liquidity, maintaining that the real need was for adjustment. The dollar exchange standard emerged as a "solution" to this problem. (Strange, *International Monetary Relations*, pp. 93–96; Block, *Origins of International Economic Disorder*, chap. 5; Richard Cooper, "Prolegomena to the Choice," p. 86; and Benjamin J. Cohen, in this volume.)

[91] In essence, Triffin argued that if the United States corrected its balance of payments deficit, the result would be world deflation because gold production at $35 an ounce could not adequately supply world monetary reserves. But if the United States continued running a deficit, the result would be the collapse of the monetary standard because U.S. foreign liabilities would far exceed its ability to convert dollars into gold on demand. Robert Triffin, *Gold and the Dollar Crisis* (New Haven: Yale University Press, 1960), which was largely a reprint of two journal articles that appeared the year before.

under-secretary of the treasury, called "outer perimeter defenses" for the dollar. Roughly speaking, these measures were designed to make gold conversion financially unattractive, to increase the capacity of the IMF to supply liquidity, and to increase the capacity of central banks to neutralize the flow of speculative capital. The U.S. also undertook limited domestic measures to reduce its payments deficits and pressured surplus countries to revalue their currencies. By 1968, however, the dollar had become in effect inconvertible into gold; it was declared formally inconvertible in 1971.

The rise and fall of the gold-convertible dollar has placed the monetary regime in a paradoxical predicament from beginning to end. It has altered profoundly central instruments of the regime having to do with the creation of international liquidity, the system of currency reserves, and the means of ultimate settlement. It has also violated procedural norms, as unilateral action usurped collective decision. But, at the same time, it seems to have been understood and acknowledged all around that, under the material and political conditions prevailing, the substantive norms of Bretton Woods, the compromise of embedded liberalism, would not have been realized in the first place by any other means. So the regime today remains stuck with the undesired consequences of means that helped bring about a desired end. What of the long-term alternatives? Several have emerged in embryonic form. Were they to be instituted more fully, all would imply a reduced official role for the dollar and a return to the kinds of mechanisms anticipated by Bretton Woods. An internationally created reserve asset exists in the form of the special drawing right (SDR). A multiple-currency reserve system is slowly coming into being, and a dollar-substitution account has been under negotiation in the IMF. The U.S. views the SDR with disfavor and actively opposes the substitution account. It has no objection to other currencies playing a larger reserve role. As they do, however, the pressure may be expected to increase both for a substitution facility covering all reserve currencies and for a noncurrency reserve asset.

With respect to the problem of adjustment, as we saw, few provisions for international measures to affect the economic policies of deficit or surplus countries survived the Bretton Woods negotiations. And once the new creditor-debtor relationships became established in the late 1950s, the mechanism of exchange rate changes also failed to operate effectively. There existed no means to compel surplus countries to appreciate, and among the largest deficit countries, Great Britain resisted depreciation fiercely in a vain attempt to preserve an international role for sterling while the United States, as the "Nth country," necessarily remained passive. Thus, the only real international leverage for adjustment was the conditionality provision developed by the Fund. The burden of domestic adjustment measures, therefore, fell disproportionately on the developing countries. The adjustable peg system became intolerable when imbalances in the external trade account came to be overshadowed, both as a source of problems and as a response to them, by massive movements of short-term speculative funds. This made it increasingly difficult for governments to conduct domestic macroeconomic policy, and to support exchange rates under pressure. When, in the late 1960s, the full attention of these funds came to be focused on the dollar as a result of dramatic deficits in the U.S. trade balance and current account, the system of fixed rates of exchange was doomed.

Shifting to floating rates required formal amendment of the Articles of Agreement of the Fund, the "slapstick comedy" act of which Triffin spoke. This is prima facie evidence of discontinuity. However, living within the Articles provided the international monetary system with an adjustment mechanism that neither functioned effectively nor fulfilled the expectations of Bretton Woods. What of the present arrangement? Three aspects bear on the argument. First, it is important to keep distinct the instrument of fixed rates from the norm of outlawing competitive currency depreciation and thus providing a framework for relatively stable exchanges. There is a good case to be made that the norm had become sufficiently well institutionalized and recourse to competitive depreciation sufficiently unnecessary given other means of influencing domestic macroeconomic factors that reliance on an increasingly burdensome instrument, which itself had begun to contribute to currency instability, could no longer be justified.[92] Moreover, experience since has shown the managed float to be capable of avoiding serious disorderliness—the early months of new administrations in Washington providing the major exceptions—and to have few if any deleterious consequences for international trade. Second, floating rates were widely perceived to provide a greater cushion for domestic macroeconomic policy, which was increasingly subjected to dislocation from speculative capital flows that were often quite out of proportion to underlying economic reality. It is clear now that the degree of insulation is less than was advertised, but in the absence of uniform and fairly comprehensive capital controls it is probably as much as can be secured. Third, as an adjustment mechanism, the managed float appears to function more symmetrically than fixed rates did. Not only have surplus countries been forced to take notice, but the precipitous depreciation of the U.S. dollar caught the attention of American policy makers in the autumn of 1978 more effectively than past balance-of-payments deficits had done.

On the evolution of the IMF we can be brief; its tendency seems to be to come full circle. One does not want to exaggerate recent changes in the Fund, especially in relation to the developing countries. Nevertheless, its financing facilities have been considerably expanded, repayment periods lengthened, and conditionality provisions relaxed somewhat as well as now requiring the Fund "to pay due regard to the domestic social and political objectives" of borrowing countries.[93] Moreover, decision-making power within the Fund has been reapportioned, at least to the extent of distributing

[92] Richard Cooper enumerates the pros and cons of these and related issues in "Prolegomena to the Choice," esp. pp. 80–81.

[93] Reported in *The New York Times,* 5 February 1980. In exploring the reasons for this change, the *Times* cites a "Washington wit" who "once said that the monetary fund had toppled more governments than Marx and Lenin combined."

veto power more equitably. These changes began in the late 1950s, to make the Fund more acceptable to the Europeans once they accepted the full obligations of IMF membership; they continued in the 1960s to reflect the economic status of the European Community and Japan; and they were accelerated and aimed increasingly at the developing countries in the 1970s, as a result of the massive payments imbalances produced by new energy terms of trade and subsequent fears about the stability of the international financial system.

The evolution of the trade regime

The sense of discontinuity concerning the international trade regime is illustrated in the following excerpt from a *Wall Street Journal* article, entitled "Surge in Protectionism Worries and Perplexes Leaders of Many Lands":

> After three decades of immense increase in world trade and living standards, exports and imports are causing tense pressures in nearly every nation and among the best of allies. The U.S. sets price floors against Japanese steel, Europe accuses the U.S. of undercutting its papermakers, the Japanese decry cheap textiles from South Korea, French farmers have smashed truckloads of Italian wine, and AFL-CIO President George Meany rattles exporters world-wide by calling free trade—'a joke.'[94]

By now, even its most severe critics realize that "the new protectionism" is not simply the latest manifestation of "old-style" protectionism. "The emergence of the new protectionism in the Western world reflects the victory of the interventionist, or welfare, economy over the market economy."[95] However, they continue to have difficulty appreciating that the new protectionism is not an aberration from the norm of postwar liberalization, but an integral feature of it.

Today, tariffs on products traded among the industrialized countries are an insignificant barrier to trade. The Tokyo Round managed to institute further tariff cuts, and began to cope with nontariff barriers for the first time. It produced codes to liberalize such barriers resulting from domestic subsidies and countervailing duties, government procurement, product standards, customs valuation, and import licensing. All barriers to trade in civil aircraft and aircraft parts were removed. And preparations for a new GATT round, on investment and services, have commenced. What is more, the volume of world trade continues to increase and its rate of growth, though declining, still exceeds economic growth rates in several OECD countries. In sum, liberalization and growth have continued despite the erosion of postwar

[94] 14 April 1978, as cited in Melvyn B. Krauss, *The New Protectionism: The Welfare State in International Trade* (New York: New York University Press, 1978), pp. xix-xx.
[95] Ibid., p. 36.

prosperity, and despite the erosion of American willingness to absorb disproportionate shares of liberalized trade.[96]

Restraints on trade have also grown. Much of the time they take one of two forms: domestic safeguards, and "voluntary" or negotiated export restraints. Under the GATT, domestic safeguards may be invoked for balance-of-payments reasons (Article XII), or to prevent injury to domestic producers caused by a sudden surge of imports that can be attributed to past tariff concessions (Article XIX). The first of these has caused little difficulty, notwithstanding several deviations from prescribed procedure.[97] Article XIX lends itself to greater abuse. It permits alteration or suspension of past tariff concessions in a nondiscriminatory manner, provided that interested parties are consulted. It has been invoked with growing frequency, particularly by the U.S. and Australia. It is quite clumsy, however, because bystanders are likely to be affected and because it may involve renegotiation or even retaliatory suspension of concessions. As a result, "most governments, on most occasions, have simply short-circuited Article XIX altogether, going straight to the heart of the problem by negotiating a minimum price agreement, or a 'voluntary' export restraint with the presumably reluctant exporter who has previously been 'softened' by threats of emergency action under GATT."[98] Many of these agreements do not involve governments at all, but are reached directly between the importing and exporting industries concerned. They take place beyond the purview of the GATT and therefore are not subject to official multilateral surveillance. An attempt, made during the Tokyo Round, to conclude a safeguards code that would have provided detailed rules and procedures was unsuccessful, though negotiations are continuing. However, these problems do not afflict the entire trading order, but are sectorally specific, and a close sectoral analysis will show that there is *not* "any decisive movement toward protectionism. . . ."[99] Lastly, so-

[96] Stephen D. Krasner, "The Tokyo Round: Particularistic Interests and Prospects for Stability in the Global Trading System," *International Studies Quarterly* 23 (December 1979).

[97] For example, Article XII calls for quantitative restrictions, but as time has passed import surcharges have usually been imposed. In an extremely peculiar "non-use" of Article XII, France imposed emergency measures against imports after the 1968 disturbances, while enjoying a strong reserve position and only fearing a potential balance-of-payments problem. France asked for "sympathy and understanding" from its partners in the GATT and got it. The exceptional circumstances were stressed all around, the danger of precedent was flagged, and the measures were approved and soon thereafter discontinued. The case shows, according to Curzon and Curzon, "the complicity which exists between governments when one of them is forced to take unpopular trade measures because it has a domestic problem on its hands" ("Management of Trade," p. 222). Their characterization of the reaction of others as complicitous captures the very essence of an international regime.

[98] Ibid., p. 225.

[99] Krasner, "Tokyo Round," p. 507. Krasner examines sectoral crosspressures and finds roughly this pattern: little pressure for protectionism where there is high intrasectoral trade, and even less if the sector is highly internationalized; protectionist pressures from import-competing sectors, which, however, may be balanced off by countervailing pressure from export sectors; high protectionist pressure when import competition is largely asymmetrical (pp. 502–7). Lipson, elsewhere in this volume, relates protectionist pressures to the production characteristics of sectors and finds that "sectoral protectionism is most likely in standardized, basic industries,

called orderly marketing arrangements, of which the Longterm Textile Agreement of 1962 was the first multilateral variant, have also proliferated vastly. However, each of these has provided for a regular expansion of exports, though of course more limited than would have been obtained under conditions of "free" trade. In sum, the impact of these restraints on international trade, even by the GATT's own reckoning, has been relatively modest.[100] Their purpose, moreover, has not been to freeze the international division of labor but to slow down structural change and to minimize the social costs of domestic adjustment.

With respect to the institutional role of the GATT, legal scholars in particular have lamented the passing of "effective and impartial" dispute settlement mechanisms.[101] However, these mechanisms had begun to fall into disuse by the late 1950s—that is, just as production and trade began to soar and serious tariff reductions were contemplated. Bilateral consultations and negotiations among instructed representatives of the disputants have since been the norm.[102] It requires an extremely optimistic view of the possibilities for international law and conciliation to expect interventionist governments to behave otherwise.

Assessment

This review does not argue that the world it describes is the best of all possible worlds. I have only argued that the world has to be looked at as it is: when the regimes for money and trade are viewed in this light, the hypothesis of norm-governed change accounts for more of the variance than claims of fundamental discontinuity. Much of the observed change has been at the level of instrument rather than norm. Moreover, in most cases the new instruments are not inimical to the norms of the regimes but represent adaptations to new circumstances. And in some cases the collective response by governments to changing circumstances reflects a greater affinity to the ex-

---

or those with high capital requirements. It is least likely in industries where R&D is high and is oriented to changing market opportunities, where innovation in products and processes is rapid, and where the rents attributable to proprietary knowledge are short-lived" (draft manuscript).

[100] Two figures are pertinent here. First, the GATT estimated in the late 1970s that import restrictions already in place or seriously threatened would affect some 3%–5% of world trade—which its Director General took to represent a threat to "the whole fabric of postwar cooperation in international trade policy." *IMF Survey,* 12 December 1977, p. 373. The second concerns the declining portion of world trade subject to MFN principles; here it must be pointed out that the overwhelming share of this decline is accounted for by customs unions and free trade areas, which, for better or for worse, have been sanctioned by the GATT. A more fundamental problem could emerge as a result of the Tokyo Round, insofar as the codes for government procurement, subsidies, and safeguards (if the last materializes) will apply only to signatories of each individual code. At this point, however, the long-term significance of this proviso remains unclear.

[101] See the literature cited in Lipson's article in this volume.

[102] Curzon and Curzon, "Management of Trade," chap. 3.

pectations of original regime designs than did the arrangements that prevailed in the interval.

This analysis suggests that far more continuity can attend hegemonic √ decline than would be predicted by the hegemonic stability thesis, provided that social purposes are held constant.[103] And, since social purposes in turn reflect particular configurations of state-society relations, it suggests further that fundamental discontinuity in these regimes *would* be effected by an erosion in the prevailing balance of state-society relations among the major economic powers. Ironically, then, the foremost force for discontinuity at present is not "the new protectionism" in money and trade, but the resurgent ethos of liberal capitalism.

5. Stress, contradiction, and the future

One question remains. How enduring is embedded liberalism? Specifically, will it survive the current domestic and international economic malaise? A central ingredient in the success of embedded liberalism to date has been its ability to accommodate and even facilitate the externalizing of adjustment costs. There have been three major modes of externalization: an intertemporal mode, via inflation; an intersectoral mode, whereby pressure on domestic and international public authorities is vented into the realm of private markets; and what, for the sake of congruity, we might call an interstratum mode, through which those who are "regime makers" shift a disproportionate share of adjustment costs onto those who are "regime takers." Each of these has emerged virtually by default as a means to avoid a still worse outcome.[104] The accumulated effects of these practices, however, have produced severe stresses in the world political economy. As a result, some manner of renegotiating the forms of domestic and international social accommodation reflected in embedded liberalism is inevitable. Its future, then, depends on how this is brought about. I take up the three modes of externalization in reverse order.

The compromise of embedded liberalism has never been fully extended to the developing countries. They have been disproportionately subject to the orthodox stabilization measures of the IMF, often with no beneficial results in export earnings but substantial increases in import bills and con-

[103] The fit between hypothesis and real world obviously is not perfect, because factors other than those examined here are also at work in the evolution of the postwar regimes. Moreover, the notion of declining American hegemony itself is very imprecise and, indeed, easy to exaggerate. See, respectively, Keohane, "Theory of Hegemonic Stability," and Susan Strange, "Still an Extraordinary Power," in Ray Lombra and Bill Witte, eds., *The Political Economy of International and Domestic Monetary Relations* (Ames: Iowa State University Press, 1982).

[104] I am here generalizing from Fred Hirsch's brilliant dissection of the social functions of inflation: "The Ideological Underlay of Inflation," in Fred Hirsch and John H. Goldthorpe, eds., *The Political Economy of Inflation* (Cambridge: Harvard University Press, 1978), esp. p. 278.

sequent increases in domestic prices. Moreover, the liberalization produced by the GATT has benefited relatively few among them. On the whole, the developing countries did well in the 1960s, as an adjunct to expansion in the OECD area; in the 1970s, they suffered as much from export losses to OECD markets as they did from the direct impact of increased oil prices. For a time in the mid 1970s, the developing countries managed to sustain both rates of growth and imports from the industrialized countries through additional private borrowing (their upper tranches in the IMF were left virtually untouched). However, neither could be continued indefinitely. Recent IMF reforms are important, as we have noted, but they cannot initiate economic recovery in the Third World. Nor are other means forthcoming in abundance. Thus, unlike the pattern under laissez-faire liberalism in the 19th century, under embedded liberalism lending and investment in the peripheral areas has been both relatively lower and positively correlated with core expansion rather than counterpoised to it. From the point of view of the future of embedded liberalism, the accumulated effects of this practice are not fatal—though they may prove to be very nearly fatal for some of the poorer developing countries.[105] From the point of view of the established system as a whole, these effects are more in the nature of lost opportunities whose realization could have contributed to the resolution of the current economic malaise.

A second mode of externalizing adjustment costs in recent decades has been to channel pressure away from domestic and international public authorities into the domain of private markets. A prime example is the vastly increased role of international financial markets in balance-of-payments lending, as analyzed by Cohen in this volume. I argued above that the success of the monetary and trade regimes may be said to have depended in some measure on this practice, even before the recycling problems of the 1970s. But it has also come to pose a source of serious stress and potential contradiction for the monetary regime, particularly as the control of inflation has become the leading economic objective of governments. One of its consequences, discussed by Cohen, is at least a partial loss of control by governments over the process of international liquidity creation. Perhaps even more important, in attempting to achieve significant restraint in the expansion of credit and money stock effected by these markets, governments may find that the domestic economy now must shoulder a disproportionate share of the burden of adjustment. Higher domestic interest rates may have to be employed than would be warranted by domestic conditions alone, in order to compensate for the more rapid rate of expansion of the Eurofund component of the consolidated domestic and international markets. "Today the mass is still relatively small, but the speed is high. Mass times speed, as the physi-

---

[105] Hollis B. Chenery notes this exception in his otherwise optimistic outlook, "Restructuring the World Economy: Round II," *Foreign Affairs* 59 (Summer 1981).

cists like to say, equals momentum.''[106] From the vantage point of our concerns, then, what has served as a handy and even necessary vent is threatening to undergo a means-ends reversal, with potentially serious consequences for domestic and international financial stability.

Lastly, I turn to the most pervasive and the most serious mode by which adjustment costs have been externalized, inflation. It is the most serious because it is the most likely to lead to a direct renegotiation of the modus vivendi that has characterized embedded liberalism. The international regimes for money and trade have increasingly accommodated inflation, in parallel with inflation's becoming the dominant domestic means of dealing with distributional strife in advanced capitalist societies.[107] On the monetary side, the release of domestic and international money supplies from their metallic base established the essential permissive condition, facilitated by subsequent developments in the monetary regime. The primacy of domestic objectives over external financial discipline was established in the interwar period. The Bretton Woods adjustment process, when it worked, worked primarily to devalue the currencies of deficit countries and consequently to increase their domestic prices. With inconvertible reserve currencies and floating rates, whatever counterforce may have existed in the pressures that previously led to gold outflows now leads to a fall in exchange rates and thus to increases in prices and costs. On the side of the trade regime, the structure of trade that it has encouraged and the minimization of domestic adjustment costs that it allows have both had inflationary consequences, by sacrificing economic efficiency to social stability. Hirsch's conclusion concerning the monetary regime is equally applicable to both: ''Critics who see these international . . . arrangements as embodying a ratchet effect for world inflation are probably right. But the relevant question is whether a liberal international economy could have been purchased at any more acceptable price.''[108] This dilemma will not be easily resolved.[109] However, so long as it remains understood that it is a dilemma, both parts of which have to be accommodated, the normative framework of embedded liberalism will endure as a central institutional feature of the international economic order.

[106] Henry C. Wallich, ''Why the Euromarket Needs Restraint,'' *Columbia Journal of World Business* 14 (Fall 1979), p. 17. Wallich estimates that the Euromarkets are expanding at two to three times the rate of growth of the domestic markets of major countries (p. 23).

[107] Hirsch and Goldthorpe, *Political Economy of Inflation,* especially the chapters by Hirsch; Goldthorpe, ''The Current Inflation: Towards a Sociological Account,'' pp. 186–214; and Charles S. Maier, ''The Politics of Inflation in the Twentieth Century,'' pp. 37–72. The following discussion of the monetary regime draws heavily on Hirsch.

[108] Ibid., p. 279.

[109] Recent enthusiasm for simply discrediting Keynesian management and reverting to earlier monetary and fiscal ''discipline'' has begun to dampen under the weight of its apparent consequences. For example, in a postmortem of the 1981 summer riots across England, a junior member of the Tory government chose words that could have been taken directly from Polanyi: ''This is what happens when you separate economic theory from social policy and pursue the one at the expense of the other.'' (Cited by David S. Broder, ''Britain Offers a Grim Reminder,'' *Manchester Guardian Weekly,* 26 July 1981, p. 16.)

The transformation of trade:
the sources and effects
of regime change

Charles Lipson

Understanding international economic regimes is essentially a twofold problem. Aside from specifying an issue's salient features, the first difficulty is to understand why regimes form, endure, and change. Regimes are thus approached as dependent variables that can vary in several ways: in the actors' adherence to rules, norms, and principles; in the coherence and pervasiveness of agreed procedures; and in the degree to which actors share convergent expectations. With the dependent variable specified (but without any sure scale to measure its variations), most analysis has focused on the predictive accuracy and causal sufficiency of models purporting to explain regime change.[1]

This understandable quest to explain regime change has ignored a second problem, the impact of regimes on behavior within an issue-area. What is the relationship between regimes, considered as normative and regulatory frameworks (or, for Keohane, as meta-agreements), and the volume and character of some putatively regulated activity? In this perspective, regimes are seen as intervening variables standing between some underlying distribution of capabilities and some volume of transactions, such as trade flows, arms sales or debt repayment. This perspective is consistent with Jer-

I am grateful to the conference participants for their vigorous discussion of the trade regime. Several colleagues also offered detailed comments on earlier drafts. I especially wish to thank John Barceló III, Benjamin J. Cohen, Stephen Haggard, Roger Hansen, Raymond Hopkins, Robert Keohane, Stephen Krasner, Lynn Mytelka, John Odell, Robert Pastor, Gilbert Winham, and Mark Zacher. The Rockefeller Foundation generously supported this research through its International Affairs Fellowship.

[1] Robert O. Keohane and Joseph S. Nye, *Power and Interdependence: World Politics in Transition* (Boston: Little, Brown, 1977); Stephen D. Krasner, "State Power and the Structure of International Trade," *World Politics* 28 (April 1976), pp. 317–47.

International Organization 36, 2, Spring 1982
0020-8183/82/020417-39 $1.50

vis's observation that international institutions can shape behavior only if the connection between outcomes and national power is indirect and mediated.[2]

Regimes, in other words, may be analyzed either as outcomes to be explained or as social institutions mediating economic and political intercourse.

The two perspectives, although complementary, raise different research questions. When the trade regime, for example, is studied as a dependent variable (as most regimes are), an overriding question is why a relatively liberal regime formed after World War II but not after World War I. Why has this relatively liberal regime weakened over the past decade? If, on the other hand, we study regimes as mediating social institutions, then our questions focus on the regime's distinctive impact on behavior. Do changes in the liberal trade regime really affect the daily flow of goods across borders? Are national commercial policies shaped by the presence of a regime?

This analysis takes up both kinds of questions about the modern trade regime. First, we specify the regime's salient features and examine the causal sources of regime change and continuity. Later, we turn to the regime's impact on behavior—commercial policy and trade flows.

Both questions, it should be noted, bear on a larger analytic problem: the relationship between international political structures and international economic activities. In the modern world economy, political structures such as the rules and institutions dealing with trade are typically artifacts of state action.[3] The General Agreement on Tariffs and Trade (GATT), for example, was begun under strong American leadership and continues now under the multilateral auspices of the U.S., the European Community (EC), and to a lesser extent Japan. Economic activities, by contrast, are typically decentralized, privately controlled, and market-oriented.[4] This disjunction between interstate political structures and decentralized economic activity forms a central problematic for the study of international political economy.[5]

---

[2] See Robert Jervis's article in this volume.

[3] The centrality of state actors is not absolute; for example, the regime dealing with international debt repayment is based largely on commercial bank lenders and the International Monetary Fund. See the author's "The International Organization of Third World Debt," *International Organization* 35, 4 (Autumn 1981), pp. 603–631.

[4] In manufactured goods, most imports and exports are handled by private firms, either in arms-length trading or in intrafirm transactions. While state agencies and parastatal enterprises are becoming more important traders, their rise probably does not undermine our juxtaposition of an interstate political framework for trade and a more disaggregated, market-oriented framework for decisions about imports and exports, for two reasons. First, parastatal enterprises often operate under incentives and constraints similar to those facing private firms. Second, they are far removed from direct control by central foreign-policy bureaucracies. It is these bureaucracies, together with trade ministries, that represent states in formulating international commercial rules. Thus, even though parastatal enterprises may be playing a greater role in commerce, there remains a disjunction between traders and trade regulators.

[5] The point is raised most clearly by Robert Gilpin in *U.S. Power and the Multinational Corporation* (New York: Basic Books, 1975), pp. 4–5, 19, 40–42; and Aristide R. Zolberg, "International Migrations in Political Perspective," in Mary Kritz, Charles Keely, and Silvano Tomasi, eds., *Global Trends in Migration: Theory and Research on International Population Movements* (New York: Center for Migration Studies, 1981), pp. 3–27.

Thus, to ask how the trade regime affects imports and exports is to raise the more general question of how interstate structures interact with and shape transactions in global markets. Moreover, to examine the causal sources of the modern trade regime is to ask, among other things, what distributions of state capabilities give rise to mediating political structures that facilitate (or impede) private, transnational flows of goods.

The most prominent causal model of regime change is the hegemonic model, which relates regime strength to the concentration of international capabilities.[6] In a broad sense, it accurately predicts changes in the postwar trade regime. In terms of rule adherence, multilateral coordination, and progressive tariff reductions, the regime appears strongest during the 1950s and 1960s, near the apex of American economic power. The model also accurately predicts increasing strains on liberal trade during the 1970s and 1980s, as American economic power declined relative to Japan and the European Community.[7] While trade barriers continue to be reduced in some areas, a proliferation of trade disputes and rule violations does indicate some weakening of the trade regime.

The model's causal connections also seem plausible in the case of the trade regime. The GATT's origins are to be found in Washington; its early elaboration came in talks between the Americans and the British.[8] The U.S. also set the pace and limits of tariff reductions within the GATT. Multilateral negotiations have always followed the President's authorization by Congress to begin such talks, and the terms of congressional authorization have always established the limits of multilateral trade liberalization. Equally important, the United States made disproportionate tariff concessions during the GATT's early stages to induce multilateral tariff reductions and incorporate more states within the GATT.[9] Over the past decade, however, the U.S., no longer a hegemon, has refused to bear the disproportionate costs of hegemonic leadership in trade and other areas. Significantly, the Americans demand and get full compensation for any trade concessions made to Europe or Japan.

In all these ways, then, the hegemonic model offers plausible accounts of the mechanisms of regime change and roughly accurate predictions. Still, some complexities in the trade regime elude the hegemonic model's sparse rendering.

According to the model, declining American hegemony should impede

---

[6] Gilpin, *U.S. Power*; Charles P. Kindleberger, *The World in Depression* (Berkeley: University of California Press, 1973) and "Systems of International Economic Organization," in David P. Calleo, ed., *Money and the Coming World Order* (New York: New York University Press for the Lehrman Institute, 1976); Krasner, "State Power" and "The Tokyo Round: Particularistic Interests and Prospects for Stability in the Global Trading System," *International Studies Quarterly* 23 (December 1979), pp. 491–531.

[7] See, for example, "U.S., Common Market on Blowup Path," *Wall Street Journal,* 18 November 1981, p. 27.

[8] Richard N. Gardner, *Sterling-Dollar Diplomacy* (Oxford: Oxford University Press, 1956), chaps. 6, 8, 14, and 17.

[9] F. V. Meyer, *International Trade Policy* (New York: St. Martin's, 1978), p. 142.

and perhaps reverse the multilateral reduction of trade barriers; yet the Tokyo Round of trade negotiations, completed in 1979, was considered a significant success by its major participants. Advanced capitalist states virtually eliminated tariffs on most manufactured goods, and for the first time they extended multilateral regulations to cover many nontariff barriers to trade. These agreements were struck during a period of declining hegemony, which the negotiations frankly acknowledged. Bargaining and trade concessions among the major economic powers were fully symmetrical.[10] The costs of regime maintenance, in other words, were being shared more broadly than in the GATT's early years, and, perhaps as a result of this sharing, the regime has not collapsed. Its continuity suggests that while a hegemonic distribution of economic resources may be crucial to regime formation (possibly because the hegemon alone is willing and able to bear the high start-up costs), the lower costs of sustaining an ongoing regime may be shared effectively. In any case, there may well be distinctive logics to regime initiation and regime maintenance.[11]

A second predictive problem is that the regime's weakening is highly uneven. Trade restrictions vary markedly across industrial sectors and are most prominent in mature, basic industries such as steel, textiles, shoes, and autos. While the regime's general weakening may be comprehensible in terms of hegemonic decline, the explanation for this sectoral variation must lie elsewhere.

One explanation is that there are systematic differences in the capacity of producers to adapt to increased imports. Producers who can successfully adapt are unlikely to oppose liberal trade. In fact, they may well support it in order to exploit foreign markets themselves, especially when the firms are multinational, with integrated global networks of production and intrafirm trade.[12] By contrast, producers who are unable to adapt commercially are likely to seek state aid, including barriers to imports.

Best situated are industries where firms make differentiated goods, spend heavily for research, and develop new products and production methods. Their response to import competition is fundamentally market-based and self-reliant. Faced with growing imports, firms in such industries seek out profitable new areas of specialization in related product lines. By specializing in subsectors where they hold comparative advantages, these firms are often able to export successfully. Thus, some industries with subsectoral specialization may be characterized by simultaneously high levels of imports and exports (known as intra-industry trade).

Even if import competition is strong, the simultaneous presence of exports is likely to divide an industry's stance on trade policy. Such internal

---

[10] Krasner, "Tokyo Round."

[11] Keohane and Nye suggest this point when they discuss an "international organization model" of regime continuity. See *Power and Interdependence*, pp. 54–58 and 146–53.

[12] See the work of G. K. Helleiner, especially *Intra-Firm Trade and the Developing Countries* (New York: St. Martin's, 1981).

divisions confer greater autonomy on state policy makers,[13] and in advanced states with highly interdependent economies that seldom leads to increased protection. In general, commercial adaptation to imports, the secular rise in intrafirm transactions, and the growth of intra-industry trade are significant sources of continuing support for liberal trade rules.

Commercial adaptation to imports is much more difficult, however, in standardized, price-competitive sectors. Faced with rapidly growing foreign competition, these sectors' predominantly national firms tend to favor trade barriers and protected home markets. They rely on state intervention to control the pace and costs of adjustment, through tariffs, quotas, subsidies or preferential purchasing. Their dilemma and their characteristic response are reminiscent of the embattled Junkers of Bismarckian Germany, who, according to Moore, needed to "rely on political levers to prop up a tottering economic position."[14] Then, as now, the chosen lever was trade policy.

Sectoral variations in protection may be related, therefore, to the specific characteristics of industrial production, particularly the market-based ability of producers to adapt to import competition. If they are so related, a sectoral account of trade barriers could usefully supplement a hegemonic model and could help explain the juxtaposition of weakness and strength in the modern trade regime.

Whether this uneven weakening of the trade regime actually dampens trade flows is another matter—and a curious one. The answer must be considered problematic, because world trade has continued to grow while trade restraints have been tightened. Among these restraints to trade, the spread of sectoral protection and discriminatory practices has been especially significant. Various forms of "managed trade," notably the use of Voluntary Export Restraints (VERs), have proliferated. Not surprisingly, many trade specialists have argued that the liberal trade regime is slipping and protectionism growing.[15] On the other hand, world trade continues to grow. Indeed, its growth easily outstrips manufacturing growth worldwide.[16]

[13] This point is a central conclusion of Bauer, Pool, and Dexter in *American Business and Public Policy* (New York: Atherton Press, 1963).

[14] Barrington Moore, *Social Origins of Dictatorship and Democracy* (Boston: Beacon Press, 1966), p. 35.

[15] Examples are numerous. One very clear statement is by John H. Jackson, "The Crumbling Institutions of the Liberal Trade System," *Journal of World Trade Law* 12 (March–April 1978), pp. 93–106. Another is by Gary Sampson of UNCTAD, who argues that "there is a 'hardening' of protectionist measures with an increasing reliance on price controls, quantity control and domestic subsidies." Sampson, "Contemporary Protectionism and Exports of Developing Countries," *World Development* 8 (February 1980), p. 113.

[16] The only recent exception was during the deep recession of 1975, when world exports fell 3% in real terms compared to a 1% drop in total output. From 1963 to 1973, trade volume grew 8.5% annually, compared to a 6% growth in output. The figures for manufacturing alone were slightly higher: an 11% annual growth in trade compared to a 7% annual growth in output. Since 1973 the rate of growth has been slower. Exports grew 4.5% annually between 1973 and 1979; production grew 3.5% annually. For manufacturing, the figures for annual trade growth are slightly higher—5% compared to 4% growth of output. All these figures are considerably higher than those in the half-century before the GATT. From 1913 to 1948, trade grew only 0.5%

Between 1975 and 1979, for instance, world trade volume (a measure that cancels out price inflation) grew by one-third.[17] Even in 1980, a year when petroleum trade dropped by 10 percent, world trade as a whole grew slightly.[18] Trade in manufactures—the core of the GATT arrangements—grew by 5.5 percent in 1979 (compared to 5% for manufacturing output) and by 3 percent in 1980 (compared to 1% for output).[19]

As a consequence, imports and exports have been rising relative to the production of goods.[20] In 1960, for example, U.S. exports equaled 11.5 percent of production, by 1970 they had expanded to 14.4 percent, and the figure for 1979, the most recent available, is 25.3 percent.[21] The ratios differ for other major industrial countries, but the trend is similar (see Table 1). Whether one looks at export volume or market penetration, trade has grown rapidly, much more rapidly than has been recognized in either public discussion or policy formation.[22] That it has grown at all is quite remarkable. The 1970s were, after all, years of sluggish economic growth, energy crises, uncertain monetary arrangements, and volatile currency fluctuations. Trade interdependence has thus risen despite unfavorable economic conditions, sectoral restraints, and discriminatory practices.

A narrow focus on GATT rule violations obscures this increasingly dense web of commerce. Yet it is precisely the coexistence of rising trade flows and rising trade restraints that is so interesting. The juxtaposition raises larger questions about the nature of the regime and its impact on behavior. At the very least, recent trade growth is not due to sharply lower trade barriers or sectoral liberalization. In fact, the causal arrow probably points in the other direction: trade growth may well explain some illiberal trends in the regime. Increasing import penetration has dislocated some domestic producers, leading them to support greater restraints and to resist

---

annually, only one-quarter the pace of production. Richard Blackhurst, Nicolas Marian, and Jan Tumlir, *Trade Liberalization, Protectionism, and Interdependence,* GATT Studies in International Trade no. 5 [hereafter called *GATT Study no. 5*] (Geneva: GATT, 1977), p. 7; GATT, *International Trade 1979/80* (Geneva, 1980), Table 1, p. 2.

[17] *Wall Street Journal,* 28 May 1981, p. 44.

[18] *IMF Survey,* 23 March 1981, p. 81.

[19] Ibid., pp. 81, 89.

[20] Trade figures are often compared to GNP rather than to production of goods, as we have done here. The comparison to GNP, however, is misleading because a steadily rising share of GNP involves services, which are not generally traded. Production covers all goods originating in agriculture, forestry, hunting, fishing, mining, quarrying, and manufacturing.

[21] U.S. Department of Commerce, *International Economic Indicators and Competitive Trends,* vol. 2 (December 1976), p. 58; vol. 7 (June 1981), Table 36.

[22] Harald B. Malmgren, "Interaction of Financial and Commercial Markets: Challenge for Policy Makers," *The World Economy* 3 (November 1980), p. 289. This rise in trade relative to production and income runs counter to the generalizations of Karl W. Deutsch and Alexander Eckstein in "National Industrialization and the Declining Share of the International Economic Sector, 1890–1959," *World Politics* 13, 2 (January 1961), especially pp. 296–97. Deutsch and Eckstein put forward a number of generalizations concerning the relationship between "stages of industrialization" and the share of trade in the national economy. Their data, unfortunately, are colored by dramatic differences in trade barriers during the period they consider and by radical changes in the world trade regime—points they fail to recognize.

Table 1. Ratios of exports to production (excluding services) for major industrial countries

Period	U.S.	France	F.R.G.	Italy	U.K.	Japan	Canada
1960	11.5	23.4	31.2	27.6	38.5	18.8	42.9
1970	14.4	30.6	40.5	41.8	50.4	22.1	70.5
1979	25.3	52.2	54.8	60.3	74.9	29.2[a]	87.0

[a]1978 figure

If exports are compared to Gross National Products rather than to production levels, the ratios are substantially lower because nontraded services are such a large element of GNP. Still, the ratio of trade to GNP shows a strong growth trend (especially during the 1970s) for all advanced states except Japan. In the U.S., for instance, exports were only 4% of GNP in 1960 and 4.3% in 1970. They nearly doubled over the next decade—to 8.2% in 1980. Imports climbed even more rapidly—from 3% of U.S. GNP in 1960 to 4% in 1970 to 9.6% in 1980. For the principal U.S. trading partners, the ratios are higher and the growth rates lower. In 1960, the Federal Republic's exports were 15.9% of their GNP, roughly four times the U.S. ratio. Over the next twenty years, West German exports grew to 23.3% of GNP, a figure that is about three times the U.S. ratio. The only aberrant case is Japan. Its exports were 9.4% of GNP in 1960. They peaked in 1976 at only 11.9% of GNP and have since declined to 10.2% (1979 figures). In fact, of the large trading states only the U.S. and Japan have import and export sectors well below 20% of GNP. West Germany, Italy, Britain, and Canada are all in the 20% to 25% range for both imports and exports. France is in the 17% to 19% range. In 1960, by contrast, the same states had import and export ratios of between 10% and 15% (a figure that is still well above today's U.S. ratio).

Sources: U.S. Department of Commerce, *International Economic Indicators and Competitive Trends,* vol. 2 (December 1976), p. 58; vol. 7 (June 1981), Tables 36, 37. The trend for imports, available from the same sources, is similar. (There are some technical differences between U.S. and other figures: U.S. imports are quoted on an f.a.s. basis, others on a c.i.f. basis; U.S. exports are quoted on an f.a.s. basis, others on an f.o.b. basis.)

further liberalization. As a consequence, trade growth, which has always been a consensual goal underlying the regime, may carry the seeds of restraint in some sectors. Beyond this irony, the sustained growth of trade in spite of new restraints casts doubts on the regime's impact on commercial flows. But that is a much larger point, deserving of closer scrutiny.

How liberal is the modern trade regime?

Just how liberal is the modern trade regime? Has it changed significantly in recent years? In what ways has it weakened? Our answers must come in several parts. First, a balanced assessment of the regime should include not only new trade barriers but also the durable features of liberal trade. Tariff reductions must be considered alongside nontariff restrictions. In addition, the domain, duration, and purposes of the nontariff barriers need careful examination. Second, the regime's limitations in promoting free trade must be measured against earlier commercial arrangements and the regime's own basic principles. It is oversimple to consider the modern regime a pale reflection of nineteenth-century free trade since the basic principles differ.

The GATT regime does not contemplate a world in which commercial policies are based on the austere pursuit of comparative advantage. It is, moreover, a misleading analogy, because the modern regime has proven more stable politically and longer lasting.

Trade liberalization in historical perspective

In the nineteenth century and the twentieth, the most durable aim of trade liberalization has been the reduction of tariffs.[23] The point is easily missed today because so much attention is paid to quotas, Voluntary Export Restraints, and formal market-sharing. Tariffs are no longer an overriding trade issue. But that, in itself, is noteworthy. Tariffs have receded from view because they have receded as obstacles to commerce. They have been cut deeply and repeatedly in multilateral negotiations, most recently in the Tokyo Round of GATT trade talks.

The Tokyo Round was the seventh multilateral trade negotiation and the third major effort at reducing tariffs. The first, in 1947, accompanied the negotiation of the original GATT treaty. The second came during the Kennedy Round, concluded in 1967. Both times industrial tariffs were cut by at least one-third. The Tokyo Round, though not primarily concerned with tariffs, cut them by another third, leaving industrial tariffs at about 5 percent on a trade-weighted basis.[24] After thirty-five years of negotiations, tariffs have been virtually eliminated as major trade barriers.

---

[23] Jock Finlayson and Mark Zacher argue that the "norm of liberalization or free trade is often regarded as central to the GATT regime, but it did not have the paramountcy of nondiscrimination in the immediate postwar years. Liberalization was regarded as important by many American officials, but it was not a primary goal of most other industrial and developing countries." Finlayson and Zacher's contribution to this volume, p. 282. This conclusion is misleading. Certainly nondiscrimination was important in the GATT's founding: the Americans, in particular, especially wanted to dismantle Commonwealth Preferences. But in the end the U.S. not only allowed existing preferences to remain but allowed European reconstruction to be built upon regional discrimination against the dollar. Tarriff-cutting, by contrast, was an important goal to most industrial countries from the earliest days of the GATT. Karin Kock, citing documents from the International Trade Organization's 1946 Preparatory Committee meeting in London, says that "the ultimate objective of the negotiations was 'to bring about the substantial reduction of tariffs and the elimination of tariff preferences.'" Kock, *International Trade Policy and the Gatt, 1947–1967* (Stockholm: Almqvist and Wiksell, 1969), p. 63. Robert Hudec, noting that the GATT grew out of ITO preparatory sessions, points out that the GATT "was not intended to be a comprehensive world organization. It was a temporary side affair meant to serve the particular interests of the major commercial powers who wanted a prompt reduction of tariffs among themselves." Hudec, *The GATT Legal System and World Trade Diplomacy* (New York: Praeger, 1975), p. 30. Liberalization thus seems to rank alongside nondiscrimination as a central GATT principle from the earliest days. Finlayson and Zacher provide a useful summary of other GATT norms. On the substantive side, they list reciprocity, safeguarding against import surges, and economic development. Procedurally, they list multilateral negotiations and a special role for states with major trading interests.

[24] According to the GATT's figures, which are based on ten developed import markets, the Tokyo Round reduced tariffs on industrial products 33% on a weighted basis, 38% on a simple-

This is a historic achievement, and central to any assessment of the postwar trade regime. It is rivaled only by Great Britain's international push for free trade in the mid-nineteenth century.[25] The British achievement differs from the modern trade regime, however, in two principal respects. First, mid-Victorian Britain, unlike any modern capitalist state, was genuinely committed to orthodox free trade. As a matter of basic policy, Britain was far less concerned about moderating the domestic costs of adjustment to imports; nor was the government especially concerned about redistributing these costs within society as a whole. Modern capitalist states, by contrast, measure the value of an open trading regime against domestic social goals. In Ruggie's illuminating phrase, their liberalism is "embedded" rather than orthodox.[26] They value open trade for its contribution to employment and income but they recognize that changes wrought by trade affect the whole society. As a rule, dislocations due to imports weigh heavily in any political calculation of net benefits. Indeed, they have effectively excluded agriculture from modern trade liberalization.

The GATT tries less to override these domestic political calculations than to moderate their impact on the larger network of liberal trade. Since the GATT's inception it has been acknowledged that trade liberalization can impose significant adjustment costs on politically important domestic actors. The GATT system has always permitted its contracting parties to take steps to dampen these costs, even when that meant reverting to higher trade barriers for selected products.

These references to the GATT call attention to other differences between British-sponsored free trade and the modern trade regime. The two regimes differ markedly in their institutionalization and multilateral backing.

Britain's commitment to orthodox free trade may have been solid at home, but it was fragile and poorly institutionalized abroad. It rested largely on a series of commercial treaties, each containing a most-favored-nation clause.[27] Modeled on the Anglo-French treaty of 1860 (the Cobden-Chevalier

---

average basis. On a weighted basis, post-multilateral trade negotiation tariffs on finished manufactures are 6.9%; on semimanufactures, 4.1%. GATT, *The Tokyo Round of Multilateral Trade Negotiations* (Geneva, 1979), pp. 117–20.

[25] James Kurth offers an explanation of Britain's free trade policies based on sectoral economic changes. See James Kurth, "The Creation and Destruction of International Regimes: The Impact of the World Market," paper delivered at the American Political Science Association meeting, Washington, D.C., August 1980. While Kurth's emphasis is on national policies, his focus on differences in sectors' adaptation to international competition parallels a theme in this article.

[26] John Gerard Ruggie's article in this volume. Ruggie's term is a useful interpretative device, especially in distinguishing modern trade politics from that of the nineteenth century, but it does raise problems. One is to define the forms of illiberal protection. The second is to differentiate embedded liberalism from illiberalism in practice. Unless one is examining a long-term trend, it may be impossible to tell whether specific trade barriers are (1) illiberal steps toward broader protection, or (2) simply efforts to moderate the impact of the world market on domestic society ("embedded liberalism").

[27] If two nations, A and B, have a most-favored-nation treaty, then neither can import the same items from nation C at lower tariffs. Given a network of such treaties, any bilateral tariff reduction becomes a multilateral reduction.

treaty), these treaties soon embraced most of Europe. Breaking radically and irreversibly with pre-industrial mercantilism, they generalized tariff concessions among the major trading powers.[28] But support for free trade was still thin on the Continent, and the liberal treaty system did not survive the economic downturn and industrial nationalism of the late 1870s and the 1880s. The decisive turn to protection came in Germany, once a leader in lowering tariffs. Bismarck's Tariff of 1879, and its extension in 1885 and 1888, not only forged a ruling coalition of iron and rye[29] but also set the stage for a succession of protectionist tariffs throughout Europe.[30] In a difficult environment, the liberal treaties of the 1860s offered little help in coordinating trade policies, limiting retaliation, or tempering the growth of nationalist tariffs in Germany, France, Italy, and elsewhere.

The GATT-centered regime, by contrast, has longstanding deliberative mechanisms. Like its nineteenth-century forerunner, it includes most-favored-nation clauses to spread tariff concessions and ensure nondiscrimination. But unlike its predecessor, it is built on multilateral commitments, organized around regular consultations and periodic negotiations.

Its fundamental institutional logic—and a crucial source of its political stability—is that it facilitates openness without ignoring domestic aspects of trade policy. There is no commitment to free-trade orthodoxy, and hence no falling away from it. GATT bargaining, adjudication, and enforcement all recognize that no state can long sustain agreements that disrupt important economic sectors. GATT trade rounds thus involve a delicate balance between multilateral bargains and a limited right to escape from them. If there is to be bargaining at all, the contracting parties must put forward reliable proposals. Yet without some legitimate means of escape from import disruption, states will be reluctant to make significant concessions in the first place. The escape provisions, then, are not simple protectionist devices. If properly limited, they allow risk-averse policy makers to undertake bolder liberalization efforts.

When these efforts cause major adjustment problems or prove politically unsustainable, several escapes are available. GATT members can modify their tariff schedules (Article XXVIII), safeguard their domestic pro-

---

[28] Barrie M. Ratcliffe, "The Origins of the Anglo-French Commercial Treaty of 1860: A Reassessment," in Ratcliffe, ed., *Great Britain and Her World, 1750–1914* (Manchester, England: Manchester University Press, 1975), pp. 125–51; A. A. Iliasu, "The Cobden-Chevalier Commercial Treaty of 1860," *Historical Journal* 14 (1971), pp. 67–98; D. C. M. Platt, *Finance, Trade, and Politics: British Foreign Policy 1815–1914* (Oxford: Oxford University Press, 1968), pp. 85–101; Gerard Curzon, *Multilateral Commercial Diplomacy* (London: Michael Joseph, 1965), pp. 15–20.

[29] The classic treatment is Alexander Gerschenkron, *Bread and Democracy in Germany* (Berkeley, 1943; New York: Howard Fertig, 1960), esp. pp. 21–88; see also Helmut Böhme, "Big Business Pressure Groups and Bismarck's Turn to Protectionism, 1873–79," *Historical Journal* 10 (1967), pp. 218–36.

[30] For a comparative analysis of national policies, see Peter Alexis Gourevitch, "International Trade, Domestic Coalitions and Liberty: Comparative Responses to the Crisis of 1873–1896," *Journal of Interdisciplinary History* (Autumn 1977), pp. 281–313.

ducers from material injuries (Article XIX), or ask for outright waivers from certain GATT obligations. Each is an institutionalized recognition that trade policy, like all foreign policy, is made subject to the domestic stability of the bargains.

Fortunately for the regime's liberality, these escape hatches have not dominated the GATT process. Rather, they have been limited in several ways. With one notable exception (the U.S. waiver for agricultural products in 1955), the remedies have tended to cover product subcategories rather than broad commodity groups. They have not been used indiscriminately. Most significantly, retaliation by trading partners has been rare.

The availability of such remedies is a recognition of the social embeddedness of trade policy. Their circumscription in use shows an attachment to the principles of liberalism and multilateralism.[31] Perhaps the best proof of this principled commitment is the sharp, cumulative reduction in industrial tariffs.

Although this steady reduction is important in its own right, it is even more remarkable because it came as international competition was growing for still other reasons. The tariff reductions accommodated, rather than resisted, long-term trends toward lower communication and transportation costs. Price competition from imports naturally increased as a result. At the same time, more producing states (with newer plants and lower labor costs) were entering the world market. Because of their most-favored-nation status, they profited passively from tariff concessions exchanged among developed countries. In addition, they have been given special reductions under the Generalized System of Preferences.[32] The newly industrializing countries of Latin America and East Asia (the NICs) have been especially vigorous in exploiting the ensuing export opportunities.

questionable

---

[31] This broad consensus about the proper pace and limits of trade liberalization does not imply agreement about specific acts of protection. It does, however, reduce the likelihood that, through miscommunication, some act of trade protection would lead to a deteriorating withdrawal of prior concessions. (From different analytic perspectives, both Keohane and Ruggie stress the communicative aspects of regimes.) The newly industrializing countries (NICs) have not yet joined this broad consensus, perhaps because their fast-rising exports face a thicket of barriers. Among developed countries, there are dark mutterings that the NICs misunderstand the GATT process, offer few concessions themselves (a kind of passive unilateralism), and threaten the liberalization process by exporting aggressively and then demanding rigid adherence to prior trade concessions.

[32] The GSP is a literal violation of nondiscrimination but hardly a mortal blow. National concessions under the program have been limited by product, by producer, and in their overall size. Moreover, as tariffs are reduced on a multilateral basis, the GSP offers a smaller margin of preference. It is best understood as a limited program, congruent with the GATT's principled support for economic development, designed to widen international participation in trade. In terms of nondiscrimination, a more serious problem is the persistence and extension of regional trading arrangements. While some regional arrangements are explicitly permitted under the GATT, there is certainly a tension between them and the norm of nondiscrimination. The problem is worsened when regional groups like the EC extend preferential arrangements to third states (their former colonies in Africa, the Caribbean, and the Pacific, the so-called ACP countries). The impact of these extra-regime arrangements on behavior is captured in the economists' distinction between trade creation and trade diversion.

Their success has undoubtedly strained the liberalization process. The problems would be much worse, however, if there were not some important offsetting factors. First, despite the NICs' success, developed countries actually receive a declining share of their imports from nonoil less developed countries (LDCs). In the first half of the 1950s, 29 percent of developed country imports came from nonoil LDCs. By the late 1970s that figure had sunk to 15 percent, and it continues to decline slowly.[33] Second, developed countries have consistently run huge trade surpluses with nonoil LDCs. In 1979, they amounted to $46.8 billion (versus $13 billion in 1970).[34] These large imbalances require financing and, in the absence of massive concessionary grants, that translates into heavy borrowing and a growing debt burden. At the end of 1980, nonoil LDCs owed $195 billion to foreign banks; their annual exports stood at only $247 billion.[35] To service these debts (plus other official loans), the debtors must increase both their borrowing and their future export earnings. With so much debt at stake and with trade surpluses running so high, the politics of protection in developed countries has become much more complex. Import-competing industries are now pitted against exporters and financial institutions with a major stake in continued openness.

Trade protection and sectoral variations

But perhaps the most important limit to modern protection is a sectoral one. A recent GATT study observes, quite correctly, that most of the new trade restrictions "are concentrated in a few manufactured product groups: textiles; clothing and shoes; steel; transport equipment, mainly ships; and such diverse light-engineering products as TV apparatus, ball-bearings, thermionic valves, dry-cell batteries and so forth."[36] To that list could be added leather goods, pulp and paper, and consumer electrical products. In a recent study of the EC, for example, Franko found that three-quarters of all actions to restrict imports under safeguard, surveillance, and antidumping provisions dealt with only three product groups: steel, textiles, and clothing.[37] Trade protection, in other words, is highly product-specific.

These protected sectors share a number of salient features. Production

---

[33] *IMF Survey*, 23 February 1981, p. 59.

[34] Ibid., p. 61.

[35] Bank for International Settlements, *1981 Annual Report*, table, p. 105.

[36] *GATT Study no. 5*, p. 44. An extensive IMF study makes much the same point by focusing on steel, textiles and clothing, footwear, and shipbuilding. See Bahram Nowzad, *The Rise in Protectionism*, International Monetary Fund Pamphlet Series no. 24 (1978).

[37] Lawrence G. Franko, "Current Trends in Protectionism in Industrialized Countries: Focus on Western Europe," in G. K. Helleiner, Franko, Helen B. Junz, and Peter Dreyer, *Protectionism or Industrial Adjustment?* (Paris: Atlantic Institute for International Affairs, 1980), pp. 32–33. Also see Jacques Pelkmans, "The European Community and the Newly Industrializing Countries," *Journal of European Integration* 4, 2 (1981), pp. 140–41.

involves standardized, labor-intensive processes. Markets are typically mature and price-competitive. Producers are usually local firms or, sometimes, local firms acting as international subcontractors. (Multinational corporations have few advantages in standardized, price-competitive production.) Locational advantages in such production have shifted rapidly, and the lowest-cost producers are now either in the NICs or in the newest, most efficient plants in the U.S., the EC or Japan.

In such basic industries, growing imports are bound to cause severe adjustment problems. Outmoded, inefficient production facilities are a well-known difficulty. Moreover, the markets themselves are usually slow growing, so domestic producers will be displaced by even moderate increases in imports. One strategy, to adapt to imports by subsectoral specialization, is prevalent in industries with higher research and development, greater innovation, and more rapidly changing markets. In basic industries, however, it may be difficult to find special niches where domestic producers hold a competitive edge, and the niches (such as specialty steel) may not be large. Finally, in basic industries, imports have an impact on employment out of proportion to their value because the processes are labor-intensive. These employment effects, especially when combined with the industries' high regional concentrations, add substantially to the political impact of imports.

These circumstances overdetermine resistance to import growth by inefficient producers. They will try to insulate their domestic markets from international competition rather than cut capacity or write down their capital. As local firms, they cannot shift production to their own plants abroad, nor will their workers want to bear transitional adjustment costs. This coincidence of interests often leads to a tactical alliance on trade issues between import-competing firms and their unions. Both prefer some solution to stabilize or even increase their market shares, such as Voluntary Export Restraints and Orderly Marketing Agreements (OMAs); a number have been reached since the mid 1970s.

These sectoral restraints should not be allowed to obscure the larger picture. As the GATT study indicated, they cover only a narrow band of industrial production. Moreover, the Tokyo Round agreements as well as repeated tariff cuts signal a basic acceptance of growing international competition. This acceptance is accompanied by a desire—broadly shared among major trading powers—to regulate the domestic impact of trade, generally through nontariff barriers. These are not and are not meant to be insurmountable barriers to imports.[38] They aim at controlling the pace of adjustment, slowing import growth in mature markets, subsidizing domestic producers to revivify them, and, in the most general terms, sharing the costs of sectoral adjustment to imports.

[38] This point is emphasized in Robert Pastor, *Congress and the Politics of U.S. Foreign Economic Policy, 1929–1976* (Berkeley: University of California Press, 1980), chaps. 3–6.

Protection vs. liberalization: the use of nontariff barriers

This analysis, which emphasizes the growing role of nontariff barriers in a limited number of sectors, is not meant to gloss over the problems they pose for trade liberalization. They are serious, even if the effects are notoriously difficult to measure. Whatever form the nontariff barriers take—quotas, VERs, OMAs—they help comparatively disadvantaged domestic producers maintain their share of the home market. As a result, they impede the shift of production to the world's lowest-cost producers.

Tariffs have the same effect, but there is an important difference. Tariffs change an import's price, which affects resource allocation, but they work through the price system and leave that system unimpaired. Quotas may not.

Because quotas become less permeable over time for efficient producers, they corrupt market adjustment mechanisms.[39] A fixed quota acts like a variable levy, giving domestic producers more protection as they become less and less competitive. As cost advantages shift to foreign producers, the quota insulates domestic producers from any need to respond.[40]

This corruption of the market adjustment mechanism is one reason why the GATT, which presumes an effective price system as the basis for trade, has always favored tariffs when protection was unavoidable.[41] The incipient systems of sectoral protection, by contrast, rely almost entirely on quotas and other nontariff mechanisms. As a result, they mark a departure both from the GATT's goal of liberalization and from its preferred means of regulating trade flows.

The long-term effects of nontariff barriers are especially pertinent because they are rarely temporary, no matter what their sponsors promise. Take the case of textiles, the first postwar instance of multilateral market-sharing. The initial agreements took effect in 1962. They have been renewed ever since and their coverage has been expanded from cotton textiles to all fibers. For those who saw market-sharing as a relatively liberal, short-lived response to sectoral adjustment problems, the experience has been sobering. The agreements failed to prevent bilateral confrontations,[42] lacked effective surveillance, and became increasingly rigid and contentious.[43] For the past

---

[39] Franko, "Current Trends in Protectionism," p. 37.

[40] Richard Blackhurst, Nicolas Marian, and Jan Tumlir, *Adjustment, Trade and Growth in Developed and Developing Countries,* GATT Studies in International Trade no. 6 (Geneva: GATT, 1978), p. 72.

[41] Melvyn B. Krauss, *The New Protectionism: The Welfare State and International Trade* (New York: New York University Press for the International Center for Economic Policy Studies, 1978), pp. 35–36.

[42] The most prominent bilateral dispute was between the U.S. and Japan; for a full account see I. M. Destler, Haruhiro Fukui, and Hideo Sato, *The Textile Wrangle: Conflict in Japanese-American Relations, 1969–1971* (Ithaca: Cornell University Press, 1979).

[43] Lalith Athulathmudali, "Forthcoming Negotiations on the Multi-fibre Arrangement," *The World Economy* 3 (June 1980), pp. 1–12; Patrick Smith, "The Fibres of Protectionism," *Far Eastern Economic Review*, 15 May 1981, pp. 74–76; Chris Farrands, "Textile Diplomacy: The Making and Implementation of European Textile Policy, 1974–1978," *Journal of Common Market Studies* 18 (September 1979), pp. 22–39.

two years their proposed renewal has been bogged down in bitter disputes between importers and exporters.

This conspicuous failure has undoubtedly raised resistance to other proposed OMAs. In fact, despite their obvious attractions to declining producers, no other formal, global market-sharing arrangements have been adopted.[44] Protection has come instead in the form of unilateral and bilateral restrictions. As the International Monetary Fund (IMF) recently observed, "[I]n such key sectors as iron and steel and textiles and clothing, mechanisms to control low-cost imports [have become] institutionally entrenched."[45]

Curiously, these mechanisms seldom violate GATT rules, which deal only with discriminatory *import* controls. Technically, the new restrictions are applied by exporting countries to their own products. As might be expected, bilateral bargaining plays a prominent part here. To curb the pace of market penetration, advanced importers often threaten some form of unilateral market closure. Exporters are then faced with a highly constrained and painful choice between voluntary restraints or even tougher mandatory controls. The "voluntary" export restraints that result are little more than clever evasions of GATT rules and outright violations of the principle of nondiscrimination.[46]

The whole issue of discriminatory safeguards was discussed thoroughly during the Tokyo Round. But unlike negotiations over government procurement, customs valuation, subsidies, and countervailing duties, this negotiation did not lead to a comprehensive code. The Europeans demanded safeguards that could be used selectively against import surges from one or two countries. The Japanese and the NICs, the most likely targets of such safeguards, strongly supported the customary GATT principle that remedies should apply uniformly to all exporters. In the end, no code was adopted, although discussions have continued in a special GATT committee.

The stalemate has far-reaching implications. It reveals a deep ambivalence about the principle of nondiscrimination, at least as it applies to these import restraints. It leaves VERs unaffected and so, by implication, permits still more bilateral bargaining over trade barriers.[47] It therefore touches on the GATT's principles of multilateralism and progressive liberalization.

VERs and OMAs may be the most visible of nontariff barriers, but others also present significant obstacles to trade. State subsidies are among the most significant. Their variety is bewildering, and their importance has grown markedly as states take on more extensive economic responsibilities.

---

[44] Ingo Walter, "The Protection of Industries in Trouble—The Case of Iron and Steel," *The World Economy* 2 (May 1979), p. 185.

[45] IMF, *Annual Report on Exchange Arrangements and Exchange Restrictions, 1980*, p. 6. A rare counterexample (but perhaps a signal of future policy) is President Reagan's lifting of U.S. quotas on shoes imported from Taiwan and South Korea. *New York Times,* 1 July 1981, p. 1.

[46] For a discussion of the differences between VERs and the GATT's favored method of protecting against import surges, Article XIX, see Brian Hindley, "Voluntary Export Restraints and the GATT's Main Escape Clause," *The World Economy* 3 (November 1980), pp. 313–41.

[47] I wish to thank Stephen Haggard for his comments on this point.

Their recent coverage by a Tokyo Round code represents a major victory for multilateral coordination and a major extension of GATT rules.

The most obvious problems in controlling these subsidies are their pervasiveness and their status as basic elements of public policy. Indeed, their impact on trade may be merely a by-product of their narrowly domestic aim. The GATT codes wisely limit themselves to these trade effects but, even so, many problems remain. One is that subsidies are often difficult to detect. They thus violate the GATT's principle of transparency: all producers and their governments should be aware of existing trade barriers. Moreover, as states play a larger economic role, their subsidies are inevitably embedded more deeply and more subtly in domestic life. Controlling their effects is thus a much more complicated task than regulating border taxes.

Even the subsidizing states themselves cannot always control their impact on the market. This lack of control has important implications for the trade regime. As Zysman has shown in his study of French industrial policy,[48] state interventions are most successful in frustrating market-oriented adjustment in sectors characterized by standardized products and processes, national producers, price competition, and low levels of innovation. These are precisely the areas where sectoral protection has grown.

In these basic sectors, advanced states can employ a variety of effective instruments. Where price competition is crucial, either they can raise the cost of imports through discriminatory taxes or regulations, or they can lower the costs of domestic production through subsidies. (State-subsidized capital, for example, can confer genuine competitive advantages in industries such as steel or shipbuilding, where fixed investments are substantial.)[49] Finally, since these products typically have long lives and stable production functions, centralized state intervention need not inadvertently create an obsolete industry.

In technologically sophisticated sectors with fast-moving international markets and differentiated products (e.g., microelectronics), protectionist state intervention is more likely to be self-defeating. Attempts to intervene in such sectors can easily create hothouse industries, lagging badly in new products and production methods, and dependent on continuing state subsidies and a captive market. The state cannot, as a rule, adroitly manipulate fast-moving technology; the lone exception involves economies of scale associated with long production runs. Where such economies exist, the first

[48] John Zysman, "The French State in the International Economy," in Peter Katzenstein, ed., *Between Power and Plenty* (Madison: University of Wisconsin Press, 1978), and Zysman, *Political Strategies for Industrial Order: State, Market and Industry in France* (Berkeley: University of California Press, 1977).

[49] This point is developed in Krauss, *The New Protectionism*, chap. 4. Note, however, that these are net advantages relative to foreign producers only if they are not offset by higher taxes or other state-imposed requirements that raise marginal costs. According to Krauss, state intervention generally corrupts the mechanisms of market adjustment and so is likely to deteriorate into protectionism. There is a logic there, but he fails to answer why, if it is the overriding logic, Scandinavian countries with large state sectors have been such bulwarks of trade liberalism.

producers to achieve mass production will dominate a market and preempt the entrance of competitors. Exporters with only a slight technological lead may hold a decisive cost advantage, preventing the development of local competition. Temporary protection of the home market might allow local producers to achieve competitive, low-cost production. Japan has pursued this strategy in both semiconductors and computers.[50] The risks of hothouse production are minimized in Japan's case by its export-oriented corporate culture. Still, the whole strategy depends upon asymmetrical access to foreign markets and so raises troubling questions about reciprocity.

These efforts to protect high-technology industries are exceptional. The vast majority of new trade barriers deal with standardized, basic industries. They are much less likely where markets change quickly, innovation is rapid, and the rents attributable to proprietary knowledge are short-lived. When protection does occur in such sectors, it is most likely to be temporary—a helping hand along the learning curve. Thus, differences in sectoral protection derive from the production characteristics of traded goods. They suggest important limits to state-directed sharing of international markets and, indeed, some sectoral segmentation in the regime itself.

Dispute settlement in the modern trade regime

So far our assessment has concentrated on the regime's basic rules and principles and its emerging sectoral differentiation. There is more to the regime, however, than its prescribed guides for conduct. The political organization of trade also involves, as Dam has observed, "a set of procedures, adapted to the subject matter and designed to resolve disputes that cannot be foreseen at the moment when those procedures are established."[51] The GATT has such procedures but their effectiveness has varied dramatically over time.

The early GATT was quite successful in creating a stable, explicitly rule-guided framework for the conduct of world trade. Its success was founded on a judicious combination of detailed rules and flexible procedures. That combination worked well because the major trading states shared a common vision of liberal world trade and because their economies were highly market-oriented. The precise, rigid set of rules offered a clear guide to desirable commercial conduct. The procedural flexibility offered states some room to maneuver in the face of exchange shortfalls and domestic pressures.

Rules cannot anticipate all contingencies and, even if they could, some differences of interpretation are bound to arise. Resolving such differences

[50] *Business Week*, 1 June 1981, p. 80.
[51] Kenneth W. Dam, *The GATT: Law and International Economic Organization* (Chicago: University of Chicago Press, 1970), p. 4.

was the GATT's special strength during its first decade. The original treaty may have spelled out formal rules and fostered common expectations, but the initial consensus was reinforced and refined by subsequent discussions of the rules' applicability. The whole process was facilitated by the contracting parties' representatives, most of whom had helped draft the treaty and held shared understandings about the rules' implicit aims and meanings.[52] Their sustained communication created an informal case law and eroded any false antithesis between legalism and pragmatism—an antagonism that had once surrounded the treaty.[53]

The GATT was evolving from a document into a working organization that kept pace with the commercial problems of the day. Nowhere was its effectiveness more evident than in its dispute-settlement procedures, where third-party adjudication developed.[54] The dispute panels revealed a prudent recognition of the limits of international law: they aimed at persuasion rather than authoritative decisions. Ultimately, they relied on the GATT's community of purpose.[55] Indeed, the GATT owes much of its early success to this combination of shared purpose and adaptive rule-making, backed by American leadership.

By 1958, according to Hudec, the GATT's "collection of ad hoc arrangements had grown together into a loose, informal, but clearly functioning international organization."[56] At the time, the GATT was performing three important tasks of trade liberalization: first, it facilitated multilateral consideration of commercial policy issues; second, it served as a forum for lowering tariff barriers; and third, it incorporated a legal system to regulate commercial conduct and conciliate disputes. In the 1960s, however, the GATT proved far less successful in its third task than in its first two.

The Kennedy Round showed that the GATT was more useful than ever as a multilateral forum for lowering tariffs. It was marred only by the exclusion of agricultural trade.[57] In the legal arena, on the other hand, the GATT's early success faded rapidly. By the late 1950s, the early agenda had been supplemented by new problems on which no consensus emerged. Japan's accession to the GATT, to take one important example, encountered resistance in Europe.[58] The problems only increased as Japan rebuilt its exporting

[52] The theme of shared understandings is developed by Hudec in *The GATT Legal System,* Parts II and III.

[53] Dam, *The GATT,* pp. 3–9.

[54] Robert Hudec, *Adjudication of International Trade Disputes,* Thames Essay no. 16 (London: Trade Policy Research Centre, 1978), p. 3.

[55] James Fawcett, *International Economic Conflicts* (London: Europa Publications for the David Davies Memorial Institute of International Studies, 1977), pp. 47–49. Fawcett emphasizes the underlying consensus on the desirability of a liberal economic order and a willingness to seek compromises between domestic producer claims and the requirements of economic integration. Hudec's works strongly underscore the same point.

[56] Hudec, *The GATT Legal System,* p. 60.

[57] Ibid., p. 199.

[58] At the GATT Annecy Conference in 1949, for example, the U.S. unsuccessfully proposed most-favored-nation treatment for Japan. "[T]he United Kingdom informed the American Embassy in London that it could not consider an M-F-N agreement for Japan until after the estab-

capacity while continuing to refuse to open its own growing market. There were trade problems in Europe, too. The formation of the European Economic Community, though permissible under the GATT, introduced another new actor and formidable difficulties, such as its variable agricultural levies[59] and capacity for trade diversion. Membership among less developed countries was also rising. Even though their power was sharply limited, their membership meant that the GATT could no longer serve as a closed forum for the major trading powers. In sum, the number of actors was growing, their cohesion diminishing.

All these changes produced a sharp decline in the GATT's legal capacities. Antilegalism became more prominent; compliance with GATT rules fell.[60] Whether one concentrates on dispute settlement, the fashioning of new rules, or the rule-guidedness of the contracting parties' behavior, it is clear that the GATT's legal structure weakened considerably during the 1960s and 1970s.

Noncompliance with GATT rules has now become a serious problem and has raised doubts about the entire legal framework.[61] Jackson calls the

---

lishment of an exchange rate and sufficient time to show the effect of the new rate. Conversations in The Hague and Brussels indicated that the Benelux countries would oppose such an agreement at Annecy and conversations in Annecy indicated that other countries, including the key trading countries were also opposed. It became apparent that any working party which might be set up to consider such an agreement would be opposed to the proposal." *Foreign Relations of the United States, 1949,* vol. 1 (Washington, D.C.: GPO, 1976), p. 718, from "Confidential Report by the Chairman of the United States Delegation (Willoughby) to the Secretary of State." Also see ibid., 658–61, 670–72, 694–95.

[59] The EC's agricultural policies, protective from the beginning, grew increasingly restrictive during the 1960s. They met with strong American opposition, and their legality under the GATT was challenged. Several points about these agricultural policies are relevant to our discussion of the trade regime. First, agriculture had never been an integral part of the liberal trade regime. "GATT draftsmen," according to Hudec, "had taken it for granted that governments would manage and support agricultural prices, and that they would need to protect these price-support programs against imports" (*The GATT Legal System,* p. 200). The result was a compromise rule that permitted quantitative restrictions but also sought to encourage imports. The compromise ultimately failed because it was inconsistent with domestic price-support schemes, which entailed surpluses well above domestic requirements. Second, the first prominent rule violations came from the regime leader—the U.S. With the Dairy Quota case in 1951 and the demand for a complete waiver from GATT agricultural obligations in 1955, the U.S. openly disregarded GATT rules. Third, the pattern of rule violation in agriculture included even the most liberal traders, such as the Scandinavians. Fourth, while the EC's Common Agricultural Policy proclaimed virtual autonomy in agriculture, it was not ruled illegal by the GATT's contracting parties. Their timorousness on the issue may have reflected the prior breakdown of rules governing agricultural trade. It may also have reflected a genuine legal ambiguity, since variable levies had not been anticipated when the GATT was drafted and so were not prohibited. Finally, the breakdown of rules in agriculture proved less than catastrophic: there was little retaliation despite several threatening situations; some agreements were made regarding agricultural exports to third markets; and agricultural trade volume continued to grow, partly because of government moderation in imposing restraints, partly because agricultural demand was outpacing subsidized domestic supply (*The GATT Legal System,* pp. 200–203).

[60] Robert Hudec, "GATT Dispute Settlement After the Tokyo Round," *Cornell International Law Journal* 13 (Summer 1980), p. 153.

[61] Hudec, *Adjudication of International Trade Disputes,* pp. 2–3.

whole system a "state of nature"[62] and, if his conclusion is exaggerated, it does at least draw attention to the increasing frequency and gravity of rule violations. The litany is a familiar one: import deposit schemes, quotas, licensing arrangements, trigger price systems, concessionary export financing, surveillance schemes, arbitrary customs valuation, and so on. Although many of these tactics are covered by Tokyo Round codes, most are deeply rooted trade distortions that will not die easily.

The lack of reliable dispute-settlement procedures makes these violations all the more dangerous to the rule system. The GATT's dispute mechanisms, which had been extensively used in the early 1950s, were virtually abandoned after 1958.[63] One reason may have been the replacement of European national delegations by the EC, which refused to file a GATT complaint until 1973.[64] In spite of sporadic U.S. efforts to revive the adjudication procedures, they lay dormant for over two decades. The Tokyo Round agreement aims to revive them, but the undertaking is ambitious and the outcome uncertain.

The new agreement includes elaborate and still untested dispute procedures for each nontariff code. The two key mechanisms are standing committees, which are associated with each code, and *ad hoc* panels, which are assembled for individual cases. If disputants cannot resolve an issue bilaterally, they have an automatic right to a third-party panel. The panel hears the case and then assists the committee in making recommendations or rulings. It is still too early to tell whether disputants will lay aside their distrust of the GATT legal system and refer their disputes to the panels and committees.

The code arrangements are supplemented by a new "Framework for the Conduct of World Trade," which updates and clarifies the old dispute procedures. It includes an "agreed description" of customary GATT dispute practices; provisions for better consultation and surveillance; procedures regarding notification of trade measures (aiming at more transparency); and detailed provisions on the establishment, composition, prerogatives, and functions of complaint panels.

These panels have always been the instrument of dispute resolution, and they have long suffered from serious problems. Foremost is a widespread lack of faith in the fairness of the process. Before the new agreements, the panels were also handicapped by their ambiguous legal status and by poorly defined implementation procedures. To make matters worse, disputants could usually delay proceedings long enough to affirm a *fait accompli*.[65] As a result, the dispute procedure has played no role in most

---

[62] Jackson, "Crumbling Institutions," p. 98.

[63] Hudec, *The GATT Legal System*, p. 193.

[64] Hudec, "GATT Dispute Settlement," p. 181.

[65] John H. Jackson, "Governmental Disputes in International Trade Relations: A Proposal in the Context of GATT," *Journal of World Trade Law* 13 (January–February 1979), pp. 5–6. Also see Jackson, "Crumbling Institutions," p. 97.

trade conflicts and has done little to ensure the integrity of the GATT's rule system.

Although amending the rules is surely slow, clumsy, and difficult, this legal disintegration is no mere technical phenomenon. Rather, it reflects the collapse of the substantive consensus underlying the early GATT. Lacking a consensus to shape and implement a modern legal framework, the GATT's contracting parties have put aside one rule after another, leaving a structure with a significant number of inoperative rules and *ad hoc* solutions.[66]

The overriding effect has been to introduce substantial confusion and uncertainty over the conduct of world trade.[67] This uncertainty reaches well beyond today's transactions. Perhaps its most important effect is the additional risk it adds to long-term investments in production for export. These "uncertainty effects," like the sectoral restraints and bilateralism discussed earlier, have their greatest impact on newly industrializing countries. Investment flows to their export sectors are very likely diminished by continued uncertainty over what levels of exports will be allowed in the future. This nexus of trade barriers, uncertainty about the future, and capital expenditures suggests at least one link between economic behavior and the regime's strength and content.

The decline in dispute settlement procedures is clear, then, but how are we to explain it? How, for that matter, are we to explain the other major changes in the regime: the rise of sectoral barriers and the countervailing trends toward liberalization? In general, how are we to explain the regime's changing strength and content? Such questions are obviously central to any analysis of the trade regime considered as a dependent variable. Having identified some significant changes and divergent trends within the regime, we now consider their most prominent explanation.

Explaining regime change

The limits of the hegemonic model

The dominant explanation of regime change, in trade as in other areas, is the hegemonic model. That model, developed in the work of Gilpin, Kindleberger, and Krasner, specifies that stable, open international economic structures are causally associated with a hegemonic distribution of state power.[68] Hegemonic powers, in other words, give rise to strong international regimes. The underlying logic, according to Kindleberger, is that international openness (liberal trade and payments) is a public good that is

---

[66] Hudec, *The GATT Legal System*, pp. 193–94.
[67] *GATT Study no. 5*, p. 9.
[68] Gilpin, *U.S. Power*; Kindleberger, *The World in Depression*; Kindleberger, "Systems of International Economic Organization"; Krasner, "State Power."

costly to provide.[69] Although the logic is not developed rigorously, the inference is that, according to the size principle, such public goods are more likely to be provided in systems where there is one very large state than where there are several medium-sized ones.

Krasner defines a hegemonic system as "one in which there is a single state that is much larger and relatively more advanced than its trading partners."[70] His conclusion, based on an analysis of nineteenth and twentieth century trade data, is that "a hegemonic distribution of potential economic power is likely to result in an open trading structure."[71] Following Krasner, the recent decline in hegemonic power should, therefore, be associated with a weaker, less open international trade regime. Disputes should be more likely and rule violations more frequent.[72]

That there has been a decline in hegemonic power seems plain enough. While there is no single obvious measure of relevant power resources, it is clear that the United States' status as the dominant trading nation of the 1940s and 1950s no longer holds. In manufactured exports, for instance, Germany surpassed the U.S. around 1970, and Japan achieved parity eight years later.[73] By whatever measure one chooses, the U.S. has lost its dominance in trade. A hegemonic model would therefore predict weakening in the trade regime.

That prediction accurately captures the central tendency of the

[69] Robert Keohane is surely correct when he observes that it is not a pure public good since states may be excluded from the GATT or from Most-Favored-Nation status. Keohane, "The Theory of Hegemonic Stability and Changes in International Economic Regimes, 1967–1977," in Ole Holsti, Randolph Siverson, and Alexander L. George, eds., *Change in the International System* (Boulder, Col.: Westview, 1980), fn. 10, p. 158. Nevertheless, the public good notion is heuristically interesting, in part because it associates some narrowly self-interested state actions with free ridership. It also suggests, persuasively for both the postwar United States and 19th century Britain, that the hegemon's policies may be directed toward the long-term goal of regime maintenance (for which it is willing to assume short-term costs, even if other states will not or cannot share them) rather than toward short-term economic advantages.

The public-good concept of hegemonic stability is suggested by Kindleberger's work on the Great Depression. Interestingly, however, Kindleberger introduces a powerful element of national voluntarism into his discussion. The capacity to act as a hegemon (that is, a hegemonic international structure of resources) does not necessarily imply stability for Kindleberger since a prospective international leader may still pursue policies appropriate to a free rider. That is largely his evaluation of American international economic policies in the 1920s and 1930s. This element of policy choice means that his model incorporates features from both national and international levels. Stephen Krasner, on the other hand, attempts to explain open trading systems by focusing more rigorously on the *structure* of hegemonic and nonhegemonic systems. Still, Krasner discusses reasons why a hegemonic power is likely to favor openness and thus to pursue it. See Krasner, "State Power," pp. 322–23.

[70] Krasner, "State Power," p. 322.

[71] Ibid., p. 318. Actually Krasner's data and his interpretation are considerably more equivocal than he suggests in this summary (see ibid., p. 335).

[72] Krasner develops this point in "The Tokyo Round." Summarizing his views, he argues that "as U.S. power has declined its leaders have become more concerned with specific national economic interests, making their behavior more similar to the behavior of policy makers in other states. This has led to a differentiated trading regime with some sectors characterized by greater liberality and others by more closure" (p. 491).

[73] U.S. Department of Commerce, *International Economic Indicators and Competitive Trends* 7, 2 (June 1981), table 28.

regime—the emergence of sectoral barriers, the decline of dispute settlement procedures, and the increasing evasion of GATT rules, especially those bearing on the principle of nondiscrimination. On the other hand, it does not capture other features of the regime that are only slightly less important: the GATT's continuity as a multilateral forum; the Tokyo Round's success under trying economic conditions; and the persistent reduction of tariffs (and some nontariff barriers) during the 1960s and 1970s.

There is, unfortunately, no agreed means of conflating these disparate trends into a single measure of regime strength. Indeed, experts differ considerably in their assessments of current trading arrangements. Compare recent comments by Franko and Burenstam-Linder. According to Franko, "The half decade that has passed since the oil crisis . . . has seen an increase in protectionist measures . . . unprecedented since the 1930s."[74] Burenstam-Linder agrees that protectionism has spread but he stresses equally the moves toward liberalization. He calls the situation "contradictory."[75] Baldwin, Mutti, and Richardson reach a similar conclusion: "The U.S.," they say, "has just completed one of the most comprehensive rounds of multilateral trade negotiations. Yet it is paradoxically facing stronger pressures for protection than at any time since the 1930s. Most other developed countries are in the same position."[76]

The trends are indeed mixed, but as a summary judgment one would have to agree with the GATT and IMF that there has been some increase in protection and some decline in rule adherence. These trends are best understood as changes *within* the regime, not changes *of* the regime. Although there is growing ambivalence about nondiscrimination, none of the other basic principles has been seriously threatened.

On the whole, then, the regime has weakened, and the hegemonic model accurately predicts its weakening.[77] The real questions are whether the model's causal inferences are plausible and whether the prediction is any more than roughly accurate.

The connection between hegemonic power and regime type is most apparent in the early GATT. The initial agreement followed U.S. talks with the British and, indeed, represented a multilateral extension of the 1938 trade agreement between the two countries.[78] Not surprisingly, the basic assumptions and goals of the GATT also reflected the American position. In par-

[74] Franko, "Current Trends in Protectionism," p. 29.
[75] Staffan Burenstam-Linder, "How to Avoid a New International Economic Disorder," *The World Economy* 3 (November 1980), p. 275.
[76] Robert E. Baldwin, John H. Mutti, and J. David Richardson, "Welfare Effects on the United States of a Significant Multilateral Tariff Reduction," *Journal of International Economics* 10 (1980), p. 405.
[77] Keohane, in "Theory of Hegemonic Stability," notes that U.S. power resources, as measured by shares of world trade among major states, have changed less in trade than in money or oil. Since the regime also changed less, he notes that the hegemonic stability theory is not disconfirmed. He does, however, challenge the causal argument linking this tangible resource change to changes in the regime, a point we take up later in this article.
[78] Meyer, *International Trade Policy*, p. 142; Charles Kindleberger, "Government Policies and Changing Shares in World Trade," *American Economic Review* 70 (May 1980), pp. 293–94.

ticular, they strongly emphasized the efficiency of open markets and sought the progressive liberalization of trade.[79]

America's hegemonic role in organizing the trade regime extends well beyond its disproportionate resources and its active diplomacy. A central feature of the new American hegemony was its defeat of the Axis powers— powers whose trade was conspicuously organized into closed regional systems under extensive state direction.[80] American leaders saw a profound connection between the cartelization of world trade in the 1930s and the origins of World War II, and they aimed to prevent a recurrence. In a sense, implementing the Bretton Woods accords represented the fruits of victory: the attachment of Germany and Japan to a liberal economic order based on market principles, restricted state intervention, multilateralism, and nondiscrimination. Thus, if the GATT's charter members had congruent purposes,[81] their fundamental unity can hardly be disentangled from America's decisive military victory or America's crucial role in rebuilding war-shattered economies and polities. In the case of Japan, for example, the U.S. not only managed reconstruction but also played an essential role in Japan's joining the GATT. To secure Japan's accession to the General Agreement, says Meyer, "the U.S. was willing to give twice as much by way of scheduled concessions as she received, just as she had done to secure the general agreement in the first place in 1947."[82] Acting very much like a hegemonic leader, the U.S. also persuaded Canada, Denmark, Finland, Italy, Norway, and Sweden to make trade concessions to Japan in return for American concessions to them.[83]

As Meyer suggests, American leadership was also decisive in early GATT tariff cutting. Only twice in the first two decades did GATT rounds lead to major tariff cuts. Both the 1947 Geneva Round and the Kennedy Round twenty years later followed new U.S. trade laws allowing the President to halve U.S. tariffs.[84]

The persistence of tariff cutting as U.S. power has diminished tends to cast doubt on the linkage, however. Until the Kennedy Round, the U.S. was willing to reduce its tariffs more than proportionately in order to extend lib-

---

[79] Krauss, *The New Protectionism,* p. 18. The tenor of the U.S. position is best shown by a secret statement made by the U.S. representative to the GATT's Torquay negotiations in November 1950. First, he praised the British for liberalizing restrictions against imports from certain soft-currency countries. Then he added, "We have recognized this action as a step in progress towards a worldwide multilateral trading system and convertibility of currencies. We have felt that it was taken in conformity with the spirit in which all of us have entered into the GATT that restrictions, particularly discriminatory restrictions, are the exception to the rule and should be relaxed as the situation which led to their imposition improved and should be removed when the circumstances which led to their imposition have been corrected." *Foreign Relations of the United States, 1950,* vol. 1 (Washington, D.C.: GPO, 1977), p. 769.

[80] Albert O. Hirschman, *National Power and the Structure of Foreign Trade* (Berkeley: University of California Press, 1945).

[81] On the congruence of purpose, see Ruggie in this volume.

[82] Meyer, *International Trade Policy,* p. 142.

[83] Ibid., p. 141.

[84] Ibid., p. 137.

eral world trade. According to the GATT's reciprocal bargaining, other countries "paid" for U.S. concessions by pledging their own. "Overall," says Meyer, "the U.S. gave about two scheduled concessions for every one received."[85] But both the Kennedy and Tokyo Rounds, where tariffs were cut by about one-third, were based on fully reciprocal bargaining among industrial countries. U.S. leadership may have been essential to the early rounds, but, in tariff-cutting at least, the decline of hegemony has not had the expected effects.

The predictions of a hegemonic model are little more accurate regarding sectoral protection and the breakdown of GATT's dispute procedures. The dispute procedures appear to have failed by the late 1950s, when American leadership was very much intact. This timing is at least perplexing in terms of a hegemonic model. Nor can an exclusive focus on international structure explain why trade protection has arisen in certain sectors while liberal trade continues in others. Even though the model can accurately predict a gross decline in trade openness, it cannot comprehend the issue of sectoral unevenness.

Beyond these predictive issues is the problem of causality in the hegemonic model. Keohane raises the issue pointedly. He documents the hegemonic model's general predictive accuracy in the oil, money, and trade regimes, but in trade especially he denies the causal linkage. He argues that protectionism is basically a domestic phenomenon related to structural weaknesses and maladjustments. He also notes the rise of LDC manufacturing exports and the recession of the mid 1970s as sources of protectionism.[86]

As important as these adjustment problems are, the issue must not be reduced too swiftly to a levels-of-analysis problem. Keohane is certainly correct in suggesting that no interstate political model can adequately comprehend the domestic sources of national trade policies. But neither do adjustment problems hold uniform consequences for the international regime. Their effects depend not only on domestic policy-making structures but also on the state's capacity to implement such policies internationally. In fact, current adjustment problems carry such serious trade implications because all advanced states have tried to shift the burdens internationally via sectoral protection policies. The GATT, which has institutionalized America's liberal trade policies, can no longer deter such policies or even resolve the disputes they engender. Not only is hegemony gone, so is the international consensus produced by American victory and reconstruction.[87]

---

[85] Ibid., p. 138.

[86] Keohane, "Theory of Hegemonic Stability," pp. 152–54.

[87] The relationship between American hegemony and the postwar consensus is complex. But Europe's support for liberal trade closely followed American initiatives and could hardly be termed autonomous, even if it did have strong domestic roots. To begin with, America's victory wiped out Germany's closed regional trade system. The regionalism that replaced it had extensive American involvement and was intended as an interim step toward multilateral trade and payments. The U.S. played a major role in the formation of postwar governments, and naturally

The continuity of trade: its economic underpinnings

The basic prediction of the hegemonic model—that the trade regime will progressively weaken—stems from its preoccupation with American decline. That preoccupation is a powerful theoretical simplification. The model posits that regime strength depends on the international distribution of state power. It thus ignores domestic politics, other types of actors, and, significantly for us, the type of activity being regulated (whatever its particular characteristics). The model can be criticized, as we have done, on the grounds that its predictions are only roughly accurate and that its causal links are not always compelling. But the most glaring predictive problem is that the regime has not weakened uniformly. Rule-guided behavior has declined markedly in some sectors but not in others.

A hegemonic explanation of the regime's differentiation would look not at specific sectors but at specific exporting countries. Protection, in this view, is less a matter of restricting particular products than of restricting particular countries' exports. With the weakening of the overall regulatory framework, presumably due to hegemonic decline, multilateral conventions are replaced by bilateral negotiations. Given the asymmetries of national resources, LDCs are particularly disadvantaged in such talks. It is not surprising, then, that they accede to VERs, or that a weakening regime is characterized by such selectivity.

This explanation captures a significant dimension of modern trade politics. Tough bilateral bargaining is common between LDCs and advanced states, and it is not always constrained by the regime's rules or principles. Of course, there is nothing unusual about tough bargaining, but in trade talks between advanced states there are additional elements of caution. Advanced states rely heavily on their mutual trade, and they are well aware of the scope for mutual retaliation. Beyond the specific dispute, they know that either party could act to undermine the larger system of rules—with far-reaching consequences.

This explanation misses, and in fact cannot comprehend, the rise of sectoral protection among advanced countries. Steel and automobiles are good examples.[88] The basic disputes involve the U.S., the EC, and Japan. As late as 1971, the most important textile dispute was between the U.S. and

---

paid special attention to their foreign policy positions. The U.S. established the institutions of liberal internationalism and those of Atlantic cooperation. It aimed at, and succeeded in, demolishing the protective network of Depression-era tariffs. This is not meant to imply that Europe was a *tabula rasa* for American designs or that governments there did not freely support these policies and institutions. But their support was clearly structured at every level by the magnitude of the American victory, the disparity of resources (and Europe's desperate need for them), and Europe's profound dependence on American foreign policy.

[88] Gilbert Winham, *The Automobile Trade Crisis of 1980* (Halifax, Nova Scotia: Dalhousie University Centre for Foreign Policy Studies, 1981); Walter, "Protection of Industries in Trouble"; [Allen Schlosser,] "Autos Dominated Congress' Trade Agenda during 1980," *JEI* [Japan Economic Institute] *Report*, 9 January 1981.

Japan. Again, it is worth noting that these disputes have involved certain types of products and have not spread to the full range of trilateral commerce. This suggests some sectoral differentiation of the regime, with the rules applying unevenly across product groupings. When steel, shoes, clothing or textiles are involved, the regime's weakness is more apparent, regardless of the exporting country. Because so many of the NICs' exports are in such sectors, they feel the regime's weakness with special force.[89]

These sectors, as we have already noted, can be characterized in general terms. They are wage-sensitive, produce standardized, price-competitive products, use relatively standard technologies, and are under the direction of national firms. They are labor-intensive, so employment is high relative to the value of production. Other things being equal, this increases their importance to trade policy makers and raises the human cost of adjustment. Because producers cannot relocate abroad as multinational firms can, they have a powerful stake in the effective protection of their domestic markets. On this point at least, there is a conjunction of interest between import-competing firms and their workers. That, too, increases the political impact of these sectors.

If we invert these sectoral characteristics, we identify the sectors that have contributed powerfully to the growth of world trade and especially to its institutional continuity. These are producers of differentiated goods with high research and development, relatively short product lives, and often increasing returns to scale. Because their proprietary knowledge of processes and products is short-lived, such producers find that access to foreign markets is essential to capture the full rents.

Such sophisticated and differentiated products are often associated with a peculiarity of national trade statistics: the simultaneous import and export of very similar goods. Such trade is poorly understood by the conventional Heckscher-Ohlin-Samuelson theory, which assumes constant returns to scale and common production functions. As a result, economists studying intra-industry trade have relaxed some of these simplifying assumptions so that they conform to "product-cycle" and "technology-gap" goods, as well as to production with increasing returns to scale (where scale usually means the length of production runs rather than plant size).

The findings, though still tentative, are suggestive. They indicate, for example, that producers in some industries respond to the loss of competitiveness in one product-line by shifting production to another closely related product—one in which they might develop proprietary skills or carve out a

---

[89] The size of the textile and clothing sector is especially important. For Hong Kong, textiles and apparel account for nearly half of all exports; for South Korea, about one-third. Smith, "The Fibres of Protectionism," p. 74. For LDCs as a whole, they represent over one-third of all exports to advanced countries. Donald B. Keesing, "World Trade and Output of Manufactures: Structural Trends and Developing Countries' Exports," *World Bank Working Paper* no. 316 (January 1979), Table 18, p. 25 (figures are for 1976). At the same time, many LDC producers are developing increasing sophistication in their manufacturing and exporting capabilities.

special niche in oligopolistic markets. According to the Heckscher-Ohlin model, market signals serve to shift resources out of noncompetitive industries into more efficient ones. But in the case of intra-industry trade, market signals serve to shift production into closely related products within the same industry.

Intra-industry trade thus implies a pattern of adjustment quite different from that assumed by economists working with simplified Heckscher-Ohlin models. The traditional models of trade, from Smith and Ricardo on, imply the relocation of production in response to differences in relative factor prices. The studies of intra-industry trade, on the other hand, suggest that certain types of import-competing industries are not extinguished and need not invoke state aid to frustrate market-imposed adjustments. They can adapt, specialize, and export their own goods.[90]

It is difficult to exaggerate the importance of such trade for the economic integration of advanced capitalist states. It suggests reasons why economies with basically similar factor endowments, such as the U.S. and the EC, might trade so extensively with each other. Moreover, it implies that the difficulties of adjustment may be less formidable for some producers than conventional trade theory would suggest. The reason for these prospectively lower adjustment costs is that intra-industry trade (unlike *inter*-industry trade) does not take place through conventional national specialization in certain sectors. Rather, increased trade occurs in products belonging to the same industry.[91]

Measuring such trade is a difficult and controversial matter, since the levels of intra-industry trade will depend upon the data's level of aggregation. Most measures, however, show extensive and growing intra-industry trade. Grubel and Lloyd, measuring at the three-digit Standard International Trade Classification (SITC) level, found that over half the 1967 OECD trade in manufactures was intra-industry trade; the proportion has since increased.[92] Aquino, using 1972 figures and somewhat different statistical

---

[90] The literature on intra-industry trade is rapidly growing. The best place to begin is Herbert G. Grubel and P. J. Lloyd, *Intra-Industry Trade: The Theory and Measure of International Trade in Differentiated Products* (New York: Wiley, Halsted Press 1975). The most recent work in the area, by some of the best-known scholars, is collected in Herbert Giersch, ed., *On the Economics of Intra-Industry Trade* (Tübingen: J. C. B. Mohr [Paul Siebeck], 1979).

[91] Grubel and Lloyd, *Intra-Industry Trade*, p. 9.

[92] Ibid., chap. 3. All commodities are categorized according to the SITC system. The first digit in a commodity's SITC number refers to the broadest product grouping. The second, third, and fourth digits entail successively finer gradations. Category 7, for instance, includes all machinery and transport equipment; 72 refers to machines designed especially for particular industries; 721 is all agricultural machinery except tractors; 721.4 is egg-handling machinery and parts. Three points are relevant to our discussion. First, the SITC numbers do not consistently categorize commodities according to their inputs or end-uses. Hence, they are not necessarily identical to industry groupings, even though they are used to measure inter-industry and intra-industry trade. Moreover, if inputs are dissimilar, then imports and exports within the same SITC category may be perfectly consistent with the Heckscher-Ohlin model of trade. Finally, the amount of intra-industry trade depends upon the level of statistical disaggregation. A country might export egg-handling equipment (721.4) and import all dairy machinery (721.3). At the

techniques, found that intra-industry trade was over 70 percent for Canada and most of western Europe, and about 57 percent for the United States.[93]

Not only are these figures high, they are growing. Separate studies by Grubel and Lloyd, Aquino, and Hesse all point to the same conclusion: intra-industry trade has tended to increase as a proportion of total trade throughout the postwar era.[94] Balassa, whose studies of trade within the EC stimulated much of this work, has also found increasing similarities in the export structures of Community members.[95] This finding is especially noteworthy when compared to the conventional expectation: liberalizing trade should lead to greater national specialization, sectoral relocation, and nationally divergent export structures. Balassa's work and a growing body of other studies support the contrary hypothesis that trade liberalization promotes intra-industry rather than inter-industry specialization.[96]

It is likely that intra-industry trade and trade liberalization are mutually reinforcing. Trade liberalization among advanced states tends to stimulate intra-industry trade, while the efficiency gains and low adjustment costs tend to reinforce the liberalization enterprise. This may be why GATT liberalization exercises have focused increasingly on areas where intra-industry trade is likely. As Hufbauer and Chilas persuasively argue, "GATT negotiations very much favor intra-industry over inter-industry specialization."[97]

4-digit level, no intra-industry trade is found. At the 3-digit level, however, the same trade pattern would be considered simultaneous imports and exports of agricultural machinery. Most studies of intra-industry trade classify industries at the 3- or 4-digit SITC level.

[93] Antonio Aquino, "Intra-Industry Trade and Inter-Industry Specialization as Concurrent Sources of International Trade in Manufactures," *Weltwirtschaftliches Archiv* 114 (1978), pp. 275–95.

[94] "The facts on intra-industry trade can be briefly stated," according to trade economist W. M. Corden. "(1) Intra-industry trade as a proportion of total trade in manufactured commodities is very high for the leading industrial nations. . . . (2) The proportion of intra-industry trade in total trade has tended to increase." Corden, "Intra-Industry Trade and Factor Proportions Theory," in Giersch, *On the Economics of Intra-Industry Trade,* p. 3. In the same volume (p. 242) Jan Tumlir of the GATT reports that intra-industry trade accounts for much of the large expansion of postwar trade. See also Aquino, "Intra-Industry Trade and Specialization"; Grubel and Lloyd, *Intra-Industry Trade*; and Helmut Hesse, "Hypotheses for the Explanation of Trade between Industrial Countries, 1953–1970," in Herbert Giersch, ed., *The International Division of Labour: Problems and Perspectives* (Tübingen: J. C. B. Mohr, 1974), pp. 39–59.

[95] Bela Balassa, "Intra-Industry Trade and the Integration of Developing Countries in the World Economy," in Giersch, *On the Economics of Intra-Industry Trade,* pp. 245–46.

[96] See, for example, Grubel and Lloyd, *Intra-Industry Trade,* chap. 9; Gary C. Hufbauer and John C. Chilas, "Specialization by Industrial Countries: Extent and Consequences," in Giersch, *International Division of Labour,* pp. 3–38.

[97] Hufbauer and Chilas, "Specialization by Industrial Countries," p. 6. The less important role played by intra-industry trade in commerce between LDCs and developed countries implies higher adjustment costs for any given volume of trade and may be an additional source of protectionist pressure. As Rudolf Loertscher and Frank Wolter concluded from their study, "As expected, intra-industry trade intensity across countries increases with a decreasing development stage differential; a decreasing market size differential; increasing average market size; and decreasing distance between trading partners" ("Determinants of Intra-Industry Trade: Among Countries and Across Industries," *Weltwirtschaftliches Archiv* 116, 2 [1980], p. 268). Except for the distance factor, all of these variables suggest a low intra-industry trade intensity for DC-LDC trade. In an article which, on the whole, deemphasizes the disruption of

The growth of intra-industry trade and its encouragement by multilateral tariff reductions remind us that the trade regime may have weakened but it has not collapsed. Instead, it has been quietly subdivided by a series of *ad hoc* solutions: VERs and "managed" trade for some sectors, greater liberalization in others. These differences largely reflect the varied circumstances of producers in advanced states. Now that the institutions of liberal trade can no longer constrain the protection of declining industries, these sectoral differences are revealed more sharply. They point to a patchwork arrangement for world trade that is neither openness nor autarky—a regime of profound discontinuities.

The impact of the trade regime

What effects do these discontinuities have on the conduct of world trade? The answer must be sought on two levels: the regime's impact on national trade policies and its impact on trade flows.

Typically, the analysis of regimes traces the impact of national capabilities and policies on a regime's strength and content. The hegemonic model, for instance, predicts the regime's weakening based on the relative decline of American economic capabilities. The connection between regimes and nation-states is not unidirectional, however. It is mutually conditioning. An ongoing regime forms a significant context for the framing of national policies. Multilateral arrangements and institutions may constrain the policy process, provide new opportunities and sources of support for some policy makers, and ultimately influence the choice of national policies.[98]

These "regime-effects" are important in the case of U.S. trade policy. The presence of a GATT-based trade regime has served as a catalyst for nearly all major postwar trade legislation. Most proposals have been designed, quite explicitly, either to initiate GATT negotiations or to implement the results. The 1962 Trade Expansion Act, for instance, was the prelude to the Kennedy Round and staked out America's initial positions there. Like other U.S. trade legislation, it authorized the reduction of trade barriers if others reciprocated. The 1974 Trade Act did the same for the Tokyo Round.

LDC exports to DCs, Carl Hamilton and Mordechai E. Kreinin nevertheless observe that such trade "probably generates much *inter*-industry specialization, which is presumably subject to higher adjustment cost than the increase in intra-industry specialization in trade among industrial countries themselves" ("The Structural Pattern of LDCs' Trade in Manufactures with Individual and Groups of DCs," *Weltwirtschaftliches Archiv* 116, 2 [1980], p. 274, emphasis mine). One possible offsetting feature of LDC trade is its vertical specialization in unskilled-labor intensive operations and its subsequent incorporation in intra-*firm* flows across borders. See Balassa, "Intra-Industry Trade," p. 267.

[98] Ronald I. Meltzer, "The Politics of Policy Reversal: The U.S. Response to Granting Trade Preferences to Developing Countries and Linkages between International Organizations and National Policy Making," *International Organization* 30, 4 (Autumn 1976), pp 649–68.

The Trade Agreements Act of 1979 (the title is instructive) ratified the Tokyo Round accords and incorporated them into domestic law.

The whole process of preparing for multilateral negotiations and then ratifying the results helps to structure U.S. trade policy making. It periodically centralizes discussion of all major trade questions. By raising trade to the top of the policy agenda, it mobilizes the usually diffuse support for liberal trade.[99] At the same time, the overriding need to produce a comprehensive negotiating package (or to seal the resulting multilateral bargain) facilitates other kinds of concessions to declining industries. The aim, shared by all postwar administrations, is to prevent the formation of a protectionist coalition by passing out side-payments and exceptions. Declining industries may be given more-than-equal treatment, but they are carefully segregated.

The need to conduct multilateral negotiations on a reciprocal basis also creates incentives to harmonize domestic laws and practices with those prevailing abroad. The need for conformity is especially great when domestic laws plainly contravene the regime's approved practices. U.S. laws on safeguards and countervailing duties are a good example. They were prominent targets during the Tokyo Round precisely because they were prominent exceptions to GATT rules and norms. Trading partners can play important roles in such cases. They can offer concessions to induce conformity, or they can threaten retaliation if the violations continue. In the Tokyo Round, they did both—successfully. U.S. laws were brought into conformity with regime-approved practices.

Despite this success, harmonization is inherently difficult, and even strenuous efforts may fail. The Johnson administration, for instance, agreed to participate in a new GATT antidumping code even though it was substantially at variance with U.S. law. It also agreed to end an idiosyncratic and objectionable method of customs valuation known as the "American Selling Price." The Congress, which was not consulted, killed both agreements.[100] The outcome showed that negotiations over nontariff barriers require continual consultation between Executive and Congress. The domestic side of tariff negotiations, by contrast, is much more concentrated in the Executive. The outside limits of Executive negotiating authority are set in advance by Congress and any agreement within those limits (e.g., a 40% tariff cut) is automatically approved. Nontariff barriers are too complex to permit this kind of *a priori* authorization. The continuing involvement of Congress, in turn, assures import-competing industries of continual access to trade policy making. Thus, the complex subject matter of modern trade policy—if not the regime itself—structures the relationship between the Executive, the Congress, and the affected industries.

[99] See Pastor, *Congress and U.S. Foreign Economic Policy,* esp. pp. 192–93.
[100] I. M. Destler and Thomas R. Graham, "The United States Congress and the Tokyo Round: Lessons of a Success Story," *The World Economy* 3 (June 1980), p. 54.

No one has understood this point better than Robert Strauss, America's negotiator during the final stages of the Tokyo Round. He maneuvered the agreements through a reluctant Congress largely by making side-payments (some say judiciously, others say extravagantly) to a variety of adversely affected industries.[101] The resulting trade law not only adopted the GATT's codes on customs valuation and government procurement, it also incorporated the GATT standard that "material injury" must be shown before countervailing duties are applied.[102] The adoption of this injury test over the strong opposition of the steel industry shows how participation in an international regime can shape domestic law.[103]

The courts, too, have been sensitive to U.S. participation in the GATT. The most famous case was Zenith's $900 million antitrust suit against Japanese television manufacturers. Zenith charged that Japan's rebates of its Value Added Taxes (VAT) were illegal under U.S. law. It asserted that the VAT rebates, which were permitted under the GATT, were a "grant or bounty" under U.S. statutes and required the imposition of countervailing duties. Its position seemed strong, based on existing U.S. trade law (Section 303 of the Tariff Act of 1930) and domestic case law (Supreme Court rulings in 1903 and 1915). The Treasury and Carter administration were vigorous in their opposition; any other reaction would have jeopardized the Tokyo Round, threatened the entire network of GATT rules, and affected as much as 60 to 70 percent of all U.S. imports. When the U.S. Customs Court ruled in Zenith's favor in April 1977, the decision "was widely viewed as a potentially explosive threat to international trade relations, precipitating a series of trade restrictions that would either follow this precedent or retaliate against its effect."[104] The GATT Council took the unusual step of warning the U.S. formally that any application of countervailing duties in this case would be illegal under the GATT and would invite reprisals. Acting quickly, the Carter administration tried to resolve the issue by negotiating an OMA—another instance where an extra-GATT arrangement was made to avoid violating the GATT's formal rules. Zenith was not appeased and pressed its side of the appeal. The Carter administration announced that it would seek new countervailing duty legislation if it lost in the higher courts; once again, the legislative agenda was being set by GATT participation. Actually, the Carter administration would probably have lost its case in

[101] Gilbert Winham, "Robert Strauss, the MTN, and the Control of Faction," *Journal of World Trade Law* 14 (September–October 1980), pp. 377–97.

[102] Harold Brandt and Wilhelm A. Zeitler, "Unfair Import Trade Practice Jurisdiction: The Applicability of Section 337 and the Countervailing Duty and Antidumping Laws," *Law and Policy in International Business* 12 (1980), p. 105.

[103] Destler and Graham, "U.S. Congress and Tokyo Round," p. 66; John J. Barceló III, "Subsidies, Countervailing Duties and Antidumping After the Tokyo Round," *Cornell International Law Journal* 13 (Summer 1980), pp. 269–70.

[104] Ronald I. Meltzer, "Dynamics of Trade Adjustment Difficulties: Color TVs and U.S.-Japanese Relations," paper presented at International Studies Association convention, Washington, D.C., 1978. This treatment of the Zenith case relies on Meltzer's discussion.

Congress, but it won on appeal. In July 1977, in a decision that was to stand, the U.S. Court of Customs and Patent Appeals overturned the lower court ruling. Strauss rightly called it "a major legal victory." Any other decision, he said, would have been a "serious threat to trade harmony and the success of trade liberalization negotiations in Geneva."[105] In the end, the courts subordinated existing domestic legislation and case law to the requirements of multilateral policy making and regime participation.

If the presence of a trade regime affects commercial law and policy making, it also affects actual commerce. In the most immediate sense, the competitiveness of traded goods (and hence the level of trade flows) is affected by the size of trade barriers. Over the longer run, those barriers influence the location and composition of production.

We have already indicated two longer-run effects: the distortion of NIC exporting sectors and the promotion of intra-industry trade. Uncertainty over future trade barriers probably dampens investments in NIC exporting sectors. Certainly the growth of nontariff barriers has affected the composition of NIC exports. Quotas, which are a common affliction for the NICs, limit the number of imports but not their value. As a result, they encourage foreign producers to shift from simple, cheap exports to more demanding products with higher value-added. Since quotas are also highly product specific, they accelerate the diversification of NIC exports.

The regime's evolution has also encouraged intra-industry trade (and its associated pattern of industrial specialization) by biased GATT tariff concessions. In this case, the relationship between trade flows and tariff structure appears dialectical. The reductions systematically favor intra-industry trade and the ensuing growth of that trade encourages more bias in future reductions. Even if producers dominate the process of tariff cutting, they are more likely to consent to lower barriers if they anticipate export growth to offset imports. That is the promise of intra-industry trade, and the reason for its ascendancy within the GATT. This persistent bias, according to Hufbauer and Chilas, may contribute to convergent industrial structures in advanced states.[106] Likewise, the mutually reinforcing combination of intra-industry trade and biased tariff concessions helps explain why convergent industrial structures have been associated with more trade, not less.

Whatever bias the tariff cuts may have had, they have surely stimulated international commerce. In general terms, the reductions are "one of the most important influences on trade during the [postwar] period."[107] Estimating the size of that influence is a more difficult task, and an inherently imprecise one. There is, however, a common theme running through the

---

[105] Ibid., p. 17.

[106] Hufbauer and Chilas, "Specialization by Industrial Countries," p. 6.

[107] A. D. Morgan, "Export Competition and Import Substitution: The Industrial Countries, 1963 to 1971," in R. A. Batchelor, R. L. Major, and A. D. Morgan, *Industrialisation and the Basis for Trade* (Cambridge: Cambridge University Press for the National Institute of Economic and Social Research, 1980), p. 76.

quantitative studies made since the late 1950s. Discrete acts of trade liberalization produce only modest gains in trade volume.[108]

That finding also seems to hold for the Tokyo Round. Kreinin and Officer have compared the results of five econometric studies, all pointing in this direction. Most, unfortunately, were made before the Round's conclusion and relied on formulas other than the one finally agreed upon. Still, on this basic point they are all agreed: the Tokyo Round tariff cuts are unlikely to produce substantial trade expansion. Cline, for instance, estimates that a 50 percent linear tariff cut (which is larger than the agreed formula) would have increased American imports by $3 billion in 1974 dollars. EC imports would have increased by $3.8 billion and Japan's by $1.5 billion. Stone, who also assumes a 50 percent cut, predicts trade increases about one-half that size and somewhat differently distributed.[109] To put these figures in perspective, world imports in 1980 were around $2 trillion, those of industrial countries $1.375 trillion.[110] "Compared to existing levels of trade and employment," say Kreinin and Officer, "all the estimated gross changes are small.[111]

Brown and Whalley reached the same conclusion with a more sophisticated general equilibrium model. They found that none of the Tokyo Round proposals would have increased world trade by more than 2 percent.[112] They calculated that the Swiss proposal, which was finally adopted by the major countries, would raise U.S. and EC imports by 1.6 percent, Japanese imports by 0.9 percent, and the rest of the world's by 1.2 percent.[113]

These modest gains from tariff reductions must be balanced against the increasing incidence of nontariff barriers. Good quantitative estimates of their effects are not available, but some general indicators are. In late 1977, the Secretary-General of the GATT, Olivier Long, estimated that some 3 to 5 percent of world trade was "being adversely affected by import restrictions introduced, or seriously threatened, by the industrially-advanced countries."[114] Along the same lines, Olechowski and Sampson have estimated that over 11 percent of U.S. import categories are traded under nontariff

[108] Mordechai Kreinin and Lawrence Officer report that these findings are made in studies by Krause (1959), Kreinin (1961), Balassa and Kreinin (1967), Officer and Hurtubise (1969), and Finger (1976) ("Tariff Reductions under the Tokyo Round: A Review of Their Effects on Trade Flows, Employment, and Welfare," *Weltwirtschaftliches Archiv* 115 [1979], p. 551 fn).

[109] Ibid., p. 551.

[110] *IMF Survey*, 23 March 1981, p. 81.

[111] Kreinin and Officer, "Tariff Reductions," p. 551. In a more recent study, Baldwin, Mutti, and Richardson also examine a 50% tariff cut by all advanced countries (but excluding imports, such as textiles, that are subject to quantitative restrictions). Their findings are similar to the studies reviewed by Kreinin and Officer. Under both fixed and flexible exchange rates, U.S. imports and exports each increase $1.75 billion in 1967 dollars. Baldwin, Mutti, and Richardson, "Welfare Effects on the U.S.," esp. p. 417.

[112] Fred Brown and John Whalley, "General Equilibrium Evaluations of Tariff-Cutting Proposals in the Tokyo Round and Comparisons with More Extensive Liberalisation of World Trade," *Economic Journal* 90 (December 1980), p. 865.

[113] Ibid., p. 862.

[114] Address by Olivier Long, secretary-general of the GATT, to the Zürich Economic Society, 9 November 1977, as cited in Nowzad, "The Rise of Protectionism," p. 4.

barriers; for the EC and Japan the figures are 5.4 percent and 3.1 percent. Most are quantitative controls in textiles and footwear.[115] Brown and Whalley's figures indicate higher barriers in Europe and Japan than in America. Using 1973 data, they computed *ad valorem* equivalents for major product categories. In the U.S. they found few nontariff barriers for durable manufactures, but in Japan they found shipbuilding subsidies and quotas for computers, transistors, and communications equipment roughly equal to a 9 percent tariff for durable manufactures. In the EC, the equivalent figure for subsidies, restrictive standards, and quotas in durable manufactures was 16.8 percent.[116]

The gaps in these data are readily apparent. They are very highly aggregated, do not reveal the impact of nontariff barriers on trade flows or on static welfare, and give no sense of changes over time, including the effects of the Tokyo Round. They certainly do not measure lost trade, or a diminished rate of trade growth. What they suggest, in a very clear way, is that nontariff barriers have become a major obstacle to trade in certain manufactured products.

These restraints on trade flows have impeded the geographic redistribution of production and have otherwise depressed trade growth in some products. On the other hand, in areas where tariffs have been liberalized, trade has been slightly stimulated. In both cases, there appears to be some connection between changes within the trade regime and private commercial transactions.

Conclusions

Let us now characterize in summary form the changes in the trade regime and consider their consequences for international trade flows.

First, the central norm of nondiscrimination has been violated with increasing frequency and boldness despite rhetorical conformity to the GATT. The rise of discriminatory trading arrangements opens the possibility that the regime will become geographically segmented. Its future boundaries may be drawn tightly around the advanced states, which have similar export structures and which deal with each other on a reciprocal basis. The NICs would then be relegated to a peripheral role, not only in decision making (that already exists) but also in sharing the benefits of trade openness. The Tokyo Round codes are a significant step toward such geographical segmentation. Signatories to the various nontariff codes promise to extend benefits only to each other, not to all most-favored-nations.[117] Since few LDCs have ap-

[115] Andrzej Olechowski and Gary Sampson, "Current Trade Restrictions in the EEC, the United States and Japan," *Journal of World Trade Law* 14 (May–June 1980), p. 227.

[116] Brown and Whalley, "General Equilibrium Evaluations," Table 4, p. 848.

[117] I wish to thank Raymond Vernon for his comments on this point. See also G. C. Hufbauer, J. S. Erb, and H. P. Starr, "The GATT Codes and the Unconditional Most-Favored-Nation Principle," *Law and Policy in International Business* 12 (1980), p. 61.

proved the codes, these provisions will, in practice, widen the fissure in the trade regime between advanced and newly industrializing states.

Second, most regime norms other than nondiscrimination are still intact. Reciprocity, multilateralism, transparency of trade barriers, the right to safeguard against import surges, and the goal of liberalizing trade barriers are still the basic tenets of modern trade relationships. Moreover, the GATT is still the institutional mechanism for making rules and coordinating the reduction of trade barriers.

If regime change entails fundamental changes in basic norms and principles, then the postwar trade regime still stands. Its evolution is, for the most part, consistent with its longstanding norms. Rather, change is to be found in its rules and shared expectations, in major states' conformity to the rules, and in the sectorally differentiated treatment of traded goods.

These changes within the regime are extensive. First, the shared expectation of secular decreases in trade barriers, especially strong in the 1960s, has been shaken by the proliferation of nontariff barriers in declining, import-competing sectors. Second, these nontariff barriers violate the GATT rule (embodied in Article XI) that trade should be regulated by tariffs and not by quantitative mechanisms. The rise of nontariff barriers in general, and quantitative restrictions in particular, is a profound challenge to the GATT's rules. Third, these barriers tend to be quite product-specific. They affect a number of basic industrial sectors but leave many others untouched. They disproportionately affect exports from less developed countries, largely because of their sectoral composition. Fourth, the procedures of dispute settlement decayed during the 1960s and 1970s after being used extensively in the 1950s. The Tokyo Round attempts to revive these mechanisms, as yet with uncertain results. Finally, despite some overall weakening of the regime, there are many areas in which liberalization continues. The GATT remains an important multilateral forum, as the Tokyo Round showed. The nontariff codes negotiated there should help reduce or control a number of trade barriers such as discriminatory government procurement. Tariffs continue to be reduced and are no longer a serious obstacle for most manufactures. Beyond these specific achievements, the Tokyo Round's success indicates that the major trading powers still support a relatively open trading order despite protectionist pressures and a difficult economic environment.

This is a complex picture of the trade regime, and not a simple one to explain. The simplest explanation focuses on the decline of American economic power. Such an explanation captures the broad outlines of regime change: America did play a crucial role in founding the regime and extending its scope, and the regime does appear strongest near the apex of American economic power, weaker as American power has waned. The uneven timing of the regime's decline, however, raises questions about the hegemonic model's causal sufficiency. The GATT's dispute settlement procedures failed while the U.S. still held a dominant position in the international economy. On the other hand, multilateral tariff reductions have continued well after the start of America's relative decline.

The continuous reduction of tariffs and the persistence of rules and institutional mechanisms suggest that the logic of regime maintenance may be distinct from that of regime initiation. Existing international organizations and networks of political interaction facilitate burden-sharing. Furthermore, the costs of regime maintenance are lower than those of establishing a new regime. Communicative networks do not have to be created or common understandings established. A rule-system need not be invented, justified, and imposed; it is already in place. New decisions are typically incremental, made within an established framework of principles, rules, and institutions. These lower costs of regime maintenance undoubtedly facilitate the transition to shared leadership within existing institutions. In the case of trade, the norm of reciprocity also helps. In addition, the cooperative process is encouraged by the fearful risks of undermining an extensive network of trade relationships in which all advanced economies are embedded. If the GATT helped foster these relationships, they now help foster the GATT.

The hegemonic model obscures these organizational aspects of regime maintenance. What it does do, however, is predict that any shared process of regime maintenance would entail a decline in rule adherence. There has been some rise in rule violations, it is true, but the regime's weakening appears less pronounced than the decline in relative U.S. economic power. Furthermore, the hegemonic model cannot adequately account for another central feature of the trade regime: its sectoral differentiation. Declining rule-adherence and rising ambivalence about nondiscrimination affect basic industries with special force. This cleavage within the regime points to the need for a supplementary account of regime change—one based on international market structures and the relative ability of sectors to adapt competitively.

The literature on intra-industry trade is germane here because it stresses systematic differences in sectors' capacities to specialize, and hence to adapt to imports under existing market conditions. The choice, ultimately, is between adaptation and protection. If industries can adapt to imports by developing their own exports, they may be able to preserve the positions of existing firms, unions, suppliers, and workers. Yet such adaptation is not equally possible for all sectors. The limited sectoral domain of intra-industry trade may help explain why protectionist pressures and sectoral "solutions" (such as VERs and OMAs) have been strongest in standardized, wage-sensitive industries. At the same time, intra-industry trade provides a powerful new source of multilateral interest in the liberal trade regime: diminished adjustment costs in some sectors, and higher net gains from trade as a result.

These net gains and the preservation of existing economic actors lend political and economic support to the current trade regime. These underpinnings are reinforced, as we noted earlier, by the high risks and costs associated with regime breakdown. Fear of the unknown plus growing trade dependence (much of it in intra-industry and intra-firm trade) are important sources of support for the present regime. The regime may be a patchwork, but it continues to provide benefits valued by the major trading states.

In summary, the hegemonic model may parsimoniously predict the overall propensity toward closure, but it obscures the organizational processes and market structures that are causally associated with maintenance of the trade regime.

The benefits (and strains) of maintaining the regime can be found in its effects on its members and on commercial transactions. That brings us back to the regime's significance as an intervening variable.

The presence of a trade regime is unmistakably felt in U.S. trade policy making. Major postwar trade legislation has aimed at starting new GATT negotiations or ratifying their conclusions. These aims give the legislation transcendent significance and mobilize a broad array of affected constituencies. Cast aside are the ordinary politics of piecemeal protectionism, dominated by the narrow claims of declining sectors. Instead, by raising the salience of trade issues and consolidating them in a single bill, the GATT-oriented legislative process catalyzes the usually latent support for liberal trade. Import-competing industries are not excluded, of course, but the logic of their position is changed. Their claims are significant only when they bear on the larger trade package. At that point, they are isolated and partially satisfied. Their satisfaction generally involves administrative concessions, rather than legislative protection, and so permits greater flexibility and discretion in its subsequent administration.[118] The courts, too, have been influenced by American participation in the GATT. In trade policy as in all foreign policy, they have hesitated to encroach on the Executive's diplomatic responsibilities. The crucial case of VAT rebates confirmed that the judiciary was willing to defer to the Tokyo Round negotiations and regime participation.

The regime's impact on trade flows is more difficult to establish, primarily because the rules, norms, and principles are such a pervasive and slow-changing feature of modern commerce. Certainly, the relative liberality and stability of the arrangements have provided a congenial environment for the long-term growth of trade and the development of industries that depend on international markets. The regime's internal differentiation—favoring intra-industry trade—has promoted the growth of such trade. That, in turn, promotes convergence of industrial structures in advanced states.

At the same time, trade in basic manufactures has grown in spite of nontariff barriers. The most plausible interpretation is not that the regime is irrelevant to these trade flows but that shifts in comparative advantage have, so far, outpaced restrictive measures. In any case, the proliferation of quantitative restrictions has a variety of indirect effects on investment risks, on the diversification of NIC exports, and on their prices and sophistication.

---

[118] Pastor, *Congress and U.S. Foreign Economic Policy,* esp. pp. 192–93.

Reducing the quantitative barriers would doubtless stimulate trade. But most recent studies indicate that further tariff cuts would add little to trade volume. This finding demonstrates the extent of the regime's prior liberalization and confirms that most static gains in trade volume have already been achieved.

The connection between the Tokyo Round and trade volumes may seem weak, but it appears much stronger if we consider the most pertinent counterfactual: the regime's collapse. Econometric studies consistently show that further reductions in trade barriers add only slightly to trade volumes. It should be recognized, however, that such studies implicitly compare trade volumes under pre–Tokyo Round conditions with trade under new, lower barriers. Thus, to conclude that the Tokyo Round only affects trade volumes marginally is to assume—wrongly—that the *status quo ante* was stable and that trade could have continued as before under those conditions. In fact, the Tokyo Round's success was an essential bulwark against a proliferation of new trade barriers. Those new barriers would probably have been quantitative and would have immediately limited trade. Given the concurrent doubling of oil prices and widespread economic stagnation, the failure to reach agreement could easily have degenerated into beggar-thy-neighbor policies, a collapse of basic regime norms, and an outright contraction of trade flows. Indeed, in one major area where no agreement was reached— safeguards—bilateralism and discriminatory practices have proliferated.

As recent events show, it is quite possible for a regime like that in trade to erode without necessarily producing an absolute decline in the activities it regulates and facilitates. In the case of trade, that is because the political framework is only one factor among many needed to estimate trade volumes. Any model for estimating aggregate trade between two or more countries would include, among other things, the national incomes of importing and exporting countries, the national-income elasticities of imports and exports, and the costs of transportation. Jointly, these could dominate changes in trade barriers, even if those changes had significant effects of their own.

In fact, the changing pattern of trade barriers does seem to have significant independent effects. In sectors where the regime is strong, intra-industry trade is growing. This growth, in turn, adds to the regime's continuity and reinforces the existing biases in trade liberalization. In sectors where the regime is weaker, new nontariff barriers have diminished hypothetical trade growth, though they have seldom aimed at a permanent rollback in market shares or trade volume. It is a complex, uneven pattern, but in areas of both strength and weakness the regime still helps shape the level and composition of world trade.

The GATT and the regulation of trade barriers: regime dynamics and functions

Jock A. Finlayson and Mark W. Zacher

During the latter stages of World War Two the United States and the United Kingdom began extensive bilateral discussions concerning the shape of the postwar international economic order. One outcome of these discussions and subsequent multilateral negotiations was the creation in July 1944 of the International Monetary Fund and its associated rules regarding exchange rates and the balance of payments. Almost four years later, in March 1948, over fifty countries signed the Havana Charter for the International Trade Organization (ITO). The charter contained a comprehensive set of rules designed to regulate the policies of national governments in several trade-related issue areas, and included chapters dealing with tariff and nontariff barriers, restrictive business practices, economic reconstruction and development, and intergovernmental commodity agreements.[1]

The U.S. Congress failed to approve American participation in the ITO; ironically, the most fervent proponent of a comprehensive code of international law to govern trade policies was itself largely responsible for the demise

The authors would like to thank the Donner Canadian Foundation and the Social Sciences and Humanities Research Council of Canada for financial assistance.

This paper was delivered at the Conference on International Regimes in Palm Springs, California, 26–28 February 1981. The authors wish to thank the conference participants for their insights on the study of international regimes, and on this essay. Particular thanks go to Stephen Krasner, Peter Katzenstein, John Barcelo, and Laura Tyson.

[1] For a comprehensive analysis of the ITO, consult W. A. Brown, *The United States and the Restoration of World Trade* (Washington, D.C.: Brookings, 1950). Also useful, especially for the perspective of a U.S. participant in the negotiations, is Clair Wilcox, *A Charter for World Trade* (New York: Macmillan, 1949).

International Organization, 35,4, Autumn 1981
0020-8183/81/0004-0561 $01.00

of the ambitious ITO scheme.[2] All that remained after years of intensive negotiations was a trade agreement negotiated in October 1947, "designed to record the results of a tariff conference that was envisioned at the time as being the first of a number of such conferences to be conducted under the auspices of the ITO."[3] The 1947 conference had been held at the urging of U.S. officials anxious to take advantage of the president's tariff-cutting authority before it expired. The results were codified in the General Agreement on Tariffs and Trade (GATT); which consisted of the tariff concessions agreed to by the twenty-three signatories and most of the trade barrier rules that later were incorporated into the commercial policy chapter of the ITO Charter. These trade barrier rules were included to ensure that the tariff concessions would have legal status and not be undermined by other trade measures before the comprehensive ITO entered into force. When the ITO failed to materialize, the GATT was transformed from a temporary agreement into a normative-institutional framework in which governments pursued multilateral regulation and discussed trade policy.

Had the ITO actually become the global trade-policy forum and legal framework that it was envisioned to be, one could perhaps speak of *the* postwar international trade regime. The GATT, however, was never intended to be the basis for the postwar trade order and was not even conceived of as an international organization.[4] Thus, a large number of trade matters are neither discussed in, nor subject to regulation and supervision by, this peculiar and entirely accidental international institution. We suggest that the GATT is at the center of a particular international trade regime, which has for the most part been concerned with one international trade issue area, namely, trade barriers, which are *state* policies or practices that impede the access countries enjoy to each other's markets for their exports. Other trade matters, such as prices and earnings deriving from the export of primary commodities or the effect of private business practices on trade—which were both brought within the ambit of the ITO—were not addressed by the 1947 General Agreement. They have not since been brought within the GATT's regulatory-consultative framework to any significant extent.

The GATT regulatory framework has been virtually coterminous with what we term the global (or quasiglobal) trade barriers regime. Several UN bodies (e.g., the General Assembly, UNCTAD, and FAO) have concerned themselves with barrier issues, but their deliberations have not been particularly influential and have certainly not resulted in binding legal instruments. Insofar as these bodies have affected treaty obligations in the issue area, it is

---

[2] This fascinating story is told in William Diebold, *The End of the ITO,* Essays in International Finance no. 16 (Princeton University, 1952).

[3] Kenneth Dam, *The GATT—Law and International Economic Organization* (1970; New York: Midway Reprint, 1977), p. 11.

[4] In fact, in the technical legal sense it can be argued that the GATT is not even an international organization today. Dam, *The GATT,* p. 335; John H. Jackson, *World Trade and the Law of GATT* (Indianapolis: Bobbs-Merrill, 1969), pp. 119–22.

largely because they have been taken into account by national negotiators at the GATT. There are, of course, many regional or bilateral accords on trade barriers, but not only do they link small numbers of states, they have often been shaped to conform with GATT rules. The fact that the number of states associated with the GATT is just over one hundred has detracted somewhat from the labeling of the GATT as the global trade barriers regime.[5] However, the only important trading states not in the GATT are several communist countries (especially the USSR), and some outsiders accept many GATT rules in any case.

Our objectives in this essay are to describe the GATT trade barriers regime, to assess its strength, and to explore some of the regime's functions in international trade and political relations. We are not seeking to explain why the regime changed over time, although some insights on this matter are inevitably included in the essay. Prior to undertaking these tasks, it is necessary to present our definition of a "regime" and to comment on some of the analytical problems involved in assessing the evolution and strength of a regime.

A recent conference of international relations scholars accepted the following definition of regime.[6]

A regime is composed of sets of explicit or implicit principles, norms, rules, and decision-making procedures around which actor expectations converge in a given area of international relations and which may help to coordinate their behavior.

1. Principles are beliefs of fact, causation, and rectitude.
2. Norms are standards of behavior defined in terms of general rights and obligations.
3. Rules are specific prescriptions and proscriptions regarding behavior.
4. Decision-making procedures are the prevailing practices for making and implementing collective choices.

This definition, while considerably more extensive than past ones, leaves room for amplification and interpretation.[7]

---

[5] GATT, *Basic Instruments and Selected Documents* (hereinafter *BISD*), 26th Supp., 1980, p. viii. Countries with full membership rights and obligations are known as contracting parties, of which there are currently 85. Two countries have acceded provisionally. A third category, which at present includes 30 countries, is referred to as "Countries applying the General Agreement on a *de facto* basis." These are former colonies that have not yet decided whether to join the GATT. They generally do not participate in GATT affairs except during trade rounds. Interviews, Ottawa, September 1980.

[6] This definition was accepted by the contributors to this volume. The conference took place in October 1980 in Los Angeles.

[7] Three shorter definitions can be found in Robert O. Keohane and Joseph S. Nye, *Power and Interdependence: World Politics in Transition* (Boston: Little, Brown, 1977), p. 19; Ernst B. Haas, "Why Collaborate? Issue-Linkage and International Regimes," *World Politics* 32 (April 1980), p. 358; and Oran R. Young, "International Regimes: Problems of Concept Formation," *World Politics* 32 (April 1980), p. 332. Young does elaborate at some length on the terms included in his definition of regimes (pp. 333–39).

The *principles* of a regime are those prevailing beliefs that underlie states' policy orientations to a variety of issue areas. They might, for example, encompass both a desire to minimize infringements on the policy-making autonomy of states and a belief that free trade enhances the welfare of all countries. Principles do not constitute specific legal or policy guidelines in an issue area. They underlie, and may provide explanations for, states' acceptance of behavioral prescriptions and proscriptions in an area of international relations, but they are not part of a regulatory framework *per se*.

It is the *norms* that provide the foundation of a regime since they constitute the general obligations and rights that are to guide states' behavior in designing decision-making procedures and in formulating and implementing rules. They can be divided into *substantive* norms, which provide standards for drawing up specific behavioral prescriptions, and *procedural* norms, which provide guidelines regarding how states should design and use decision-making mechanisms. These decision-making or *procedural mechanisms* define who participates in different types of decisions and whose consent is necessary for the formulation of rules and their implementation. We posit that together the norms and procedural mechanisms constitute the *decision-making framework* of a regime.

Second, norms can be classified according to their strength or salience. States almost always attach greater weight to certain norms than to others, and their relative importance changes over time. In large part, the evolution of a regime's rules can be explained by alterations in the importance of its norms.

Third, norms can be distinguished according to whether they are derived from the traditional structure of international politics (sovereignty norms), or from international interdependencies in particular issue areas that incline states to maximize welfare through collaboration (interdependence norms).[8] A recognition of this distinction is crucial in evaluating the *strength* of an issue-area regime. If sovereignty norms clearly dominate in an issue area, then one cannot ascribe a great deal of behavioral impact to the regime—it merely reflects "politics as usual." On the other hand, if interdependence norms are judged to have a significant impact on the formulation and implementation of rules, one can ascribe a certain degree of autonomy to the regime. Students of regimes differ over the degree of constraining effect these interdependence norms must have before one may proclaim that a regime "exists."[9] In fact, some scholars would state that an issue-area regime exists even if its norms

[8] The authors would like to thank Peter Katzenstein and Lynn Mytelka for their suggestions of terms to describe these two sets of norms.

[9] The distinction between sovereignty and interdependence norms is not made by other authors. However, they do implicitly address the issue of how much constraint nonsovereignty norms would have to exert in order to state that a regime exists. In the articles included in this volume Young and Puchala and Hopkins basically take the point of view that regimes exist in all issue areas, whereas Keohane, Stein, Jervis, and Haas are concerned that a significant constraining effect of nonsovereignty or interdependence norms be established before one concludes that a regime exists.

mirror the norms of the classic, fragmented system of sovereign nation-states, in which *ad hoc* bargaining and the influence of the powerful prevail. While this view is correct (in that there exist identifiable norms in the issue area), it is important to point out that scholars study regimes because they are interested in trends and behavior that diverge from what is presumed to exist in the "traditional" interstate system. Given this, it is desirable to equate regimes with regulatory systems in which "interdependence norms" are prominent, and to analyze the strength or autonomy of regimes in terms of the importance of interdependence norms.

Two final components of a regime that merit brief discussion are the *rules* and *rule implementation*. These are its most observable dimensions since rules are generally codified and activities to implement them can usually be observed. They constitute the regime's *programs,* and we suggest that they are largely determined by the regime's norms and procedural mechanisms. By employing this framework we hope that the internal dynamics of regime change can be better understood.

The essay is divided into two sections. The first and larger describes the regime's decisionmaking framework and programs, explores the impact of the former on the latter, and evaluates the strength of the regime. It offers analyses of how each of the seven substantive and procedural norms has increased or decreased in importance since 1947 and how their relative significance has shaped the procedural mechanisms and the programs (i.e., rules and rule implementation). The second and final part of the essay focuses on some of the most important functions or effects of the GATT regime.

Our rationale for organizing the first section around the norms is that they constitute the fundamental or underlying structure of a regime. One dimension of the regime excluded from the section is principles. As previously noted, principles generally apply to many issue areas, and it is beyond the scope of an essay of this length to examine the variety of beliefs of fact, causation, and rectitude that have impinged on the trade barriers regime.

This section will highlight a major problem in the analysis of regimes. While the influence of norms at different times shapes the programs, it is the characteristics of these programs which provide the first and best evidence of their changing relative importance. It is virtually impossible to escape this problem of circularity, although efforts to explain interrelationships among factors and to gather additional evidence on states' policies in the issue area can lessen it.

Regime dynamics: evolution of framework and programs

The central substantive and procedural norms of the GATT trade barriers regime have been relatively few in number. They have varied in importance to the regime at particular times, and the salience of some of them has changed quite markedly over the almost three and a half decades since the signing of the General Agreement in 1947. The substantive norms concern nondiscrimination, liberalization, reciprocity, the right to take "safeguard" action, and economic development. The procedural norms relate to multilateralism and the role of states with "major interests" in trade relations. The regime programs, which have been affected by these norms, are discussed after an overview of each norm, and include rules concerning the utilization of nontariff barriers (NTBs), tariff "bindings," and various rule-implementation activities.

Substantive norms

1. Universal application of trade barriers: the nondiscrimination norm

The former Director-General of GATT, Eric Wyndham-White, has written that the principle of nondiscrimination was the "cornerstone" of the GATT.[10] In the immediate postwar era it was regarded as the crucial GATT norm, if only because the immensely powerful United States saw it as necessary for both the expansion of its own trade and the forestalling of hostile economic blocs. However, nondiscrimination has since suffered severe and regular blows, which have had a significant cumulative effect. Most of the original GATT rules regarding nondiscrimination remain "on the books"; but they are often disobeyed, and the GATT does little to promote their implementation. The norm still has a role in the regime; but it tends to be important in fewer trade contexts and is in general a less powerful restraint on behavior than once was the case.

The basic GATT commitment to nondiscrimination—or "unconditional most-favored-nation" (MFN) treatment, as it is usually termed—appears in Article I:1 of the General Agreement and requires that "any advantage, favour, privilege, or immunity granted by any contracting party to any product originating in or destined for any other country shall be accorded immediately and unconditionally to the like product originating in or destined for the territories of all other contracting parties." This MFN clause applies to all tariffs, whether or not a concession has been negotiated, as well as to all other GATT rules. The fact that unanimous consent is required to amend Article I underlines the importance attached to nondiscrimination at the time of GATT's formation. Additional statements of the nondiscrimination obligation appear in a host of other articles of the General Agreement.[11]

Despite the importance of the norm in 1947, many exceptions to it were

[10] Eric Wyndham-White, "Negotiations in Prospect," in C. Fred Bergsten, ed., *Toward A New World Trade Policy: The Maidenhead Papers* (Lexington, Mass.: D.C. Heath, 1975), p. 321.

[11] For example, in Article XIII:1 (nondiscriminatory application of quantitative restrictions), Article XVII:1 (state trading practices), and Article XVIII:20 (economic development measures). For a fuller list, see Jackson, *World Trade,* pp. 255–56.

accepted. The British and French refused to dismantle their extant preference schemes, and the U.S. was consequently forced to agree to a permanent exception (Article I:2) allowing for their continued existence, although preference margins (i.e., the difference between the MFN and preferential tariff rates) were frozen. Another exception, which in retrospect appears enormously significant, permitted discrimination in the form of customs unions, free trade areas, and "interim" arrangements during a period of transition. Article XXIV of the General Agreement recognizes "the desirability of increasing freedom of trade by the development, through voluntary agreements, of closer integration between the economies of the countries parties to such agreements." The U.S. and other countries concerned about the weakening of the nondiscrimination norm insisted that, in order to be eligible for the Article XXIV exception to MFN, proposed schemes would have to require the abolition of tariffs and other restrictions on "substantially all trade" among participants. In addition, trade barriers for each member of a free trade area and for a union could not, "on the whole," be more restrictive after the formation of such schemes than they were before.[12] Other exceptions in the General Agreement allow discrimination in connection with quotas imposed to safeguard the balance of payments, the imposition of antidumping and countervailing duties against dumped or subsidized goods, and the withdrawal of previous "concessions" in retaliation for the "nullification or impairment" of any benefits enjoyed by a contracting party.[13]

Throughout the history of the GATT regime the major source of erosion of the nondiscrimination norm has come from "regional" (and other) trade arrangements that involve discrimination in the use of trade barriers against nonmember contracting parties. Most have been presented by proponents as basically meeting the rather strict criteria spelled out in Article XXIV but, according to one legal scholar, of the dozens of schemes put before GATT members for examination and approval only one, the 1965 United Kingdom-Ireland Free Trade Area, has been in essentially complete accord with the article's requirements.[14] The drafters of the General Agreement had no conception of the popularity that political and economic arguments in support of "economic regionalism" would attain in later decades; nor could they foresee what this trend would portend for the "sacrosanct" MFN obligation in the GATT.

Undoubtedly the most important regional scheme to be considered by GATT members was the EEC customs union outlined in the Treaty of Rome. Because the United States announced its unambiguous political backing for the "discriminatory" EEC plan—as it had done previously in connection with West European discrimination against "dollar area" imports and with the

---

[12] Ibid., pp. 502–503; Dam, *The GATT,* pp. 276–83.
[13] Articles XIV, VI, and XXIII, respectively.
[14] Dam, *The GATT,* p. 290.

European Coal and Steel Community scheme of the early 1950s[15]—the legal issue of whether the proposed customs union conformed with GATT rules was fudged, and the EEC went into operation in 1958 without obtaining the formal approval of the GATT membership. The GATT committee scrutinizing the Treaty of Rome concluded that "examination and discussion of the legal issues involved . . . could not usefully be explored at the present time."[16] A precedent was thus set: the nondiscrimination norm notwithstanding, regional trade arrangements would not have to conform to GATT rules, and multilateral supervision of regional schemes would be lax since the "rules" were implicitly discarded. Thus the European Free Trade Area in the 1960s, the free trade treaties between the EEC and other developed West European states, and the enlargement of the EEC itself in the 1970s have undermined the MFN obligation, partly because participants perceive little need to meet the GATT rules regarding regional exceptions to MFN.

But regional trade among developed countries was not the only preferential onslaught the nondiscrimination norm had to bear. Beginning with the EEC's "reverse" preferential arrangements with former African colonies, codified in the Yaoundé Convention of 1963, a potpourri of EEC–LDC preferential schemes has sprung up, the most recent being the second Lomé Convention of 1979 between the enlarged Community and fifty-eight African, Caribbean, and Pacific LDCs.[17] These arrangements violate the GATT's original rules regarding regional exceptions to MFN. Many GATT members— including the United States since the early 1960s—have voiced sharp opposition to the Community's myriad preference schemes with LDCs and "Mediterranean" states but, as the Curzons comment, "too many members of GATT had preferential leanings of one kind or another" by the mid 1960s for there to exist a workable political consensus to reassert the primacy of nondiscrimination over preferences of various kinds.[18] Discriminatory preferences were recognized in the Tokyo Round "framework" agreement, which accepted the permanent legitimacy of the Generalized System of Preferences (GSP) for LDCs. (The GSP violation of nondiscrimination had earlier been authorized by a ten-year GATT waiver in 1971.) Intra-LDC preferences, also authorized temporarily by a 1971 waiver, were similarly accorded permanent legal status as a result of the Tokyo Round.[19]

---

[15] *BISD,* 2nd Supp., 1954, pp. 101–109.

[16] *BISD,* 7th Supp., 1959, pp. 69–71.

[17] Alfred Tovias, *Tariff Preferences in Mediterranean Diplomacy* (London: Macmillan, 1977); *Lomé II,* Overseas Development Institute Briefing Paper no. 1 (London: ODI, 1980).

[18] Gerard and Victoria Curzon, "The Management of Trade Relations in the GATT," in Andrew Shonfield, ed., *International Economic Relations of the Western World, 1959–71,* volume 1: *Politics and Trade* (Oxford: Oxford University Press, 1976), p. 231

[19] *BISD,* 18th Supp., 1972, pp. 24–28 for the 1971 waivers. See Tracy Murray, *Trade Preferences for Developing Countries* (London: Macmillan, 1977), for an analysis of GSP, and H. Espiel, "GATT: Accommodating Generalized Preferences," *Journal of World Trade Law* 8 (May–June 1974), for a discussion of GATT's response to the GSP. See *BISD,* 26th Supp., 1980, pp. 201–11 for the Tokyo Round decisions on GSP and preferences among LDCs.

At the very least this proliferation of regional, developed-developing country, and intra-LDC trade preferences has "greatly lessened the amount of trade" covered by the nondiscrimination norm.[20] Over one-fifth of the world's trade now takes place within a huge West European preferential trade zone.[21] In 1955, about 90 percent of GATT trade took place at MFN tariff rates; this had fallen to 77 percent by 1970,[22] and to perhaps 65 percent in 1980.[23] The recent Tokyo Round nontariff barrier codes may provide an additional fillip to trade discrimination. Implicitly, these codes (on subsidies and countervailing measures, customs valuation, import licensing, technical barriers to trade, government procurement, and a new version of the 1967 Antidumping Code) envisage a bifurcated regime membership: signatories and nonsignatories. The U.S. has made it clear that the provisions of the Subsidies and Government Procurement codes will not necessarily be applied to nonsignatories in U.S. law.[24] Other signatories are likely to take a similar view.[25] That a further lessening in the influence of the nondiscrimination norm and a further relative reduction in the proportion of GATT trade conducted on an MFN basis will result, seems inevitable.[26]

Finally, another trend clearly unfavorable to nondiscrimination in the GATT regime is the growing popularity of "voluntary" export restraints (VERs) as instruments of trade control.[27] The increasing resort to VERs stems significantly from the GATT's generally permitting only nondiscriminatory emergency import controls (discussed under "the safeguards norm," below). VERs, on the other hand, allow for selectivity in taking action against the (alleged) sources of "market disruption,"[28] and for this reason are attractive to some states.[29] Although with the exception of the textile-restraint accords VERs are not undertaken within the GATT regime (a testimony to weakness

---

[20] Robert E. Baldwin, *Beyond the Tokyo Round Negotiations,* Thames Essay no. 22 (London: Trade Policy Research Centre, 1979).

[21] Rachel McCulloch, "Trade and Direct Investment: Recent Policy Trends," in Rudiger Dornbusch and Jacob A. Frenkel, eds., *International Economic Policy: Theory and Evidence* (Baltimore: Johns Hopkins University Press, 1979), p. 90.

[22] Curzon, "Management of Trade Relations," p. 229.

[23] Interviews, Ottawa, September 1980.

[24] Section 102(f) of the 1974 Trade Act allows the president to recommend to Congress that the U.S. implementing law for the codes apply only to signatories. U.S., Senate, Committee on Finance, Subcommittee on International Trade, *MTN Studies,* vol. 4, Part 1 (Washington, D.C.: Government Printing Office, 1979), pp. 220–24 (hereinafter *MTN Studies*); Stephen D. Krasner, "The Tokyo Round: Particularistic Interests and Prospects for Stability in the Global Trading System," *International Studies Quarterly* 23 (December 1979), p. 515.

[25] Interviews with U.S. and Canadian trade officials.

[26] *MTN Studies,* vol. 4, p. 4; Krasner, "Tokyo Round," pp. 500–24.

[27] C. Fred Bergsten, "On the Non-Equivalence of Import Quotas and 'Voluntary' Export Restraints," in Bergsten, ed., *New World Trade Policy,* p. 242; OECD, *Policy Perspectives for International Trade and Economic Relations: Report by the High-Level Group on Trade and Related Problems* (Paris, 1972), p. 82.

[28] Bergsten, "On Non-Equivalence"; Jagdish Bhagwati, "Market Disruption, Export Market Disruption, Compensation and GATT Reform," in Jagdish Bhagwati, ed., *The New International Economic Order: The North-South Debate* (Cambridge: MIT Press, 1977).

[29] Curzon, "Management of Trade Relations," pp. 274–78.

in the regime, to be sure), the general trend contributes to the erosion of non-discriminatory trade.

The various currents that have undermined the norm of nondiscrimination in the GATT have not succeeded in completely stripping it of influence. Several key trading nations—the U.S., Canada, Japan, and a few others—continue to pay homage to it. Moreover, the very low industrial tariffs prevailing in most West European countries tend to lessen the trade significance of preferential European arrangements,[30] while the structure of donor countries' GSP schemes indicates that the volume of trade affected has not been and is not likely to be high.[31] However, we find it difficult to dissent from the conclusion of one eminent observer, that it is becoming increasingly "difficult to sustain that the unconditional most-favored-nation clause is a basic pillar of the international trading system."[32]

2. Reduction of trade barriers: the liberalization norm

The norm of liberalization or free trade is often regarded as central to the GATT regime, but it did not have the paramountcy of nondiscrimination in the immediate postwar years. Liberalization was regarded as important by many American officials, but it was not a primary goal of most other industrial and developing countries. Following European recovery in the late 1950s the norm achieved a fairly high profile (particularly in the manufactures sector), but receded somewhat in importance in the 1970s. The decline of support for freer trade has been reflected not so much in the results of the Tokyo Round, which in fact made some progress in reducing nontariff barriers, as in actions and agreements taken outside the GATT, which in many instances contravene GATT rules and escape its supervision. The norm remains relevant to trade in manufactured products among the industrial countries and to trade in unprocessed commodities, but outside these areas protectionism has had a significant impact.

Although the Preamble of the General Agreement refers to reductions in trade barriers as one means to achieve economic growth, full employment, and increasing incomes, the signatories recognized that domestic stabilization and full employment took precedence over liberalization. This was enshrined in Article XII, and was implicit in "the many loopholes in the name of balance-of-payments difficulties, domestic unemployment, and the lack of effective demand."[33] Support for liberalization in the immediate postwar years was not widespread, and this was reflected in the first set of tariff negotiations.

When the General Agreement was drawn up in 1947, an initial "round" of tariff negotiations was undertaken simultaneously by twenty-three coun-

[30] McCulloch, "Trade and Direct Investment," p. 90.
[31] Murray, *Trade Preferences,* passim.
[32] White, "Negotiations," p. 323.
[33] Curzon, "Management of Trade Relations," p. 148.

tries. A large number of tariff reductions ("concessions" in GATT parlance) were negotiated between pairs of countries (123 in all), and those by the U.S. were quite extensive.[34] The Europeans made more modest concessions, but these were temporarily vitiated by a wholesale resort to exchange and import controls because of war-ravaged economies and bankrupt treasuries.[35] Tariff conferences held in 1949 and 1951 (the Annecy and Torquay Rounds) resulted in very minor tariff reductions,[36] and similarly the fourth conference (the 1956 Geneva Round) saw little progress in barrier reduction.[37] It was not until the late 1950s that a more "positive" attitude toward freer trade became pervasive.[38] As the Curzons comment, this development "had its roots in the fundamental change in the economic environment between 1947 and 1958": economic recovery in Europe and growth elsewhere, as well as the "technological and industrial explosion of the 1960s," combined to generate a much larger "political constituency" for freer trade.[39] Although tariff reductions in the 1960–62 Dillon Round were modest owing to limited U.S. tariff-cutting authority (20 percent), the effects of the U.S. "peril point" procedure, and uncertainties caused by the EEC's efforts to negotiate on the basis of its new Common External Tariff,[40] the momentum for liberalization was not slowed.

The sixth GATT tariff conference (the Kennedy Round) began with a ministerial agreement on the key objectives in May 1963 and did not conclude until June 1967. It is generally regarded as the most successful exercise in trade barrier liberalization in the GATT's history.[41] The Trade Expansion Act granted the U.S. executive a 50 percent tariff-cutting authority, on an across-the-board (linear) basis instead of item by item, and permitted elimination of duties of 5 percent and less.[42] The "peril point" procedure that had bedeviled U.S. negotiators in previous rounds was also removed. In addition, sentiment in most developed non-EEC countries—especially the U.S.—strongly favored a major multilateral exercise in tariff reductions in order to mitigate the apparent and feared trade division occasioned by European integration.[43] After protracted haggling over the formula for making linear tariff reductions and what products to exclude, sixteen industrial countries did make linear cuts of almost 40 percent on manufactured products.[44] Large tariff reductions were

[34] F. V. Meyer, *International Trade Policy* (London: Croom Helm, 1978), pp. 137–38.

[35] Article XII of the General Agreement permits the use of quotas for balance-of-payments purposes. Dam, *The GATT*, pp. 150–53.

[36] Meyer, *Trade Policy*, pp. 138–40; Karin Kock, *International Trade Policy and the GATT: 1947–67* (Stockholm: Almqvist and Wiksell, 1969), pp. 95–96.

[37] Meyer, *Trade Policy*, p. 142; Kock, *International Trade Policy*, p. 99.

[38] Curzon, "Management of Trade Relations," pp. 149–50; Dam, *The GATT*, p. 57.

[39] Curzon, "Management of Trade Relations," pp. 149–50.

[40] Ibid., pp. 168–75; Meyer, *Trade Policy*, pp. 146–47; Dam, *The GATT*, p. 67.

[41] Curzon, "Management of Trade Relations," p. 170; Ernest H. Preeg, *Traders and Diplomats: An Analysis of the Kennedy Round of Negotiations Under the General Agreement For Tariffs and Trade* (Washington, D.C.: Brookings, 1970), p. 12.

[42] Ibid., pp. 47–49.

[43] Ibid., p. 29.

[44] Canada, New Zealand, South Africa, Australia, and the LDCs were not participants in the linear tariff negotiations. Dam, *The GATT*, pp. 72–73.

accepted by the four major participants—the U.S., EEC, the U.K., and Japan.[45] Important, but far smaller, reductions in agricultural duties were also agreed to by the major countries, on the order of 20 percent,[46] but their effect was undermined by nontariff obstacles in the sector. Finally, for the first time since 1947 an important nontariff barrier to trade, antidumping measures, was subject to negotiation in a.GATT trade round.[47]

While the norm of trade barrier liberalization enjoyed perhaps its greatest support in the closing years of the 1960s (particularly from industrial countries), the 1970s witnessed a marked resurgence of strongly protectionist pressures in most developed countries, especially in the period since the 1973–74 oil crisis and the ensuing recession. Sectors complaining loudly about import competition included both older, capital-intensive heavy industries (e.g. steel, shipbuilding) and light, standardized manufactures and consumer durables (e.g. textiles and clothing, footwear, and electrical manufactures). Two points of relevance to the GATT regime and the liberalization norm stand out.[48] First, the "new protectionism" largely relies on various nontariff obstacles to imports, both because they are more effective protective devices than tariffs (which operate through the price system) and because tariffs have been markedly reduced and usually "bound" during GATT negotiations. Many of these protectionist measures are patent violations of GATT nontariff barrier rules, especially the GATT prohibition of quotas, but arc taken outside the regime and thus are not subject to multilateral scrutiny. The best-known examples are VERs, which involve often secret accords between an importing country and firms or the government in exporting countries to restrict exports to prescribed levels over a period of time. Second, the recent protectionism has focused on manufactures and has hit hardest at developing countries, especially newly industrializing countries, which have expressed increasing concern about this trend and the GATT's failure to secure implementation of its rules.[49] Trade liberalization in textiles and clothing, a key export sector for LDCs and the only sector subject to special GATT supervision,[50] has been

[45] Derived from Preeg, *Traders and Diplomats,* pp. 208–11 (Tables 13-1, 13-2, 13-3, 13-4).

[46] Ibid., p. 251.

[47] On the Antidumping Code consult Dam, *The GATT,* pp. 174–77; and Peter Lloyd, *Antidumping Actions and the GATT System,* Thames Essay no. 9 (London: Trade Policy Research Centre, 1977). See also the first report of the GATT committee of signatories, *BISD,* 17th Supp., 1970, pp. 43–46.

[48] Recent treatments of the current protectionist drift include Bela Balassa, "The 'New Protectionism' and the International Economy," *Journal of World Trade Law* 12 (September–October 1978); Susan Strange, "The Management of Surplus Capacity," *International Organization* 33 (Summer 1979); and R. Blackhurst, N. Marian, and J. Tumlir, "Trade Liberalization, Protectionism and Interdependence," *GATT Studies in International Trade* no. 5 (November 1977). The next two paragraphs draw heavily on Balassa. He estimates that industrial countries' "new" protective measures affected 3–5% of world trade, or $30–50 billion, in 1976 and 1977, and that, partly as a result, world trade growth was more than halved in 1977 over 1976 (pp. 418, 429).

[49] *BISD,* 25th Supp., 1979, pp. 32–33; *BISD,* 26th Supp., 1980, pp. 276–79.

[50] Following the establishment of a Working Party on "Market Disruption" in 1959, a Long-Term Arrangement Regarding International Trade in Cotton Textiles (LTA) was agreed to in 1962,

undermined by practices and policies in developed countries taken under the rubric of the GATT textile arrangements.

In the most recent (Tokyo) Round, the average tariff reduction on all industrial products by developed countries was one-third, while that on manufactures of interest to LDCs was substantially less, about one-quarter. In general, "the deepest cuts have been concentrated in non-electrical machinery, wood products, chemicals and transport equipment"[51]—areas where intra-OECD trade is high. Sectoral free trade was attained in an Agreement on Trade in Civil Aircraft, signed by the main industrial countries, which "offers a clear example of how intrasectoral cross-cutting cleavages can create an atmosphere favorable" to barrier reduction.[52] In agriculture, support of liberalization has never been forthcoming from the EEC or Japan,[53] and "major breakthroughs in protectionist agricultural trade policies were not obtained . . ."[54] Failure to negotiate a new agreement "to bring within the GATT ambit the increasing number and variety of safeguards—and pseudo-safeguards—which are in use, and to improve on them," must be counted as a major setback to any reassertion of a *general* (as opposed to sectoral) commitment to liberalization.[55] On the other hand, the nontariff barrier codes negotiated do lend some support to the norm of barrier reduction, particularly the Government Procurement Code, which deals with a major lacuna in GATT's normative thrust toward liberalization.[56] The codes on Import Licensing, Technical

---

under the auspices of the GATT (which struck a committee to administer the Arrangement); the LTA was extended for three years in 1967 and again in 1970. A broader arrangement to ensure the so-called "orderly expansion" of trade in virtually all classes of textiles and clothing, the Multi-Fibre Arrangement (MFA), was negotiated in 1973 and renegotiated to cover the period 1978–82. Membership in the committee and participation in the various textile agreements have been open to both members and nonmembers of GATT. For evaluation and description of these schemes, consult Dam, *The GATT,* pp. 296–315; Strange, "Surplus Capacity," pp. 310–18; and H. Taake and D. Weiss, "The World Textile Arrangement: The Exporters' Viewpoint," *Journal of World Trade Law* 8 (November–December 1974). For the contrasting views of exporters and importers on the impact and utility of the recent MFA, see GATT Doc. COM.TEX/15, 5 February 1980, and *BISD,* 26th Supp., 1980, pp. 340–53.

[51] *The Tokyo Round of Multilateral Trade Negotiations: Report by the Director-General of GATT* (Geneva: GATT, April 1979), pp. 120–21 (hereinafter *Tokyo Round*).

[52] Krasner, "Tokyo Round," p. 511.

[53] T. K. Warley, "Western Trade in Agricultural Products," in Shonfield, ed., *International Economic Relations,* vol. 1, pp. 287–404; T. E. Josling, *Agriculture in the Tokyo Round Negotiations,* Thames Essay no. 10 (London: Trade Policy Research Centre, 1977).

[54] *MTN Studies,* vol. 2, p. 63 and passim. Also see Sidney Golt, *The GATT Negotiations 1973–79: The Closing Stage* (Washington, D.C.: British-North American Committee, 1979), pp. 28–29; Krasner, "Tokyo Round," pp. 518–21; Josling, *Agriculture in Tokyo Round; Tokyo Round,* pp. 143–47, 156–64, 177–79.

[55] Golt, *GATT Negotiations,* p. 25; Krasner, "Tokyo Round," pp. 521–23; *Tokyo Round,* pp. 90–95.

[56] See Krasner, "Tokyo Round," pp. 512–15; *Tokyo Round,* pp. 75–82. Article VIII of the code permits exclusion of defense-related purchases, and of purchases in connection with public health and safety practices, from the new rules. *BISD,* 26th Supp., 1980, p. 51. Krasner (pp. 514–15) reports that 85% of U.S. government purchases will not be covered by the code. See also Dam, *The GATT,* pp. 199–221.

Barriers, and Customs Valuation are also congruent with the trade liberalization norm in that they tighten up existing GATT rules that regulate the protective potential of government laws and practices in these areas. The same can be said of the renegotiated version of the 1967 Antidumping Code. Finally, the Code on Subsidies and Countervailing Duties prohibits the use of direct export subsidies on industrial products (not primary products). The United States accepted the requirement that an injury test be employed before countervailing duties are levied, and its trading partners are likely to construe this as a gain for trade liberalization. But on balance it appears that the code aims to regularize the use of primary-product export subsidies, make more transparent the use of domestic subsidies (which are pervasive), and provide for consultation and dispute-settlement procedures, rather than in any significant sense to remove subsidies as a trade barrier.[57]

A continuing commitment to trade barrier reduction is evidenced by the tariff cuts negotiated in the Tokyo Round and in the serious efforts to tackle NTBs through new codes that improve on existing GATT rules. However, the scope of this commitment and its importance vis-a-vis other regime norms are unclear. In agriculture, there is little likelihood that the strong belief in "the sanctity of internal farm policies" will soon disappear.[58] The proliferation of VERs and extralegal restrictions on exports from developing to developed countries, and the failure to bring these practices within the regime's system of multilateral surveillance, are testimony to the fragility of the liberalization norm in the GATT. Ironically, many LDCs are now strong proponents of more liberal trade policies, having gone through a long period when import-substitution industrialization was popular.[59] They are constantly pressing the advanced industrial countries to liberalize access for LDC exports within GATT forums.[60]

3. Exchange of trade concessions: the reciprocity norm

Reciprocity, long identified as a central norm of the GATT regime, has had a major influence on rules concerning trade barriers and on rule interpretation. The notion that a country that benefits from another country's lowering of trade barriers should reciprocate, preferably to an equivalent ex-

---

[57] Krasner, "Tokyo Round," pp. 515–17; *MTN Studies,* vol. 6, part 1, pp. 100–102.

[58] Josling, *Agriculture in Tokyo Round,* p. 11.

[59] Bela Balassa, *The Structure of Protection in Developing Countries* (Baltimore: Johns Hopkins Press, 1971); Carlos Diaz-Alejandro, "Trade Policies and Economic Development," in Peter Kenen, ed., *International Trade and Finance: Frontiers for Research* (Cambridge: Cambridge University Press, 1975).

[60] "The representative of a developing country stated that even though his country had liberalized almost completely its trade regime and imports had consequently greatly expanded, difficulties of access impeding the expansion and diversification of exports were being experienced in some developed country markets." *BISD,* 26th Supp., 1980, p. 277 (Report of the Committee on Trade and Development, November 1978).

tent, has had a profound impact on almost all agreements in the GATT. But since the advent of linear tariff negotiations and NTB codes in the 1960s, the norm has been more difficult to operationalize; and with the symbolic waiver of the reciprocity requirement for developing countries in 1965, the GSP in 1971, and the "enabling clause" in 1979, it has suffered some weakening. However, despite these trends there can be little doubt about the continuing importance of reciprocity in trade bargaining within the GATT.

One reason for the prominence of reciprocity may be traced to the history of U.S. trade policy and legislation. Until the passage of the Trade Expansion Act by Congress in 1962, American negotiators were required both to conduct tariff negotiations on an "item-by-item" or "product-by-product" basis and to achieve reciprocity in concessions negotiated with each relevant trading partner. In passing trade legislation to authorize American participation in the Kennedy and Tokyo Rounds, Congress broadened the definition of reciprocity so that the results could be assessed more as a "package,"[61] but the belief that, as Harry Hawkins once put it, there should be "a dollar's worth of increased exports for every dollar's worth of increased imports"[62] remains strong among U.S. legislators. And as the Curzons astutely observe, "what the U.S. negotiating team is obliged to obtain by law, other countries' teams strive to achieve by instinct and tradition."[63]

While observers are unanimous in proclaiming the influence of the reciprocity norm, no one knows quite what it means in concrete terms. The text of the General Agreement is not particularly helpful in clearing up the confusion since it only alludes briefly to the norm. Article XXVIII bis, added in 1955, states that negotiations are to be conducted "on a reciprocal and mutually advantageous basis. . . ." In practice, "trade coverage" has been used to determine reciprocity in the GATT; it involves measuring the volume of imports "covered" by an agreed tariff cut. In the Rounds, "the custom grew up of attempting to balance the trade coverage of concessions made by each party to a particular negotiation."[64] The depth of tariff cuts has also been considered in calculations of reciprocity since the early 1960s.[65]

Most observers argue that reciprocity is a requirement imposed on trade negotiators by fundamentally political imperatives.[66] Governments feel compelled to justify their tariff "concessions" to instinctively mercantilist domestic audiences by pointing out that major trading partners have made at

---

[61] Dam, *The GATT,* pp. 67–68; *MTN Studies,* vol. 6, part 1, pp. 23, 48–49. Reciprocity is implicit in section 126 of the 1974 Trade Act.

[62] Cited in John Evans, *The Kennedy Round and American Trade Policy: The Twilight of the GATT?* (Cambridge: Harvard University Press, 1971), pp. 21–22.

[63] Curzon, "Management of Trade Relations," p. 156.

[64] Dam, *The GATT,* p. 59.

[65] Curzon, "Management of Trade Relations," p. 160.

[66] Ibid., p. 159; Evans, *Kennedy Round,* pp. 24–25; Harry Johnson, *Trade Negotiations and the New International Monetary System* (Geneva: Graduate Institute of International Studies, 1976) pp. 16–18.

least equivalent "sacrifices." As one critic has lamented, governments "cannot ignore the pervasive belief that, when a country grants a tariff concession, it incurs a cost that must be compensated."[67] Clearly, this way of thinking about reducing trade barriers owes little to liberal economic theory, which stresses the benefits accruing to the country that lowers barriers, even unilaterally. There are macroeconomic arguments in favor of reciprocity, such as the view that with a "balanced" increase in imports and exports a deficit in the balance-of-payments and a net rise in unemployment are less likely. These considerations certainly affect governments' broad bargaining strategies; however, it is the political salience of reciprocity that stands out.[68] As Kenneth Dam has commented, the GATT's trade bargaining vocabulary is suggestive of a political battle: "an original tariff reduction is a 'concession,' whereas a reciprocal reduction is 'compensation.' Even the word 'round' suggests a competition in which one side must 'win,' a boxing match with two parties locked in combat."[69]

The major effect of the reciprocity norm (in tandem with the "major interests" procedural norm) is that it assures that rules reflect the interests of the major trading nations in GATT Rounds. Since reciprocity dictates that states receiving tariff reductions for their exports be able to offer lower barriers and markets to their negotiating partners, leverage on barrier reductions requires that states have both large domestic markets and a high volume of trade with countries whose barriers they want lowered. And since the industrialized states have the biggest domestic markets and are each other's major trading partners, they—particularly the U.S., the EEC, and Japan—have shaped the GATT's rules in large part to serve their commercial goals.[70] These states have the ability to offer "reciprocal" concessions and are consequently reciprocity's strongest adherents.

A more specific effect of the norm of reciprocity with its strongly mercantilist cast is that GATT members rarely reduce tariffs unilaterally. Even tariffs that have "no intrinsic economic value" can serve as bargaining chips with which a country can help to satisfy its trading partners' need for reciprocity without hurting its own economic interests.[71] Reciprocity had a com-

---

[67] Evans, *Kennedy Round,* p. 25.
[68] Curzon, "Management of Trade Relations," pp. 158–59; Johnson, *New Monetary System,* pp. 16–18. Johnson notes (p. 23) that flexible exchange rates undermine "the balance-of-payments rationale for . . . reciprocity." Johnson has elsewhere contrasted the liberal and instinctively mercantilist ways of viewing tariff reductions: "An Economic Theory of Protectionism, Tariff Bargaining, and the Formation of Customs Unions," *Journal of Political Economy* 73 (1965): 256–82.
[69] Dam, *The GATT,* p. 65.
[70] Golt (*GATT Negotiations*) pictures the Tokyo Round as essentially a triangular bargaining process among the "big three," with Canada, the LDCs, and a few other countries occupying minor roles except when specific issues (e.g., tropical products for the LDCs) were discussed. Preeg similarly discusses the Kennedy Round as if the only players of consequence were the U.S., Japan, the EEC, and the U.K., the latter not then a member of the Community.
[71] Evans, *Kennedy Round,* pp. 24, 31.

parable effect on negotiations in the 1960s over the removal of quantitative restrictions: certain states took the position that they would not end practices contrary to GATT rules unless they were compensated with reciprocal concessions.[72] The lesson is that any barrier reduction has a price.

While problems in determining reciprocity have arisen in negotiations over linear cuts and the NTB codes, the norm has not lost its significance. Concerning the bargaining over linear reductions in the Kennedy Round, the Curzons remark that a balance of concessions between any two large traders remained "as central as ever to the bargaining process."[73] Commercial policy officials have testified that the expectation that all major trading powers had to offer roughly comparable concessions exercised a tremendous influence in negotiations of the NTB codes during the Tokyo Round.[74] Although the difficulties of measuring reciprocity were magnified in the case of NTB negotiations, no one was prepared to abandon the concept. According to some observers, the NTB codes were basically assessed as a "package" by the OECD countries.[75]

The implementation of rules has also been affected by the reciprocity norm. For example, much attention in dispute settlement is focused on "containing" disputes rather than on determining whether a rule has been violated and what punishment to mete out. Indeed, the major purpose of dispute settlement in GATT "is to maintain, or to restore, the balance of advantages in trade terms."[76] Hudec complains that rather than revise the rules or promote greater compliance, the "leading GATT governments" have usually chosen "to divert attention from rules altogether and to substitute whatever *ad hoc, pragmatic procedures* seemed to offer the best prospect of a *reasonable accommodation of interests.*"[77] The norm best suited to attain such an "accommodation" has been reciprocity. The primary concern when supervising rule implementation has not been to "punish" transgressors but rather to maintain the delicate balance of reciprocal advantages that constitutes the most valued achievement of the GATT regime.

A final point concerning reciprocity relates to the longstanding argument of the LDCs that the norm ought not to apply to them. When Part IV was added to the General Agreement in 1965, the industrial countries committed themselves not to seek reciprocity in negotiations with LDCs. Most developing countries, however, expressed dissatisfaction with the results of the Kennedy Round and claimed that developed contracting parties continued to bargain according to the norm of reciprocity.[78] Within the "Framework Group"

[72] Dam, *The GATT*, p. 19.
[73] Curzon, "Management of Trade Relations," p. 161; Dam, *The GATT*, pp. 68–77.
[74] Interviews, Ottawa, September 1980; interview, U.S. trade officials, November 1980.
[75] Golt, *GATT Negotiations*, pp. 22–23; Krasner, "Tokyo Round," pp. 514–18; interviews, Ottawa, September 1980.
[76] Curzon, "Management of Trade Relations," p. 206.
[77] Robert E. Hudec, *Adjudication of International Trade Disputes*, Thames Essay no. 16 (London: Trade Policy Research Centre, 1978), p. 17; emphasis added.
[78] Preeg, *Traders and Diplomats*, pp. 227–30; Kock, *International Trade Policy*, p. 245.

established in the Tokyo Round, several LDCs favored a legal consolidation and strengthening of various GATT provisions for "differential treatment" of LDCs, including a more precise commitment to and definition of *non-reciprocity*.[79] The agreed "enabling clause" offered a clearer statement of nonreciprocity,[80] but whether it will have a major impact is—to say the least—problematical. In the NTB code negotiations, LDCs were not asked to "contribute" on a scale anywhere near what developed countries were expected to offer,[81] yet only a handful of LDCs have signed the codes;[82] and complaints have been made about the "graduation clause" attached to the decision on differential treatment, which envisages LDCs in GATT "gradually" developing to a point where reciprocity is expected of them.[83] Thus, whatever concessions are offered to LDCs as a result of nonreciprocal bargaining (and they have been quite modest to date) are to be regarded as temporary. Reciprocity is still a dominant norm in the system.

4. Waiving rules in cases of economic difficulty: the safeguard norm

"Exceptions," "loopholes," "escape clauses," or "safeguard clauses" in international agreements give states the flexibility not to comply with certain rules when changes in the domestic or international environment mean that compliance would seriously undermine the well-being of part or all of their population. Such exceptions threaten the order that nations are trying to promote, but on the other hand little order would be possible if states felt they were locking themselves into rigid compliance with all the substantive rules of an accord. In the case of the GATT, it has been noted that without the exceptions the signatories "would not have signed the Agreement in the first place."[84] However, the exceptions did not simply give members the right to opt out at will: specifying criteria for the exercise of the right and procedural hurdles did pose some constraints. Since the founding of GATT these constraints have been eroded through interpretation and lack of collective action. Strictures on the taking of safeguard action still do exist, but they have been frequently been applied in a less stringent fashion than one would expect from a reading of the General Agreement.

In the General Agreement a number of trade spheres are exempted *permanently* from GATT regulations. These are government procurement practices,

---

[79] The submissions of the LDCs to the "framework" negotiating group can be found in GATT Docs. MTN/FR/W/14 (Mexico), MTN/FR/W/9 (India), MTN/FR/W/7 (Pakistan), and MTN/FR/W/1 (Brazil).

[80] *BISD,* 26th Supp., 1980, p. 204.

[81] Bela Balassa, *The Tokyo Round and Developing Countries,* World Bank Staff Working Paper no. 370 (February 1980).

[82] Interview, Ottawa, September 1980.

[83] *BISD,* 26th Supp., 1980, p. 205. The graduation concept envisages an improvement in LDCs' "trade situation" to the point where they are expected "to participate more fully in the framework of rights and obligations under the General Agreement."

from the MFN rules; customs unions and free trade areas, from the MFN rules; agriculture and fisheries, from the prohibition on quotas (provided domestic production control is practiced); export subsidies on primary products, from the prohibition on export subsidies; and actions taken in connection with national security imperatives and policies related to health, safety, and public morals, from GATT rules generally.[85] In addition, thanks to the "grandfather clause," states only accede to the GATT "provisionally," and are thereby allowed to continue trade practices domestically legislated at the time of accession.[86] However, this section focuses on GATT authorizations to take safeguard action or waive compliance with particular substantive rules *on a temporary basis*—as a result of "emergency," "extraordinary," or "exceptional" situations. These can be classified under the headings of balance of payments, economic development, market disruption, and other "exceptional circumstances."[87] (Economic development is treated in detail under the next norm, special and differential treatment for developing countries.)

A crucial exemption or escape clause is provided for countries whose balance of payments is in deficit. Article XII permits the imposition of quantitative restrictions—generally prohibited in Article XI—to safeguard the balance of payments. Article XVIII:B provides more generous treatment of LDCs in this regard, and its provisions were further liberalized in the Tokyo Round.[88] Up through the 1950s the developed West European countries used the safeguard extensively while employing quotas and exchange restrictions during economic recovery.[89] In fact, the Balance of Payments Committee was the most active body in GATT during these years.[90] Since the early 1960s developed states in payments difficulties have tended to eschew quotas and instead impose tariff surcharges, since they are easier to administer and dismantle.[91] (These surcharges violate Article II, but members have usually been willing to grant waivers under Article XXV.)[92] Since the mid 1960s the LDCs have been the only states to employ quotas frequently because of payments deficits,

[84] Curzon, "Management of Trade Relations," p. 152.

[85] Articles III:3, XXIV, XI:2, XVI:3, XX, XXI.

[86] Jackson, *World Trade*, pp. 60–64.

[87] These other minor, temporary escape clauses concern the withdrawal or modification of tariff concessions (Article XXVIII) and the authorization of "exceptional" duties in cases where dumping or subsidization allegedly occurs (permitted by Article VI, the Kennedy and Tokyo Round Antidumping Codes, and the Tokyo Round Subsidies/Countervailing Duties Code).

[88] *BISD*, 26th Supp., 1980, pp. 205–209.

[89] Gerard Curzon, *Multilateral Commercial Diplomacy* (London: Michael Joseph, 1965), p. 137.

[90] Interview, Ottawa, September 1980.

[91] Balassa, "The 'New Protectionism,' " p. 422; Dam, *The GATT*, pp. 33–34.

[92] Dam, *The GATT*, pp. 32–34; Curzon, "Management of Trade Relations," pp. 217–20. See the report of the Working Party that examined a 1971 Danish surcharge, where it was concluded that, although "not explicitly covered by any provision of the GATT," the Danish surcharge was consistent with the "spirit" of GATT. It was further noted: "Quantitative restrictions provided for in Article XII would have had a more serious effect on the interests of its trading partners." *BISD*, 19th Supp., 1973, pp. 129.

usually under the generous provisions of Article XVIII:B.[93] The criteria in this article have been applied rather loosely to LDCs, but they have still exerted a constraining influence on their policies.

The right to waive the rules in cases of market disruption (Article XIX) is the most important escape clause or safeguard provision in the General Agreement. It stipulates that GATT members can impose quotas or alter bound tariffs if three conditions are met: first, actual or threatened "serious injury" to a domestic industry resulting from GATT obligations is shown; second, the parties concerned consult; and third, the import restraints are imposed in a nondiscriminatory fashion. Resort to emergency restraints under Article XIX has become more frequent and the use of quotas more popular.[94] However, this legal way of meeting threats from low-cost producers has tended to be replaced by approaches that violate the General Agreement and stretch the accepted scope of safeguard action. Countries have increasingly tended to abjure invoking Article XIX when establishing import restraints because of doubts about their ability to show "serious injury," their perceived need to impose the restraints "selectively" against certain countries, and their wish to avoid retaliation (under Article XIX:3[a]).[95] A common tactic has been to negotiate often-secret "voluntary export restraints,"[96] which are undoubtedly more common than invocations of Article XIX. In the Tokyo Round the developing countries and Japan pushed for a new safeguards code to curb the arbitrary shelving of GATT rules, but the negotiations came to naught—largely because of the EEC's insistence on the right to apply restraints "selectively." The consensus on the right of states to take safeguard action to prevent market disruption remains strong, but there are serious differences on the conditions under which it is legitimate and on the extent of multilateral control desirable.

In designing an international agreement states try to anticipate all of the situations in which they might want waivers, but normally they recognize their foresight is limited. In the General Agreement this recognition appears in Article XXV:5, which states that "in exceptional circumstances not elsewhere provided for in this Agreement," obligations may be waived by two-thirds majority of the votes cast. This has been termed "the equivalent of a large hole in the hull below the water line,"[97] and has been used on almost sixty occasions to exempt contracting parties from a variety of GATT obligations, usually on

[93] For example, all the contracting parties having recourse to quantitative restrictions under the balance-of-payments safeguard provision in 1976, 1977, 1978, and 1979 have been LDCs, and all have done so under Article XVIII.

[94] GATT Doc. L/4679, "Modalities of Application of Article XIX," 5 July 1978.

[95] Jan Tumlir, "A Revised Safeguard Clause for GATT?" *Journal of World Trade Law* 7 (July–August 1973), p. 405 and passim; Gerald Meier, "Externality Law and Market Safeguards: Applications in the GATT Multilateral Trade Negotiations," *Harvard International Law Journal* 18 (Summer 1977), pp. 496–97, 523; Bhagwati, "Market Disruption."

[96] Bhagwati, "Market Disruption," p. 169; Meier, "Externality Law," p. 523.

[97] Curzon, "Management of Trade Relations," p. 152.

a temporary basis (or so it is thought).[98] GATT members have often interpreted "exceptional circumstances" in a flexible and vague fashion. Many essentially permanent waivers have been granted, especially with respect to agricultural policies and quotas inconsistent with Article XI[99] and preference schemes inconsistent with Article I but not acceptable under Article XXIV (customs unions and free trade areas). The membership evidently has regarded and still regards such an open-ended waiver as providing a needed element of flexibility in the regime.

The GATT's provisions to permit the taking of safeguard action have grown somewhat obsolete since 1947. It is doubtful, for example, that the industrial countries fully anticipated the extent to which certain of their economic sectors would require protection to survive. Similarly, the drafters of the General Agreement would probably be surprised at the incidence of severe payments imbalances in certain countries. Unanticipated trends and events have increased the size of the "holes" provided by the GATT's safeguard rules, as in the frequently loose application of safeguard provisions. More important, however, has been the tendency to avoid multilateral supervision by taking actions outside the regime framework. This has *de facto* broadened the scope of safeguard action in the trade barrier issue-area.

5. Special treatment of LDC trade: the development norm

The norm obligating the developed countries to provide special treatment to the trade of developing nations in order to assist their economic development has grown gradually in importance since the founding of the GATT. In the late 1940s and early 1950s it played a minor role in the trade regime, in part because of the demise of the International Trade Organization (with its extensive provisions on economic development). From the mid 1950s to the mid 1960s it slowly achieved greater prominence as a result of the significant increase in the number of Third World GATT members and the heightened political sensitivity of the western countries to their demands. With the addition of Part IV to the GATT in 1965 this trend accelerated, with significant

---

[98] Waivers are listed in the cumulative index, *BISD,* 26th Supp., 1980, pp. 387–92. Jackson (*World Trade,* p. 548) argues that waivers were intended to be temporary, but have become permanent in many cases.

[99] In 1955, the U.S. obtained a waiver to permit the use of import quotas regardless of whether production controls were employed, as required by the Agricultural Adjustment Act. This was "a grave blow to GATT's prestige" (Dam, *The GATT,* p. 260), and was the first major step to remove agriculture from GATT rules. Jackson (*World Trade,* p. 548) notes that because of the size of the U.S. market, the impact of this waiver "on world trade has probably been more extensive" than that of any other. The Community's Common Agricultural Policy has no doubt been infinitely more disruptive, but it is not covered by a waiver. Evans notes that "Community producers are insulated from the effect of any price competition with the outside world" (*Kennedy Round,* p. 84).

subsequent events being the acceptance of the Generalized System of Preferences in 1971 and the adoption of a variety of provisions in the accords accepted at the end of the Tokyo Round in 1979. However, it is still what we might call a subsidiary norm since the major trading states appear willing to make only limited sacrifices to promote the trade interests of the developing countries.

In the 1950s, the developing countries in the GATT were basically concerned with the "import side" of GATT rules, that is, with ensuring that they could deviate from these rules in order to protect their infant industries and precarious foreign exchange reserves, in accordance with the contemporary economic orthodoxy of import-substituting industrialization.[100] The single GATT article (XVIII) dealing with special dispensations from GATT rules was revised in 1955 to grant LDCs greater latitude to restrict trade for developmental purposes,[101] but those developing countries that were members of the regime were dissatisfied with the limited recognition of their special economic problems.

Following a 1958 experts' report examining a variety of trade issues, including the export prospects of developing countries, the GATT membership became more interested in the "export side" of LDCs' trade interests. The question was whether the norm of special treatment could or should be applied to the export side. A start was made in late 1958 with the launching of an "Action Program" to expand trade. A committee (known simply as Committee III) was established to examine obstacles restricting LDC exports.[102] An inventory of trade barriers in developed countries was compiled, and the developed states were pressed to eliminate them. The extent of success, however, was "disappointing."[103]

Meanwhile, a large number of newly independent underdeveloped countries joined the GATT in the early 1960s, and pressure to broaden the scope of the norm of special treatment intensified. The creation of UNCTAD in 1964 facilitated this Third World campaign to reform GATT rules. In February 1965, a new chapter on trade and development—known as Part IV of the General Agreement—was added.[104] Part IV strengthened the norm of special treatment and was a victory of at least a symbolic nature for the developing countries. It consists of three articles, none of which imposes binding obligations on the developed contracting parties,[105] but which taken together articulate a significant *symbolic* acceptance of the special character of LDCs'

---

[100] Dam, *The GATT,* p. 227; Kock, *International Trade Policy,* p. 237.
[101] Ibid., p. 230.
[102] *BISD,* 7th Supp., 1959, p. 28.
[103] Dam (*The GATT,* pp. 229–35) provides an excellent survey of Committee III's work.
[104] GATT Press Release 962 (1966).
[105] Jackson describes the legal obligations contained in Part IV as "soft" (*World Trade,* p. 647). Dam notes that the new chapter contains "a great deal of verbiage and very few precise commitments" (*The GATT,* p. 237).

rights and obligations within the regime. Perhaps the best-known element of the new chapter on trade and development is Article XXXVI:8, which states that "The developed contracting parties do not expect reciprocity for commitments made by them in trade negotiations to reduce or remove tariffs and other barriers to the trade of less-developed contracting parties." Article XXXVII spells out "commitments" accepted by developed countries to reduce trade barriers (including internal taxes) "currently or potentially of particular interest to less-developed countries." However, this is qualified by the phrase "to the fullest extent possible," which makes it impossible to regard these "commitments" as binding "obligations."[106]

In recent years efforts have been made to strengthen the relative importance of the economic development norm in the GATT, with respect both to LDCs' ability to deviate from certain rules related to imports and to the conditions under which their exports enjoy access to developed-country markets. LDCs have proposed that "in any new safeguard system, special rules should be provided for developing countries, including the general rule that these countries be excluded from the application of safeguard measures by developed countries."[107] Predictably, this suggestion has gone nowhere, since the developed countries regard certain Third World countries as the major source of "market disruption." LDCs have achieved greater success in their attempts to benefit from discriminatory trade preferences. As noted earlier, waivers to permit both the General System of Preferences and intra-LDC trade preferences were obtained in 1971. Under the GSP each industrial country has established preferential tariffs for particular LDC imports, although the effects have been quite limited. After the conclusion of the Tokyo Round, the contracting parties accepted an "enabling clause" that permits "differential and more favorable treatment" of developing countries. This decision made "legal" both the GSP and trade preferences among LDCs, and thus obviated the need for further waivers for these schemes.[108] It also granted LDCs greater latitude to use trade barriers for developmental purposes.

Special treatment for LDCs is also provided for in the Tokyo Round NTB codes.[109] The Subsidies Code exempts LDCs from the prohibition of export subsidies for nonprimary commodities, and from countervailing action if their employment of export subsidies "leads to the displacement of the exports of another signatory in third-country markets." Their obligations under the code remain "vague."[110] Under the Agreement on Government Procurement, LDCs are permitted to participate in the agreement without opening up their

[106] Ibid., p. 239.
[107] *Tokyo Round*, p. 93.
[108] *BISD*, 26th Supp., 1980, p. 203; "GATT: A Legal Guide to the Tokyo Round," *Journal of World Trade Law* 13 (September–October 1979), pp. 443–44.
[109] *BISD*, 29th Supp., 1980, p. 203; Balassa, *Tokyo Round and Developing Countries*, pp. 28–30.
[110] Ibid., pp. 15–20.

own procurement practices, thanks to generous exclusion provisions for LDCs in Article III of the code. The Technical Barriers Code states that LDCs signing the agreement "should not be expected to use international standards as a basis for their technical regulations or standards . . . which are not appropriate to their development, financial and trade needs" (Article XXI:4), and they can be granted "exceptions in whole or in part from obligations under this Agreement" (Article XXI:8). The Customs Valuation Code grants LDCs who accede to it technical assistance and permits delays in implementing the code. All the codes call for special consideration of LDCs' needs by developed signatories.[111]

The Tokyo Round appears to have enshrined special treatment of LDCs as a central norm of the regime, although the effect on trade bargaining is unclear. It remains questionable whether the GATT regime, which is focused on trade barrier reduction and regulation in pursuit of mutual commercial advantages, will prove to be a hospitable forum in which new practices can be developed to guide North-South economic relations.[112] To date the industrialized states have made concessions at the normative level and the level of very general rules, but the concrete effects of their "sacrifices" have been very modest.

Procedural norms and mechanisms

At the heart of the procedural component of a regime are the norms that provide guidelines as to how decisions are to be made. The mechanisms, which Young has described as the "institutional arrangements specialized to the resolution of problems of social choice arising within the framework of particular regimes,"[113] are shaped by the norms. Hence the impact of procedural norms on actual regime programs is mediated by the mechanisms. Our analysis will focus on the evolution of the two central procedural norms and their impact on mechanisms and regime programs, but first it is necessary to provide an overview of the GATT's institutional mechanisms.

The GATT's two most important institutions are the annual meetings of contracting parties and the Council (open to all states). Under the Council—which meets at least six times a year—there are a variety of committees and *ad hoc* working parties, which monitor and make recommendations on particular issues. There are also two different types of dispute settlement bodies. Panels of Conciliation are composed of experts appointed by the Director General, and they are charged with submitting specific proposals for resolving conflicts. Working Parties are more "political" and include representatives of the two disputants as well as outside parties; they are supposed to encourage agree-

---

[111] Ibid., passim.
[112] See Sidney Golt, *Developing Countries and the GATT System,* Thames Essay no. 13 (London: Trade Policy Research Centre, 1978).
[113] Young, "International Regimes," pp. 336–37.

ment between the conflicting parties. Since the 1960s Working Parties have been used more frequently than Panels.[114] In addition, there are now committees that will oversee the new NTB codes; these are limited to signatories.

In large part, the permanent institutions are concerned with rule implementation (including dispute settlement) and general reviews of trade relations, but the Council and the annual meetings of contracting parties also deal with amendments to the General Agreement and "decisions" that establish policy directions for the organization. Amendments to the most-favored-nation clause and the tariff schedules (Articles I and II) and Article XXX require unanimity; amendments to other articles require the approval of a two-thirds majority, but only become effective for those countries accepting them.[115] "Decisions" can be taken by a simple majority. Voting in the meetings of contracting parties and the Council is not common, and there is a strong preference for operating by consensus.[116]

While this ongoing network of GATT bodies is mainly charged with the promotion of rule implementation, it is the periodic conferences (seven since 1947) or "Rounds" that are responsible for rule making. The administrative aspects of these conferences are handled by a committee-of-the-whole, the Trade Negotiations Committee, but specific accords on tariffs and nontariff barriers are formulated by two or more states. During the first five conferences, between 1947 and 1962, the mode of decision-making was dominantly bilateral, and the agreements were "the result of essentially bilateral concessions, which accumulate and are automatically made multilateral by the most-favored-nation clause."[117] With the advent of linear tariff cuts and the formulation of NTB codes in the Kennedy and Tokyo Rounds, an important multilateral element has been introduced. However, trade agreements still depend on a group of states coming together voluntarily—and not on a decision of a particular deliberative body. GATT rounds resemble more a stock exchange than a legislature. The participants operate within the framework of certain rules, but "deals" are generally made between two or among a limited number of states. It is this feature that sets off the GATT from most other international organizations.

1. Collective decision making: the multilateralism norm

Certain of the substantive norms identified above are clearly in conflict (e.g., liberalization vs. safeguards), and in the case of the two procedural norms this is even more true. Multilateralism signifies the willingness of

[114] Jackson, *World Trade,* chapter 8; Dam, *The GATT,* chapter 19; Hudec, *Adjudication of International Trade Disputes,* pp. 1–25.

[115] Jackson, *World Trade,* pp. 77 and 122–23.

[116] Gerard and Victoria Curzon, "GATT: Traders' Club," in Robert W. Cox and Harold K. Jacobson, eds., *The Anatomy of Influence: Decision-Making in International Organization* (New Haven: Yale University Press, 1973), p. 302.

[117] Ibid., p. 314.

governments to participate in rule-making conferences and to allow multi-lateral surveillance of, and even a degree of control over, their trade policy. It symbolizes regime members' acceptance of the proposition that they have a legitimate interest in each other's policies and behavior. What we call the major interests norm, on the other hand, stems from a contrasting belief that participation in certain aspects of decision making ought to be restricted to those most affected or most influential, or both, in respect of the issue being dealt with. That a tension exists between these two procedural norms is obvious.

Two major aspects of decision making are identified here: rule making and the promotion of rule implementation. The latter category in turn includes several distinct types of activity, of which we discuss three: the monitoring of state behavior, the interpretation of rules, and the settlement of disputes. In the case of the multilateralism norm, its impact on rule making in the GATT was minimal until the advent of linear tariff negotiations in the mid 1960s and, especially, the deliberations concerning nontariff codes of conduct. Insofar as the promotion of rule implementation is concerned, the multilateralism norm has exercised an important influence on the monitoring of behavior, although this has declined somewhat in the past decade or so. Rule interpretation and dispute settlement have also been affected by the belief in multilateral procedures in the regime, but here the competing major interests norm has perhaps been dominant. We first discuss the role of multilateralism in rule making, then the indicators and evolution of the norm with respect to rule implementation.

Rule making (i.e., the negotiation of binding agreements concerning tariffs and NTBs) was dominantly bilateral in character during most of the GATT's first two decades. Tariff conferences typically "commenced as networks of bilateral negotiations"[118] (discussed under the major interests norm, below). Near the close of negotiations, a "last-minute balancing" of "offers" and "concessions" would occur in order to get countries that would benefit secondarily from the nondiscriminatory application of agreed tariff reductions to "pay" for these benefits.[119] This constituted the only multilateral element in rule making. However, the development of linear tariff negotiations and, even more so, the growing importance of NTBs in recent bargaining rounds have introduced a stronger component of multilateralism into decision making in the GATT. True, the major trading states continue to dominate the rule-making process, but more regime members now participate in any given negotiation, particularly in the case of NTBs.

The impact of the belief in multilateral supervision and decision making is perhaps easiest to adduce from the monitoring of behavior, which is the major aspect of rule implementation in the regime. In connection with this, mention should be made of both the consultation and the notification requirements of

---

[118] Dam, *The GATT,* p. 61.
[119] Ibid., pp. 62–63.

the GATT. The General Agreement contains a host of provisions that obligate members to consult, if requested by other members, in the case of such actions as the modification of tariff schedules, actions taken to support "infant industries," the imposition of emergency quotas, and many other matters. Jackson lists nineteen "clauses" that require consultations between contracting parties or between a party initiating a certain action and the membership as a whole.[120] Frequent consultations clearly facilitate the close monitoring of behavior by the membership. The GATT's various textile accords have also contained elaborate consultation clauses that require importing states to justify their policies to those countries that are members of the Textiles Committee. The Tokyo Round NTB agreements provide for extensive consultations regarding matters that pertain to the subjects of the individual codes. And the Understanding Regarding Notification, Consultation and Dispute Settlement, adopted in November 1979, reaffirms the faith of GATT members in the efficacy of consultation and indicates a commitment to the regulatory system as a whole.[121]

The GATT's numerous notification requirements are also indispensable to the close monitoring of behavior that lies at the heart of effective rule implementation. Contracting parties are obligated to *report* (which involves more than simply *consulting*) regularly on actions taken under certain "escape clauses," such as those permitting the formation of customs unions and free trade areas (Article XXIV), the furtherance of economic development (Article XVIII), and the safeguarding of the balance of payments (Article XII). In addition, once waivers are granted, recipients are in most cases required to make annual reports and generally show that they are in compliance with the terms of the waiver. Further, notifications and the provision of information are required not only in relation to escape-clause actions and waivers, but in connection with many other aspects of state behavior in the trade barrier field. A recent GATT Secretariat document has enumerated the numerous escape-clause and other notification provisions that reflect the importance of multilateralism in the regime (Table 1). To this extensive list one would now have to add the new notification and reporting obligations contained in the Tokyo Round's NTB agreements, as well as the more general notification commitment made in the "enabling clause" decision of November 1979.[122]

Although the extent of compliance with these notification obligations has varied over time and between individual provisions, the record has in fact been reasonably good.[123] Compliance with the obligation to provide information concerning trade barrier policies helps immeasurably to increase the transparency of policy in this issue area. Observers of the GATT often argue that improving the quality and quantity of information about international trade

---

[120] Jackson, *World Trade*, pp. 164–65.
[121] *BISD*, 26th Supp., 1980, p. 211.
[122] *BISD*, 26th Supp., 1980, p. 210.
[123] GATT Doc. MTN/FR/W17.

Table 1. GATT notification requirements

Article or Decision	Particular Matter Requiring Notifications
II	Adjustment of "specific" duties.
VI:6	Imposition of antidumping and countervailing duties in certain cases.
X	Publication of trade regulations and of new regulations.
XII:4, XVIII:12	Restrictions imposed to safeguard the balance of payments.
XVI:1	Use of subsidies.
XVII	Products traded by state enterprises.
XVIII:A	Modification of concessions by LDCs to foster new industries.
XVIII:C	Other measures by LDCs to establish new industries.
XIX:2	Emergency actions to protect domestic industry.
XXII:2	Notification of bilateral consultations.
XXIV:7	Customs unions, free trade areas, initial and ongoing reports.
XXVIII:1 and 4	Modification or withdrawal of concessions (non-LDCs).
XXVIII:5	Reserve right to modify concessions in the future.
XXXVII:2	New barriers on LDC exports.
March 1965	Review of implementation of Part IV.
December 1970	Changes in border tax adjustments.
March 1955	Liquidation of strategic stockpiles.
November 1958	Legislation regarding marks of origin.

policy has been one of the regime's major contributions.[124] More importantly, without the provision of data and information concerning members' trade policies, behavior could not be effectively monitored and therefore the ability to implement regime rules would suffer.

Multilateral rule implementation has also involved the interpretation of regime rules by GATT bodies. Students of the GATT are often "struck by the extent to which 'legalism' was dominant in the drafting of the original General Agreement . . . and . . . 'pragmatism' has governed the interpretation and administration" of GATT rules.[125] Most GATT members have preferred a pragmatic, flexible approach to rule interpretation, but on many occasions this has not been inconsistent with multilateral decision making. The numerous GATT bodies that have existed over the years have frequently reinterpreted GATT rules in light of changing circumstances and state preferences. Legal scholars have expressed some dismay at the tendency "informally" to reinterpret rules and even to ignore the rules in certain instances, a tendency that has become more marked since the early 1960s.[126] However, the fact that a rather pragmatic approach to rule interpretation has existed in the regime does not vitiate the argument that rule interpretation has exhibited a multilateral char-

[124] Jackson, *World Trade,* p. 124.

[125] Dam, *The GATT,* p. 4.

[126] Hudec, *Adjudication of International Trade Disputes;* John H. Jackson, "The Crumbling Institutions of the Liberal Trade System," *Journal of World Trade Law* 12 (March–April 1978), and "Governmental Disputes in International Trade Relations: A Proposal in the Context of GATT," *Journal of World Trade Law* 12 (Jan.–Feb. 1979); Thomas Roschke, "The GATT: Problems and Prospects," *Journal of Law and Economics* 12 (1977).

acter. Moreover, it must be emphasized that many "reinterpreted" rules have in fact achieved the status of new, although uncodified, law in the GATT.[127]

Another dimension of multilateral rule interpretation relates to the various decisions of the contracting parties. The granting of waivers is the most obvious example of collective decision making that may involve rule interpretation in some cases. For example, the several waivers permitting states to impose tariff surcharges for balance-of-payments reasons, in spite of their illegality under GATT rules, indicate that the membership has "reinterpreted" GATT obligations.[128] Similarly, waivers to permit LDCs to benefit from preferences have amounted "to new thrusts of regulation designed to support completely new policies."[129] GATT members also make collective decisions that have the effect of altering, reinterpreting, or adding to the corpus of regime rules; the most recent example is of course the set of "decisions" concerning the GATT's legal framework, agreed to in November 1979 after intense negotiations during the Tokyo Round.

Finally, rule implementation has also manifested a degree of multilateralism in connection with dispute settlement. Article XXIII authorizes the contracting parties to consider complaints from a GATT member about the behavior of another member. Upon investigation, a ruling or recommendation may be handed down. In the 1950s in particular, GATT Panels quite successfully addressed a number of disputes. Since then, the use of adjudicatory bodies has declined and members have instead relied on bilateral settlement techniques or, alternatively, have resolved their differences in the context of Working Parties, where matters are generally settled with only limited reference to existing rules. Nonetheless, between 1947 and 1977 some thirty collective "decisions of sorts" were issued by the membership or subsidiary bodies in instances of disputes between contracting parties.[130] However, as discussed below, dispute settlement in the GATT has tended to be highly bilateral during most of the regime's history.

In assessing the evolution of the multilateralism norm, it must be admitted that the monitoring and surveillance of members' compliance with GATT rules have suffered from the proliferation of actions taken outside the regime's framework (e.g., VERs), from the extremely superficial scrutiny given to many regional trading arrangements that harm the trade interests of nonparticipants, and from the marked inclination to treat much agricultural trade as a special sector to which GATT disciplines do not apply. In addition, the conscious encouragement of bilateral dispute resolution by many regime members has limited the scope for multilateral decision making in relation to dispute settlement. Thus, while multilateralism has grown more prominent in

[127] Jackson, *World Trade*, p. 757.
[128] Dam, *The GATT*, pp. 30–32.
[129] Jackson, *World Trade*, pp. 30–31.
[130] Hudec, *Adjudication of International Trade Disputes*, p. 5.

the rule-making process in the GATT, the impact of the norm on the various facets of rule implementation has at the same time suffered some attenuation.

2. Trading interests and decision-making roles: the major interests norm

What we call the major interests norm of the GATT reflects the belief of many members that those with the most obvious stake in a given issue or negotiation should exercise paramount influence in related decision making. To some extent it also signifies a belief, or perception, that the most powerful states have, almost by definition, the largest stakes in regime negotiations and activities, and therefore are entitled to exert a degree of influence proportionate with this role. In addition, the "efficiency" benefits of conducting decision making among the parties most concerned also appear to have supported states' acceptance of the norm. The Curzons suggest that bilateral negotiations have been "the key to GATT's relative success as a forum for tariff negotiations" because they limit "the effective negotiators to those who have a genuine interest in the subject under discussion . . ."[131] Restricting the number of participants in decision making also ensures that the fragile multilateral machinery is not overloaded with matters that can more easily be settled in a bilateral or limited multilateral context.

This major interests norm has been important in shaping both rule making and rule implementation throughout the GATT's history. Its impact has clearly been diminished in the former case by the introduction of more multilateral rule-making techniques, but it has remained extremely important for most aspects of regime activity and continues to enjoy the support of many regime members, especially the most powerful.

Perhaps the best example of the impact of this norm is the techniques employed for negotiating tariff reductions prior to the Kennedy Round. The first bargaining Round in 1947 had established the precedent that tariff concessions would be negotiated bilaterally on a product-by-product basis.[132] A GATT document noted that the "principal supplier rule" was to govern the exchange of tariff concessions and this "rule" dictated a manifestly bilateral bargaining procedure: "the importing country negotiates its tariff rate with its principal supplier and not with all suppliers of the same product." This was to prevent "an unnecessary multiplicity of negotiations on the same product."[133] Under this system, an importing country was normally only prepared to offer concessions to a principal supplier since this latter state, as primary beneficiary, would be more willing than secondary suppliers to "pay" for concessions.[134]

---

[131] Curzon, "GATT: Traders' Club," p. 134.

[132] Ibid., p. 137; Dam, *The GATT*, p. 61. Note that this technique was made necessary by U.S. law.

[133] Cited in Kock, *International Trade Policy*, p. 100.

[134] Dam, *The GATT*, p. 62.

This negotiating technique was not, strictly speaking, bilateral, since "secondary" suppliers were expected to offer reciprocal concessions once the bilateral bargaining had concluded. This minor balancing at the close of a conference "constituted the only truly multilateral element of the negotiations."[135] Prior to the 1956 conference it was agreed that countries could join together to request concessions on products of which they *collectively* were the major suppliers to an importing country.[136] By the time of the Dillon Round (1960–62), it was accepted that a country supplying more than 10 percent of a product to an import market would be asked to "reciprocate" or "pay" for a concession received on this product, although it would not itself negotiate such a concession, that task being restricted to the importing country and the principal supplier.[137] In general, however, it must be recognized that GATT tariff bargaining procedures "served to reinforce as well as to reflect the bilateral character of pre-Kennedy Round trade negotiations."

> The basic assumption . . . was that each party to a particular negotiation would be in a position both to grant and to receive concessions. The principal supplier rule provided in effect that only countries that were the principal suppliers of products were in a position to receive concessions. Therefore, the principal supplier rule operated to exclude from meaningful tariff negotiations . . . those countries that were not the principal suppliers of any products.[138]

Thus, small countries, especially LDCs, that did not have large import markets to "offer" and that were not major suppliers of most traded goods were effectively stripped of significant influence in the negotiation of tariff reductions.

With the advent of linear, across-the-board tariff reductions in the Kennedy Round and the growth of interest in negotiating NTB codes, this bilateral technique was discarded for a greater degree of multilateralism. But the ability of those few countries that are the major suppliers of most products and that possess the largest import markets to determine the extent of linear tariff cuts, the sectors to be excluded from such cuts (e.g., textiles, agriculture), and the new rules governing the use of NTBs, remains striking.[139] The crucial bargaining now occurs in a *"petit sommet"* of a few states, where such essential issues as the tariff-cutting formula to be adopted or the outline of a new subsidies agreement will be resolved.[140] In the view of observers of the Tokyo Round, the "big three" (the U.S., the EEC, and Japan) are an overwhelming presence during most facets of contemporary trade barrier negotiations in the regime,[141]

[135] Ibid.
[136] *BISD,* 4th Supp., 1956, p. 80.
[137] Curzon, "Management of Trade Relations," p. 173.
[138] Dam, *The GATT,* p. 62.
[139] Ibid., pp. 61–77; *MTN Studies,* vol. 2, pp. 34–35.
[140] Curzon, "Management of Trade Relations," p. 205.
[141] Golt, *GATT Negotiations,* passim.

although there has been some modest sharing of influence—especially in NTB code negotiations.

The major interests norm has also influenced the monitoring of state behavior, which is the most important aspect of rule implementation in the regime. For example, supervision of countries' compliance with the rules and their general behavior is explicitly bilateral according to GATT articles dealing with emergency import restrictions (Article XIX), the modification of past tariff bindings (Article XXVIII), and the alleged "nullification or impairment" of benefits accruing to a member under the General Agreement.[142] The absence of guaranteed multilateral surveillance in regard to emergency actions taken against imports causing "market disruption" is particularly significant in this context. Several observers have criticized the paucity of multilateral supervision and control of countries' behavior in imposing emergency import restrictions, which is occasioned by the "bilateral" negotiating bias of Article XIX.[143] And, of course, the proliferation of extralegal "voluntary" export restraints and "orderly" marketing schemes outside the regime's supervisory framework is also a telling indication of certain states' eagerness to "regulate" behavior in a bilateral setting, where major interests and the superior leverage of the powerful are given freer rein than in the GATT.

It is evident that rule interpretation and dispute settlement should be discussed together, for while there is no formal provision for nonmultilateral rule interpretation or reinterpretation in the GATT, nonetheless the strongly bilateral character of dispute settlement in the regime may lead to highly informal types of rule interpretation on the part of two or a small number of concerned states. Of major importance here is GATT members' *obligation* to seek bilateral resolution of a dispute before invoking the regime's multilateral machinery (Article XXII).[144] A bias in favor of "containing" disputes through bilateral or limited multilateral discussions is striking.[145] The norm of reciprocity has clearly affected the approach taken toward disputes in the GATT and has supported the major interests norm in this area. Observers note that the central goal of dispute settlement in the regime is not to develop a sophisticated jurisprudence or to ensure that behavior is perfectly consonant with the rules, but rather to restore the previous "balance of advantages"— that is, reciprocity.[146] This has irked legal scholars and several smaller GATT members, who fear that resolving disputes according to the major interests and reciprocity imperatives puts weaker powers at a disadvantage and undermines the integrity of the rule system.[147] The Tokyo Round accords appear to reflect

[142] Curzon, "Management of Trade Relations," p. 205.
[143] Jan Tumlir, "A Revised Safeguards Clause for GATT?" *Journal of World Trade Law* 7 (July–August 1973), p. 407; Bhagwati, "Market Disruption."
[144] Curzon, "Management of Trade Relations," p. 205.
[145] Curzon, "GATT: Traders' Club," p. 316.
[146] Curzon, "Management of Trade Relations," p. 206.
[147] Hudec, *Adjudication of International Trade Disputes;* George A. Maciel, *The International Framework for World Trade: Brazilian Proposals for GATT Reform* (London: Trade Policy Research Centre, 1977), pp. 11–12.

a more multilateral approach to dispute settlement, but it is unclear whether the pattern established in the 1950s—when multilateral techniques of adjudication were quite successful and popular—will once again develop in the regime.[148] One is entitled to be skeptical.

In sum, while rule making in the regime has become more multilateral in character since the mid 1960s, the monitoring of behavior and other elements of rule implementation have been increasingly affected by the competing major interests norm. The ongoing battle between the procedural norms of multilateralism and major interests warrants close scrutiny by students of the GATT, since the balance between them provides in some respects an index to the strength of the regime.

Conclusion

This discussion has highlighted a number of major characteristics of the GATT trade barriers regime; these are in turn of some interest for the study of regimes generally. Three basic conclusions emerge from the analysis of GATT's normative structure and evolution. First, it must be emphasized that it is the norms of a regime, and the importance the most influential members attach to them, that largely determine the regime's rules and rule implementation as well as its decision-making mechanisms. In the case of the GATT's procedural norms, their impact on regime programs is mediated through their effect on the decision-making mechanisms, a point of some import for students of international organizations who seek to understand why decision-making bodies evolve in certain ways and how they are related to the broader structure of international collaboration in various issue areas.

Second, recognition of the fact that the relative importance of regime norms varies over time is critical for an adequate understanding of regime evolution. These normative dynamics are a major cause of changes in regime programs. The reasons for the rise and fall of regime norms are of course to be found in the shifting power resources and policy objectives of regime members, particularly the most influential ones. But changes in the relative significance of norms do not necessarily indicate that the regime has "broken down" or ceased to regulate state behavior effectively, at least if the interdependence norms continue to exert some influence in the regime.

Third, norms do not live in isolation; many are either mutually supportive or to some extent in conflict. Rule making can in some senses be conceived as the product of a "dialectical struggle" between conflicting norms, leading sometimes to "victories" by one norm but more frequently to tradeoffs and compromises. Of course underlying the "victory" or "defeat" of a given norm are the views, priorities, and relative strengths of the states that comprise the regime's membership. Nonetheless, interesting tensions are bound to exist as a result of conflicts among regime norms. In the case of the GATT, the

---

[148] Hudec, *Adjudication of International Trade Disputes*, pp. 7–11.

development norm is manifestly incompatible with certain other regime norms, nondiscrimination and reciprocity in particular. Another interesting set of tensions exists between liberalization on one hand and reciprocity and nondiscrimination on the other. Reciprocity, while in some respects a political necessity if barrier reduction is to succeed, does work to constrain progress toward liberalization by ensuring that concessions requested by state A will only be offered by state B to the extent that B can in turn obtain concessions from A. Nondiscrimination supports liberalization because it extends all negotiated reductions to all regime members, but it also limits the willingness of countries to liberalize because of their fear that "free riders" who do not contribute will nonetheless benefit as a consequence of the MFN obligation.[149] Moreover, as Andrew Shonfield has written, nondiscrimination and reciprocity always threaten to undermine the liberalization already achieved:

> M.f.n. is in fact a ready-made instrument for setting in motion a downward spiral in the process of bargaining . . . for a dispute between two countries which leads one of them to withdraw a trade concession . . . is almost bound to inflict some injury on the trading interests of other countries who happen to be exporters of the products affected. Assuming that everyone insists on . . . reciprocity, there is no end to the series of consequent adjustments that may have to be made.[150]

Some norms are also mutually supportive. The relationship between reciprocity and the major interests norm—both of which derive from generally prevailing beliefs and practices in the international system—is one example. The nondiscrimination norm has helped to strengthen multilateralism by increasing the number of GATT members with a commercial stake in any bilateral or limited multilateral trade bargain. Others could be enumerated, but the point is clear: norms affect each other, and the tradeoffs or mutually supporting relationships that may develop help to determine the rules and rule implementation of a regime.

Of overriding concern to students of international collaboration is (or should be) the strength or autonomy of a regulatory regime. Earlier we distinguished between *sovereignty norms* and *interdependence norms*. It is the prominence, both relatively and over time, of the *interdependence* norms that is the fundamental indicator of regime strength. Table 2 provides some rough judgments concerning the strength of the GATT's norms since the founding of the regime (these assessments, we hasten to add, are offered with some trepidation; we recognize that many observers of the GATT's colorful history will differ with at least some of our categorizations). Table 2 indicates both the evolution of individual norms and their approximate relative standing within the

---

[149] William Cline et al., *Trade Negotiations in the Tokyo Round* (Washington, D.C.: Brookings, 1978), p. 30.

[150] Shonfield, "International Economic Relations of the Western World: An Overall View," in Shonfield, ed., *International Economic Relations,* vol. 1, pp. 47–48.

Table 2. The strength of interdependence and sovereignty norms in the GATT regime

	1950s	1960s	1970s
A. INTERDEPENDENCE NORMS			
1. Nondiscrimination	Very strong—the central pillar of the early GATT; temporary discrimination by European states was not seen as undermining the primacy of the norm.	Strong—with the exception of "regional" preference schemes it was strong among industrialized states; undermined somewhat by EEC Yaoundé Convention and a few rather ineffective inter-LDC schemes.	Moderately strong—EEC's schemes with LDCs and Mediterranean states proliferated; hurt by VERs and OMAs, GSP, and NTB codes; still important for trade among OECD countries.
2. Liberalization	Weak to moderately strong—very dependent on U.S. willingness to cut tariffs.	Strong—Kennedy Round saw major cuts by industrialized countries (weak in agriculture).	Moderately strong to strong—rise of some protectionism directed especially at NICs and Japan; the Tokyo Round made real progress on NTB codes—and to a lesser extent on tariffs.
3. Economic development	Very weak—only a few LDCs in GATT, and they were quite unassertive.	Weak—Part IV raised status of norm, but real effects were minor. Many LDCs joined GATT.	Weak to moderately strong—GSP and parts of NTB codes are most noteworthy manifestations of higher profile.
4. Multilateralism			
a. Rule making	Weak—tariffs negotiated bilaterally on a product-by-product basis; "last minute balancing" and collegial pressure did add a multilateral dimension.	Weak to moderately strong—linear cuts introduced some multilateralism, but confined to a group of industrial countries.	Moderately strong—combination of linear cutting procedure and formulation of NTB codes among all OECD states and some LDCs strengthened multilateral element.
b. Rule implementation	Strong—extensive monitoring to ensure behavior accords with rules. Use of adjudicatory Panels common. Rule implementation breaks down on EEC issue, however.	Moderately strong—monitoring and surveillance weaken somewhat, especially regarding regional trade arrangements. Less reference to rules in dispute resolution.	Moderately strong—extralegal VERs, OMAs, weaken the norm; still considerable collective surveillance. Tokyo Round may signal strengthening of norm.

X X

Table 2. The strength of interdependence and sovereignty norms in the GATT regime (Continued)

	1950s	1960s	1970s
B. SOVEREIGNTY NORMS			
1. Reciprocity	Very strong—however, U.S. was lenient in demanding concessions and their implementation for political reasons.	Very strong—somewhat more difficult to calculate in linear cuts; foreswearing of reciprocity in Part IV was largely symbolic.	Strong—Tokyo Round strengthens special treatment and nonreciprocity vis-a-vis LDCs. Impact on bargaining limited, however. Still a key norm.
2. Safeguard	Moderately strong—grounds for resorting to safeguard action are vague in some cases and more specific in others; procedures for securing approval pose real constraints; compliance reasonably good.	Moderately strong—granting of waivers relatively frequent, especially for LDCs under more lenient criteria, but compliance with procedures is quite extensive.	Strong—constraints on taking safeguard action weakened, especially through actions outside of regime. Tokyo Round fails to develop new safeguard code.
3. Major interests			
a. Rule making	Very strong—especially with respect to setting tariffs in "Rounds."	Strong—impact of linear cutting procedure added some multilateralism.	Strong—Tokyo Round broadened the number of participants in decision making but influence still in hands of major traders.
b. Rule implementation	Weak to moderately strong—bilateral consultation and dispute settlement, albeit in accordance with GATT rules, were common; EEC preference scheme in contravention of GATT rules was "accepted" for political reasons.	Moderately strong—use of nonadjudicatory procedures of dispute settlement and failures to apply GATT rules to new preference schemes increased, although many aspects of multilateral system were used frequently.	Moderately strong—failure to respond to certain violations of GATT rules, but multilateral monitoring still important.

regime. Our determinations of the strength of norms are largely based on this criterion: what importance did those states *with the ability to implement the norms* attach to them? Thus it is the views and activities of the major trading states that count most in our assessment of norm strength. While most of the regime members included under this label are developed market economy states, some LDCs, particularly the newly industrializing countries, have begun to enjoy more influence in the GATT.

In the trade barriers regime the sovereignty norms have always occupied a very influential position. This reflects the fact that the issue area is a highly salient one in contemporary international economic relations. Also, the regime is embedded in an international system in which states prize their autonomy and vary considerably in their control of resources. Only in relatively unimportant spheres of international life might one expect the clear supremacy of interdependence norms, and even there, as functionalists have learned, "progress" is very slow in coming.

But to say that sovereignty norms such as reciprocity, the right to take safeguard action, and the rule of major interests have occupied preeminent positions is not to say that interdependence norms have been meaningless. As our previous discussion has indicated, they certainly have not. Members' adherence to nondiscrimination has suffered somewhat but their belief in liberalization has increased. In addition, the economic development norm has exerted a great impact, although that norm can, in reality, be seen as a double-edged sword in judging the strength of a regime. While imposing some constraints on the developed countries, it also provides LDC regime members with greater freedom to jettison GATT rules (i.e., to take safeguard action). In this sense it is both an interdependence and a sovereignty norm.

To identify the constraining influence of *substantive* interdependence norms is an important aspect of evaluating a regime's strength. However, despite the fact that these norms indicate members' willingness to regularize or standardize their behavior along certain lines, they are indications of consensuses based in part on perceptions of self-interest at a particular time, which can later be rejected if states see fit. More central to an evaluation of a regime's strength is the standing of the *procedural* interdependence norm of multilateralism. In the words of a GATT official, this "principle of multilaterality" stands for a belief in "common responsibilities, joint decisions, and international surveillance—the continuous presence of a concerned forum in which a country can complain and seek mediation for its grievances. . . ."[151] Without a fairly strong commitment to this norm, rule-governed change, with its concomitant attributes of predictability and order, is likely to break down in a dynamic environment. Kenneth Dam has commented more generally on the salience of the norm to any legal system:

[151] Jan Tumlir, "Emergency Action Against Sharp Increases in Imports," in Hugh Corbet and Robert Jackson, eds., *In Search of a New World Economic Order* (London: Croom Helm, 1974), p. 266.

Law is not solely, or even primarily, a set of substantive rules. It is also a set of procedures, adapted to the subject matter and designed to resolve disputes that cannot be foreseen at the moment when those procedures are established. Perhaps more important than serving to settle disputes, law viewed as procedures and process serves to identify the common interest in complex situations and to formulate short-term policies for the achievement of long-term objectives.[152]

A more telling insight on the importance of multilateralism (and implicitly on the need for the study of international organizations) would be difficult to find.

It is precisely because of the importance of multilateralism for regimes that we judge that the trade barriers regime has weakened in the past two decades. The attenuation the norm has suffered in the issue area is unquestionable. The belief that trade problems touching on GATT rules should be studied and resolved within its forums no longer has the bite it once had. The constraints that flow from the norm are still real (and may be on the increase as a result of the Tokyo Round accords) but the reliance on and growth of actions contrary to the rules, actions that are ignored by GATT bodies, must be recognized. Perhaps we should be surprised that the inclusion of so many developing countries and the worldwide economic problems of the 1970s have not done more damage to multilateralism; but damage they have done!

Functions of the GATT regime

International regimes as social phenomena warrant scholarly attention because of the perception that they shape in some significant ways the behavior of the actors (usually states) participating in them. We have discussed the continuing "strength" of the GATT trade barriers regime by examining the evolution of its "interdependence" norms. In this final section, we briefly explore the major *functions* of the GATT regime. We ask how the regime has affected states' trade policies and international trade relations. By scrutinizing the functions performed by the GATT regime we hope that some more general insights into this dimension of international regimes may be suggested. Four functions are analyzed: the "facilitative" function, the "constraint" function, the "diffusion of influence" function, and the "promotion of interaction" function. An important point to emphasize is that these functions are interrelated and tend mutually to support one another. Moreover, the last function —the "promotion of interaction"—in large part depends upon the performance of the first three.

During three and one half decades of the GATT's existence, seven conferences (or "Rounds") have been held under its auspices at which tariffs have been reduced significantly and the use of NTBs controlled. The way in which

[152] Dam, *The GATT*, pp. 4–5.

these agreements concerning the reduction and control of trade barriers have been achieved offers crucial insights into the GATT's role in postwar trade relations. It has basically served as a framework within which specific accords and agreements among a limited number of interested states are reached. In this sense the GATT fits Cox and Jacobson's definition of a "forum organization," one that creates "a framework for member states to carry on many activities ranging from the exchange of views to the negotiation of binding legal instruments."[153] That the GATT has facilitated the reaching of agreements to lower trade barriers and regulate their use is partly attributable to the fact that it operates to reduce what Keohane calls the "organization costs" of negotiating accords and "deals."[154] This is achieved by bringing together skilled negotiators from a large number of interested countries to bargain in a familiar setting with well-known and respected conventions and rules. The GATT has also performed its facilitative function by encouraging the "side payments" necessary to any successful bargaining process.[155] The construction of the "package deals" indispensable during the GATT Rounds has only been possible because regime members have been willing to make often complex tradeoffs in the context of wide-ranging negotiations. (The reciprocity norm of course explicitly incorporates the notion of side payment or tradeoff.) Thus, the institutional and normative setting of the GATT regime has clearly facilitated the negotiation of commercial accords. The GATT has helped states to achieve important trade policy goals related to liberalization and the growth of trade by making it easier and less costly to reach concrete agreements.

For an international regime to exert a meaningful impact on the behavior of states, a pattern of compliance with regime prescriptions and proscriptions must be in evidence. In the case of the GATT regime, its evolving code of trade conduct has clearly constrained the policies of member governments, although there have of course been many violations of specific rules. It is impossible to know how many protectionist actions have *not* been undertaken because of the existence of GATT obligations, but it is not unreasonable to suggest that there may have been quite a few. It may be interesting to ask why states comply with GATT rules (or with those of other regimes). Obviously, calculations of self-interest are one crucial part of any explanation of compliance, but self-interest is by no means the only important factor at work. As Oran Young has ably demonstrated, factors such as a sense of obligation to other regime members, social pressures from these members, and the influence of habit and custom increase the likelihood of compliance with "behavioral prescriptions."[156] These have unquestionably been present during the GATT's history and have con-

[153] Robert Cox and Harold Jacobson, "Introduction," in Cox and Jacobson, eds., *The Anatomy of Influence,* pp. 5–6.

[154] See Keohane's article in this volume.

[155] Keohane also notes that this is a function of regimes.

[156] Oran R. Young, *Compliance and Public Authority: A Theory With International Applications* (Baltimore: Johns Hopkins University Press, 1979), pp. 18–25.

tributed to the ability of the regime to constrain the behavior of its members.[157] Many analysts have commented on the atmosphere of "cosy give-and-take" that prevails in the regime,[158] and this atmosphere has promoted policies of restraint on the part of governments. Although one should resist placing too much weight on such nebulous factors when seeking to explain the reasons for compliance with rules and constraint, to overlook the impact of habit or perceptions of mutual obligation would do a disservice to a rather fascinating aspect of the GATT.

Another way of examining how the GATT regime has contributed to the fulfillment of what we term the constraint function involves asking how the existence of the GATT's rules and norms affects governments' and bureaucratic actors' ability to bargain with opposing forces or actors favoring protectionist policies. John Jackson has noted that the simple fact that a country is a member of the GATT and thus has certain legal obligations provides its government with some useful "argumentative ammunition" when doing battle with domestic groups demanding trade restrictions.[159] "Governments can cite . . . established rules to counter parochial short-run interest group demands that in the long run might damage national and world economies."[160] It has also been suggested that the staging of a round of GATT trade negotiations allows governments to erect "a buffer against pressures for protectionism" while the bargaining proceeds.[161]

That a state has GATT obligations may also assist certain government officials to make a stronger case for constraint than would be possible in the absence of such obligations. Robert Hudec has observed that the GATT's legally articulated rules "add to the weight of those officials who decide to advocate the GATT policy position. In debate within the government there are limits to the force with which an official may advocate personal preferences or views. . . . Defence of an international rule commands more attention. . . ."[162] Evidence gathered in interviews tends strongly to confirm Hudec's contention that the existence of the GATT's many rules and norms has helped commercial policy officials in arguing in favor of constraint and adherence to GATT "law" within government councils.[163]

As is true of most areas of international relations, the largest and most powerful states in the GATT trade barrier regime have exercised a decisive influence over its evolution. Most observers link power within the GATT to the size of domestic markets to which improved access can be offered in a trade

---

[157] Interviews.

[158] Shonfield, "An Overall View," p. 126; Curzon, "GATT: Traders' Club," passim.

[159] Jackson, "Governmental Trade Disputes," p. 2.

[160] Jackson, "The Birth of the GATT-MTN System," p. 26.

[161] Evans, *Kennedy Round,* p. 318.

[162] Hudec, *Adjudication,* p. 36.

[163] Interviews with Canadian trade policy officials, September 1980, and with U.S. officials, November 1980.

bargaining context.[164] Since the early 1970s, the regime has been dominated by the "big three"—the U.S., the EEC, and Japan.[165] In spite of the undoubted power of the largest trading nations, one can plausibly argue that the existence of the GATT regulatory-consultative framework has given smaller regime members a greater opportunity to pursue their interests than would have been the case had no regime for this issue area come into being. For example, by ensuring that a high degree of "transparency" is attained insofar as members' trade policies are concerned, the regime has functioned in a way that clearly benefits weaker states that are unable to ferret out detailed commercial policy information on their own. By providing a standing institutional forum in which the weak may probe for information and press for changes in the policies of other states, the GATT has probably permitted such members to exert more influence over the regulation of international trade barriers than one would expect given their inferior position as trading powers. The GATT's norms and rules are of course largely the product of the preferences of the strong, but once established an international regime may well limit the policy freedom of those who originally created it. To a modest degree, this appears to be true in the case of the GATT. Further, as legal scholars frequently emphasize, the fact that international rules exist at all is likely to benefit the weak more than the powerful. Great powers typically have less to fear from the absence or decline in the integrity of international rules. "When rules break down, the bargaining advantage of those already rich and powerful may be significantly enhanced."[166] Finally, it should be mentioned that the extension of all negotiated tariff concessions and other trade barrier agreements to the entire GATT membership through the MFN obligation opens markets to smaller members unable to negotiate for such improved access themselves, although it is not clear that this increases their influence within the regime in any significant way.

By facilitating the conclusion of commercial accords, encouraging constraint on the part of members, and offering many smaller states a modest opportunity to influence the international regulation of trade barriers, the GATT regime has performed three important specific functions. Particularly insofar as the regime has functioned to increase the likelihood that trade agreements will be reached and to promote constraint, it has assisted in the performance of what we term the "promotion of interaction" function. The type of "interaction" that is "promoted" in the GATT is of course trade exchanges.

The basic *raison d'être* for the regime is the belief, shared by virtually all members, that the expansion of international trade flows benefits all states. Thus it does not seem unreasonable to suggest that the key function of the regime has been to promote such an expansion. But in order for the GATT to

---

[164] Curzon, "GATT: Traders' Club," pp. 325–26, for a discussion of influence in the GATT.
[165] Golt, *GATT Negotiations,* passim.
[166] *MTN Studies,* vol. 4, p. 7.

have played this role, its performance of the more narrowly conceived functions identified earlier had to yield significant results. Specifically, its sponsorship of multilateral deliberations had to lead to a reduction in trade barriers; and its encouragement of compliance had to promote a reduction of uncertainty in international trade relations. In fact, several analysts have suggested that uncertainty may well be the single most important trade barrier and thus its lessening, the major achievement of the GATT.

> Rules and regulations that serve to limit the uncertainty surrounding international transactions are . . . crucial . . . uncertainty is a highly effective non-tariff barrier to international trade, in particular because it discourages long-term investments whose profitability depends on secure access to foreign markets or on assured supplies of low-cost foreign inputs. The absence of observed international rules insuring stability . . . would stunt the contribution which other economic forces . . . can make to the growth of trade.[167]

By serving to promote constraint within the context of an evolving code of rules, the GATT has greatly contributed to the growth of trade—or the promotion of interaction.[168] In addition, a measure of predictability has been introduced into international trade relations by the fact that the resolution and avoidance of trade disputes has been a notable feature of the regime. A significant depoliticization of trade relations appears to have been one legacy of the GATT's existence. Whether the regime will continue to perform in an effective way the various functions discussed above is of course open to question. However, there can be little doubt that the GATT has had an important role in the evolution of postwar international trade relations.

---

[167] Blackhurst, Marian and Tumlir, "Trade Liberalization," p. 9.

[168] Between 1948 and 1973, the volume of world trade increased sixfold, growing at an average annual rate of 7%. This growth rate surpassed that of world production, which was also growing rapidly. Since 1973, growth rates have slowed, but trade has generally continued to expand faster than production. See ibid., pp. 7-19, and Richard Cooper, *The Economics of Interdependence* (New York: McGraw-Hill, 1968), chap. 3.

Balance-of-payments financing: evolution of a regime

Benjamin J. Cohen

In few areas of international economic relations has there been as much change in recent years as in the area of monetary relations. At the start of the 1970s, the international monetary system was still essentially that established at Bretton Woods, New Hampshire, a quarter of a century earlier. Exchange rates were still "pegged" within relatively narrow limits around declared par values. Currency reserves were still convertible, directly or indirectly, into gold at the central-bank level. And the main source of external financing for balance-of-payments deficits was still the International Monetary Fund (IMF).

A decade later, all that has changed. Exchange rates of major currencies are no longer pegged; they float. Currency reserves are no longer convertible into gold; they are inconvertible. And the main source of balance-of-payments financing is no longer the IMF but private banking institutions. The role of the private banks in international monetary relations has been greatly enhanced as a result of repeated increases in oil prices since 1973, which have generated enormous financing problems for many oil-importing countries (the petrodollar recycling problem). The recycling of the surplus earnings of OPEC countries, via bank credits and bond issues, to nations in balance-of-payments deficit has, in lieu of commensurate increases in financing from official sources, fallen primarily to private credit markets. As a result, the markets have come to play a role once reserved (in principle) exclusively for official institutions such as the Fund. As one former central banker has put it, "the private banking system took over the functions proper to an official institution possessed of the power to finance balance-

International Organization 36, 2, Spring 1982
0020-8183/82/020457-22 $1.50

of-payments disequilibria through credit-granting and to create international liquidity. . . . The function of creating international liquidity has been transferred from official institutions to private ones." [1]

Not that the practice of private lending for balance-of-payments purposes is entirely new. Even in the late 1960s, as much as one-third of all payments financing was intermediated by banking institutions between surplus countries (in those days, mainly countries of the Group of Ten) and deficit countries. But up to 1973, the private markets' role tended to be relatively modest. It was only with the emergence of the petrodollar recycling problem that the markets came into their own as an alternative source of payments financing. A special report to the OECD in 1977 (the McCracken Group Report) perhaps best described the development in historical perspective:

> The shift to increased reliance on private lenders for official financing purposes marked the culmination of a secular transformation of the process of liquidity creation. This transformation had already been going on for some time. Its roots lay in the development of the international financial markets—in particular, the growth of the Euro-dollar market—which gradually made it easier for governments to rely on private international financial intermediation rather than on the deficits of reserve centres to obtain new monetary reserves. The international markets act as worldwide financial intermediaries between the lenders and borrowers of loanable funds (including official as well as private lenders and borrowers). Private capital and the accumulated reserves of surplus countries flow into the market and then ultimately are lent on to countries in balance-of-payments difficulties. Increases of demand for credit in borrowing countries are financed by the markets, within the usual institutional and legal constraints, by borrowing or attracting deposits from the banking systems of surplus countries with available loanable funds. The events of 1974–76 simply confirmed and accelerated a trend in the process of liquidity creation that had been evident well before the oil price increases of 1973. [2]

This may be only a change of degree—but it is a change of degree so profound that it appears to border on a transformation of kind. This seeming transformation of the regime governing access to balance-of-payments financing is the subject of this article.

I shall first summarize the role of balance-of-payments financing in in-

---

[1] Guido Carli, *Why Banks Are Unpopular*, The 1976 Per Jacobsson Lecture (Washington: IMF, 1976), pp. 6, 8.

[2] *Towards Full Employment and Price Stability,* A Report to the OECD by a Group of Independent Experts, chaired by Paul McCracken (Paris: OECD, 1977), para. 159. In a still longer historical perspective, Charles Kindleberger has pointed out that—on an intermittent basis—private bankers at least since the Medici have made a practice of last-resort lending to governments at times of financial crisis; see his *Manias, Panics, and Crashes: A History of Financial Crises* (New York: Basic Books, 1978), chap. 10. Only with the growth of the Eurocurrency market, however, has balance-of-payments lending from private sources tended to become a *regular* practice.

ternational monetary relations, and then describe the key elements of the
financing regime that was established at Bretton Woods. Next, the evolution
of the regime will be analyzed, and I shall argue that no matter how profound
the regime's recent change may appear, it does not in fact add up to a transformation of kind. Rather, to borrow John Ruggie's phrase, it represents an
example of "norm-governed change." At the level of principles and norms,
the regime remains very much as it was. In the final two sections of the
article, I shall briefly consider what inferences may be drawn from the analysis regarding, first, the relationship between the financing regime and behavior; and second, the jurisdictional boundaries between this and other international economic regimes.

The role of financing

The regime for payments financing encompasses the set of implicit or
explicit principles, norms, rules, and decision-making procedures governing
access to external credit for balance-of-payments purposes. This is clearly a
very disaggregated notion of a substantive issue-area. In fact, payments
financing as an issue is firmly embedded in the broader question of balance-
of-payments adjustment (which in turn is embedded in the still broader
question of the structure and management of international monetary relations in general). My choice of issue-area for analysis is based on conve-
nience for a relatively narrow case study; it implies no claim regarding what
may or may not be the most appropriate level of aggregation for the study of
regimes in other international issue-areas.

Payments financing arises as an issue essentially because of the insistence of national governments on their sovereign right to create money. The
existence of separate national moneys requires some integrative mechanism
to facilitate economic transactions between states. In practical terms, this
function is performed by the foreign-exchange market, which is the medium
through which different national moneys are bought and sold. The basic role
of the foreign-exchange market is to transfer purchasing power between
countries—that is, to expedite exchanges between a local currency and
foreign currencies ("foreign exchange"). This role will be performed effectively so long as the demand for foreign exchange in any country (representing the sum of the demands of domestic importers, investors, and the
like, all of whom must normally acquire foreign currencies in order to consummate their intended transactions abroad) and the supply of foreign exchange (representing the sum of demands by foreigners for domestic goods,
services, and assets, which must be paid for with local currency) remain
roughly in balance at the prevailing price of foreign exchange—that is, so
long as the exchange market is in *equilibrium*. Difficulties arise when demand and supply do not tend toward balance at the prevailing price—that is,
when the market is in *disequilibrium*. Then, either the price of foreign ex-

change (the exchange rate) must be brought to a new equilibrium level or other actions must be taken or tolerated in order to remove or suppress the disequilibrium. This is the problem of balance-of-payments adjustment.

Structural adjustment

When confronted by a payments disequilibrium, national governments have two basic policy options. Either they may *finance* the disequilibrium, or they may *adjust* to it. Adjustment implies that the authorities are prepared to accept an immediate reallocation of productive resources (and hence of exchanges of real goods, services, and investments) through changes of relative prices, incomes, exchange rates, or some combination thereof. In effect, they are prepared to accept a reduction of domestic spending on goods, services, and investments (in technical terms, real domestic absorption) relative to national output (real national income). Financing, by contrast, implies that the authorities prefer to avoid an immediate reallocation of resources or a reduction of the ratio of real absorption to production by run-

> inflation

ning down their international monetary reserves or borrowing from external credit sources or both. Politics aside, decisions by individual governments regarding the preferred mix of these two options tend to reflect the comparative economic costs of each.

The economic costs of adjustment have both macroeconomic and microeconomic dimensions. At the macroeconomic level, there may be a decline in the overall level of employment of resources, an increase in the rate of price inflation, or both. At the microeconomic level, there may be a decline in the overall productivity of resources because of distortions introduced into the pattern of resource allocation, as well as frictional costs of the sort that occur whenever resources are reallocated. The magnitude of the costs of adjustment will depend not only on the macroeconomic and microeconomic conditions of the economy but also on the particular strategy of payments adjustment that is chosen—whether that strategy relies most heavily on income changes via variations of monetary policy and fiscal policy (expenditure-reducing policies), or on relative price changes via a modification of the exchange rate, or on direct restrictions on trade or capital movements (expenditure-switching policies). The distinguishing characteristic of adjustment costs is that they must be borne currently, whatever happens to the balance of payments in the future (even if subsequently the causes of the deficit should prove to have been transitory).

The costs of financing, by contrast, are borne not in the present but in the future, when monetary reserves must be replenished and foreign debts repaid. The country will then have to generate a greater net volume of exports to gain the requisite increment of foreign exchange. But until that time, no reduction of current absorption relative to production is required.

The choice between adjustment and financing thus reduces to a choice between reducing the absorption-production ratio today and reducing it tomorrow. Put differently, it reduces to a (necessarily subjective) evaluation of the present values of two different kinds of cost, one (the cost of adjustment) to be borne in the present and one (the cost of financing) in the future—a classic discounting problem.

For political and other reasons, governments often prefer to attach a rather high discount rate to future costs as compared with present costs; that is, they prefer to postpone nasty decisions for as long as possible. Consequently, the greater the level of their reserves or access to external credit or both, the greater is the risk that they may be tempted to alter their policy mix away from adjustment and toward financing—even in situations where an immediate reallocation of resources might be the more appropriate response. Thus it has long been felt that, on principle, governments ought not to enjoy unlimited access to balance-of-payments financing. That principle was formally incorporated into the design of the international monetary system established by a conference of forty-four allied nations at Bretton Woods in 1944.

The Bretton Woods system

The Bretton Woods conference represented the culmination of more than two years of planning, particularly in the Treasuries of Great Britain and the United States, for reconstruction of the monetary system after World War II. In agreeing on a charter for an entirely new international economic organization, the International Monetary Fund, the conferees in effect wrote a constitution for the postwar monetary regime—what later became known as the Bretton Woods system.[3]

Provision of supplementary financing

One of the cardinal principles established at Bretton Woods was that nations should be assured of an adequate supply of international liquidity. Since it was widely believed at the time that the interwar period had demonstrated (to use the words of one authoritative source) "the proved disadvantages of freely fluctuating exchanges,"[4] the conferees decided that countries should be obligated to declare a par value (a "peg") for their currencies and to intervene in the exchange market to limit fluctuations within relatively narrow margins. But since, at the same time, it was also widely recognized that exchange-market intervention "presupposes a large volume of . . . reserves for each single country as well as in the aggregate," the conferees agreed that there should be some "procedure under which international liquidity would be supplied in the form of prearranged borrowing facilities."[5] It was in order to ensure the availability of such supplementary financing that the IMF was created.

[3] Comprehensive histories of the wartime discussions and Bretton Woods conference can be found in J. Keith Horsefield, ed., *The International Monetary Fund, 1945–1965*, vol. 1: *Chronicle* (Washington: IMF, 1969), Part I; and Richard N. Gardner, *Sterling-Dollar Diplomacy* (Oxford: Clarendon Press, 1956), chaps. 5, 7.
[4] League of Nations, *International Currency Experience* (1944), p. 211.
[5] Ibid., pp. 214, 218.

Access to the IMF's resources, however, was not to be unlimited. On the contrary, access was to be strictly governed by a neatly balanced system of subscriptions and quotas. In essence, the Fund was created as a pool of national currencies and gold subscribed by each member country. Members would be assigned quotas, according to a rather complicated formula intended roughly to reflect each country's relative importance in the world economy, and would be obligated to pay into the Fund a subscription of equal amount. The subscription was to be paid 25 percent in gold or currency convertible into gold (effectively the U.S. dollar, which was the only currency still convertible directly into gold) and 75 percent in the member's own currency. In return, each member would be entitled, when short of reserves, to "purchase" (i.e., borrow) amounts of foreign exchange from the Fund in return for equivalent amounts of its own currency. Maximum purchases were set equal to the member's 25 percent gold subscription (its "gold tranche") plus four additional amounts each equal to 25 percent of its quota (its "credit tranches"), up to the point where the Fund's holdings of the member's currency would equal 200 percent of its quota.[6] (If any of the Fund's holdings of the member's initial 75% subscription in its own currency were to be borrowed by other countries, the member's borrowing capacity would be correspondingly increased: this was its "super-gold tranche.") The member's "net reserve position" in the Fund would equal its gold tranche (plus super-gold tranche, if any) less any borrowings by the country from the Fund. Net reserve positions were to provide the supplementary financing that the Bretton Woods conferees agreed was essential.[7]

Formally, within these quota limits, governments were little constrained in their access to Fund resources. The IMF charter simply provided that "the member desiring to purchase the currency [of another member] represents that it is presently needed for making in that currency payments which are consistent with the provisions of the Agreement"[8]—for example, that it "avoid competitive exchange depreciation" and that it "correct maladjustments in [its] balance of payments without resorting to measures destructive to national or international prosperity."[9] In short, the member would play by the agreed rules of the game. It was only with the passage of time that access to financing from the Fund came to be governed explicitly by what has become known as policy "conditionality."[10]

---

[6] Although the original Fund charter contained a provision prohibiting members in most circumstances from borrowing more than 25% of quota in any twelve-month period, in practice, as IMF operations evolved, this provision was frequently waived and was finally eliminated entirely in the Second Amendment of the Articles of Agreement of the IMF in 1976.

[7] As a result of the Second Amendment in 1976, gold was eliminated from the Fund system of subscriptions and quotas. In lieu of gold, members now subscribe Special Drawing Rights or national currencies; and in lieu of a gold tranche, members now have a reserve tranche.

[8] *Articles of Agreement of the International Monetary Fund,* Art. V., Section 3 (a) (i). The original Articles are reprinted in Horsefield, *The IMF,* vol. 3: *Documents,* pp. 185–214.

[9] *Articles of Agreement,* Art. I (iii) and (v).

[10] For the evolution of the concept of policy conditionality, see Horsefield, *The IMF,* vol. 2: *Analysis,* chaps. 18, 20, 21, 23; Joseph Gold, *Conditionality,* IMF Pamphlet Series, no. 31

As such, the word "conditionality" does not appear anywhere in the IMF Articles of Agreement. Indeed, in the Fund's early years, there was some question whether the organization even had a legal authority to make borrowing subject to conditions; and for a time debate raged over the issue. Very soon, however, as a result of accumulating experience and precedent, a recognized interpretation of the Fund's prerogatives did in fact emerge to govern members' access to credit. Two landmark decisions of the Fund's governing Board of Executive Directors[11] stand out in this connection. In the first, in 1948, the Board agreed that the IMF could challenge a member's request for finance on the grounds that *inter alia* it would not be "consistent with the provisions of the Agreement," and indeed that the Fund could "postpone or reject the request, or accept it subject to *conditions*."[12] In the second, in 1952, "conditions" were defined to encompass "policies the member will pursue . . . to overcome the [balance-of-payments] problem"[13]—in other words, policies that promise a genuine process of adjustment to external deficit. Since 1952, this has been the accepted meaning of the term "conditionality."

The 1952 decision was also important for establishing a practical distinction between a member's gold tranche and its four credit tranches, by ruling that borrowing in the gold tranche (plus the super-gold tranche, if any) would receive "the overwhelming benefit of any doubt."[14] Subsequent practice also created a distinction between a member's first credit tranche and its remaining ("upper") credit tranches, as summarized in the Fund's 1959 *Annual Report:*

> The Fund's attitude to requests for transactions within the first credit tranche . . . is a liberal one, provided that the member itself is also making reasonable efforts to solve its problems. Requests for transactions beyond these limits require substantial justification.[15]

Integral to the evolution of these distinctions were two further developments in IMF practice—stabilization programs and stand-by arrangements.

(Washington: IMF, 1979); Manuel Guitian, "Fund Conditionality and the International Adjustment Process: The Early Period, 1950–70," *Finance and Development* 17, 4 (December 1980), pp. 23–27; and Frank A. Southard Jr., *The Evolution of the International Monetary Fund,* Essays in International Finance, no. 135 (Princeton: Princeton University, International Finance Section, 1979), pp. 15–21.

[11] Formally, the Fund is governed by its Board of Governors, consisting of one Governor (usually the Finance Minister or central-bank Governor) from each member-country. However, since the Board of Governors only meets once a year, in practice most of its powers have been delegated to the Executive Board, which functions in continuous session. Executive Directors now (1981) number twenty-two, seven representing the five largest members of the Fund together with Saudi Arabia (one of the Fund's two largest creditors) and China, and fifteen representing various constituencies comprising collectively the remaining membership.

[12] Decision No. 284-4, 10 March 1948, reprinted in Horsefield, *The IMF,* 3:227. Italics supplied.

[13] Decision No. 102-(52/11), 13 February 1952, reprinted in Horsefield, *The IMF,* 3:228.

[14] Ibid., p. 230.

[15] IMF, *Annual Report,* 1959, p. 22.

Over the course of the 1950s, the Fund evolved a practical expression of policy conditionality in the form of stabilization programs, which members were obliged to submit when applying for financing in their credit tranches. Such a program may be quite comprehensive, covering monetary, fiscal, credit, and exchange-rate policies as well as trade and payments practices. In the case of a request in the first credit tranche, members may express their policy intentions at a relatively high level of generality. But for upper credit tranches, programs have to be correspondingly more precise and rigorous in design. Common to most stabilization agreements are, first, a "letter of intent" from the member-government to the Fund spelling out its program to correct its external deficit; and, second, the use of "performance criteria" to express, in quantitative terms, the policy objectives of its program.

Also over the course of the 1950s, the Fund evolved what has become one of the primary instruments used in applying policy conditionality—the stand-by arrangement. Under a stand-by, a member is assured of access to a specified amount of Fund resources for a fixed period of time under agreed conditions, without further consideration of the member's position beyond that provided for in the initial agreement. A key characteristic of most stand-bys is "phasing," which provides that specified amounts of finance will be made available at specified intervals during the stand-by period. At each interval the member's access to finance is made dependent on compliance with the performance criteria spelled out in its stabilization program. These criteria usually operate automatically to suspend (in Fund terminology, "interrupt") the member's access to finance if the policy objectives of its program are not being observed.[16]

Stand-bys normally originate from negotiations between a mission composed of officials of the Fund Secretariat, operating under the instructions of the Fund's Managing Director, and representatives of the member-government. From these negotiations, which may be quite protracted, a letter of intent emerges, usually signed by the member's Finance Minister or central-bank Governor (or both). The Fund Secretariat then, through a decision process involving both "area" departments (responsible for individual countries and regions) and "functional" departments (responsible for individual policy issues such as exchange and trade restrictions, fiscal or monetary policy, etc.), formulates the stand-by arrangement by reference to the letter of intent. That arrangement in turn is submitted by the Managing Director to the Executive Board for final approval. The Board then makes its decision, usually without benefit of a formal vote. If a formal vote is required, Executive Directors vote on behalf of all the members, with the vote of each member weighted in proportion to its individual quota.[17]

---

[16] For a model stand-by arrangement, see Joseph Gold, *Financial Assistance by the International Monetary Fund: Law and Practice,* IMF Pamphlet Series, no. 27 (Washington: IMF, 1979), Appendix B.

[17] For more on the Fund's decision-making procedures, see Horsefield, *The IMF,* 2, chap. 1; and Southard, *Evolution of IMF,* pp. 2–15.

The regime for payments financing embedded in the postwar Bretton Woods system can be readily summarized in terms of the four elements of the definition offered in the introduction to this volume.

Principles. The basic principle underlying the regime was that nations should be assured of an adequate but not unlimited supply of supplementary financing for balance-of-payments purposes. The principle was formally articulated in the IMF Articles of Agreement and backed by explicit organizational arrangements in the Fund.

Norms. Standards of behavior were defined in terms of formally articulated treaty rights and obligations accepted by each nation pursuant to its membership in the Fund. Rights consisted of access to IMF resources within quota limits. Obligations consisted of the general pledge to avoid policies inconsistent with the provisions of the IMF charter (i.e., to play by the agreed rules of the game).

Rules. Specific prescriptions or proscriptions for action derived from the Fund's prerogative of policy conditionality. Members' access to financing, particularly in the upper credit tranches, was subject to explicit conditions embodied in Fund stabilization programs and stand-by arrangements.

Decision-making procedures. Arrangements for determining the amount of financing to be made available and the policy conditions, if any, to be imposed in individual instances combined bargaining (in negotiations between the deficit country and the Fund), administrative decision making (within the Fund Secretariat) and, if necessary, voting (in the Executive Board).

Evolution of the regime

The regime remained relatively intact until barely more than a decade ago. What accounted for its creation and subsequent maintenance for more than a quarter of a century? And what then explains its dissipation and subsequent changes in the 1970s?

Creation

To a certain extent, creation of the postwar financing regime may be attributed to enlightened self-interest on the part of the forty-four nations represented at Bretton Woods. All understood the need for adequate liquidity in any exchange-rate regime other than a pure float. All remembered the so-called "gold shortage" of the 1920s—a by-product of extreme price inflation in almost all countries during and immediately after World War I, which had sharply reduced the purchasing power of monetary gold stocks (then still valued at their prewar parities). And all remembered the financial chaos of the 1930s that had ensued when Britain was forced to depart from the gold standard in 1931. None wanted to risk repeating any of that dismal history.

But all understood as well the need to set some upper limit on the availability of supplementary financing for balance-of-payments purposes. The question was, what form should that limit take?

Planning for the postwar monetary system was dominated by the two great reserve centers of the day, Great Britain and the United States. Prior to Bretton Woods the British government, in the person of John Meynard Keynes, had pushed hard for the establishment of an international clearing union endowed with some characteristics of a central bank and in particular, with authority to create a new international currency (''bancor'') for lending to countries in deficit. Access to financing, within very broad and flexible limits, would have been automatic and repayment would have followed only after the external imbalance had been reversed. But the Keynes plan was opposed by the American government—in particular, by the chief American negotiator, Harry Dexter White—as being excessively biased in favor of financing rather than adjustment. A much firmer limit on borrowing was needed, White felt: financing should be conditional rather than automatic, and repayment should be at a set time rather than indefinite.

The respective positions of the two governments reflected, in good measure, their national concerns. Britain, facing an enormous task of reconstruction, did not want to be hampered by an inability to finance prospective payments deficits. The United States, by contrast, potentially the largest creditor in the system, did not want in effect to write a blank check. For America, the problem was to avoid financing a massive ''giveaway'' of U.S. exports. For the U.K., the problem was to avoid constraints on the process of postwar recovery.

In the end, the American position prevailed—reflecting, of course, the predominant position of the United States among the allied nations during World War II. What was agreed at Bretton Woods was a compromise between the Keynes and White plans. But as one author has put it, ''the compromise contained less of the Keynes and more of the White plans.''[18] A contractarian route was used, in effect, to legitimate America's view of what constituted rectitude in monetary affairs. Supplementary financing would be made available to deficit countries, but only subject to strict quantitative limits and contingent upon appropriate policy behavior. Hence the Fund's neatly balanced system of subscriptions and quotas.

Only in one respect did the American position on borrowing not prevail at Bretton Woods, and that was on the issue of repayment. In a compromise with the British, the United States initially agreed to an ''automatic'' provision requiring members to repay credits only when their reserves were rising

[18] Sidney E. Rolfe, *Gold and World Power* (New York: Harper & Row, 1966), p. 78.

(with repayments normally to equal one-half the net increase of reserves in each year).[19] But not long thereafter (in 1952), under U.S. pressure, the Fund's Executive Board agreed to a more precise and rigorous temporal limit, requiring repayment within three to five years at the outside.[20] Thus here, too, America's view ultimately won out.

Maintenance

Two factors were principally responsible for the maintenance of the postwar financing regime in the 1950s and 1960s. On the demand side, the need for supplementary financing generally did not exceed what the IMF could provide. On the supply side, there were few alternative sources of financing to compete with the Fund or compromise its authority to exercise policy conditionality.

The demand side. Implicit in the original charter of the IMF was a remarkable optimism regarding prospects for monetary stability in the postwar era. Underlying the choice of a pegged-rate exchange regime seemed to be a clear expectation that beyond the postwar transition period (itself expected to be brief) payments imbalances would not be excessive. The pegged-rate regime was manifestly biased against frequent changes of exchange rates, reflecting the bitter memory of the 1930s, yet nations were left with few instruments under the charter other than capital controls to deal with external disturbances. Few of the conferees at Bretton Woods appeared to doubt that the new Fund's resources would be sufficient to cope with most financing problems.

As matters turned out, this optimism was not entirely justified, at least not in the near term. In fact, in the immediate postwar period monetary relations were anything but stable, and the Fund's resources were anything but sufficient. Most nations were too devastated by war—their export capacities damaged, their import needs enormous, their monetary reserves exhausted—to pay their own way; and their financing needs far exceeded what the IMF could offer. Consequently, the initial burden fell instead to the United States, which in the years 1946 to 1949 disbursed $26 billion through the Marshall Plan and other related aid programs for deficit countries. Fund lending, meanwhile, after a short burst of activity during its first two years, mainly to the benefit of European nations, shrank to an extremely low level. In 1950, the Fund made no new loans at all.[21]

By the mid 1950s, however, the situation had altered substantially.

---

[19] *Articles of Agreement*, Art. V, Section 7.

[20] See, e.g., Southard, *Evolution of IMF*, pp. 16–17.

[21] Inadequacy of resources was not the only reason for the Fund's meager contribution during these years. In addition, there was the running debate over conditionality, which was not finally resolved until the Executive Board's landmark 1952 decision. See Southard, *Evolution of IMF*, p. 17.

Economies had recovered from wartime destruction and reserve levels were increased by the U.S. balance-of-payments deficit (which averaged approximately $1.5 billion annually between 1950 and 1956). Thereafter, until the emergence of the petrodollar recycling problem in the 1970s, payments imbalances of most countries tended to be more manageable than formerly, and financing needs tended not to strain Fund resources unduly—particularly after 1962, when the Fund's potential lending authority was substantially augmented by negotiation of an arrangement with ten of its main industrial members (the "General Arrangements to Borrow") to borrow additional amounts of their currencies when necessary.[22] During these years, monetary relations corresponded much more closely than previously to the expectations of the conferees at Bretton Woods. And this in turn reinforced the regime that had been designed there.

The supply side. The regime was also reinforced by the absence of important alternative sources of balance-of-payments financing. Some alternative sources did exist, but none seriously threatened to undermine the central role of the Fund.

For example, from 1950 to 1958 the countries of Western Europe enjoyed access to a limited amount of payments financing through the European Payments Union.[23] Similarly, in the 1960s the larger industrial countries could avail themselves of short-term credit through the network of central-bank swap lines initiated by the American Federal Reserve System as well as through other special arrangements at the Bank for International Settlements (BIS) at Basle (e.g., the special stand-bys arranged for Great Britain between 1964 and 1968).[24] And of course a number of countries also had the standing to obtain a certain amount of financing in private credit markets via bank credits or bond issues. But none of these sources was ever posed as a competitor to conditional lending by the Fund. Indeed, most were designed to complement rather than to substitute for IMF credit.

The existence of these alternatives did, of course, bias the system somewhat in favor of the relatively small group of rich industrial countries able to take advantage of them. In effect, only the poorer countries of Europe and Third World nations were fully subject to the ostensible rules of the game. The richer countries had room for a certain amount of "cheating," by borrowing either from one another or (to a limited extent) from the private markets. But it should also be noted that the room for such cheating was not unlimited; witness the fact that Britain required $3.6 billion of IMF loans during the 1964–68 period, despite its access to other lines of credit through the Federal Reserve and the BIS. In any event, the most important of these al-

---

[22] The text of the arrangement is reprinted in Horsefield, *The IMF*, 3:246–56.

[23] For more detail on EPU, see Robert Triffin, *Europe and the Money Muddle* (New Haven: Yale University Press, 1957), chaps. 5–6.

[24] For more detail on the various support operations arranged for Britain during this period, see Benjamin J. Cohen, *The Future of Sterling as an International Currency* (London: Macmillan, 1971), pp. 97–98.

ternative sources of financing were still official rather than private, thus tending to ensure, in practice, no great inconsistency with Fund conditionality.

In fact, there was only one country at the time that truly had the capacity to avoid Fund conditionality through access to an alternative source of financing. That, ironically enough, was the principal author of the postwar regime, the United States, through the central role of the dollar in international monetary affairs. Because other countries, eager to build up their currency reserves, were largely prepared to accumulate America's surplus dollars (in effect, America's IOUs), the United States was for the most part freed from any balance-of-payments constraint to spend as freely as it thought necessary to promote objectives believed to be in its national interest. In brief, the United States could simply "liability-finance" its deficits. Not that this meant that America's "exorbitant privilege" (as Charles De Gaulle called it) necessarily exploited or disadvantaged others. In fact, as I have argued elsewhere, the element of mutual self-interest in this arrangement was very strong.[25] But it did mean that the regime was potentially vulnerable to abuse by the reserve center, and eventually, as we know, America's deficits did indeed become too great for the postwar system to bear.

Dissipation

With the emergence of the petrodollar recycling problem in the 1970s, changes occurred on both the demand side and the supply side to alter substantially the appearance of the postwar regime. On the demand side the need for supplementary financing expanded enormously, overwhelming what the IMF alone could provide, while on the supply side the private credit markets emerged as an increasingly important rival to the Fund as a source of such financing.

The demand side. Once oil prices began to rise in late 1973, it was clear that oil-importing countries as a group would for some time face extremely large current-account deficits in their relations with oil producers. Some of the largest members of OPEC simply could not increase their imports of goods and services as quickly as their revenues: their "absorptive capacity," at least in the short term, was too low. Accordingly, the balance of their earnings—their "investable surplus"—perforce would have to be invested in foreign assets or otherwise lent back to oil-importing nations as a group.[26] But since reflows of funds from OPEC could not be counted upon to

---

[25] Benjamin J. Cohen, *Organizing the World's Money* (New York: Basic Books, 1977), pp. 95–97.

[26] In fact, OPEC's absorptive capacity after the first round of oil price increases in 1973–74 surpassed expectations, and by 1978 its investable surplus (which averaged some $45 billion annually, 1974–76) had fallen to below $10 billion. But with the second round of price increases starting in late 1978, the surplus soared to $68 billion in 1979 and $112 billion in 1980. Most

match up precisely with the distribution of deficits among oil importers, some of the latter (industrialized as well as developing countries) were bound to find themselves in serious payments difficulties. The aggregate need of such countries for supplementary financing far exceeded what the IMF alone could provide.

The IMF tried, of course. What was needed, plainly, was not just an increase of quotas (which in fact occurred twice during the 1970s), but, even more importantly, an increase of members' access to Fund resources beyond the strict limit set by their quotas. Precedent for this already existed in two special facilities that had been created during the 1960s to help members cope with particular types of payments problems. The Compensatory Financing Facility was established in 1963 to assist countries, particularly producers and exporters of primary products, experiencing temporary shortfalls of export revenues for reasons largely beyond their own control. The Buffer Stock Financing Facility was established in 1969 to assist countries participating in international buffer-stock arrangements designed to stabilize the price of a specific primary product. Each of these two facilities initially permitted a member to borrow an amount equal to 50 percent of its quota over and above its regular credit tranches.[27]

Building on these precedents, the Fund in the 1970s erected several more special facilities in an effort to cope with its members' increased need for financing. These included a temporary one-year Oil Facility (1974), to help countries meet the initial balance-of-payments impact of higher oil prices; a second one-year Oil Facility (1975); an Extended Fund Facility (1974), to provide financing for longer periods (up to ten years) and in larger amounts (up to 140% of quota) for members experiencing "structural" balance-of-payments problems; a Trust Fund (1976), to provide special assistance to the Fund's poorest members (for up to ten years) out of the proceeds of sales of a portion of the Fund's gold holdings; and a Supplementary Financing Facility (1979), also known as the Witteveen facility, to provide extra credit to members experiencing very large deficits in relation to their quotas. By 1979, as a result of these initiatives, a country could in principle borrow as much as 467.5 percent of its quota, as compared with the 125 percent authorized under the original Articles of Agreement.[28]

But even this was not enough. Although the Fund found itself lending

---

observers expect this OPEC surplus to persist for much longer. See, e.g., Morgan Guaranty Trust Company, *World Financial Markets,* September 1980, pp. 1–13, and May 1981, pp. 3–5; *Citibank Monthly Economic Letter,* April 1981, pp. 5–6; IMF, *World Economic Outlook* (Washington, D.C., June 1981).

[27] More recently, the Compensatory Financing Facility has been liberalized to permit borrowings up to 100% of quota.

[28] For more detail on the Fund's various special facilities, see Gold, *Financial Assistance;* and *IMF Survey,* May 1981, "Supplement on the Fund," pp. 6–10. It should be noted that of these facilities, only three—the Compensatory Financing Facility, the Buffer Stock Financing Facility, and the Extended Fund Facility—represent *permanent* additions to the IMF's lending authority.

more money to more countries than ever before, the magnitude of deficits after 1973 was simply too great,[29] and much of what the Fund did was really a case of too little and too late. Deficit countries had to look elsewhere. What they found were the private credit markets.

The supply side. The increased role of the private markets as an alternative source of payments financing was a natural consequence of OPEC's comparatively low absorptive capacity. Insofar as the imports of the largest oil exporters failed to keep pace with their revenues, their investable surplus had to be placed somewhere; and the most attractive options were to be found in Western financial markets. Coincident with the weakening of domestic investment demand in industrialized countries, this in turn spurred Western banking institutions to search for new outlets for their greatly enhanced liquidity. Seemingly among the most attractive of such outlets were countries in need of supplementary financing for balance-of-payments purposes.

After 1973, accordingly, private lending to deficit countries increased enormously, primarily by way of bank credits or bonds issued in national or international (offshore) markets. Private banking institutions came to represent, in quantitative terms, the single most important source of payments financing in the world.[30] Not all countries were able to avail themselves of such financing, of course. Poorer less developed countries, lacking any standing at all in the markets, still had to rely on official bilateral or multilateral sources for most of their foreign borrowing. But for developing countries that were regarded by private lenders as sufficiently "creditworthy," as well as for most industrial countries, the bulk of external assistance now came from private sources. Much as in the manner of the United States after World War II, the markets took over from the IMF the main burden of providing supplementary financing for payments purposes.

The result appeared fundamentally to challenge the IMF's presumed role as final arbiter of access to such financing. Private banking institutions had neither the legal authority nor (usually) the inclination to make loans to sovereign governments subject to policy conditions. As a consequence, countries that were regarded by the markets as creditworthy were formally unconstrained in their access to financing, so long as they were willing and able to pay the going rate of interest. This created a danger that some countries might be tempted by the availability of such relatively "easy" (i.e., unconditional) financing to postpone painful—even if necessary— adjustment measures. Put differently, it suggested that the cardinal principle underlying the postwar financing regime—that governments ought not to enjoy unlimited access to balance-of-payments financing—might have been fatally compromised.

---

[29] For more detail, see Benjamin J. Cohen, *Banks and the Balance of Payments,* in collaboration with Fabio Basagni (Montclair, N.J.: Allenheld, Osmun, 1981), chap. 1.
[30] Ibid.

The danger was widely acknowledged. Said Wilfried Guth, a prominent German banker, in 1977: "The banks as today's main international creditors are unable to bring about by themselves a better balance between external adjustment and financing."[31] His sentiment was echoed by Arthur Burns, chairman of the Federal Reserve Board of Governors, who admitted that "Countries thus find it more attractive to borrow than to adjust their monetary and fiscal policies."[32] The problem was best summarized by the IMF:

> Access to private sources of balance-of-payments finance may . . . in some cases permit countries to postpone the adoption of adequate domestic stabilization measures. This can exacerbate the problem of correcting payments imbalances, and can lead to adjustments that are politically and socially disruptive when the introduction of stabilization measures becomes unavoidable.[33]

Nor was the danger merely hypothetical. In fact, the IMF was describing what actually came to pass in a number of individual instances. In Peru, for example, in 1976, at a time when the country's balance of payments was under severe pressure owing to plummeting prices for copper (a major Peruvian export) as well as to a mysterious disappearance of anchovy stocks from offshore waters (essential for fishmeal, another major Peruvian export), the government used a new $385 million syndicated bank credit to avoid painful adjustment measures, such as credit restraints or cutbacks of fiscal expenditures. The government even announced, less than a month after the credit was negotiated, plans to purchase $250 million worth of fighter-bombers from the Soviet Union. The result was further deterioration of Peru's external balance, domestic social and political unrest, and eventually stringent austerity measures when the government was finally obliged to adopt an effective stabilization program in 1978.[34]

Similar cases could be cited elsewhere, for example, in both Turkey and Zaïre after 1975. In these countries, access to market financing apparently encouraged the authorities to postpone needed adjustment measures, with consequences ultimately very much like those in Peru.

But not all countries yielded to the temptation to postpone needed adjustment measures. In fact, for any example such as Peru, one could cite a variety of counterexamples of countries that at one time or another used

---

[31] Wilfried Guth, in Guth and Sir Arthur Lewis, *The International Monetary System in Operation,* The 1977 Per Jacobsson Lecture (Washington: IMF, 1977), p. 25.

[32] Arthur F. Burns, "The Need for Order in International Finance," in *International Banking Operations,* Hearings before the Subcommittee on Financial Institutions Supervision, Regulation, and Insurance of U.S., Congress, House Committee on Banking, Finance and Urban Affairs (Washington, D.C., March-April 1977), p. 860.

[33] IMF, *Annual Report,* 1977, p. 41.

[34] For more detail on the Peruvian and other examples cited in this section, see Cohen, *Banks and the Balance of Payments,* chap. 4 and Appendix.

their access to market financing to underwrite immediate and effective actions to restore balance-of-payments equilibrium. Particularly impressive was the case of South Korea following the rise of oil prices in 1973 and the onset of recession in its principal export markets in the United States and Japan in 1974. While relying on borrowing in international credit markets to bridge a widening balance-of-payments gap, the Korean authorities instituted an intensive program of export promotion supplemented by a modest relaxation of monetary and fiscal policy to cushion the domestic impact of recession in foreign markets. In effect, market financing was used to give the economy a breathing space to reallocate resources to the export sector in a context of continuing real growth. Similar cases could be cited, such as Argentina in 1976 and Spain in 1977.

Still, little comfort could be drawn from such "success stories." As the Peruvian case demonstrated, the danger inherent in the availability of relatively "easy" financing from the markets was real—and no one was more aware of it than private banking institutions themselves. Certainly the banks recognized that it was not in their interest to make loans to any country that would do little to ensure its future capacity to service such debt. They had no wish to throw good money after bad, but the problem from their point of view was one of leverage. What, in practice, could they do to ensure that sovereign borrowers would indeed undertake policies that promised a genuine process of adjustment to external deficit?

Variations of terms on offer in the marketplace (e.g., a rise of interest rates or a shortening of maturities) seemed to have little influence on the policies of borrowing governments. As one central banker conceded, it was difficult to "regard this as more than a very marginal contribution to adjustment."[35] Potentially more effective might have been variations of *access* to the market (whatever the terms on offer)—that is, shifts in market sentiment regarding a sovereign borrower's creditworthiness. But the difficulty with that approach was that it might cut off a country's access to financing just when it was most needed. It was certainly not in the banks' interest to force a nation into outright default on its foreign debt.

An alternative approach might have been to exert discipline directly on a borrower through imposition of comprehensive policy conditions. In fact, this was attempted only once—in the syndicated credit to Peru in 1976, which was split into two installments, the first to be drawn immediately and the second in early 1977. Peru's creditors thought that they could ensure adherence to an effective stabilization program by establishing a system for continuous monitoring of the Peruvian economy and by making the second installment of their loan formally contingent upon satisfactory performance. The effort was unique. It was also a failure. In the end, when the loan's second installment came due, no delay was ever seriously mooted despite

[35] J. A. Kirbyshire, "Should Developments in the Euro-Markets be a Source of Concern to Regulatory Authorities?", *Bank of England Quarterly Bulletin* 17, 1 (March 1977), p. 44.

Peru's evident failure to meet its policy commitments. The banks, as private institutions, simply did not have the legal or political leverage to dictate policy directly to a sovereign government. Since that episode, they have not even tried.

Instead, private lenders have turned increasingly to the IMF, the one lender that, as a multilateral institution backed by formal treaty commitments, *does* have such legal and political leverage. In a growing number of instances, where doubts have developed regarding a country's prospective policy stance, borrowers have been told to go to the IMF first: formally or informally, new financing from the markets has been made contingent upon negotiation of a satisfactory stabilization program with the Fund. As a result, the Fund has come to play a role as a de facto certifier of creditworthiness in the markets—the official issuer of an unofficial "Good Housekeeping Seal of Approval."[36] As one banker has said: "Conditional credit from the Fund is increasingly viewed as an 'international certificate of approval' which enhances the ability of a country to borrow in the private market place."[37] The procedure is favored by lenders because of the Fund's high professional standards, access to confidential information, and—above all—recognized right to exercise policy conditionality. The procedure is acceptable to the Fund because, in effect, it "gears up" the IMF's own lending while ensuring that new financing in such cases will indeed be used to support a well-conceived process of adjustment.

To this extent, therefore, the Fund's role as arbiter of access to financing has been preserved: for countries whose creditworthiness comes into doubt, it is still the Fund that formally imposes specific prescriptions or proscriptions for action. This suggests that the change in the regime is really less than it first appears.

That profound change has occurred is clear. At the level of decision-making procedures, the amounts or conditions of lending are in most instances no longer a matter for negotiation solely between the authorities of a country and the IMF. Now a third set of actors is often prominently involved—private banking institutions. And in the many instances where a borrower's policy stance has not come into doubt, the IMF may not be involved at all. To that extent the Fund's monitoring role has indeed been eroded.[38] Nonetheless, I would argue that this falls short of a transformation of kind.

[36] See, e.g., Giovanni Magnifico, "The Real Role of the IMF," *Euromoney*, October 1977, pp. 141–44; Charles Lipson, "The IMF, Commercial Banks, and Third World Debts," in Jonathan David Aronson, ed., *Debt and the Less Developed Countries* (Boulder, Col.: Westview Press, 1979); and Carl R. Neu, "The International Monetary Fund and LDC Debt," in Lawrence G. Franko and Marilyn J. Seiber, eds., *Developing Country Debt* (New York: Pergamon Press, 1979).

[37] Richard D. Hill, in *International Debt,* Hearings before the Subcommittee on International Finance of U.S., Congress, House Committee on Banking, Housing and Urban Affairs (Washington, D.C., 1977), p. 127.

[38] There seems little to be done to reverse this erosion, at least by way of formal reforms, without losing the acknowledged benefits of private lending for balance-of-payments purposes. See Cohen, *Banks and the Balance of Payments,* pp. 171–76.

In the first place, just as the practice of private lending for balance-of-payments purposes is itself not entirely new, neither is the role of the Fund as informal certifier of creditworthiness in the markets. Even as far back as the 1950s, cases could be cited where an IMF stabilization program proved the key to unlocking supplementary financing from private sources.[39] Admittedly, use of that procedure prior to 1973 was relatively infrequent. Still, the very fact that it existed at all suggests that there has been more of an element of continuity in the financing regime than might have been thought.

Even more importantly, there has been a strong element of continuity in the basic principles and norms underlying the regime. The idea that deficit countries ought not to enjoy unlimited access to balance-of-payments financing has not been fatally compromised; nor have commonly agreed standards of behavior been significantly altered. Rather, what has happened is that all the key players—governments, banking institutions, the IMF— have made operational adaptations to the changed circumstances on both the demand and the supply sides of the system. True, as a result norms and rules have tended to become somewhat less formally articulated than before; decision-making procedures have become more ambiguous; and the room for cheating (for countries with unquestioned creditworthiness) now is greater than it used to be. But these are changes of degree only—"norm-governed changes," once again to borrow Ruggie's phrase. The important point is that all players, even while making their operational adaptations, still acknowledge the fundamental need to play by the rules of the game. In its maintenance of a balance of recognized rights and obligations for deficit countries, the financing regime remains very much the same as before. In its deeper tenets, it has not in fact changed.

The relationship between regime and behavior

What conclusions may we draw, from this stylized sketch of the evolution of the postwar financing regime, regarding the relationship between the regime and behavior?

At the time of its creation, it is clear, the regime was the product not of actual behavior but rather of other, endogenous factors—in particular, the experiences of the interwar period and World War II. The interwar experience had generated a broad consensus in favor of establishing some kind of mechanism to provide limited amounts of supplementary payments financing. World War II had confirmed the economic and political predominance of the United States. The fact that a regime emerged from Bretton Woods at all reflected the allies' collective perception of self-interest in monetary affairs. The specific shape of that regime reflected largely the individual concerns and influence of the United States.

[39] See, e.g., Peter B. Kenen, *Giant Among Nations* (New York: Harcourt, Brace, 1960), pp. 93–94.

Moreover, over the next quarter of a century, it was mostly the regime that influenced behavior rather than the reverse. Deficit countries, with the important exception of the United States, did in fact generally respect IMF policy conditionality when availing themselves of supplementary payments financing—although, to be sure, this reflected conditions on both the demand and the supply sides of the system as much as it did the influence of the regime as such. Governments played by the formal rules agreed at Bretton Woods not only because they were legally committed to do so by an international agreement but also because their need for supplementary financing did not in general exceed what the IMF could provide and because there were few alternative sources of financing to compete with the Fund. Maintenance of the regime in the 1950s and 1960s was attributable as much to the general absence of either need or means to circumvent the regime as it was to the enlightened self-interest of nations.

Conversely, when conditions changed dramatically in the 1970s, so did behavior. The vast increase in the need for financing led countries to search for new sources of external credit; the vast increase of liquidity in financial markets led banking institutions to search for new customers. The result was a profound change in the appearance of the regime as the markets emerged as a major alternative source of financing for deficit countries. No longer did the IMF stand alone as arbiter of access to payments support.

But this cannot be regarded as a transformation of kind. Owing to the informal working relationship that has gradually developed between the IMF and the markets whereby private lenders, in cases of serious payments difficulties, treat negotiation of a Fund stand-by (with attendant policy conditionality) as a prerequisite for lending, the basic principle underlying the regime as well as commonly agreed standards of behavior for deficit nations have, for the most part, been preserved. While rules and decision-making procedures admittedly have become somewhat vaguer than they were, and for some countries the room for cheating has been increased, these changes have been for the most part "norm-governed" in character. In its essential purpose, the financing regime continues to have a real effect on behavior.

Jurisdictional boundaries of the regime

Finally, it is of interest to consider the impact of recent events on the jurisdictional boundaries of the financing regime.

Originally, a very clear division of labor was intended to distinguish the work of the IMF from that of its sister organization created at Bretton Woods, the World Bank (formally, the International Bank for Reconstruction and Development). The mandate of the Fund was to lend for relatively short periods of time to help maintain international payments equilibrium. The mandate of the Bank was to lend for much longer periods to help support postwar economic recovery and, subsequently, economic development in poorer countries. The regime to govern access to IMF financing was firmly embedded in the broader question of balance-of-payments adjustment. The regime to govern access to Bank financing was firmly embedded in the broader question of development assistance.

More recently, however, as a result of repeated increases in world oil prices since 1973, the line dividing the Fund's mandate from the Bank's has grown rather more ambiguous. In fact, the Fund has come under a great deal of pressure to extend increased amounts of credit to deficit countries—particularly in the Third World—for longer periods and with more flexible policy conditions.[40] In an era of persistent OPEC surpluses, it is argued, deficits in nonoil developing countries cannot be treated simply as a short-term phenomenon caused by faulty domestic policies and amenable to traditional policy prescriptions (e.g., devaluation or monetary and fiscal restraint). Oil-induced deficits perforce must be expected to continue for much longer periods, until such time as the nations involved can make the necessary "structural" adjustments to the altered relative cost of energy. In the meantime, the Fund should make a greater effort to supplement private lending by reforms of its own lending policies, such as making more money available for longer-term, structural measures to narrow net dependence on oil imports and to broaden the foreign-exchange earning capacity of deficit countries.

To some extent, the Fund has tried to respond to these pressures. In 1979, the Executive Board issued a new set of guidelines on policy conditionality explicitly acknowledging that adjustment in many cases might require a longer period of time than traditionally assumed in Fund stabilization programs, and pledging to "pay due regard to . . . the circumstances of members, including the causes of their balance of payments problems."[41] And in 1980 and 1981 a new policy of "enlarged access" to the Fund's resources was brought formally into effect, along with a 50 percent increase of all members' quotas. Under the new policy, the maximum amount that a country may in principle cumulatively borrow from the Fund has been raised from 467.5 percent of its quota to 600 percent.[42] In addition, an increasing

---

[40] See, e.g., Group of 24, *Outline for a Program of Action on International Monetary Reform*, reprinted in *IMF Survey*, 15 October 1979, pp. 319–23; *North-South: A Programme for Survival*, Report of the Independent Commission on International Development Issues, chaired by Willy Brandt (Cambridge: MIT Press, 1980), chap. 13; and Sidney Dell and Roger Lawrence, *The Balance of Payments Adjustment Process in Developing Countries* (New York: Pergamon Press, 1980). I have associated myself with this point of view in Benjamin J. Cohen, "Balancing the System in the 1980s: Private Banks and the IMF," in Gary Clyde Hufbauer, ed., *The International Framework for Money and Banking in the 1980s* (Washington: International Law Institute, 1981).

[41] See *IMF Survey*, 19 March 1979, pp. 82–83; and Gold, *Conditionality*, pp. 14–37.

[42] In practice the limit is even higher, since the 600% figure does not take into account loans from either the Compensatory Financing Facility or the Buffer Stock Financing Facility. See *IMF Survey*, May 1981, "Supplement on the Fund," p. 10. The first country to borrow up to this new maximum was Turkey, in June 1980. See *IMF Survey*, 25 June 1980, p. 177. The IMF had never previously lent more than 400% of a member's quota.

proportion of Fund lending is now being directed through the Extended Fund Facility, thus making available more financing for longer periods of time than had generally been available in the past.

However, as these changes have been carried out, the Fund has found itself moving closer to the traditional province of the World Bank—just as, simultaneously, the Bank has been moving the other way. Also under pressure to do more for countries hit hard by the increased relative cost of energy, the Bank in 1979 began to shift from its usual emphasis on long-term project lending to more, relatively short-term, program lending for "structural adjustment" purposes. The object of such lending, in the words of a senior Bank official, is "to provide support for member countries already in serious BOP [balance-of-payments] difficulties, or faced in the years ahead with the prospect of unmanageable deficits arising from external factors which are not likely to be easily or quickly reversed."[43] This sounds remarkably similar to the IMF's explanations of its own lending policies.

In fact, we are witnessing a partial convergence of the roles of the Fund and the Bank—that is, a partial overlapping of the regimes governing access to payments financing and development assistance. Here, in the blurring of the jurisdictional boundary between these two regimes, is perhaps the most significant impact of the events of the 1970s. In the 1980s it will be increasingly difficult to maintain a clear distinction between these two forms of lending.

[43] E. Peter Wright, "World Bank Lending for Structural Adjustment," *Finance and Development,* September 1980, p. 21.

Cave! hic dragones:
a critique of regime analysis

Susan Strange

The purpose of this relatively brief article is rather different from that of others in this volume. Instead of asking what makes regimes and how they affect behavior, it seeks to raise more fundamental questions about the questions. In particular, it queries whether the concept of regime is really useful to students of international political economy or world politics; and whether it may not even be actually negative in its influence, obfuscating and confusing instead of clarifying and illuminating, and distorting by concealing bias instead of revealing and removing it.

It challenges the validity and usefulness of the regime concept on five separate counts. These lead to two further and secondary (in the sense of indirect), but no less important, grounds for expressing the doubt whether further work of this kind ought to be encouraged by names as well-known and distinguished as the contributors to this volume. The five counts (or "dragons" to watch out for) are first, that the study of regimes is, for the most part a fad, one of those shifts of fashion not too difficult to explain as a temporary reaction to events in the real world but in itself making little in the way of a long-term contribution to knowledge. Second, it is imprecise and woolly. Third, it is value-biased, as dangerous as loaded dice. Fourth, it distorts by overemphasizing the static and underemphasizing the dynamic element of change in world politics. And fifth, it is narrowminded, rooted in a state-centric paradigm that limits vision of a wider reality.

Two indirect criticisms—not so much of the concept itself as of the

The title translates as "Beware! here be dragons!"—an inscription often found on pre-Columbian maps of the world beyond Europe.

International Organization 36, 2, Spring 1982
0020-8183/82/020479-18 $1.50

tendency to give it exaggerated attention—follow from these five points. One is that it leads to a study of world politics that deals predominantly with the status quo, and tends to exclude hidden agendas and to leave unheard or unheeded complaints, whether they come from the underprivileged, the disfranchised or the unborn, about the way the system works. In short, it ignores the vast area of nonregimes that lies beyond the ken of international bureaucracies and diplomatic bargaining. The other is that it persists in looking for an all-pervasive pattern of political behavior in world politics, a "general theory" that will provide a nice, neat, and above all simple explanation of the past and an easy means to predict the future. Despite all the accumulated evidence of decades of work in international relations and international history (economic as well as political) that no such pattern exists, it encourages yet another generation of impressionable young hopefuls to set off with high hopes and firm resolve in the vain search for an El Dorado.

Not wishing, however, to be entirely destructive, I conclude the article by suggesting an alternative and, to my mind, more valuefree, more flexible, and more realistic approach to the study of what I take to be everyone's underlying concern—which is, "Where (and how) do we go from here?" This approach is both to the "left" of most of the other contributors and to the "right" of some who would call themselves liberal internationalists.

It is to the "left" of the majority in that it starts from a frankly structuralist perception of the international system (in the sense in which Marxists and neomarxists use the word structuralist). This does not mean the political system dominated by territorial states but the structure of a world economy in which the relationships between those states are largely determined by the relations of production and the other prevalent structural arrangements for the free movement between states of capital, knowledge, and goods (but not labor) that make up a world market economy.

And it is to the "right"—as they would see it—of most liberal internationalists in that it is skeptical of the achievements to be expected of international organizations and collective decision making, that is, it is realist in the sense of continuing to look to the state and to national governments as the final determinants of outcomes.

 ## Five criticisms of the concept of regimes

 ### A passing fad?

The first of my dragons, or pitfalls for the unwary, is that concern with regimes may be a passing fad. A European cannot help making the point that concern with regime formation and breakdown is very much an American academic fashion, and this is reflected in the fact that all the other contributors to this volume work in American universities. They share a rather striking common concern with the questions posed about regimes. A comparable group in Europe—or in most other parts of the world, I would suggest—would have more diverse concerns. Some would be working on questions of moral philosophy, some on questions of historical interpretation. (Europeans generally, I would venture to say, are more serious in the attention they pay to historical evidence and more sensitive to the possibilities of divergent interpretations of "facts.") Europeans concerned with matters of strategy and security are usually not the same as those who write about structures affecting economic development, trade, and money, or with the prospects for particular regions or sectors. Even the future of Europe itself never dominated the interests of so large a group of scholars in Europe as it did, for a time, the American academic community. Perhaps Europeans are not generalist enough; perhaps having picked a field to work in, they are inclined to stick to it too rigidly. And conversely, perhaps Americans are more subject to fads and fashions in academic inquiry than Europeans, more apt to conform and to join in behind the trendsetters of the times. Many Europeans, I think, believe so, though most are too polite to say it. They have watched American enthusiasm wax and wane for systems analysis, for behavioralism, for integration theory, and even for quantitative methods indiscriminately applied. The fashion for integration theory started with the perceived U.S. need for a reliable junior partner in Europe, and how to nurture the European Communities to this end was important. The quantitative fashion is easily explained by a combination of the availability of computer time and the finance to support it and of the ambition of political scientists to gain as much kudos and influence with policy makers as the economists and others who had led the way down the quantitative path. Further back we can see how international relations as a field of study separate from politics and history itself developed in direct response to the horrors of two world wars and the threat of a third. And, later, collective goods theories responded to the debates about burden-sharing in NATO, just as monetarism and supply-side economics gained a hearing only when the conditions of the 1970s cast doubts on Keynesian remedies for recession, unemployment, and inflation.

The current fashion for regimes arises, I would suggest, from certain, somewhat subjective perceptions in many American minds. One such perception was that a number of external "shocks," on top of internal troubles like Watergate and Jimmy Carter, had accelerated a serious decline in American power. In contrast to the nationalist, reactionary response of many Reaganites, liberal, internationalist academics asked how the damage could be minimized by restoring or repairing or reforming the mechanisms of multilateral management—"regimes." A second subjective perception was that there was some sort of mystery about the uneven performance and predicament of international organizations. This was a connecting theme in Keohane and Nye's influential *Power and Interdependence,* which struck responsive chords far and wide.

But the objective reality behind both perceptions was surely far less dramatic. In European eyes, the "decline" arises partly from an original overestimation of America's capacity to remake the whole world in the image of the U.S.A. In this vision, Washington was the center of the system, a kind of keep in the baronial castle of capitalism, from which radiated military, monetary, commercial, and technological as well as purely political channels carrying the values of American polity, economy, and society down through the hierarchy of allies and friends, classes and cultural cousins, out to the ends of the earth. The new kind of global empire, under the protection of American nuclear power, did not need territorial expansion. It could be achieved by a combination of military alliances and a world economy opened up to trade, investment, and information.

This special form of nonterritorial imperialism is something that many American academics, brought up as liberals and internationalists, find it hard to recognize. U.S. hegemony, while it is as nonterritorial as Britain's India in the days of John Company or Britain's Egypt after 1886, is still a form of imperialism. The fact that this nonterritorial empire extends more widely and is even more tolerant of the pretensions of petty principalities than Britain was of those of the maharajahs merely means that it is larger and more secure. It is not much affected by temporary shocks or setbacks. Yet Americans are inhibited about acknowledging their imperialism. It was a Frenchman who titled his book about American foreign policy *The Imperial Republic*.[1]

Moreover, Americans have often seemed to exaggerate the "shocks" of the 1970s and the extent of change in U.S.-Soviet or U.S.-OPEC relations. Nobody else saw the pre-1971 world as being quite so stable and ordered as Americans did. Certainly for Third-Worlders, who had by then lived through two or three recent cycles of boom and slump in the price of their country's major exports—whether coffee, cocoa, tin, copper, sugar or bananas—plus perhaps a civil war and a revolution or two, the "oil-price shock" was hardly the epoch-making break with the stable, comfortable, predictable past that it seemed to many Americans. If one has been accustomed for as long as one can remember to national plans and purposes being frustrated and brought to nothing by exogenous changes in the market, in technology or in the international political situation between the superpowers—over none of which your own government has had the slightest control—then a bit more disorder in a disorderly world comes as no great surprise.

To non-American eyes therefore, there is something quite exaggerated in the weeping and wailing and wringing of American hands over the fall of the imperial republic. This is not how it looks to us in Europe, in Japan, in Latin America or even in the Middle East. True, there is the nuclear parity of the Soviet Union. And there is the depreciated value of the dollar in terms of gold, of goods, and of other currencies. But the first is not the only factor in the continuing dominant importance to the security structure of the balance

---

[1] Raymond Aron, *The Imperial Republic: The U.S. and the World, 1945–1973* (Englewood Cliffs, N.J.: Prentice-Hall, 1974).

of power between the two superpowers, and the second is far more a sign of the abuse of power than it is of the loss of power. The dollar, good or bad, still dominates the world of international finance. Money markets and other markets in the United States still lead and others still follow; European bankrupts blame American interest rates. If the authority of the United States appears to have weakened, it is largely because the markets and their operators have been given freedom and license by the same state to profit from an integrated world economy. If Frankenstein's monster is feared to be out of control, that looks to non-Americans more like a proof of Frankenstein's power to create such a monster in the first place. The change in the balance of public and private power still leaves the United States as the undisputed hegemon of the system.[2]

To sum up, the fashion for regime analysis may not simply be, as Stein suggests,[3] a rehash of old academic debates under a new and jazzier name—a sort of intellectual mutton dressed up as lamb—so that the pushy new professors of the 1980s can have the same old arguments as their elders but can flatter themselves that they are breaking new ground by using a new jargon. It is also an intellectual reaction to the objective reality.

In a broad, structuralist view (and using the broader definition of the term) of the structures of global security, of a global credit system, of the global welfare system (i.e., aid and other resource transfers) and the global knowledge and communications system, there seems far less sign of a falling-off in American power. Where decline exists, it is a falling-off in the country's power and will to intervene with world market mechanisms (from Eurodollar lending to the grain trade) rather than significant change in the distribution of military or economic power to the favor of other states. Such change as there is, has been more internal than international.

The second subjective perception on the part of Americans that I wish to address is that there is some mystery about the rather uneven performance in recent times of many international arrangements and organizations. While some lie becalmed and inactive, like sailing ships in the doldrums, others hum with activity, are given new tasks, and are recognized as playing a vital role in the functioning of the system. I would personally count the GATT, FAO, and UNESCO in the first group, the World Bank and the regional banks, the BIS, and IMCO in the second. The IMF holds a middle position: it has largely lost its universal role but has found an important but more specialized usefulness in relation to indebted developing countries.

The mixed record of international organizations really does need explaining. But Americans have been curiously reluctant, to my mind at least,

---

[2] For a more extended discussion of this rather basic question, see my "Still an Extraordinary Power," in Ray Lombra and Bill Witte, eds., *The Political Economy of International and Domestic Monetary Relations* (Ames: Iowa State University Press, 1982); James Petras and Morris Morley, "The U.S. Imperial State," mimeo (March 1980); and David Calleo, "Inflation and Defense," *Foreign Affairs* (Winter 1980).

[3] See Arthur Stein's article in this volume, p. 116.

to distinguish between the three somewhat different purposes served by international organizations. These can broadly be identified as *strategic* (i.e., serving as instruments of the structural strategy and foreign policy of the dominant state or states); as *adaptive* (i.e., providing the necessary multilateral agreement on whatever arrangements are necessary to allow states to enjoy the political luxury of national autonomy without sacrificing the economic dividends of world markets and production structures); and as *symbolic* (i.e., allowing everybody to declare themselves in favor of truth, beauty, goodness, and world community, while leaving governments free to pursue national self-interests and to do exactly as they wish).

In the early postwar period, most international organizations served all three purposes at once. They were strategic in the sense that they served as instruments of the structural strategies of the United States. Also, they were often adaptive in that they allowed the United States and the other industrialized countries like Britain, Germany, France, and Japan to enjoy both economic growth and political autonomy. Finally, many organizations were at the same time symbolic in that they expressed and partially satisfied the universal yearning for a "better world" without doing anything substantial to bring it about.

In recent years the political purposes served by institutions for their members have tended to be less well balanced; some have become predominantly strategic, some predominantly adaptive, and others predominantly symbolic. This has happened because, where once the United States was able to dominate organizations like the United Nations, it can no longer do so because of the inflation of membership and the increasing divergence between rich and poor over fundamentals. Only a few organizations still serve U.S. strategic purposes better than bilateral diplomacy can serve them; they are either top-level political meetings or they deal with military or monetary matters in which the U.S. still disposes of predominant power. In other organizations the tendency toward symbolism, expressed in a proliferation of Declarations, Charters, Codes of Conduct, and other rather empty texts, has strengthened as the ability to reach agreement on positive action to solve real global problems has weakened. This applies especially to the United Nations and many of its subsidiary bodies, to UNCTAD, IDA, and many of the specialized agencies. The one growth area is the adaptive function. The integration of the world economy and the advance of technology have created new problems, but they also have often enlarged the possibility of reaching agreement as well as the perceived need to find a solution. Such predominantly adaptive institutions are often monetary (IBRD, IFC, BIS) or technical (ITU, IMCO, WMO).

Imprecision

The second dragon is imprecision of terminology. "Regime" is yet one more woolly concept that is a fertile source of discussion simply because people mean different things when they use it. At its worst, woolliness leads to the same sort of euphemistic Newspeak that George Orwell warned us would be in general use by 1984. The Soviet Union calls the main medium for the suppression of information *Pravda* (Truth), and refers to the "sovereign independence of socialist states" as the principle governing its relations with its East European "partners." In the United States scholars have brought "interdependence" into general use when what they were describing was actually highly asymmetrical and uneven dependence or vulnerability. In the same way, though more deliberately, IBM public relations advisers invented and brought into general and unthinking use the term "multinational corporation" to describe an enterprise doing worldwide business from a strong national base.

Experience with the use of these and other, equally woolly words warns us that where they do not actually mislead and misrepresent, they often serve to confuse and disorient us. "Integration" is one example of an overused word loosely taken to imply all sorts of other developments such as convergence as well as the susceptibility of "integrated" economies to common trends and pressures—a mistake that had to be painstakingly remedied by careful, pragmatic research.[4]

In this volume, "regime" is used to mean many different things. In the Keohane and Nye formulation ("networks of rules, norms and procedures that regularize behavior and control its effects") it is taken to mean something quite narrow—explicit or implicit internationally agreed arrangements, usually executed with the help of an international organization—even though Keohane himself distinguishes between regimes and specific agreements. Whereas other formulations emphasize "decision-making procedures around which actors' expectations converge," the concept of regime can be so broadened as to mean almost any fairly stable distribution of the power to influence outcomes. In Keohane and Nye's formulation, the subsequent questions amount to little more than the old chestnut, "Can international institutions change state behavior?" The second definition reformulates all the old questions about power and the exercise of power in the international system. So, if—despite a rather significant effort by realist and pluralist authors to reach agreement—there is no fundamental consensus about the answer to Krasner's first question, "What is a regime?", obviously there is not going to be much useful or substantial convergence of conclusions about the answers to the other questions concerning their making and unmaking.

Why, one might ask, has there been such concerted effort to stretch the elasticity of meaning to such extremes? I can only suppose that scholars, who by calling, interest, and experience are themselves "internationalist" in aspiration, are (perhaps unconsciously) performing a kind of symbolic ritual against the disruption of the international order, and do so just because they

[4] Yao-so Hu, *Europe under Stress* (forthcoming).

are also, by virtue of their profession, more aware than most of the order's tenuousness.

c. Value bias

The third point to be wary of is that the term regime is value-loaded; it implies certain things that ought not to be taken for granted. As has often happened before in the study of international relations, this comes of trying to apply a term derived from the observation of national politics to international or to world politics.

Let us begin with semantics. The word "regime" is French, and it has two common meanings. In everyday language it means a diet, an ordered, purposive plan of eating, exercising, and living. A regime is usually imposed on the patient by some medical or other authority with the aim of achieving better health. A regime must be recognizably the same when undertaken by different individuals, at different times, and in different places. It must also be practised over an extended period of time; to eat no pastry one day but to gorge the next is not to follow a regime. Nor does one follow a regime if one eats pastry when in Paris but not in Marseilles. Those who keep to a diet for a day or two and abandon it are hardly judged to be under the discipline of a regime.

Based on the same broad principles of regularity, discipline, authority, and purpose, the second meaning is political: the government of a society by an individual, a dynasty, party or group that wields effective power over the rest of society. Regime in this sense is more often used pejoratively than with approval—the "ancien regime," the "Franco regime," the "Stalin regime," but seldom the "Truman" or "Kennedy" regime, or the "Attlee" or "Macmillan," the "Mackenzie King" or the "Menzies" regime. The word is more often used of forms of government that are inherently authoritarian, capricious, and even unjust. Regimes need be neither benign nor consistent. It may be (as in the case of Idi Amin, "Papa Doc" Duvallier or Jean-Bedel Bokassa) that the power of the regime is neither benign nor just. But at least in a given regime, everyone knows and understands where power resides and whose interest is served by it; and thus, whence to expect either preferment or punishment, imprisonment or other kinds of trouble. In short, government, rulership, and authority are the essence of the word, not consensus, nor justice, nor efficiency in administration.

What could be more different from the unstable, kaleidoscopic pattern of international arrangements between states? The title (if not all of the content) of Hedley Bull's book, *The Anarchical Society,* well describes the general state of the international system. Within that system, as Bull and others have observed, it is true that there is more order, regularity of behavior, and general observance of custom and convention than the pure realist expecting the unremitting violence of the jungle might suppose. But by and large the world Bull and other writers describe is characterized in all its main outlines not by discipline and authority, but by the absence of government, by the precariousness of peace and order, by the dispersion not the concentration of authority, by the weakness of law, and by the large number of unsolved problems and unresolved conflicts over what should be done, how it should be done, and who should do it.

Above all, a single, recognized locus of power over time is the one attribute that the international system so conspicuously lacks.

All those international arrangements dignified by the label regime are only too easily upset when either the balance of bargaining power or the perception of national interest (or both together) change among those states who negotiate them. In general, moreover, all the areas in which regimes in a national context exercise the central attributes of political discipline are precisely those in which corresponding international arrangements that might conceivably be dignified with the title are conspicuous by their absence. There is no world army to maintain order. There is no authority to decide how much economic production shall be public and how much shall be privately owned and managed. We have no world central bank to regulate the creation of credit and access to it, nor a world court to act as the ultimate arbiter of legal disputes that also have political consequences. There is nothing resembling a world tax system to decide who should pay for public goods—whenever the slightest hint of any of these is breathed in diplomatic circles, state governments have all their defenses at the ready to reject even the most modest encroachment on what they regard as their national prerogatives.

The analogy with national governments implied by the use of the word regime, therefore, is inherently false. It consequently holds a highly distorting mirror to reality.

Not only does using this word regime distort reality by implying an exaggerated measure of predictability and order in the system as it is, it is also value-loaded in that it takes for granted that what everyone wants is more and better regimes, that greater order and managed interdependence should be the collective goal. Let me just recall that in an early paper at the very outset of this whole project, the editor asked these questions:

"Was the 1970s really a period of significant change? Was it an interregnum between periods of stability? Does it augur a collapse or deterioration of the international economic system? Did the system accommodate massive shocks with astonishing ease or were the shocks much less severe than has been thought?

"These," he went on, "are perplexing questions without obvious answers, for the answers to these questions are related *to the most fundamental concern of social theory: how is order established, maintained and destroyed?*"[5]

Krasner's common question here is about order—not justice or effi-

---

[5] Stephen D. Krasner, "Factors Affecting International Economic Order: A Survey," mimeo (July 1979), the earliest draft of his introductory article to this volume.

ciency, nor legitimacy, nor any other moral value. In an international political system of territorial states claiming sovereignty within their respective
territories, how can order be achieved and maintained?

The questions people ask are sometimes more revealing of their perceptions of what is good or bad about a situation and of their motives, interests,
fears, and hopes than the answers they give. Yet there is a whole literature
that denies that order is "the most fundamental concern" and that says that
the objectives of Third World policy should be to achieve freedom from
dependency and to enhance national identity and freer choice by practicing
"uncoupling" or delinking or (yet another woolly buzz-word) by "collective
self-reliance."

Now, these ideas may be unclear and half-formed. But in view of the
Islamic revival and the newfound self-confidence of several newly industrialized countries (NICs), it would be patently unwise for any scholar to
follow a line of inquiry that overlooks them. Let us never forget the folly of
League of Nations reformers, busily drafting new blueprints while Hitler and
Mussolini lit fires under the whole system. Should we not ask whether this
too does not indicate an essentially conservative attitude biased toward the
status quo. Is it not just another unthinking response to fear of the consequences of change? Yet is not political activity as often directed by the desire to achieve change, to get more justice and more freedom from a system, as it is by the desire to get more wealth or to assure security for the
haves by reinforcing order?

d. Too static a view

The fourth dragon to beware is that the notion of a regime—for the
semantic reasons indicated earlier—tends to exaggerate the static quality of
arrangements for managing the international system and introducing some
confidence in the future of anarchy, some order out of uncertainty. In sum, it
produces stills, not movies. And the reality, surely, is highly dynamic, as can
fairly easily be demonstrated by reference to each of the three main areas for
regimes considered in this collection: security, trade, and money.

For the last thirty-five years, the international security regime (if it can
be so called), described in this volume by Jervis, has not been derived from
Chapter VII of the U.N. Charter, which remains as unchanged as it is irrelevant. It has rested on the balance of power between the superpowers. In
order to maintain that balance, each has engaged in a continuing and es-
calating accumulation of weapons and has found it necessary periodically to
assert its dominance in particular frontier areas—Hungary, Czechoslovakia,
and Afghanistan for the one and South Korea, Guatemala, Vietnam, and El
Salvador for the other. Each has also had to be prepared when necessary
(but, fortunately, less frequently) to engage in direct confrontation with the
other. And no one was ever able to predict with any certainty when such

escalation in armaments, such interventions or confrontations were going to be thought necessary to preserve the balance, nor what the outcome would be. Attempts to "quick-freeze" even parts of an essentially fluid relationship have been singularly unsuccessful and unconvincing, as witness the fate of the SALT agreements, the European Security Conference, and the Non-Proliferation Treaty.

In monetary matters, facile generalizations about "the Bretton Woods regime" abound—but they bear little resemblance to the reality. It is easily forgotten that the orginal Articles of Agreement were never fully implemented, that there was a long "transition period" in which most of the proposed arrangements were put on ice, and that hardly a year went by in the entire postwar period when some substantial change was not made (tacitly or explicitly) in the way the rules were applied and in the way the system functioned. Consider the major changes: barring the West European countries from access to the Fund; providing them with a multilateral payments system through the European Payments Union; arranging a concerted launch into currency convertibility; reopening the major international commodity and capital markets; finding ways to support the pound sterling. All these and subsequent decisions were taken by national governments, and especially by the U.S. government, in response to their changing perceptions of national interest or else in deference to volatile market forces that they either could not or would not control.

Arrangements governing international trade have been just as changeable and rather less uniform. Different principles and rules governed trade between market economies and the socialist or centrally planned economies, while various forms of preferential market access were practiced between European countries and their former colonies and much the same results were achieved between the United States and Canada or Latin America through direct investment. Among the European countries, first in the OEEC and then in EFTA and the EC, preferential systems within the system were not only tolerated but encouraged. The tariff reductions negotiated through the GATT were only one part of a complex governing structure of arrangements, international and national, and even these (as all the historians of commercial diplomacy have shown) were subject to constant revision, reinterpretation, and renegotiation.

The trade "regime" was thus neither constant nor continuous over time, either between partners or between sectors. The weakness of the arrangements as a system for maintaining order and defining norms seems to me strikingly illustrated by the total absence of continuity or order in the important matter of the competitive use of export credit—often government guaranteed and subsidized—in order to increase market shares. No one system of rules has governed how much finance on what terms and for how long can be obtained for an international exchange, and attempts to make collective agreements to standardize terms (notably through the Berne Union) have repeatedly broken down.

The changeable nature of all these international arrangements behind the blank institutional facade often results from the impact of the two very important factors that regime analysis seems to me ill-suited to cope with: technology and markets. Both are apt to bring important changes in the distribution of costs and benefits, risks and opportunities to national economies and other groups, and therefore to cause national governments to change their minds about which rules or norms of behavior should be reinforced and observed and which should be disregarded and changed.

Some of the consequences of technological change on international arrangements are very easily perceived, others less so. It is clear that many longstanding arrangements regarding fishing rights were based on assumptions that became invalid when freezing, sonar, and improved ship design altered the basic factors governing supply and demand. It is also clear that satellites, computers, and video technology have created a host of new problems in the field of information and communication, problems for which no adequate multilateral arrangements have been devised. New technology in chemicals, liquid natural gas, nuclear power, and oil production from under the sea—to mention only a few well-known areas—is dramatically increasing the risks involved in production, trade, and use. These risks become (more or less) acceptable thanks to the possibility of insuring against them. But though this has political consequences—imposing the cost of insurance as a kind of entrance tax on participation in the world market economy—the fact that no structure or process exists for resolving the conflicts of interest that ensue is an inadequately appreciated new aspect of the international system.

Technology also contributes to the process of economic concentration, reflected in the daily dose of company takeovers, through the mounting cost of replacing old technology with new and the extended leadtime between investment decisions and production results. Inevitably, the economic concentration so encouraged affects freedom of access to world markets and thus to the distributive consequences in world society. The nationalist, protectionist, defensive attitudes of states today are as much a response to technical changes and their perceived consequences as they are to stagnation and instability in world markets.

Since the chain of cause and effect so often originates in technology and markets, passing through national policy decisions to emerge as negotiating postures in multilateral discussions, it follows that attention to the end result—an international arrangement of some sort—is apt to overlook most of the determining factors on which agreement may, in brief, rest.

The search for common factors and for general rules (or even axioms), which is of the essence of regime analysis, is therefore bound to be long, exhausting, and probably disappointing. Many of the articles in this volume abound in general conclusions about regimes, their nature, the conditions favoring their creation, maintenance, and change, and many of the generalizations seem at first reading logically plausible—but only if one does not examine their assumptions too closely. My objection is that these assumptions are frequently unwarranted.

State-centeredness

The final but by no means least important warning is that attention to these regime questions leaves the study of international political economy far too constrained by the self-imposed limits of the state-centered paradigm. It asks, what are the prevailing arrangements discussed and observed among governments, thus implying that the important and significant political issues are those with which governments are concerned. Nationally, this is fairly near the truth. Democratic governments have to respond to whatever issues voters feel are important if they wish to survive, and even the most authoritarian governments cannot in the long run remain indifferent to deep discontents or divisions of opinion in the societies they rule. But internationally, this is not so. The matters on which governments, through international organizations, negotiate and make arrangements are not necessarily the issues that even they regard as most important, still less the issues that the mass of individuals regards as crucial. Attention to regimes therefore accords to goverments far too much of the right to define the agenda of academic study and directs the attention of scholars mainly to those issues that government officials find significant and important. If academics submit too much to this sort of imperceptible pressure, they abdicate responsibility for the one task for which the independent scholar has every comparative advantage, the development of a philosophy of international relations or international political economy that will not only explain and illuminate but will point a road ahead and inspire action to follow it.

Thus regime analysis risks overvaluing the positive and undervaluing the negative aspects of international cooperation. It encourages academics to practice a kind of analytical *chiaroscuro* that leaves in shadow all the aspects of the international economy where no regimes exist and where each state elects to go its own way, while highlighting the areas of agreement where some norms and customs are generally acknowledged. It consequently gives the false impression (always argued by the neofunctionalists) that international regimes are indeed slowly advancing against the forces of disorder and anarchy. Now it is only too easy, as we all know, to be misled by the proliferation of international associations and organizations, by the multiplication of declarations and documents, into concluding that there is indeed increasing positive action. The reality is that there are more areas and issues of nonagreement and controversy than there are areas of agreement. On most of the basic social issues that have to do with the rights and responsibilities of individuals to each other and to the state—on whether abortion, bribery, drink or drug pushing or passing information, for example, is a crime or not—there is no kind of international regime. Nor is there a regime on many of the corresponding questions of the rights and responsibilities of states toward individuals and toward other states.

In reality, furthermore, the highlighted issues are sometimes less important than those in shadow. In the summer of 1980, for example, INMARSAT announced with pride an agreement on the terms on which U.S.-built satellites and expensive receiving equipment on board ship can be combined to usher in a new Future Global Maritime Distress and Safety System, whereby a ship's distress call is automatically received all over a given area by simply pressing a button. For the large tankers and others who can afford the equipment, this will certainly be a significant advance; not so for small coasters and fishing boats. In the same year, though, millions died prematurely through lack of any effective regime for the relief of disaster or famine. Meanwhile, the Executive Directors of the International Money Fund can reach agreement on a further increase in quotas, but not on the general principles governing the rescheduling of national foreign debts.

Moreover, many of the so-called regimes over which the international organizations preside turn out under closer examination to be agreements to disagree. The IMF amendments to the Articles of Agreement, for example, which legitimized the resort to managed floating exchange rates, are no more than a recognition of states' determination to decide for themselves what strategy and tactics to follow in the light of market conditions. To call this a "regime" is to pervert the language. So it is to call the various "voluntary" export restrictive arrangements bilaterally negotiated with Japan by other parties to the GATT "a multilateral regime." Since 1978 the Multi-Fibre "Agreement," too, has been little more, in effect, than an agreement to disagree. Similarly, UNESCO's debate on freedom and control of information through the press and the media resulted not in an international regime but in a bitter agreement to disagree.

One good and rather obvious reason why there is a rather large number of issues in which international organizations preside over a dialogue of the deaf is simply that the political trend within states is towards greater and greater intervention in markets and greater state responsibility for social and economic conditions, while the major postwar agreements for liberal regimes tended the other way and bound states to negative, noninterventionist policies that would increase the openness of the world economy.

In a closely integrated world economic system, this same trend leads to the other aspect of reality that attention to regimes obscures, and especially so when regimes are closely defined, in this volume by Young and others, as being based on a group of actors standing in a characteristic relationship to each other. This is the trend to the transnational regulation of activities in one state by authorities in another, authorities that may be, and often are, state agencies such as the U.S. Civil Aeronautics Authority, the Department of Justice or the Food and Drug Administration. There is seldom any predictable pattern of "interaction" or awareness of contextual limitations to be found in such regulation.

Other neglected types of transnational authority include private bodies like industrial cartels and professional associations or special "private" and semiautonomous bodies like Lloyds of London, which exercises an authority delegated to it by the British government. This club of rich "names," underwriters, and brokers presides over the world's largest insurance and reinsurance market, and consequently earns three-quarters of its income from worldwide operations. By converting all sorts of outlandish risks into costs (the premiums on which its income depends), Lloyds plays a uniquely important part in the smooth functioning of a world market economy.

By now the limits on vision that may be encouraged as a secondary consequence of attention to regimes analysis have been implied. The aspects of political economy that it tends to overlook constitute the errors of omission that it risks incurring. I do not say that, therefore, *all* regime analyses commit these errors of omission; I can think of a number that have labored hard to avoid them. But the inherent hazard remains. They should not have to labor so hard to avoid the traps, and if there is a path to bypass them altogether it should be investigated.

I shall suggest where this path might be discovered after a word about the second indirect reason for skepticism about the value of regime analysis. This is that it persists in the assumption that somewhere there exists that El Dorado of social science, a general theory capable of universal application to all times and places and all issues, which is waiting to be discovered by an inspired, intrepid treasure-hunter. I confess I have never been convinced of this; and the more I know of political economy, the more skeptical I become. If (as so many books in international relations have concluded) we need better "tools of analysis," it is not because we will be able to dig up golden nuggets with them. Those nuggets—the great truths about human society and human endeavor—were all discovered long ago. What we need are constant reminders so that we do not forget them.

Outline of a better alternative

My alternative way of analyzing any issue of international political economy, which is likely to avoid some of these dragons, involves extending Charles Lindblom's useful clarifying work on *Politics and Markets* to the world system. Whether one chooses to apply it to sectors of the world economy or to the structures of that system, it suggests many much more open-ended and value-free questions about the relationship between authorities and markets and about the outcomes of their interaction than does regime analysis.

It thus allows serious questions to be posed for research or discussion about any issue, whether they are of interest to governments or not. Moreover, it does not take markets as part of the data, but accepts that they are creations of state policies—policies that affect transactions and buyers and sellers, both directly and indirectly, through the part played by markets in shaping basic structures of the world system such as the security structure, the production structure, the trade and transport structure, the credit and money structure, the communication and knowledge structure, and (such as it is) the welfare structure.

It involves asking a series of questions, none of which in any way pre-judges the answers. It is therefore equally adaptable to the concerns and interests of conservatives and radicals, to scholars far to the right or far to the left, or to those who want only to move more freely in the middle ground between extremes.

Not only does it liberate inquiry from the procrustean limits set by ideology, it also breaks the confining limits set when regime analysis identifies an international regime with the existence of a particular interna-tional agency or bureaucracy. Patients often abandon a regime but do not feel it necessary to eliminate the doctor; international institutions are seldom wound up, however useless. Indeed, the continued existence of the "doc-tors" on the international scene and the fairly widespread abandonment of regular regimes by the "patients" seems to me precisely what has been hap-pening in the international political economy in the latter half of the 1970s. There has been a rather marked shift from multilateral arrangements around which actors' expectations (more or less) converged toward bilateral proce-dures, negotiations, and understandings.

This shift took place in the security structure, as Jervis explains, at a relatively early date in recognition of the limited distribution of capacity to wreak global destruction by nuclear weapons and delivery systems. It can be seen gathering speed from Cuba and SALT I onwards and spilling over in the 1970s into other issues such as food. Moreover, on one important aspect of the security structure, the sale or transfer of arms to other states, there never have been any effective multilateral arrangements. Bargains have always been bilateral.

This bilateralism in security matters has recently become common in other fields. In trade, for example, the most recent report from the GATT had this to say:

> While the rules of the GATT continue to exert considerable influence on policy conduct, there is no denying that infractions and circumventions of them have tended to multiply. . . . That there has not been more open violence to the rules is also partly explained by the increasing resort to privately agreed and officially tolerated if not promoted, restraints on trade and competition. Developments in such important industrial sec-tors as steel, automobiles, synthetic fibres and perhaps other pet-rochemicals exemplify this tendency.[6]

In matters of investment for future production, too, the most notable

---

[6] GATT, *International Trade 1980–81* (Geneva: GATT, 1981), p. 11.

achievements of recent years have not come through multilateral or general processes but through an aggregation of a great deal of piecemeal bargaining. Most of the key bargains have been struck between governments (and not only governments of developing countries) and large manufacturing or processing enterprises, some state-owned, some private, some syndicates of both. Since these arrangements will radically affect future relations of production in the world economy and the relative economic prospects of states and their governments, they cannot be ignored with impunity.

Thus, asking what are the key bargains that have been made—or could conceivably be made in the future—and how they have affected outcomes will reveal rather more about the real levers of power in the system than attention to regimes. For in that system, now that transnational transactions have become so important, three points are worth noting. First, the bargaining partners often dispose of very different kinds of power; for example, one has the political power to refuse access to a market, the other the power to refuse to transfer technology. Second, each of them is vulnerable to a different kind of risk, as it might be of a palace revolution on one side or a corporate takeover on the other. So that, thirdly, the bargain struck is apt to consist of a highly variable mix of political and economic benefits conferred and opportunities opened up. Bargains will reflect both the positive goals the parties severally wish to achieve and the negative risks and threats from which they want to find some security.

In trying to draw a map of interlocking, overlapping bargains the researcher will often be drawn far beyond the conventional limits of international politics or international economics. Most likely, the map will have to include bargaining situations and their outcomes within national political economies. To illustrate the point, take Cohen's examination in this volume of the international monetary regime. He interprets this almost exclusively as concerning the regulation of exchange rate behavior. Yet his own most recent work (*Banks and the Balance of Payments*)[7] implicitly acknowledges the fundamental importance of (national) banking regulation in shaping the world's monetary system. He would probably agree that the major change in the 1970s was not the rather marginal shift from intermittently flexible fixed rates to generally managed floating rates but rather the shift in the balance of influence in international capital markets from public authorities and agencies to private operators—a shift reflected in the changing debt patterns of most NOPEC countries.

Drawing bargaining maps will therefore reveal the domestic roots of international arrangements, and tell us more about what is likely to be permanent and what will probably prove ephemeral about them.

Whether the purpose is analytical description or normative prescription, the exercise will also leave far more open the question of what values the

---

[7] Benjamin J. Cohen with Fabio Basagni, *Banks and the Balance of Payments: Private Lending in the International Adjustment Process* (Montclair, N.J.: Allenheld Osmun, 1981).

existing pattern of bargaining has produced or what values might conceivably emerge from future patterns of bargaining. Paying more attention to values would raise our vision above the horizons set by governments and their (often limited and shortsighted) perceptions of national interest; it would allow us to include those perceived by classes, generations, and other transnational or subnational social groups. The bias of regime analysis can be corrected by attention to the determining basic structures of the international political economy, the structures of security, money, welfare, production, trade, and knowledge. Each of these raises the question, "How to achieve change?", which is surely no less important than the question, "How to keep order?"

The *dynamic* character of the "who-gets-what" of the international economy, moreover, is more likely to be captured by looking not at the regime that emerges on the surface but underneath, at the bargains on which it is based. By no means all of these key bargains will be between states. For besides those between states and corporate enterprises, or between corporations and banks, there will be others between corporations and labor unions, or between political groups seeking a common platform on which to achieve political power. Having analyzed the factors contributing to change in bargaining strength or weakness, it will be easier then to proceed to look at the outcome with less egocentric and value-biased eyes.

What is the net result and for whom, in terms of order and stability, wealth and efficiency, justice and freedom; and in terms of all the opposite qualities—insecurity and risk, poverty and waste, inequity and constraint? These, it seems to me, are much more fundamental political questions, and imply an altogether broader and less culture-bound view of world politics, than the ones addressed in this volume.

Regimes and the limits of realism: regimes as autonomous variables

Stephen D. Krasner

Two realist views: billiard balls and tectonic plates

In an area of study that is not, properly speaking, a discipline and lacks agreement on what questions should be addressed and what methodology is acceptable, fads are endemic. The concept of regimes may fall within this category. It is compatible with a number of postwar Grotian formulations, such as functionalism, neofunctionalism, linkage politics, and trans-nationalism, as well as the "idealism" of the interwar period, that have channeled attention for a time but failed to launch a sustained attack on conventional structural realist perspectives. These conceptualizations have, in Ronald Rogowski's felicitous turn of phrase about another set of arguments, gradually retired "into a kind of 'old theories' home, where the senile relict . . . receives the distant veneration of the extended family and the unwilling visits of the graduate-student young."[1] The notion of regimes may well suffer the same fate.

However, what distinguishes the regime concept as it has been used in this volume from its most obvious lineage is that it has attracted a number of scholars who have been primarily identified with the realist tradition. What accounts for this?

One answer is that during the 1970s scholars working from a realist per-spective developed an alternative to the conventional billiard ball model with its focus on zero-sum state interaction. This alternative image, suggested by the metaphor of tectonic plates, shared with the more conventional approach the fundamental assumptions of a realist structural paradigm: an inter-

---

[1] Ronald Rogowski, "Rationalist Theories of Politics: A Midterm Report," *World Politics* 30, 2 (January 1978), p. 306.

International Organization 36, 2, Spring 1982
0020-8183/82/020497-14 $1.50

national system composed of egoistic sovereign states differentiated only by their power capabilities. In both images, outcomes are a function of the distribution of power in the system. However, the first is concerned solely with the political interactions among states; the second, with the impact of the distribution of state power on various international environments.

The first tradition is encapsulated in the billiard ball metaphor. The international system is composed solely of states. There is no external environment (the billiard table is ignored). States are interested in maximizing their power. Power is a relative concept. One state's increase in power capabilities inevitably decreases the capability of others.[2] The world is zero-sum. States only act to structure nonpolitical behavior if this would enhance their relative power capability. Economic policy, for instance, is not an end in itself; it is a device for enhancing the power of the state. The analysis of Nazi policy towards east and central Europe during the 1930s by Hirschman and the discussions of investment policy by Feis and Staley reflect this tradition.[3] In such a world there is no room for international regimes unless one accepts Young's concept of imposed regimes. The billiard ball approach dominated international relations scholarship through the 1960s, when security concerns and Soviet-American relations were the center of attention.

The second realist tradition envisions a more complicated universe. Here the issue is the impact of the distribution of state power on some external environment. The interaction of states may, for instance, structure the pattern of world trade, the distribution of radio frequencies, the use of outer space, or the rules governing the exploitation of deep seabed nodules. Conflict is not ignored, but the world is not zero-sum. In some areas the objectives sought by states are unaffected by the utilities achieved by other actors. Relative power capabilities are not the only state objective; economic wealth, for instance, could be an end in itself. Richard Rosecrance has recently suggested that the proper analogy for international relations in the economic literature is not microanalysis of markets but pure trade theory. Here there is an opportunity for mutual gain from international exchange so long as comparative advantage is present, but the division of benefits may vary over a range of real relative prices.[4] The opportunity to realize these gains may be a function of the ability to create effective regimes.

However, outcomes related to either regimes or behavior ultimately

---

[2] One exception is the additional acquisition of nuclear weapons in a world of assured second-strike capability. See Robert Jervis, "Why Nuclear Superiority Doesn't Matter," *Political Science Quarterly* 94, 4 (Winter 1979–80).

[3] Albert Hirschman, *National Power and the Structure of Foreign Trade* (Berkeley: University of California Press, 1981); Herbert Feis, *Europe The World's Banker, 1870–1914* (New York: Norton, 1965); Eugene Staley, *War and the Private Investor: A Study in the Relations of International Politics and International Private Investment* (Garden City, N.Y.: Doubleday, Doran, 1935).

[4] Richard Rosecrance, "International Theory Revisited," *International Organization* 35, 4 (Autumn 1981), pp. 705–706.

remain a function of the distribution of power among states. The most common proposition is that hegemonic distributions of power lead to stable, open economic regimes because it is in the interest of a hegemonic state to pursue such a policy and because the hegemon has the resources to provide the collective goods needed to make such a system function effectively. The analyses in this volume by Keohane, Stein, and Jervis extend this argument by emphasizing the conditions that provide incentives for states other than the hegemon to accept cooperative policies.

Within the framework of this analysis, there need not always be congruity between power distributions and related behavior and outcomes. A change in power distributions does not always imply a change in outcomes because regimes may function as intervening variables. Regimes may assume a life of their own, a life independent of the basic causal factors that led to their creation in the first place. There is not always congruity between underlying power capabilities, regimes, and related behavior and outcomes. Principles, norms, rules, and procedures may not conform with the preferences of the most powerful states. Ultimately state power and interests condition both regime structures and related behavior, but there may be a wide area of leeway.

This line of argument suggests the importance of periodization and uneven rates of change. Causal relationships may vary across periods of regime creation, persistence, and dissipation. Regime creation usually occurs at times of fundamental discontinuity in the international system, such as the conclusions of major wars. When regimes are first created there is a high degree of congruity between power distributions and regime characteristics: powerful states establish regimes that enhance their interests. But over time the two can drift apart. In general the basic principles and norms of regimes are very durable and, once a regime is created, adjustment is likely to involve altering rules and decision-making procedures. But power distributions are more dynamic—they are constantly changing. Thus, regimes and power distributions are not likely to change at the same rate. Over time incongruities develop. If these incongruities become too severe, there is likely to be revolutionary change as those with the greatest power capabilities move to change underlying principles and norms.

The appropriate metaphor for this perspective is not billiard balls but tectonic plates. One plate can be envisioned as the distribution of power among states, the other as regimes and related behavior and outcomes. Pressures between the plates vary over time. When regimes are first created there is little pressure. Over time pressure develops at the interface of the plates as they move at different rates. These pressures may be relieved by imperceptible incremental movements, but often the pressures build. The higher the level of incongruity, the more dramatic the ultimate earthquake that finally realigns the plates. Lenin's discussion of uneven growth and North's arguments about lateral pressure, as well as the structural realist arguments discussed in this volume, share this image of the relationship between dynamic power capabilities and more static resources and regimes.[5]

This tectonic plate image of the international system helped adherents of the realist position to explain a practical puzzle: why did things not fall apart during the 1970s? Most adherents of the realist approach have maintained that the power of the United States declined. To some extent this is manifest in overall power capabilities but, more pertinently, it is related to a decline in relative resources in specific issue-areas. Oil is the most obvious but, as the essays on trade and monetary affairs in this volume point out, the loss of power has extended to a range of issue-areas. The hegemonic argument, most common in the literature, contends that a decline in hegemonic power will lead to increasing disorder. While the 1970s have hardly been placid, there has not been a general collapse of the world economic system. Outcomes have changed, especially in oil, but many patterns of behavior have endured. Regimes offer one way to account for the persistence of behavior and outcomes even though basic causal factors associated with political power have changed.[6] Once regimes are established they assume a life of their own. Regimes do not necessarily change even though the basic causal variables that led to their creation in the first place have altered. Lags between shifts in basic causal variables, especially the distribution of power, and regimes and behavior, can become a central phenomenon of international relations.

Aside from lags, a structural analysis that emphasizes the relationship between basic causal variables and regimes and behavior suggests an even more discomforting line of reasoning. Once regimes are established they may feed back on the basic causal variables that gave rise to them in the first place. They may alter the distribution of power. They may change assessments of interest. Regimes may become interactive, not simply intervening, variables. This argument is one step further removed from the structural formulations about the causes and consequences of regimes discussed in the introduction. That discussion dealt primarily with periods of regime creation, while the discussion here deals primarily with periods of regime persistence. Once a regime is actually in place, it may develop a dynamic of its own that can alter not only related behavior and outcomes but also basic causal variables.[7]

[5] A succinct statement of Robert North's argument can be found in his "Toward a Framework for the Analysis of Scarcity and Conflict," *International Studies Quarterly* 21, 4 (December 1977). For a superlative new exposition see Robert Gilpin, *War and Change in World Politics* (New York: Cambridge University Press, 1981).

[6] It is, of course, possible to deny that any puzzle exists, to argue that there has not been any fundamental shift in power. Susan Strange takes this position in her article for this volume, as do most European scholars. In this case the higher degree of disorder would be compatible with a marginal shift in power capabilities within a structure that has remained basically hegemonic. One might also argue, as Strange does, that there has always been considerable disorder in the system.

[7] This debate in the international relations literature parallels a current debate in the literature on domestic explanations of foreign, especially foreign economic, policy. For a conventional

Regime autonomy: lags and feedback

The autonomy of regimes is derived from lags and feedback. Lags refer to situations in which the relationship between basic causal variables and regimes becomes attenuated. Regimes come to have an independent impact on outcomes and related behavior. The most common formulation refers to a situation in which power and interests change, but regimes do not. Feedback refers to processes by which established regimes alter power and interests. Both lags and feedback present serious Kuhnian puzzles for conventional theoretical orientations.[8] They can be solved by elaborating the initial paradigm, or they may lead to the conclusion that the paradigm is fundamentally flawed.

Lags

The presence of lags suggests that regimes assume a life of their own. Basic causal variables may be less important for explaining regime persistence than for explaining regime creation. While the influence of basic causal variables does not evaporate, principles, norms, rules, and decision-making procedures come to have their own exogenous impact on outcomes and behavior. The basic causal schematic posits the relations in Figure 1.

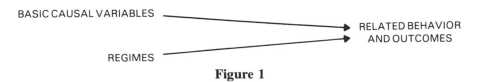

Figure 1

The significance of lags depends upon their duration. Even narrow structural formulations rarely assert that a change in power or interests will instantaneously result in a change in regimes. But they would posit fairly rapid change, especially in the international environment where rules and

---

structural analysis with economic sectors as the exogenous variable see James R. Kurth, "The Political Consequences of the Product Cycle: Industrial History and Political Outcomes," *International Organization* 33, 1 (Winter 1979). For an analysis that sees both economic interests and political institutions as independent variables see Peter A. Gourevitch, "International Trade, Domestic Coalitions, and Liberty: Comparative Responses to the Crisis of 1873–1896," *Journal of Interdisciplinary History* 8, 2 (Autumn 1977). For two articles that emphasize the interactive and autonomous roles of institutions once they are firmly implanted see Peter J. Katzenstein, "Capitalism in One Country? Switzerland in the International Economy," *International Organization* 34, 4 (Autumn 1980), and Peter J. Katzenstein, "Problem or Model? West Germany in the 1980s," *World Politics* 32, 4 (July 1980); for the same conceptualization in a Marxist framework see Raymond D. Duvall and John R. Freeman, "The State and Dependent Capitalism," *International Studies Quarterly* 25, 1 (March 1981).

[8] Lags and feedback do not present puzzles for various Grotian orientations illustrated in this volume by Haas's discussion of organic theories emphasizing turbulent fields with multiple feedback loops.

norms are not guaranteed by hierarchical authority. For conventional arguments, such as Susan Strange's, regimes are the handmaidens of more fundamental factors. Lengthy incongruence between basic causal variables and regimes is unlikely. Only if the lags between changes in interests and power and changes in regimes are extensive do they present a serious puzzle for conventional argumentation.

Lags may arise because of custom and usage, uncertainty, and cognitive failing. First, custom and usage may provide a basis of support for a well established regime. Individuals continue to adhere to particular regimes because they have done so in the past. Even if power or egoistic interests change, practices may remain unaltered, sustained by the ongoing rhythm of daily activity. Stein notes, for instance, that states do not constantly reassess their interest in the light of existing regimes. Jervis suggests that the longevity of the Concert of Europe was in part a manifestation of accepted habits that precluded the constant evaluation of new options.

Second, uncertainty may provide a basis for lags. Stein notes that actors may continue to accept an established regime because they are uncertain about the durability of environmental change. "Institutions may be required again in the future, and their destruction for short-term changes may be very costly in the long run."[9] Higher food prices in any given year may be seen as a temporary perturbation requiring no alteration in the norm of accepting dependence on food imports, or may be interpreted as an indication of long-term market change requiring greater self-sufficiency. However, the latter strategy is costly, and since it is difficult to separate cyclical and secular trends, existing norms may persist. Uncertainty is also inevitably associated with predictions about the consequences of any new regime. Actors may tolerate extant principles, norms, rules, and procedures, even if they generate some unsatisfactory outcomes, rather than launch a new enterprise the impact of which cannot be accurately assessed.

Uncertainty may also be associated with the prospects for securing acceptance for a new regime. Alexander George has argued that regime creation involves both normative and cognitive legitimation. Actors must be convinced that a new arrangement is both right and feasible. Policy makers can never be certain that they can secure consensus on such issues even if they have a clear vision of what they want. This implies a general propensity to accept extant regimes, even when there are reservations about their effectiveness.[10]

Third, cognitive failing may lead to a lag between regime change and changes in power and interests. Actors may be dissatisfied with an existing regime but unable to formulate an alternative cognitive framework. As Haas argues, knowledge can be an important variable in explaining the creation

[9] Arthur Stein's contribution to this volume, p. 138.

[10] Alexander L. George, "Domestic Constraints on Regime Change in U.S. Foreign Policy: The Need for Policy Legitimacy," in Ole R. Holsti et al., *Change in the International System* (Boulder, Col.: Westview, 1980), p. 248.

and maintenance of a regime. In the international system, stable regimes are likely to be based on consensual knowledge. Such knowledge can provide the basis for agreement on principles, norms, rules, and decision-making structures. In the absence of such shared cognitive orientations it may be impossible to conceive of an alternative regime. Even if there are powerful concerns about the dysfunctional character of an extant regime, it may be difficult to change.

Feedback

The possibility of feedback from established regimes to basic causal variables presents a more serious puzzle for conventional ratiocination. Once principles, norms, rules, and decision-making procedures are entrenched they may alter the egoistic interests and power configurations that led to their creation in the first place. Under these circumstances the set of causal relationships depicted in Figure 2 is posited.

BASIC CAUSAL VARIABLES ⟷ REGIMES ⟶ RELATED BEHAVIOR AND OUTCOMES

Figure 2

As in the case of lags there are distinctions across the cycle of regime development from creation to persistence to dissipation. This formulation is potentially significant only after a regime has been created.

There are four feedback mechanisms. First, regimes may alter actors' calculations of how to maximize their interests. Second, regimes may alter interests themselves. Third, regimes may become a source of power to which actors can appeal. Fourth, regimes may alter the power capabilities of different actors, including states.

1. Regimes and calculations of interests

The game-theoretic and microeconomic analyses of Stein and Keohane suggest that the existence of regimes can alter calculations of interest by changing "incentives and opportunities."[11] The behavior that an actor adopts to maximize a certain set of interests after a regime is in place differs from the behavior that would be followed in the absence of a regime even when interests are unchanged. (In the language of regression analysis the parameters may change even though the variables remain unaltered.)

Once a regime is established there are sunk costs. Running an old regime primarily involves variable costs; establishing a new one requires addi-

[11] Stein's contribution to this volume, p. 139.

tional fixed costs. In the first instance these costs are associated with the difficulty of securing agreement in a world of independent actors. Kenneth Arrow suggests that in general "agreements are typically harder to change than individual decisions. When you have committed not only yourself but many others to an enterprise, the difficulty of changing becomes considerable. . . . Even if experience has shown the unexpectedly undesirable consequences of a commitment, the past may continue to rule the present."[12] Similarly, Young argues that it is difficult to change regimes because "new arrangements require actors to assimilate alternative procedures or patterns of behavior and accept (initially) unknown outcomes."[13]

Keohane places particular emphasis on information channels as a form of capital investment with potential economies of scale, especially under conditions of complex interdependence. He argues that "the institutions and procedures that develop around international regimes acquire value as arrangements permitting communication, and therefore facilitating the exchange of information. As they prove themselves in this way, demand for them increases."[14] Even if power becomes more fragmented, shifting downward the supply function for regimes, regimes may persist because the demand function has been shifted upward by the informational advantages provided by extant principles, norms, rules, and decision-making procedures. For instance, regimes that make it easier to gather information about the activities of other states are particularly important in situations where it is tempting to cheat. By enhancing the flow of information, regimes discourage cheating by making discovery more likely. Since everyone is better off without cheating it is attractive to maintain the regime.[15]

2. Regimes and the alteration of interest

Regimes may change the interests that led to their creation in the first place by increasing transactions flows, facilitating knowledge and understanding, and creating property rights. (Here it is the underlying variable which changes.) If a regime increases transactions flows in a particular issue-area it can alter interests by increasing the opportunity costs of change. (Strictly speaking the causal mechanism in this instance is from the regime to behavior to basic causal variables.) Many of the authors in this volume emphasize the relationship between complexity, interconnectedness, and regimes and, especially for Haas, regimes are designed to manage such complexity. Successful management implies that states can tolerate higher levels

[12] Kenneth J. Arrow, *The Limits of Organization* (New York: Norton, 1974), p. 28.
[13] Oran Young's contribution to this volume, p. 96.
[14] Robert O. Keohane's contribution to this volume, p. 164.
[15] Vinod K. Aggarwal, "Regime Transformation: An Analysis of the International Textile/Apparel System—1955–1978," paper presented to the International Studies Association, Philadelphia, March 1981, p. 16.

of transactions flows than would be the case in the absence of regimes. But higher transactions flows alter interests. At the national level they increase the opportunity costs of changing the regime. At a disaggregated level the regime promotes the interests of some groups and damages the interests of others. For instance, an open regime for trade facilitates the development of export industries and weakens the position of import-competing industries.

Haas emphasizes that the information-generating functions of regimes may also alter interests, or at least actors' understandings of their interests. Haas's cognitive evolutionary perspective envisions a world of turbulent fields, of uncertainties and possibilities. Actor perceptions of their interests are constantly changing, partly as a result of the information disseminated by existing regime structures. This leads to new behavior by actors, which can alter international regimes. New regimes gather and disseminate different and usually more complex information, highlighting cause and effect relationships that had not previously been understood. This, in turn, leads to new perceptions of interest, which prompts a change in behavior, which may involve changes within or between regimes. Haas argues that organizations "may autonomously feed the process of change by the information and ideas they are able to mobilize."[16]

A central mechanism through which international economic regimes alter interests is by assigning property rights. If sovereignty is the constitutive principle of the international political system, property rights are the constitutive principle of the international economic system. A wide range of international regimes is designed to establish property rights. For instance, a basic norm of the international regime for civil aviation is that a country's airlines should have 50 percent of the traffic generated within that country.[17] The function of various agreements on ocean carriage is to define the obligations of shippers, carriers, insurers, and purchasers. A major objective of the United Nations Conference on the Law of the Seas is to define property rights for deep seabed nodules. World Administrative Radio Conference meetings assign property rights to different parts of the radio wave spectrum.

Regimes that establish property rights create interests. The international regime for civil aviation facilitated the development of a large number of national airlines as opposed to a small number of very large multinational airlines. The standardized contracts legitimated by international agreements on ocean carriage reduce transaction costs, a reduction that disproportionately benefits smaller firms. The Law of the Seas Treaty would establish an internationally controlled Enterprise to exploit seabed nodules. The allocation of the radio band facilitates some forms of international communication and precludes others. Hence, calculations of power or interest lead to

[16] Ernst B. Haas's contribution to this volume, p. 57.
[17] Christer Jönsson, "Sphere of Flying: The Politics of International Aviation," *International Organization* 35, 2 (Spring 1981).

the creation of international regimes, but once these regimes are in place they create new interests.[18]

3. Regimes as a source of power

A third feedback mechanism from regimes to basic causal variables involves situations in which the regime is used by actors with limited national capabilities as a source of power. The underlying resources of the actors are not changed but the ability to influence behavior is enhanced, or circumscribed, by the principles, norms, rules, and decision-making procedures of a regime. Such a situation is unlikely to arise when a regime is first created. At that time the characteristics of the regime are likely to coincide closely with the preferences of the most powerful actors in the system. Weaker actors are not likely to be able to use the regime to augment their own national power resources. However, for the reasons discussed in the section on lags, incongruities between regime characteristics and the preferences of the strong can develop over time. These incongruities can open possibilities for weaker states to enhance their influence.[19]

Extant international regimes offer a number of examples of such behavior, particularly in the area of North-South relations. The Third World has used international regimes to enhance power and control over international transaction flows in a number of issue-areas. The Third World has advocated allocative systems based on authoritative state control rather than on the market. In the area of shipping, developing countries have supported the United Nations Convention on Liner Conferences, which establishes a norm of a 40-40-20 split of cargo between exporting, importing, and third-country liners. In the area of trade, developing countries have used the General Agreement on Tariffs and Trade (GATT) and UNCTAD to press for special and differential treatment. Through international agreements on business practices and technology transfer, developing countries have sought to legitimate and thereby enhance the power of national government to regulate multinational corporations. The Law of the Seas negotiations have afforded developing states the opportunity to claim revenues from the exploitation of deep seabed nodules even though they lack the technology and capital to undertake development on their own.[20]

---

[18] John A. C. Conybeare's imaginative application of the Coase theorem to international organizations, in "International Organization and the Theory of Property Rights," *International Organization* 34, 3 (Summer 1980), emphasizes the property-rights assigning function of international organizations. It may be preferable to have such institutions create a set of property rights that internalize externalities, rather than have them directly allocate resources.

[19] See Jock A. Finlayson and Mark W. Zacher's contribution to this volume, p. 313, for an elaboration of this point in the context of the international trade regime.

[20] This argument is elaborated in Stephen D. Krasner, "Transforming International Regimes: What the Third World Wants and Why," *International Studies Quarterly* 25, 1 (March 1981).

Regimes also have an impact on the power of specific groups within states. Charles Lipson's analysis of the international regime for trade points out that principles and rules constrained protectionist pressures in the United States: those advocating liberal policies could point to the international obligations assumed by the United States. While the GATT offers a clear set of principles and norms, protectionists had no alternative cognitive framework to which they could appeal. Various multilateral trade negotiations have set the agenda for trade legislation in the United States.[21] Benjamin Cohen's analysis of the monetary regime notes that one of its central principles has been that some lenders could question the policies of borrowing states. This is reflected in the conditionality practices followed by the International Monetary Fund (IMF). In negotiating conditions for standby agreements the Fund may alter the power of different groups within a borrowing country. The Fund's proposals may be a source of strength for those advocating more restrained policies or may undermine their position if there is general rejection of the IMF's approach. In either case, the regime acts to alter the power of actors within states.

4. Regimes and actor capabilities

Finally, regimes may alter the underlying power capabilities of their members. By facilitating particular patterns of behavior, regimes can strengthen or weaken the resources of particular actors. Regimes may reinforce or undermine the power capabilities that led to their creation in the first place.

There are, for instance, major disagreements about the impact of the postwar economic regime on actors in the system. Dependency theorists have held that the regime has reinforced existing power capabilities by maintaining a set of mechanisms that allow the strong to exploit the weak. Capital flows are pernicious. Mineral investments are insulated from the rest of the economy. Transfer prices are set to evade taxation. Technology is geared to the preferences of the rich. Multinationals can leave a country with relative abandon. Labor migration is restricted. Manufactured exports from the South are subject to trade barriers. The political systems of backward areas are corrupted. Potentially progressive elements are suppressed or bought off. Right wing military establishments are maintained by foreign aid freezing authoritarian, often precapitalist power relationships. Poorer areas may experience growth, but it is conditioned by their place in the international system. The regime reinforces the underlying power capabilities of actors in the North.

A sharply contrasting view is offered by a number of writers who identify hegemony with stability and even justice. They are often labeled mer-

---

[21] Finlayson and Zacher, "The GATT," p. 312.

cantilists or neomercantilists. They argue that the United States has tended to support regimes that dissipate its own underlying power capabilities. Into the 1960s the United States tolerated asymmetric international trading arrangements, especially with Europe and Japan. Encouragement for the free movement of goods and factors created an environment in which multinational corporations flourished. However, by exporting capital and technology these corporations have weakened the economic position of the United States itself. While a fully open regime for goods and factors may initially serve the interests of a hegemonic state, over the long term it tends to undercut the hegemon's position.[22] For both dependentistas and mercantilists, regimes are significant because they alter the underlying power capabilities of actors.

The constitutive principle of the existing international system, sovereignty, may offer a powerful example of how regimes affect actor capabilities. A number of economists have recently turned their attention to the development of political arrangements. North and Thomas, for instance, argue that the development of sovereign states in Europe was a rational response to changing military technology and increasing long-distance trade. New military technology was expensive and characterized by scale economies; it asymmetrically benefited larger political units. Increased trade offered fiscal rewards to political units that provided physical security. As trade routes lengthened, effective protection required larger territorial units.[23]

Certainly through the 18th century, and possibly through the 19th, an international system based on sovereign states was highly congruent with the basic political and economic interests both of the rulers themselves and of their subjects. With the exception of the Napoleonic period the general destructiveness of wars was limited. The industrial revolution ushered in a period of unprecedented economic growth.

But the congruence between a world of sovereign states and egoistic interests has become increasingly questionable in the 20th century. As Haas points out, writers associated with the world order perspective emphasize the deleterious economic and political consequences of sovereignty in a nuclearized interdependent world. Nuclear weapons and modern delivery systems make it impossible for even the most powerful states to protect their own populations. Economic interdependence vitiates the formal powers of the state. Prosperity is hostage to external and uncontrollable variables. Governments can no longer guarantee the safety or the economic well-being of their populations.

Various environmental orientations see survival in a world of limited resources as the central issue confronting mankind. Externalities are rife.

[22] Robert Gilpin, *U.S. Power and the Multinational Corporation* (New York: Basic Books, 1975), especially chaps. 7 and 8.

[23] Douglass C. North and Robert Paul Thomas, *The Rise of the Western World: A New Economic History* (Cambridge: Cambridge University Press, 1973), chap. 1.

The tragedy of the commons is the governing metaphor. Sovereign political units are not well placed to cope with the problems of "spaceship earth."

However, these arguments, and others that could be cited, have had virtually no impact on the constitutive principle of the present international system. Why should this be the case? For one thing (referring back to the discussion of lags), no convincing alternative cognitive construct has been presented. There is no consensual knowledge about what principle might replace sovereignty. For another, there are high sunk costs in the existing regimes. Changing sovereignty would also mean a change in the regimes of virtually all other issue-areas. The uncertainties of such an enterprise would be high.

But more significantly, sovereignty itself has strongly reinforced the position of the major actor in the system it legitimates—national states functioning within specific territorial boundaries. Formally, states are the only actors with an unlimited right to act in the international system. Behaviorally, they are unquestionably the most powerful actors in the system, recent discussions of transnationalism notwithstanding. The wholesale acceptance of the principle of sovereignty has made the positions of transnational, subnational, and universal actors weaker than they would have been under a Grotian regime. The raft of new political units that have emerged from colonialism since World War II have been constituted as sovereign states, even though the area, population, and wealth of many of them are extremely limited. Especially for the very weak, abandoning the principle of sovereignty would undermine their independence and autonomy. Without sovereignty many poor and small areas would be placed in formally subservient, perhaps tributary, relationships with more powerful actors. Of all of the actors in the system, states are the least likely to be swayed by appeals to transcend sovereignty. For various critics of the existing system, the problem of moving to their desired world order is exacerbated by the feedback from the regime of sovereignty to state capability.

Conclusion

Most of the authors in this volume have adopted a structural realist perspective in approaching international regimes, or more precisely a variant of that perspective which sees environmental behavior as a function of the distribution of power among states; a world of tectonic plates and intermittent earthquakes rather than billiard balls and frequent collisions. But this exemplar, like Kuhn's paradigms, has pushed some of the analyses to the limits of a realist orientation. How long can a lagged variable lag before it is more usefully understood as exogenous rather than endogenous? If regimes alter not just calculations of interest and the weight of power but also the interests and capabilities that underlie these calculations and weights, have not principles, norms, rules, and decision-making procedures become confounded with more conventional causal variables? If feedback from the regime is positive, and power is in part a function of the nature of the regime, is it not merely tautological to assert that regimes must be closely tied to the underlying capabilities that sustain them?

Thinking about such questions may be liberating not only for structural perspectives but also for those who study them. It has been a peculiar tendency of recent social science to disparage the importance of learning, cognitive ideas, and understanding. Few theories incorporate these concepts as major explanatory variables. In a peculiar way social scientists have constantly disparaged the prescriptive utility of their work. If cognitive understanding is not used as an independent variable in explaining a particular social phenomenon, there is no explicit reason to suppose that an accurate piece of analysis will alter anyone's behavior. If individual behavior is determined or conditioned by the international system, or bureaucratic interests, or economic structures, it is not clear why reading Weber, Marx or Morgenthau should make any difference. Yet analysts have felt that their work could matter, and not just those studies that were explicitly policy-oriented. But the mechanism through which ideas could influence outcomes has been obscure.

The concept of regimes does suggest such a mechanism. It is an area where, as Haas points out, knowledge can matter. Knowledge alone is never enough to explain either the creation or the functioning of a regime. Interests and power cannot be banished. But knowledge and understanding can affect regimes. If regimes matter, then cognitive understanding can matter as well.

Index

Library of Congress Cataloging in Publication Data
Main entry under title:

International regimes.

    Includes index.
    1. International organization—Research—Addresses, essays, lectures. 2. International relations—
Research—Addresses, essays, lectures. I. Krasner, Stephen D., 1942-
JX1954.I485   1983   341.2   82-19905
ISBN 0-8014-1550-0 (cloth)
ISBN 0-8014-9250-5 (pbk.)